Praise for Plan

"Lester Brown tells us how to build a more just ~~societ~~... in a practical, straightforward way. We shou~~ld~~..."

—President Bill Clinton

"...a far-reaching thinker."

—U.S. News & World Report

"It's exciting...a masterpiece!"

—Ted Turner

"[Brown's] ability to make a complicated subject accessible to the general reader is remarkable..."

—Katherine Salant, Washington Post

"If the 2007 Nobel Peace Prize had been extended to a third recipient, the logical candidate would have been Lester Brown."

—Edward O. Wilson

"Brown is impassioned and convincing when talking about the world's ills and what he considers the four great goals to restoring civilization's equilibrium..."

—April Streeter, TreeHugger.com

"In this impressively researched manifesto for change, Brown bluntly sets out the challenges and offers an achievable road map for solving the climate change crisis."

—The Guardian

"In tackling a host of pressing issues in a single book, Plan B 2.0 makes for an eye-opening read."

—Times Higher Education Supplement

"The best big-picture summary of our environmental situation—both the problems and the solutions—I've ever read."

—Grist

"A great book which should wake up humankind!"

—Klaus Schwab, World Economic Forum

"Lester R. Brown, one of the world's preeminent eco-economists...has a solution for dealing with the threat...Plans must be periodically revised and refined, which Brown has done with insight and foresight in this volume."

—Ode

continued...

"... a highly readable and authoritative account of the problems we face from global warming to shrinking water resources, fisheries, forests, etc. The picture is very frightening. But the book also provides a way forward."

—Clare Short, British Member of Parliament

"Lester R. Brown gives concise, but very informative, summaries of what he regards as the key issues facing civilization as a consequence of the stress we put on our environment.... a valuable contribution to the ongoing debate."

—*The Ecologist*

"An enormous achievement—a comprehensive guide to what's going wrong with earth's life support system and how to fix it."

—*Grinning Planet*

"Plan B has three parts: restructuring the global economy, working to eradicate poverty and reversing environmental destruction. Tall orders, to be sure: but Plan B is here thoughtfully laid out to achieve the seeming impossible—and with an understanding of world trends and cultures too."

—*The Midwest Book Review*

"Lester R. Brown...offers an attractive 21st-century alternative to the unacceptable business-as-usual path that we have been following with regard to the environment (Plan A), which is leading us to 'economic decline and collapse.'"

— Thomas F. Malone, *American Scientist*

"Brown's overall action plan is both comprehensive and compelling."

—Caroline Lucas, *Resurgence*

"A great book about ways to improve the environment and sustain economic progress."

—*St. Petersburg Times*

"Plan B 3.0 is a great wealth of information on the environment unequaled in any other source of which I am aware."

—Walter Youngquist, author of *GeoDestinies*

"Beautifully written and unimpeachably well-informed."

—Ross Gelbspan, author of *The Heat Is On*

"The best single volume on saving the earth, period."

—Geoffrey Holland, author of *The Hydrogen Age*

PLAN B 4.0

OTHER NORTON BOOKS
BY LESTER R. BROWN

*Plan B 3.0: Mobilizing to Save
Civilization*

*Plan B 2.0: Rescuing a Planet
Under Stress and a
Civilization in Trouble*

*Outgrowing the Earth: The Food
Security Challenge in an Age
of Falling Water Tables and
Rising Temperatures*

*Plan B: Rescuing a Planet
Under Stress and a
Civilization in Trouble*

The Earth Policy Reader
with Janet Larsen and
Bernie Fischlowitz-Roberts

*Eco-Economy: Building an
Economy for the Earth*

State of the World 1984
through *2001*
annual, with others

Vital Signs 1992 through *2001*
annual, with others

Beyond Malthus
with Gary Gardner
and Brian Halweil

The World Watch Reader 1998
editor with Ed Ayres

Tough Choices

Who Will Feed China?

Full House
with Hal Kane

Saving the Planet
with Christopher Flavin
and Sandra Postel

Building a Sustainable Society

Running on Empty
with Colin Norman
and Christopher Flavin

The Twenty-Ninth Day

In the Human Interest

Earth Policy Institute® is a nonprofit environmental research organization
providing a plan for building a sustainable future. In addition to the *Plan B*
series, the Institute issues four-page *Plan B Updates* that assess progress in
implementing Plan B. All of these plus additional data and graphs can be
downloaded at no charge from the EPI Web site.

Web site: www.earthpolicy.org

PLAN B 4.0

Mobilizing to Save Civilization

Lester R. Brown

EARTH POLICY INSTITUTE

W · W · NORTON & COMPANY

NEW YORK   LONDON

Copyright © 2009 by Earth Policy Institute
All rights reserved
Printed in the United States of America
First Edition

The EARTH POLICY INSTITUTE trademark is registered in the U.S. Patent and Trademark Office.

The views expressed are those of the author and do not necessarily represent those of the Earth Policy Institute; of its directors, officers, or staff; or of any funders.

The text of this book is composed in Sabon. Composition by Elizabeth Doherty; manufacturing by Courier Westford.

ISBN 978-0-393-07103-0 (cloth) 978-0-393-33719-8 (pbk)

W. W. Norton & Company, Inc., 500 Fifth Avenue,
New York, N.Y. 10110
www.wwnorton.com

W. W. Norton & Company, Ltd., Castle House, 75/76 Wells Street,
London W1T 3QT

1 2 3 4 5 6 7 8 9 0

❀ This book is printed on recycled paper.

Contents

III. THE GREAT MOBILIZATION

Preface

Several months ago I was reading an article in *Newsweek* on climate and energy when a line jumped off the page: "Business as usual has started to read like the end of the world."

Although this conclusion may surprise many, it will not surprise the scientists who track global environmental trends such as deforestation, soil erosion, falling water tables, and rising temperature. For some time they have been saying that if these trends continue we will be in trouble. What was not clear was what form the trouble would take.

It looks now as though food is the weak link, just as it was for many earlier civilizations. We are entering a new food era, one marked by higher food prices, rapidly growing numbers of hungry people, and an intensifying competition for land and water resources that has now crossed national boundaries as food-importing countries try to buy or lease vast tracts of land in other countries.

Unlike earlier grain price hikes that were caused by singular events—a drought in the Soviet Union or a monsoon failure in India—and were typically remedied by the next harvest, this recent rise is trend-driven. Among the trends responsible are population growth, falling water tables, rising temperature, ice melting, and the use of grain to produce fuel for cars.

In decades past, when grain prices climbed, the U.S. Department of Agriculture simply returned some cropland idled under farm programs to production, but now that land is all in use. Suddenly, food security has become a highly complex issue.

Energy policy may affect future food security more than agricultural policy. Eradicating hunger may depend more on the success of family planners than that of farmers. Raising water productivity may contribute more to future food security than expanding the irrigation water supply would.

In his book *The Collapse of Complex Societies*, Joseph Tainter observes that civilizations become progressively more complex as they evolve until eventually they cannot manage the complexity. I was reminded of this as I watched Congress wrestling with the climate bill, whittling away at its goals as this book was going to press.

International institutions are also wrestling with complexity. At this writing, all eyes are on the upcoming Copenhagen climate conference in early December. From my vantage point, internationally negotiated climate agreements are fast becoming obsolete for two reasons. First, since no government wants to concede too much compared with other governments, the negotiated goals for cutting carbon emissions will almost certainly be minimalist, not remotely approaching the bold cuts that are needed.

And second, since it takes years to negotiate and ratify these agreements, we may simply run out of time. This is not to say that we should not participate in the negotiations and work hard to get the best possible result. But we should not rely on these agreements to save civilization.

Some of the most impressive climate stabilization advances, such as the powerful U.S. grassroots movement that has led to a de facto moratorium on new coal-fired power plants, had little to do with international negotiations. At no point did the leaders of this movement say that they wanted to ban new coal-fired power plants only if Europe does, if China does, or if the rest of the world does. They moved ahead unilaterally knowing that if the United States does not quickly cut carbon emissions, the world will be in trouble.

We are in a race between political tipping points and natural tipping points. Can we cut carbon emissions fast enough to save the Greenland ice sheet and avoid the resulting rise in sea level? Can we close coal-fired power plants fast enough to save the glaciers in the Himalayas and on the Tibetan Plateau, the ice melt of which sustains the major rivers and irrigation systems of

Asia during the dry season? Can we stabilize population by reducing fertility before nature takes over and stabilizes our numbers by raising mortality?

On the climate front, everything seems to be moving faster. Only a few years ago summer sea ice in the Arctic Sea was shrinking, but it was projected to last for several decades. The most recent reports indicate that it could disappear in a matter of years.

Only a few years have passed since the most recent report by the Intergovernmental Panel on Climate Change (IPCC), but already the rise in carbon dioxide emissions, the rise in temperature, and the rise in sea level are all moving faster than even the IPCC's worst-case scenario.

The good news is that the shift to renewable energy is occurring at a rate and on a scale that we could not imagine even two years ago. Consider what is happening in Texas. The 8,000 megawatts of wind generating capacity in operation, the 1,000 megawatts under construction, and a huge amount in development will give it over 50,000 megawatts of wind generating capacity (think 50 coal-fired power plants). This will more than satisfy the residential needs of the state's 24 million people.

China, with its Wind Base program, is working on six wind farm mega-complexes with a total generating capacity of 105,000 megawatts. And this is in addition to the many smaller wind farms already in operation and under construction.

Most recently, a consortium of European corporations and investment banks has announced a proposal to develop a massive amount of solar thermal generating capacity in North Africa, much of it for export to Europe. In total, it could easily exceed 300,000 megawatts—roughly three times the electrical generating capacity of France.

And we could cite many more examples. The energy transition from fossil fuels to renewable sources of energy is moving much faster than most people realize. In the United States, for example, generating capacity for wind increased by 8,400 megawatts in 2008, while that from coal increased by only 1,400 megawatts.

The question we face is not what we need to do, because that seems rather clear to those who are analyzing the global situation. The challenge is how to do it in the time available. Unfortunately we don't know how much time remains. Nature is the timekeeper but we cannot see the clock.

Plan B is ambitious simply because this is what it is going to take to turn things around. Will it be difficult? No question. Are the stakes high? No question.

The thinking that got us into this mess is not likely to get us out. We need a new mindset. Let me paraphrase a comment by environmentalist Paul Hawken in a 2009 college commencement address. In recognizing the enormity of the challenge facing us, he said: First we need to decide what needs to be done. Then we do it. And then we ask if it is possible.

Lester R. Brown
July 2009

Earth Policy Institute
1350 Connecticut Ave. NW
Suite 403
Washington, DC 20036

Phone: (202) 496-9290
Fax: (202) 496-9325
E-mail: epi@earthpolicy.org
Web site: www.earthpolicy.org

This book can be downloaded without charge from our Web site. Permission for reprinting or excerpting portions of the manuscript can be obtained from Reah Janise Kauffman at Earth Policy Institute. For additional information on the topics discussed in this book, see www.earthpolicy.org.

PLAN B 4.0

1

Selling Our Future

From time to time I go back and read about earlier civilizations that declined and collapsed, trying to understand the reasons for their demise. More often than not shrinking food supplies were responsible. For the Sumerians, rising salt levels in the soil—the result of a flaw in their irrigation system—brought down wheat and barley yields and eventually the civilization itself.[1]

For the Mayans, soil erosion exacerbated by a series of intense droughts apparently undermined their food supply and their civilization. For other early civilizations that collapsed, it was often soil erosion and the resulting shrinkage in harvests that led to their decline.[2]

Does our civilization face a similar fate? Until recently it did not seem possible. I resisted the idea that food shortages could also bring down our early twenty-first century global civilization. But our continuing failure to reverse the environmental trends that are undermining the world food economy forces me to conclude that if we continue with business as usual such a collapse is not only possible but likely.

The historic grain price climb in the last few years underlines the gravity of the situation. From mid-2006 to mid-2008, world prices of wheat, rice, corn, and soybeans roughly tripled, reaching historic highs. It was not until the global economic crisis beginning in 2008 that grain prices receded somewhat. But even then they were still well above the historical level.[3]

The world has experienced several grain price surges over the last half-century, but none like this. These earlier trends were event-driven—a monsoon failure in India, a severe drought in the Soviet Union, or a crop-shrinking heat wave in the U.S. Midwest. The price surges were temporary, caused by weather-related events that were usually remedied by the next harvest. The record 2006–08 surge in grain prices is different. It is trend-driven. This means that working our way out of this tightening food situation depends on reversing the trends that are causing it, such as soil erosion, falling water tables, and rising carbon emissions.

As a result of persistently high food prices, hunger is spreading. One of the United Nations Millennium Development Goals is to reduce hunger and malnutrition. In the mid-1990s, the number of people in this category had fallen to 825 million. But instead of continuing to decline, the number of hungry started to edge upward, reaching 915 million at the end of 2008. It then jumped to over 1 billion in 2009. With business as usual, I see a combination of the projected growth in population, the planned diversion of grain to produce fuel for cars, spreading shortages of irrigation water, and other trends combining to push the number of hungry people to 1.2 billion or more by 2015.[4]

Rising food prices and the swelling ranks of the hungry are among the early signs of a tightening world food situation. At a time when progress is seen as almost inevitable, this recent reversal on the food front is a disturbing setback. More and more, food is looking like the weak link in our civilization, much as it was for the earlier ones whose archeological sites we now study.

Food: The Weak Link

As the world struggles to feed all its people, farmers are facing several trying trends. On the demand side of the food equation are three consumption-boosting trends: population growth, the growing consumption of grain-based animal protein, and, most recently, the massive use of grain to fuel cars.

On the supply side, several environmental and resource trends are making it more difficult to expand food production fast enough. Among the ongoing ones are soil erosion, aquifer depletion, crop-shrinking heat waves, melting ice sheets and rising sea level, and the melting of the mountain glaciers that feed major rivers and irrigation systems. In addition, three resource trends are affecting our food supply: the loss of cropland to non-farm uses, the diversion of irrigation water to cities, and the coming reduction in oil supplies.

The first trend of concern is population growth. Each year there are 79 million more people at the dinner table. Unfortunately, the overwhelming majority of these individuals are being added in countries where soils are eroding, water tables are falling, and irrigation wells are going dry. If we cannot get the brakes on population growth, we may not be able to eradicate hunger.[5]

Even as our numbers are multiplying, some 3 billion people are trying to move up the food chain, consuming more grain-intensive livestock products. At the top of the food chain ranking are the United States and Canada, where people consume on average 800 kilograms of grain per year, most of it indirectly as beef, pork, poultry, milk, and eggs. Near the bottom of this ranking is India, where people have less than 200 kilograms of grain each, and thus must consume nearly all of it directly, leaving little for conversion into animal protein.[6]

Beyond this, the owners of the world's 910 million automobiles want to maintain their mobility, and most are not particularly concerned about whether their fuel comes from an oil well or a corn field. The orgy of investment in ethanol fuel distilleries that followed the 2005 surge in U.S. gas prices to $3 a gallon after Hurricane Katrina raised the annual growth in world grain consumption from roughly 20 million tons per year to more than 40 million tons in both 2007 and 2008, creating an epic competition between cars and people for grain.[7]

Turning to the supply-side constraints, soil erosion is currently lowering the inherent productivity of some 30 percent of the world's cropland. In some countries, such as Lesotho and Mongolia, it has reduced grain production by half or more over the last three decades. Kazakhstan, the site of the Soviet Virgin Lands project a half-century ago, has abandoned 40 percent of its grainland since 1980. Vast dust storms coming out of sub-

Saharan Africa, northern China, western Mongolia, and Central Asia remind us that the loss of topsoil is not only continuing but expanding.[8]

In contrast to the loss of topsoil that began with the first wheat and barley plantings, falling water tables are historically quite recent, simply because the pumping capacity to deplete aquifers has evolved only in recent decades. As a result, water tables are now falling in countries that together contain half the world's people. As overpumping spreads and as aquifer depletion continues, the wells are starting to go dry. Saudi Arabia has announced that because its major aquifer, a fossil (non-replenishable) aquifer, is largely depleted, it will be phasing out wheat production entirely by 2016. A World Bank study shows that 175 million people in India are being fed by overpumping aquifers. In China, this problem affects 130 million people.[9]

Climate change also threatens food security. After a certain point, rising temperatures reduce crop yields. For each 1 degree Celsius rise in temperature above the norm during the growing season, farmers can expect a 10-percent decline in wheat, rice, and corn yields. Since 1970, the earth's average surface temperature has increased by 0.6 degrees Celsius, or roughly 1 degree Fahrenheit. And the Intergovernmental Panel on Climate Change projects that the temperature will rise by up to 6 degrees Celsius (11 degrees Fahrenheit) during this century.[10]

As the earth's temperature continues to rise, mountain glaciers are melting throughout the world. Nowhere is this of more concern than in Asia. It is the ice melt from glaciers in the Himalayas and on the Tibetan Plateau that sustain the major rivers of India and China, and the irrigation systems that depend on them, during the dry season. In Asia, both wheat and rice fields depend on this water. China is the world's leading wheat producer. India is number two. (The United States is third.) These two countries also dominate the world rice harvest. Whatever happens to the wheat and rice harvests in these two population giants will affect food prices everywhere. Indeed, the projected melting of the glaciers on which these two countries depend presents the most massive threat to food security humanity has ever faced.[11]

According to the latest information on the accelerating melting of the Greenland and West Antarctic ice sheets, ice melt combined with thermal expansion of the oceans could raise sea level by up to 6 feet during this century. Every rice-growing river delta in Asia is threatened by the melting of these ice sheets. Even a 3-foot rise would devastate the rice harvest in the Mekong Delta, which produces more than half the rice in Viet Nam, the world's number two rice exporter. A World Bank map shows that a 3-foot rise in sea level would inundate half the rice-land in Bangladesh, home to 160 million people. The fate of the hundreds of millions who depend on the harvests in the rice-growing river deltas and floodplains of Asia is inextricably linked to the fate of these major ice sheets.[12]

As pressures on land-based food sources mounted after World War II, the world turned to the oceans for animal protein. From 1950 to 1996 the world fish catch climbed from 19 million to 94 million tons. But then growth came to a halt. We had reached the limits of the oceans before those of the land. Since 1996, growth in the world seafood supply has come almost entirely from fish farms. The spiraling demand for fish feed, most of it in the form of grain and soybean meal, is further intensifying pressure on the earth's land and water resources.[13]

Advancing deserts—the result of overgrazing, overplowing, and deforestation—are encroaching on cropland in Saharan Africa, the Middle East, Central Asia, and China. Advancing deserts in northern and western China have forced the complete or partial abandonment of some 24,000 villages and the cropland surrounding them. In Africa, the Sahara is moving southward, engulfing cropland in Nigeria. It is also moving northward, invading wheat fields in Algeria and Morocco.[14]

Farmers are losing cropland and irrigation water to nonfarm uses. The conversion of cropland to other uses looms large in China, India, and the United States. China, with its massive industrial and residential construction and its paving of roads, highways, and parking lots for a fast-growing automobile fleet, may be the world leader in cropland loss. In the United States, suburban sprawl is consuming large tracts of farmland.

With additional water no longer available in many countries, growing urban thirst can be satisfied only by taking irrigation water from farmers. Thousands of farmers in thirsty California find it more profitable to sell their irrigation water to Los Angeles and San Diego and leave their land idle. In India, villages are selling the water from their irrigation wells to nearby cities. China's farmers are also losing irrigation water to the country's fast-growing cities.[15]

Lingering in the background is the prospect of declining oil use as a result of either declining production or efforts to cut carbon emissions—or, more likely, some combination of the two. The tripling of the world grain harvest over the last half-century is closely tied to oil. Today oil figures prominently in the farm economy, used in tillage, irrigation, and harvesting. Once oil production turns downward, countries will compete for a shrinking supply as they try to keep their agriculture producing at a high level. It was relatively easy to expand world food production when oil was cheap and abundant. It will be far more difficult when the price of oil is rising and the supply is declining.[16]

Despite the growing need for new techniques to expand production, the backlog of unused agricultural technology is shrinking. In the more agriculturally advanced countries, farmers are using virtually all the available technology to raise land productivity. And agricultural scientists are not finding many new ways to raise yields. In Japan, the first country to launch a sustained rise in grain yield per hectare, rice yield increases have stalled, with little gain over the last 14 years. In China, the rapid rise in rice yields is now history. In both France and Egypt, wheat yields, which are among the world's highest, have been flat for roughly a decade. For the world as a whole, the rise in grainland productivity dropped from 2.1 percent a year from 1950 to 1990 to 1.3 percent from 1990 to 2008.[17]

Some commentators point to genetically modified crops as a way out of this predicament. Unfortunately, no genetically modified grains have dramatically raised yields. Nor are they likely to do so. Scientists using conventional plant breeding techniques have already exploited most of the genetic potential for raising crop yields.[18]

The bottom line is that harvest-expanding scientific advances are ever more difficult to come by as crop yields move closer to the inherent limits of photosynthetic efficiency. This limit in turn establishes the upper bounds of the earth's biological productivity, which ultimately will determine its human carrying capacity.[19]

As the world's farmers attempt to expand the harvest, the

trends that negatively affect production are partly offsetting advances in technology. The question now is, Could the environmental damage to world agriculture at some point entirely offset the gains from advancing technology, as it has already in Saudi Arabia and Yemen, where water shortages are shrinking grain harvests, or in Lesotho and Mongolia, where soil erosion is reducing harvests?[20]

The question—at least for now—is not will the world grain harvest continue to expand, but will it expand fast enough to keep pace with steadily growing demand.

Business as usual is no longer a viable option. Food security will deteriorate further unless leading countries collectively mobilize to stabilize population, stabilize climate, stabilize aquifers, conserve soils, protect cropland, and restrict the use of grain to produce fuel for cars.

The Emerging Politics of Food Scarcity

As world food security deteriorates, a dangerous geopolitics of food scarcity is emerging in which individual countries, acting in their narrowly defined self-interest, reinforce the negative trends. This began in late 2007 when wheat-exporting countries such as Russia and Argentina limited or banned exports in an attempt to counter domestic food price rises. Viet Nam banned rice exports for several months for the same reason. Several other minor exporters also banned or restricted exports. While these moves reassured those living in the exporting countries, they created panic in the scores of countries that import grain.[21]

At that point, as grain and soybean prices were tripling, governments in grain-importing countries suddenly realized that they could no longer rely on the market for supplies. In response, some countries tried to nail down long-term bilateral trade agreements that would lock up future grain supplies. The Philippines, a leading rice importer, negotiated a three-year deal with Viet Nam for a guaranteed 1.5 million tons of rice each year. A delegation from Yemen, which now imports most of its wheat, traveled to Australia with the hope of negotiating a long-term wheat import deal. Egypt has reached a long-term agreement with Russia for more than 3 million tons of wheat each year. Other importers sought similar arrangements. But in a seller's market, few were successful.[22]

The inability to negotiate long-term trade agreements was accompanied by an entirely new genre of responses among the more affluent food-importing countries as they sought to buy or lease for the long term large blocks of land to farm in other countries. As food supplies tighten, we are witnessing an unprecedented scramble for land that crosses national boundaries. Libya, importing 90 percent of its grain and worried about access to supplies, was one of the first to look abroad for land. After more than a year of negotiations it reached an agreement to farm 100,000 hectares (250,000 acres) of land in the Ukraine to grow wheat for its own people. This land acquisition is typical of the many that have introduced a new chapter in the geopolitics of food.[23]

What is so surprising is the sheer number of land acquisition agreements that have been negotiated or are under consideration. The International Food Policy Research Institute (IFPRI) has compiled a list of nearly 50 agreements, based largely on a worldwide review of press reports. Since there is no official point of registry of such transactions, no one knows for sure how many such agreements there are. Nor does anyone know how many there will eventually be. This massive acquisition of land to grow food in other countries is one of the largest geopolitical experiments ever conducted.[24]

The role of government in land acquisition varies. In some cases, government-owned corporations are acquiring the land. In others, private entities are the buyers, with the government of the investing country using its diplomatic resources to achieve an agreement favorable to the investors.

The land-buying countries are mostly those whose populations have outrun their own land and water resources. Among them are Saudi Arabia, South Korea, China, Kuwait, Libya, India, Egypt, Jordan, the United Arab Emirates, and Qatar. Saudi Arabia is looking to buy or lease land in at least 11 countries, including Ethiopia, Turkey, Ukraine, Sudan, Kazakhstan, the Philippines, Viet Nam, and Brazil.[25]

In contrast, countries selling or leasing their land are often low-income countries and, more often than not, those where chronic hunger and malnutrition are commonplace. Some depend on the World Food Programme (WFP) for part of their food supply. The *Financial Times* reported in March 2009 that the Saudis celebrated the arrival of the first shipment of rice produced on land they had acquired in Ethiopia, a country where the WFP is currently working to feed 4.6 million people. Another major acquisition site for the Saudis and several other grain-importing countries is the Sudan—ironically the site of the WFP's largest famine relief effort.[26]

Indonesia has agreed to give Saudi investors access to 2 million hectares (4.9 million acres) of land, much of it to grow rice. The Saudi Binladin Group was negotiating to develop 500,000 hectares of land for rice production in Indonesia's Papua province, but this has apparently been put on hold because of financial constraints.[27]

For sheer size of investment, China stands out. The Chinese firm ZTE International has secured rights to 2.8 million hectares (6.9 million acres) in the Democratic Republic of the Congo on which to produce palm oil, which can be used either for cooking or to produce biodiesel fuel—indicating that the competition between food and fuel is also showing up in land acquisitions. This compares with the 1.9 million hectares used by the Congo's 66 million people to produce corn, their food staple. Like Ethiopia and Sudan, the Congo also depends on a WFP lifeline. China is also negotiating for 2 million hectares in Zambia on which to produce jatropha, an oilseed-bearing perennial. Among the other countries in which China has acquired land or has plans to do so are Australia, Russia, Brazil, Kazakhstan, Myanmar, and Mozambique.[28]

South Korea, a leading world corn importer, is a major investor in several countries. With deals signed for some 690,000 hectares (1.7 million acres) in the Sudan for growing wheat, South Korea is one of the leaders in this food security push. For perspective, this land acquisition is nearly three fourths the size of the 930,000 hectares South Korea now uses at home to produce rice, its staple food. The Koreans are also looking at the Russian Far East, where they plan to grow corn and soybeans.[29]

One of the little noticed characteristics of land acquisitions is that they are also water acquisitions. Whether the land is rainfed or irrigated, it represents a claim on the water resources in the host country. Land acquisitions in the Sudan that tap water from the Nile, which is already fully utilized, may simply mean that Egypt will get less water from the river—making it even more dependent on imported grain.[30]

These bilateral land acquisitions raise many questions. To begin with, these negotiations and the agreements they lead to lack transparency. Typically only a few high-ranking officials are involved and the terms are confidential. Not only are many stakeholders such as farmers not at the table when the agreements are negotiated, they do not even learn about the deals until after they have been signed. And since there is rarely idle productive land in the countries where the land is being purchased or leased, the agreements suggest that many local farmers will simply be displaced. Their land may be confiscated or it may be bought from them at a price over which they have little say. This helps explain the public hostility that often arises within host countries.

China, for example, signed an agreement with the Philippine government to lease over a million hectares of land on which to produce crops that would be shipped home. Once word leaked out, the public outcry—much of it from Filipino farmers—forced the government to suspend the agreement. A similar situation developed in Madagascar, where South Korea's Daewoo Logistics had pursued rights to more than 1 million hectares of land, an area half the size of Belgium. This helped stoke the political furor that led to a change in government and cancellation of the agreement. China is also running into on-the-ground opposition over its quest for 2 million hectares in Zambia.[31]

This new approach to achieving food security also raises questions about the effects on employment. At least two countries, China and South Korea, are planning in some cases to bring in their own farm workers. Beyond this, is the introduction of large-scale commercial, heavily mechanized farming operations what is needed by the recipient countries, where unemployment is widespread?[32]

If food prices are rising in the host country, will the investing country actually be able to remove the grain it has produced on acquired land? Or will it have to hire security forces to ensure that the harvests can be brought home? Aware of this potential problem, the government of Pakistan, which is trying to sell or lease 400,000 hectares, is offering to provide a security force of 100,000 men to protect the land and assets of investors. Who will these security forces be protecting the invested assets from?

Will it be hungry Pakistanis? Or perhaps farmers whose land was confiscated to make the massive land sale to the investors?[33]

Another disturbing dimension of many land investments is that they are taking place in countries like Indonesia, Brazil, and the Democratic Republic of the Congo where expanding cropland typically means clearing tropical rainforests that sequester large quantities of carbon. This could measurably raise global carbon emissions, increasing the climate threat to world food security.

The Japanese government, IFPRI, and others have suggested the need for an investment code that would govern these land acquisition agreements, a code that would respect the rights of those living in the countries of land acquisition as well as the rights of investors. The World Bank, the U.N. Food and Agriculture Organization, and the African Union are apparently each drafting codes of conduct.[34]

Growing world food insecurity is thus ushering in a new geopolitics of food scarcity, one where the competition for land and water resources is crossing national boundaries. Many of the land acquisitions are in hunger-ridden, land-scarce countries, leaving less land to produce food for the people who live there. The risk is that this will increase hunger and political instability, leading to even more failing states.

No country is immune to the effects of tightening world food supplies, not even the United States, the world's breadbasket. For example, if China turns to the world market for massive quantities of grain, as it recently has done for soybeans, it will necessarily look to the United States, which dominates world grain exports. For U.S. consumers, the prospect of competing for the U.S. grain harvest with 1.3 billion Chinese consumers with fast-rising incomes is a nightmare scenario.[35]

In such a situation, it would be tempting for the United States to restrict exports—as it did, for example, with grain and soybeans in the 1970s when domestic food prices soared. But this is not an option with China, which now holds well over $1 trillion in U.S. debt. It is often the leading international buyer at the monthly auctions of U.S. Treasury securities that finance the growing U.S. fiscal deficit. In effect, China has become banker to the United States. Like it or not, U.S. consumers will share their grain with Chinese consumers, regardless of how high food prices rise.[36]

Our Global Ponzi Economy

Our mismanaged world economy today has many of the characteristics of a Ponzi scheme. A Ponzi scheme takes payments from a broad base of investors and uses these to pay off returns. It creates the illusion that it is providing a highly attractive rate of return on investment as a result of savvy investment decisions when in fact these irresistibly high earnings are in part the result of consuming the asset base itself. A Ponzi scheme investment fund can last only as long as the flow of new investments is sufficient to sustain the high rates of return paid out to previous investors. When this is no longer possible, the scheme collapses—just as Bernard Madoff's $65-billion investment fund did in December 2008.[37]

Although the functioning of the global economy and a Ponzi investment scheme are not entirely analogous, there are some disturbing parallels. As recently as 1950 or so, the world economy was living more or less within its means, consuming only the sustainable yield, the interest of the natural systems that support it. But then as the economy doubled, and doubled again, and yet again, multiplying eightfold, it began to outrun sustainable yields and to consume the asset base itself. In a 2002 study published by the U.S. National Academy of Sciences, a team of scientists led by Mathis Wackernagel concluded that humanity's collective demands first surpassed the earth's regenerative capacity around 1980. As of 2009 global demands on natural systems exceed their sustainable yield capacity by nearly 30 percent. This means we are meeting current demands in part by consuming the earth's natural assets, setting the stage for an eventual Ponzi-type collapse when these assets are depleted.[38]

As of mid-2009, nearly all the world's major aquifers were being overpumped. We have more irrigation water than before the overpumping began, in true Ponzi fashion. We get the feeling that we're doing very well in agriculture—but the reality is that an estimated 400 million people are today being fed by overpumping, a process that is by definition short-term. With aquifers being depleted, this water-based food bubble is about to burst.[39]

A similar situation exists with the melting of mountain glaciers. When glaciers first start to melt, flows in the rivers and the irrigation canals they feed are larger than before the melting started. But after a point, as smaller glaciers disappear and larger ones shrink, the amount of ice melt declines and the river flow diminishes. Thus we have two water-based Ponzi schemes running in parallel in agriculture.

And there are more such schemes. As human and livestock populations grow more or less apace, the rising demand for forage eventually exceeds the sustainable yield of grasslands. As a result, the grass deteriorates, leaving the land bare, allowing it to turn to desert. At some point the herds of ultimately emaciated cattle also collapse. In this Ponzi scheme, herders are forced to rely on food aid or they migrate to cities.

Three fourths of oceanic fisheries are now being fished at or beyond capacity or are recovering from overexploitation. If we continue with business as usual, many of these fisheries will collapse. Overfishing, simply defined, means we are taking fish from the oceans faster than they can reproduce. The cod fishery off the coast of Newfoundland in Canada is a prime example of what can happen. Long one of the world's most productive fisheries, it collapsed in the early 1990s and may never recover.[40]

Paul Hawken, author of *Blessed Unrest*, puts it well: "At present we are stealing the future, selling it in the present, and calling it gross domestic product. We can just as easily have an economy that is based on healing the future instead of stealing it. We can either create assets for the future or take the assets of the future. One is called restoration and the other exploitation."[41]

The larger question is, If we continue with business as usual—with overpumping, overgrazing, overplowing, overfishing, and overloading the atmosphere with carbon dioxide—how long will it be before the Ponzi economy unravels and collapses? No one knows. Our industrial civilization has not been here before.

Unlike Bernard Madoff's Ponzi scheme, which was set up with the knowledge that it would eventually fall apart, our global Ponzi economy was not intended to collapse. It is on a collision path because of market forces, perverse incentives, and poorly chosen measures of progress. We rely heavily on the market because it is in so many ways such an incredible institution. It allocates resources with an efficiency that no central planning body can match, and it easily balances supply and demand.

The market does, however, have some fundamental, potentially fatal, weaknesses. It does not respect the sustainable yield thresholds of natural systems. It also favors the near term over the long term, showing little concern for future generations. It does not incorporate into the prices of goods the indirect costs of producing them. As a result, it cannot provide the signals telling us that we are caught up in a Ponzi scheme.

In addition to consuming our asset base, we have also devised some clever techniques for leaving costs off the books—much like the disgraced and bankrupt Texas-based energy company Enron did some years ago. For example, when we use electricity from a coal-fired power plant we get a monthly bill from the local utility. It includes the cost of mining coal, transporting it to the power plant, burning it, generating the electricity, and delivering electricity to our homes. It does not, however, include any costs of the climate change caused by burning coal. That bill will come later—and it will likely be delivered to our children. Unfortunately for them, their bill for our coal use will be even larger than ours.[42]

When Sir Nicholas Stern, former chief economist at the World Bank, released his groundbreaking 2006 study on the future costs of climate change, he talked about a massive market failure. He was referring to the failure of the market to incorporate the costs of climate change in the price of fossil fuels. According to Stern, the costs are measured in the trillions of dollars. The difference between the market prices for fossil fuels and an honest price that also incorporates their environmental costs to society is huge.[43]

As economic decisionmakers—whether consumers, corporate planners, government policymakers, or investment bankers—we all depend on the market for information to guide us. In order for markets to work over the long term and for economic actors to make sound decisions, the markets must provide reliable information, including the full cost of products. But the market is giving us incomplete information, and as a result we are making bad decisions.

One of the best examples of this massive market failure can be seen in the United States, where the gasoline pump price was around $3 per gallon in mid-2009. This reflects only the cost of finding the oil, pumping it to the surface, refining it into gasoline, and delivering the gas to service stations. It overlooks the costs of climate change as well as the costs of tax subsidies to the oil industry (such as the U.S. oil depletion allowance), the burgeoning military costs of protecting access to oil in the politically unstable Middle East, and the health care costs of treating respiratory illnesses from breathing polluted air.[44]

Based on a study by the International Center for Technology Assessment, these costs now total nearly $12 per gallon ($3.17 per liter) of gasoline burned in the United States. If these were added to the $3 direct cost of the gasoline, motorists would pay $15 a gallon for gas at the pump. In reality, burning gasoline is very costly, but the market tells us it is cheap, thus grossly distorting the structure of the economy.[45]

A similar situation exists with food. If we paid the full cost of producing it—including the true cost of the oil used in producing it, the future costs of overpumping aquifers, the destruction of land through erosion, and the carbon dioxide emissions from land clearing—food would cost far more than we now pay for it in the supermarket.

In addition to ignoring indirect costs, the market does not value nature's services. This became abundantly clear in the summer of 1998 when China's Yangtze River valley, home to nearly 400 million people, was wracked by some of the worst flooding in history. The resulting damages of $30 billion equaled the value of the country's annual rice harvest.[46]

After several weeks of flooding, Beijing announced a ban on tree cutting in the Yangtze River basin. It justified this by noting that trees standing are worth three times as much as trees cut—the flood control services provided by forests were far more valuable than the lumber they contained. In effect, the market price had been off by a factor of three.[47]

The market does not respect the carrying capacity of natural systems. For example, if a fishery is being continuously overfished, the catch eventually will begin to shrink and prices will rise, encouraging even more investment in fishing trawlers. The inevitable result is a precipitous decline in the catch and the collapse of the fishery.

Today we need a realistic view about the relationship between the economy and the environment. We also need, more than ever before, political leaders who can see the big picture. And since the principal advisors to government are economists, we need either economists who can think like ecologists—Sir

Nicholas Stern and Herman Daly, a pioneer in ecological economics, are rare examples of this—or more ecological advisors.

Market behavior—including its failure to include the indirect costs of goods and services, to value nature's services, and to respect sustainable-yield thresholds—is leading to the destruction of the economy's natural support systems, our own version of a Ponzi scheme. At some point the deteriorating relationship between the economy and its natural supports begins to take a political toll, contributing to state failure.

Mounting Stresses, Failing States

After a half-century of forming new states from former colonies and from the breakup of the Soviet Union, the international community is today focusing on the disintegration of states. The term "failing state" has entered our working vocabulary only during the last decade or so, but these countries are now an integral part of the international political landscape. As an article in *Foreign Policy* observes, "Failed states have made a remarkable odyssey from the periphery to the very center of global politics."[48]

In the past, governments have been concerned by the concentration of too much power in one state, as in Nazi Germany, Imperial Japan, and the Soviet Union. But today it is failing states that provide the greatest threat to global order and stability. As *Foreign Policy* notes, "World leaders once worried about who was amassing power; now they worry about the absence of it."[49]

States fail when national governments lose control of part or all of their territory and can no longer ensure the personal security of their people. When governments lose their monopoly on power, the rule of law begins to disintegrate. When they can no longer provide basic services such as education, health care, and food security, they lose their legitimacy. A government in this position may no longer be able to collect enough revenue to finance effective governance. Societies can become so fragmented that they lack the cohesion to make decisions.

Failing states often degenerate into civil war as opposing groups vie for power. Conflicts can easily spread to neighboring countries, as when the genocide in Rwanda spilled over into the Democratic Republic of the Congo, where an ongoing civil conflict has claimed more than 5 million lives since 1998. The vast majority of these deaths in the Congo are nonviolent, most of them due to hunger, respiratory illnesses, diarrhea, and other diseases as millions have been driven from their homes. Within the Sudan, the killings in Darfur quickly spread into Chad. As *The Economist* observes, "like a severely disturbed individual, a failed state is a danger not just to itself, but to those around it and beyond."[50]

Failing states can also provide possible training grounds for international terrorist groups, as in Afghanistan, Iraq, and Pakistan, or as a base for pirates, as in Somalia. They may become sources of drugs, as in Myanmar (formerly Burma) or Afghanistan, which accounted for 92 percent of the world's opium supply in 2008, much of which is made into heroin. Because they lack functioning health care services, weakened states can become a source of infectious disease, as Nigeria and Pakistan have for polio, derailing efforts to eradicate this dreaded disease.[51]

Among the most conspicuous indications of state failure is a breakdown in law and order and a related loss of personal security. In Haiti, armed gangs ruled the streets until a U.N. peacekeeping force arrived in 2004. While the security situation has improved somewhat since then, kidnappings for ransom of local people who are lucky enough to be among the 30 percent of the labor force that is employed are commonplace. In Afghanistan the local warlords, not the central government, control the country outside of Kabul. Somalia, which now exists only on maps, is ruled by tribal leaders, each claiming a piece of what was once a country. In Mexico, drug cartels are taking over, signaling the prospect of a failed state on the U.S. border.[52]

Various national and international organizations maintain their own lists of failing, weak, or failed states. The most systematic ongoing effort to analyze failed and failing states is one undertaken jointly by the Fund for Peace and *Foreign Policy* magazine, in an index that is updated annually and published in each July/August issue of *Foreign Policy*. This invaluable service, which draws on thousands of information sources worldwide, is rich with insights into the changes that are under way in the world and, in a broad sense, where the world is heading.[53]

This analysis identifies 60 countries, ranking them according to "their vulnerability to violent internal conflict and societal deterioration." Based on 12 social, economic, political, and military indicators, it puts Somalia at the top of the list of failed states for 2008, followed by Zimbabwe, Sudan, Chad, and the Democratic Republic of the Congo. Three oil-exporting countries are among the top 20 failed states—Sudan, Iraq, and Nigeria. Pakistan, now ranking number 10 on the list, is the only failing state with a nuclear arsenal. North Korea, seventeenth on the list, is developing a nuclear capability. (See Table 1–1.)[54]

Scores for each of the 12 indicators, ranging from 1 to 10, are aggregated into a single country indicator: the Failed States Index. A score of 120, the maximum, means that a society is failing totally by every measure. In the first *Foreign Policy* listing, based on data for 2004, just 7 countries had scores of 100 or more. In 2005 this increased to 9. By 2008 it was 14—doubling in four years. This short trend is far from definitive, but higher scores for countries at the top and the doubling of countries with scores of 100 or higher suggest that state failure is both spreading and deepening.[55]

Ranking on the Failed States Index is closely linked with key demographic and environmental indicators. Of the top 20 failed states, 17 have rapid rates of population growth, several of them expanding at close to 3 percent a year or 20-fold per century. In 5 of these 17 countries, women have on average more than six children each. In all but 6 of the top 20 failed states, at least 40 percent of the population is under 15, a demographic statistic that often signals future political instability. Young men, lacking employment opportunities, often become disaffected, making them ready recruits for insurgency movements.[56]

In many of the countries with several decades of rapid population growth, governments are suffering from demographic fatigue, unable to cope with the steady shrinkage in cropland and freshwater supplies per person or to build schools fast enough for the swelling ranks of children.[57]

Sudan is a classic case of a country caught in the demographic trap. It has developed far enough economically and socially to reduce mortality, but not far enough to quickly reduce fertility. As a result, women on average have four children, double the two needed for replacement, and the population of 41 million is growing by over 2,000 per day. Under this

Table 1–1. *Top 20 Failing States, 2008*

Rank	Country	Score
1	Somalia	114.7
2	Zimbabwe	114.0
3	Sudan	112.4
4	Chad	112.2
5	Democratic Republic of the Congo	108.7
6	Iraq	108.6
7	Afghanistan	108.2
8	Central African Republic	105.4
9	Guinea	104.6
10	Pakistan	104.1
11	Côte d'Ivoire	102.5
12	Haiti	101.8
13	Burma	101.5
14	Kenya	101.4
15	Nigeria	99.8
16	Ethiopia	98.9
17	North Korea	98.3
18	Yemen	98.1
19	Bangladesh	98.1
20	Timor-Leste	97.2

Source: See endnote 54.

pressure, Sudan—like scores of other countries—is breaking down.[58]

All but 3 of the 20 countries that lead the list of failed states are caught in this demographic trap. Realistically, they probably cannot break out of it on their own. They will need outside help—and not just a scattering of aid projects but systemic assistance in rebuilding—or the political situation will simply continue to deteriorate.[59]

Among the top 20 countries on the failing state list, all but a few are losing the race between food production and population growth. Close to half of these states depend on a food lifeline from the WFP.[60]

Food shortages can put intense pressures on governments. In many countries the social order began showing signs of stress in

2007 in the face of soaring food prices and spreading hunger. Food riots and unrest continued in 2008 in dozens of countries—from the tortilla riots in Mexico to breadline fights in Egypt and tempeh protests in Indonesia—and signaled the desperation of consumers trapped between low incomes and rising food prices. In Haiti, soaring food prices helped bring down the government.[61]

In Pakistan, where wheat flour prices had doubled, an armed soldier escorted each grain truck lest it be stolen or used to illegally haul scarce wheat across the border into Afghanistan. In Kandahar, Afghanistan, market vendors were robbed at gunpoint by thieves who made off with sacks of grain. In Sudan, 110 grain-laden trucks delivering food for the World Food Programme were hijacked during 2008 before reaching the Darfur relief camps.[62]

Another characteristic of failing states is a deterioration of the physical infrastructure—roads and power, water, and sewage systems. Care for natural systems is also neglected as people struggle to survive. Forests, grasslands, and croplands deteriorate, generating a downward economic spiral. A drying up of foreign investment and a resultant rise in unemployment are also part of the decline syndrome.

In many countries, the United Nations or other international bodies are trying to keep the peace, often unsuccessfully. Among the countries where U.N. peacekeeping forces are deployed are Chad, the Democratic Republic of the Congo, and Côte d'Ivoire. Other countries supplied with multinational peacekeeping forces include Afghanistan, Haiti, and Sudan. All too often these are token forces, large enough to avoid immediate collapse but not large enough to ensure the stability needed for long-term development.[63]

Countries like Haiti and Afghanistan are surviving because they are on international life-support systems. Economic assistance, including food lifelines, is helping to sustain them. But there is not enough assistance to overcome the reinforcing trends of deterioration they are experiencing and replace them with the demographic and political stability need to sustain economic progress.[64]

In an age of increasing globalization, the functioning of the global system depends on a cooperative network of functioning nation states. When governments lose their capacity to govern, they can no longer collect taxes, much less be responsible for their international debts. More failing states means more bad debt. Efforts to control international terrorism depend on cooperation among functioning nation states, and these efforts weaken as more states fail.

In addition, protecting endangered species almost always requires close international cooperation. In countries such as the Democratic Republic of the Congo, where government agencies have collapsed, hunger is widespread, and chaos reigns, the population of mountain gorillas has dropped precipitously. This story is being repeated over and over again in Africa, where so many of the world's remaining large mammal species are concentrated.[65]

As the number of failing states grows, dealing with various international crises becomes more difficult. Actions that may be relatively simple in a healthy world order, such as maintaining monetary stability or controlling an infectious disease outbreak, could become difficult or impossible in a world with numerous disintegrating states. Even maintaining international flows of raw materials could become a challenge. At some point, spreading political instability could disrupt global economic progress, suggesting that we need to address the causes of state failure with a heightened sense of urgency.

Plan B—A Plan to Save Civilization

Plan B is the alternative to business as usual. Its goal is to move the world from the current decline and collapse path onto a new path where food security can be restored and civilization can be sustained. Just as the trends that are behind the current deterioration in the food situation go far beyond agriculture itself, so too must the response. In times past it was the Ministry of Agriculture that held the key to expanding agricultural research, expanding credit to farmers, and all the other obvious things that fall within its province, but securing future food supplies now depends on the mobilization of our entire society.

For these reasons Plan B is far more ambitious than anything the world has ever undertaken, an initiative that has no precedent in either scale or urgency. It has four components: cutting net carbon dioxide emissions 80 percent by 2020, stabilizing population at 8 billion or lower, eradicating poverty, and restoring the earth's natural systems, including its soils, aquifers, forests, grasslands, and fisheries. The ambitiousness of this plan is not driven by perceived political feasibility but by scientific reality.

The plan to cut carbon emissions involves dramatically raising energy efficiency worldwide, investing in the massive development of the earth's renewable energy resources, banning deforestation, and planting trees by the billion. Plan B essentially outlines a transition from an economy powered mainly by oil, coal, and natural gas to one powered largely by wind, solar, and geothermal energy.

The Plan B goal of stabilizing population is set at 8 billion or lower simply because I do not think world population will ever reach the 9.2 billion projected by U.N. demographers for 2050. To begin with, the vast majority of the 2.4 billion people projected to be added by 2050 will be born in developing countries—countries where the land and water resource base is deteriorating and hunger is spreading. Simply put, many support systems in these countries are already in decline, and some are collapsing. The question is not whether population growth will come to a halt before reaching 9.2 billion but whether it will do so because the world shifts quickly to smaller families or because it fails to do so—and population growth is checked by rising mortality. Plan B embraces the reduced fertility option.[66]

Eradicating poverty is a priority goal for three reasons. One, in combination with giving women everywhere access to reproductive health care and family planning services, it is the key to accelerating the global shift to smaller families. It also helps bring impoverished nations into the international community, giving them a stake in such matters as stabilizing climate. When people are not sure where their next meal is coming from, it is difficult for them to get excited about trying to stabilize the earth's climate. And third, eradicating poverty is the humane thing to do. One of the hallmarks of a civilized society is the capacity to care about others.

The fourth component of Plan B involves repairing and protecting the natural systems that support humankind. This includes conserving soil, banning deforestation, promoting reforestation, restoring fisheries, and making a worldwide effort to protect aquifers by raising water productivity. Unless we can reverse the deterioration of these systems we are unlikely to reverse the rise in hunger.

Plan B is an integrated program with four interdependent goals. We are not, for example, likely to stabilize population unless we can also eradicate poverty. Conversely, we cannot restore the earth's natural systems without stabilizing population and climate, and we are not likely to stabilize climate unless we also stabilize population. Nor can we eradicate poverty without restoring the earth's natural systems.

The ambitiousness of this save-our-civilization plan is matched by the urgency with which it must be implemented. Success depends on moving at wartime speed, restructuring the world energy economy at a pace reminiscent of the restructuring of the U.S. industrial economy in 1942 following the attack on Pearl Harbor. The United States shifted from producing cars to turning out planes, tanks, and ships within a matter of months. The current restructuring cannot be achieved without a fundamental reordering of priorities. And it will not be accomplished without sacrifice. For example, the key to the 1942 industrial restructuring was a ban on the sale of new cars, a ban that lasted nearly three years.[67]

We face an extraordinary challenge, but there is much to be upbeat about. All the problems we face can be dealt with using existing technologies. And almost everything we need to do to move the world economy off the collapse path and back onto an environmentally sustainable path has already been done in one or more countries. For example, more than 30 countries have essentially stabilized their population size.[68]

We see the components of Plan B in technologies already on the market. On the energy front, for example, we can get more energy from an advanced-design wind turbine than from an aging oil well. The new plug-in gas-electric hybrids coming to market, like the Chevrolet Volt, can get up to 150 miles per gallon. In the Plan B energy economy of 2020, most of the U.S. fleet will be plug-in hybrids and all-electric cars, and they will be running largely on wind-generated electricity for the equivalent of less than $1 a gallon of gasoline.[69]

The world is in the early stages of a revolution in lighting technology. Some time ago we learned that a compact fluorescent could provide the same lighting as the century-old incandescent bulb but would use only one fourth as much electricity. This was exciting news. Now we are looking at a still more-advanced lighting technology—the light-emitting diode (LED)—which uses 15 percent of the electricity used by an incandescent bulb. In addition, motion sensors can turn off lights in unoccupied spaces, and other sensors can adjust lighting intensity in response to the daylight available. Shifting from incandescent bulbs to LEDs and installing motion sensors and dimmers can reduce electricity used for lighting by more than 90 percent.[70]

As for Plan B models at the national level, Denmark today gets more than 20 percent of its electricity from wind and has plans to push this to 50 percent. Seventy-five million Europeans get their residential electricity from wind farms. Some 27 million Chinese homes get their hot water from rooftop solar water heaters. Iceland, which heats 90 percent of its homes with geothermal energy, has virtually eliminated the use of coal for home heating. The Philippines gets 26 percent of its electricity from geothermal power plants.[71]

We see what a Plan B world could look like in the reforested mountains of South Korea. Once a barren, almost treeless country, the 65 percent of South Korea now covered by forests has checked flooding and soil erosion, returning environmental health and stability to the Korean countryside. The United States—which over the last quarter-century retired one tenth of its cropland, most of it highly erodible, and shifted to conservation tillage practices on part of the remainder—has reduced soil erosion by 40 percent. Meanwhile, the grain harvest expanded by one fifth.[72]

Some of the most innovative leadership has come from cities. Curitiba, Brazil, began restructuring its transport system in 1974, and in the two decades that followed the city cut car traffic by 30 percent while its population doubled. Amsterdam has a diverse urban transport system where some 40 percent of all trips within the city are taken by bicycle. And the transport diversification plan in Paris that includes a prominent role for the bicycle is intended to reduce car traffic by 40 percent. London is taxing cars entering the city center and investing the revenue in upgrading public transit.[73]

The challenge is not only to build a new economy but to do it at wartime speed before we miss so many of nature's deadlines that the economic system begins to unravel. Participating in the construction of this enduring new economy is exhilarating. So is the quality of life it will bring. A world where population has stabilized, forests are expanding, and carbon emissions are falling is within our grasp.

I

THE CHALLENGES

2

Population Pressure: Land and Water

The French use a riddle to teach schoolchildren the nature of exponential growth. A lily pond, so the riddle goes, contains a single leaf. Each day the number of leaves doubles—two leaves the second day, four the third, eight the fourth, and so on. "If the pond is full on the thirtieth day, at what point is it half full?" Answer: "On the twenty-ninth day."[1]

Trends in world cropland area and irrigation water supplies suggest that we are living in the thirty-first day. After expanding modestly from 1950 to 1981, world grain area stopped growing and the area declined somewhat as land losses from erosion and conversion to nonfarm uses offset new land brought under the plow. On close to one third of the world's cropland, topsoil is eroding faster than new soil is being formed by geological processes, slowly reducing the land's inherent productivity.[2]

The world's irrigated area tripled from 1950 to 2000 but has expanded little since then. It could soon begin to decline—as it is already doing in some countries—as aquifers are depleted by overpumping and as the mountain glaciers that sustain so many of the world's rivers and irrigation systems melt and disappear.

Many irrigation systems, whether dependent on underground water or on river water, are at risk.[3]

We cannot escape the water intensity of food production. Worldwide, we drink on average close to 4 liters of water per day, either directly or in coffee, juice, soda, wine, and other beverages. But it takes 2,000 liters of water to produce the food we consume each day—500 times as much as we drink. In effect, we "eat" 2,000 liters of water each day.[4]

Soil erosion initially reduces the inherent productivity of the land and then, after a point, leads to cropland abandonment. Both effects of erosion are undermining world food security. A combination of population growth and soil erosion has caused a number of countries that were once self-sufficient in grain to become heavily dependent on imports.

With water tables now falling in almost every country that irrigates with underground water, many of these countries are facing hunger-inducing losses of irrigation water as aquifers are depleted and wells go dry. Overpumping—the pumping of aquifers that exceeds the natural recharge—presents a classic case of ecological overshoot and collapse. It is a way of satisfying current food needs that virtually guarantees a future drop in food production when aquifers are depleted. In effect, we have created a "food bubble economy." Both soil erosion and aquifer depletion reflect an emphasis on current consumption at the expense of the next generation.[5]

Civilization's Foundation Eroding

The thin layer of topsoil that covers the planet's land surface is the foundation of civilization. This soil, typically 6 inches or so deep, was formed over long stretches of geological time as new soil formation exceeded the natural rate of erosion. But sometime within the last century, as human and livestock populations expanded, soil erosion began to exceed new soil formation over large areas.

This is not new. In 1938, Walter Lowdermilk, a senior official in the Soil Conservation Service of the U.S. Department of Agriculture (USDA), traveled abroad to look at lands that had been cultivated for thousands of years, seeking to learn how these older civilizations had coped with soil erosion. He found that some had managed their land well, maintaining its fertility over long stretches of history, and were thriving. Others had failed to do so and left only remnants of their illustrious pasts.[6]

In a section of his report entitled "The Hundred Dead Cities," he described a site in northern Syria, near Aleppo, where ancient buildings were still standing in stark isolated relief, but they were on bare rock. During the seventh century, the thriving region had been invaded, initially by a Persian army and later by nomads out of the Arabian Desert. In the process, soil and water conservation practices used for centuries were abandoned. Lowdermilk noted, "Here erosion had done its worst....if the soils had remained, even though the cities were destroyed and the populations dispersed, the area might be re-peopled again and the cities rebuilt, but now that the soils are gone, all is gone."[7]

Now fast-forward to a trip in 2002 by a U.N. team to assess the food situation in Lesotho, a small country of 2 million people embedded within South Africa. Their finding was straightforward: "Agriculture in Lesotho faces a catastrophic future; crop production is declining and could cease altogether over large tracts of the country if steps are not taken to reverse soil erosion, degradation, and the decline in soil fertility." Michael Grunwald reported in the *Washington Post* that nearly half of the children under five in Lesotho are stunted physically. "Many," he wrote, "are too weak to walk to school."[8]

The U.N. team report was on the mark. During the last 10 years, Lesotho's grain harvest dropped by 40 percent as its soil fertility fell. Its collapsing agriculture leaves Lesotho heavily dependent on food supplied by the U.N. World Food Programme (WFP), its lifeline for survival.[9]

In the western hemisphere, Haiti, one of the early failing states, was largely self-sufficient in grain 40 years ago. Since then it has lost nearly all its forests and much of its topsoil, forcing it to import over half of its grain. Like Lesotho, Haiti is also dependent on a WFP lifeline.[10]

A similar situation exists in Mongolia, where over the last 20 years three fourths of the wheatland has been abandoned and wheat yields have fallen by one fourth, shrinking the harvest by four fifths. Mongolia—a country almost three times the size of France with a population of 2.6 million—is now forced to import nearly 70 percent of its wheat.[11]

Whether the land is in Lesotho, Mongolia, Haiti, or any of

the many other countries losing their soil, the health of the people living on it cannot be separated from the health of the land itself. A large share of the world's 1 billion hungry people live on soils worn thin by erosion.[12]

You do not need to visit soil-devastated countries to see the evidence of severe erosion. Dust storms originating in the new dust bowls are now faithfully recorded in satellite images. On January 9, 2005, the National Aeronautics and Space Administration released images of a vast dust storm moving westward out of central Africa. This huge cloud of tan-colored dust stretched over 5,300 kilometers (some 3,300 miles), enough to cover the United States from coast to coast.[13]

Andrew Goudie, professor of geography at Oxford University, reports that the number of Saharan dust storms—once rare—has increased 10-fold during the last half-century. Among the African countries most affected by soil loss from wind erosion are Niger, Chad, Mauritania, northern Nigeria, and Burkina Faso. In Mauritania, in Africa's far west, the number of dust storms jumped from 2 a year in the early 1960s to 80 a year recently.[14]

The Bodélé Depression in Chad is the source of an estimated 1.3 billion tons of wind-borne soil a year, up 10-fold since measurements began in 1947. The nearly 3 billion tons of fine soil particles that leave Africa each year in dust storms are slowly draining the continent of its fertility and biological productivity. In addition, dust storms leaving Africa travel westward across the Atlantic, depositing so much dust in the Caribbean that they cloud the water and damage coral reefs.[15]

People in China are all too familiar with dust storms that originate in the country's northwest and western Mongolia, but the rest of the world typically learns about this fast-growing ecological catastrophe when the massive soil-laden storms leave the region. On April 18, 2001, the western United States—from the Arizona border north to Canada—was blanketed with dust. It came from a huge dust storm that originated in northwestern China and Mongolia on April 5. Measuring 1,200 miles across when it left China, the storm carried millions of tons of topsoil, a resource that will take nature centuries to replace.[16]

Almost exactly one year later, on April 12, 2002, South Korea was engulfed by a huge dust storm from China that left people in Seoul literally gasping for breath. Schools were closed, airline flights were cancelled, and clinics were overrun with patients having difficulty breathing. Retail sales fell. Koreans have come to dread the arrival of what they now call "the fifth season," the dust storms of late winter and early spring.[17]

These two dust storms, among the 10 or so major dust storms that now occur each year in China, offer visual evidence of the ecological catastrophe unfolding in northern and western China. Overgrazing is the principal culprit.[18]

A U.S. Embassy report entitled "Desert Mergers and Acquisitions" describes satellite images showing two deserts in north-central China expanding and merging to form a single, larger desert overlapping Inner Mongolia (Nei Monggol) and Gansu Provinces. To the west in Xinjiang Province, two even larger deserts—the Taklimakan and Kumtag—are also heading for a merger. Highways running through the shrinking region between them are regularly inundated by sand dunes.[19]

Water erosion also takes a toll on soils. This can be seen in the silting of reservoirs and in satellite photographs of muddy, silt-laden rivers flowing into the sea. Pakistan's two large reservoirs, Mangla and Tarbela, which store Indus River water for the country's vast irrigation network, are losing roughly 1 percent of their storage capacity each year as they fill with silt from deforested watersheds.[20]

Ethiopia, a mountainous country with highly erodible soils, is losing close to 2 billion tons of topsoil a year, washed away by rain. This is one reason Ethiopia always seems to be on the verge of famine, never able to accumulate enough grain reserves to provide a meaningful measure of food security.[21]

Soil erosion from the deterioration of grasslands is widespread. The world's steadily growing herds of cattle and flocks of sheep and goats forage on the two fifths of the earth's land surface that is too dry, too steeply sloping, or not fertile enough to sustain crop production. This area supports most of the world's 3.3 billion cattle, sheep, and goats, all ruminants with complex digestive systems that enable them to digest roughage, converting it into beef, mutton, and milk.[22]

An estimated 200 million people make their living as pastoralists, tending cattle, sheep, and goats. Since most land is held in common in pastoral societies, overgrazing is difficult to control. As a result, half of the world's grasslands are degraded. The problem is highly visible throughout Africa, the Middle East, Central Asia, and northwest China, where the growth in livestock numbers tracks that in human numbers. In 1950, Africa was home to 227 million people and 273 million livestock. By 2007, there were 965 million people and 824 million livestock. With livestock demands now often exceeding grassland carrying capacity by half or more, grassland is turning into desert.[23]

Nigeria, Africa's most populous country, is losing 351,000 hectares (867,000 acres) of rangeland and cropland to desertification each year. While Nigeria's human population was growing from 37 million in 1950 to 148 million in 2007, a fourfold expansion, its livestock population grew from roughly 6 million to 102 million, a 17-fold jump. With the forage needs of Nigeria's 16 million cattle and 86 million sheep and goats exceeding the sustainable yield of grasslands, the northern part of the country is slowly turning to desert. If Nigeria continues toward its projected 289 million people by 2050, the deterioration will only accelerate.[24]

Iran, with 73 million people, illustrates the pressures facing the Middle East. With 8 million cattle and 79 million sheep and goats—the source of wool for its fabled rug-making industry—Iran's rangelands are deteriorating from overstocking. In the southeastern province of Sistan-Balochistan, sand storms have buried 124 villages, forcing their abandonment. Drifting sands have covered grazing areas—starving livestock and depriving villagers of their livelihood.[25]

Neighboring Afghanistan is faced with a similar situation. The Registan Desert is migrating westward, encroaching on agricultural areas. A U.N. Environment Programme (UNEP) team reports that "up to 100 villages have been submerged by windblown dust and sand." In the country's northwest, sand dunes are moving onto agricultural land in the upper reaches of the Amu Darya basin, their path cleared by the loss of stabilizing vegetation from firewood gathering and overgrazing. The UNEP team observed sand dunes 15 meters high blocking roads, forcing residents to establish new routes.[26]

China faces similarly difficult challenges. After the economic reforms in 1978 that shifted the responsibility for farming from large state-organized production teams to farm families, China's cattle, sheep, and goat populations spiraled upward. While the United States, a country with comparable grazing capacity, has 97 million cattle, China has a slightly smaller herd of 82 million. But while the United States has only 9 million sheep and goats, China has 284 million. Concentrated in China's western and northern provinces, sheep and goats are destroying the land's protective vegetation. The wind then does the rest, removing the soil and converting productive rangeland into desert.[27]

China's desertification may be the worst in the world. Wang Tao, one of the world's leading desert scholars, reports that from 1950 to 1975 an average of 600 square miles turned to desert each year. By century's end, nearly 1,400 square miles (3,600 square kilometers) were going to desert annually.[28]

China is now at war. It is not invading armies that are claiming its territory, but expanding deserts. Old deserts are advancing and new ones are forming like guerrilla forces striking unexpectedly, forcing Beijing to fight on several fronts. Wang Tao reports that over the last half-century, some 24,000 villages in northern and western China have been entirely or partly abandoned as a result of being overrun by drifting sand.[29]

Soil erosion often results from the demand-driven expansion of cultivation onto marginal land. Over the last century or so there were massive cropland expansions in two countries—the United States and the Soviet Union—and both ended in disaster.[30]

During the late nineteenth century, millions of Americans pushed westward, homesteading on the Great Plains, plowing vast areas of grassland to produce wheat. Much of this land— highly erodible when plowed—should have remained in grass. This overexpansion culminated in the 1930s Dust Bowl, a traumatic period chronicled in John Steinbeck's novel *The Grapes of Wrath*. In a crash program to save its soils, the United States returned large areas of eroded cropland to grass, adopted strip-cropping, and planted thousands of miles of tree shelterbelts.[31]

The second major expansion came in the Soviet Union beginning in the mid-1950s. In an all-out effort to expand grain production, the Soviets plowed an area of grassland larger than the wheat area of Australia and Canada combined. The result, as Soviet agronomists had predicted, was an ecological disaster—another Dust Bowl. Kazakhstan, where the plowing was concentrated, has abandoned 40 percent of its grainland since 1980. On the remaining cultivated land, the wheat yield per acre is one sixth of that in France, Western Europe's leading wheat producer.[32]

A third massive cropland expansion is now taking place in the Brazilian Amazon Basin and in the *cerrado*, a savannah-like region bordering the basin on its south side. Land in the *cerrado*, like that in the U.S. and Soviet expansion, is vulnerable to soil erosion. This cropland expansion is pushing cattle ranchers into the Amazon forests, where ecologists are convinced that continuing to clear the area of trees will end in disaster. Reporter Geoffrey Lean, summarizing the findings of a 2007 Brazilian scientific symposium in London's *Independent*, notes that the alternative to a rainforest in the Amazon would be "dry savannah at best, desert at worst."[33]

Water Tables Falling

Nowhere are falling water tables and the shrinkage of irrigated agriculture more dramatic than in Saudi Arabia, a country as water-poor as it is oil-rich. After the Arab oil export embargo in the 1970s, the Saudis realized they were vulnerable to a counter embargo on grain. To become self-sufficient in wheat, they developed a heavily subsidized irrigated agriculture based largely on pumping water from a deep fossil aquifer.[34]

After being self-sufficient in wheat for over 20 years, in early 2008 the Saudis announced that, with their aquifer largely depleted, they would reduce their wheat planting by one eighth each year until 2016, when production will end. By then Saudi Arabia will be importing roughly 15 million tons of wheat, rice, corn, and barley for its population of 30 million. It is the first country to publicly project how aquifer depletion will shrink its grain harvest.[35]

The Saudis are not alone. Scores of countries are overpumping aquifers as they struggle to satisfy their growing water needs. Most aquifers are replenishable but some are not. For example, when aquifers in India and the shallow aquifer under the North China Plain are depleted, the maximum rate of pumping will be automatically reduced to the rate of recharge.

But for fossil aquifers, like the Saudi aquifer, the vast Ogallala aquifer under the U.S. Great Plains, or the deep aquifer under the North China Plain, depletion brings pumping to an end. Farmers who lose their irrigation water have the option of returning to lower-yield dryland farming if rainfall permits. But in more arid regions, such as in the southwestern United States and parts of the Middle East, the loss of irrigation water means the end of agriculture.[36]

In Yemen, a nation of 23 million people neighboring Saudi Arabia, the water table is falling by roughly 6 feet a year as water use outstrips aquifer recharge. With one of the world's fastest-growing populations and with water tables falling everywhere, Yemen is quickly becoming a hydrological basket case. Grain production has fallen by half over the last 35 years. By 2015, irrigated fields will be a rarity and the country will be importing virtually all of its grain. Living on borrowed water and borrowed time, Yemen ranks high on the list of failing states.[37]

Falling water tables are already adversely affecting harvests in some larger countries, including China, which rivals the United States as the world's largest grain producer. A groundwater survey released in Beijing in August 2001 revealed that the water table under the North China Plain, an area that produces over half of the country's wheat and a third of its corn, was falling fast. Overpumping has largely depleted the shallow aquifer, forcing well drillers to turn to the region's deep aquifer, which is not replenishable.[38]

The survey reported that under Hebei Province in the heart of the North China Plain, the average level of the deep aquifer was dropping nearly 3 meters (10 feet) per year. Around some cities in the province, it was falling twice as fast. He Qingcheng, head of the groundwater monitoring team, notes that as the deep aquifer is depleted, the region is losing its last water reserve—its only safety cushion.[39]

A World Bank study indicates that China is mining underground water in three adjacent river basins in the north—those of the Hai, which flows through Beijing and Tianjin; the Yellow; and the Huai, the southern most of the three. Since it takes 1,000 tons of water to produce 1 ton of grain, the shortfall in the Hai basin of nearly 40 billion tons of water per year (1 ton equals 1 cubic meter) means that when the aquifer is depleted, the grain harvest will drop by 40 million tons and China will lose the food supply for 130 million of its people.[40]

As serious as water shortages are in China, they are even more serious in India, where the margin between food consumption and survival is so precarious. To date, India's 100 million farmers have drilled more than 21 million wells, investing some $12 billion in wells and pumps. In August 2004 Fred Pearce reported in *New Scientist* that "half of India's traditional hand-dug wells and millions of shallower tube wells have already dried up, bringing a spate of suicides among those who rely on them. Electricity blackouts are reaching epidemic proportions in states where half of the electricity is used to pump water from depths of up to a kilometer."[41]

As water tables fall, well drillers are using modified oil-drilling technology to reach water, going down a half mile or more in some locations. In communities where underground water sources have dried up entirely, all agriculture is now rain-fed and drinking water must be trucked in. Tushaar Shah, who heads the International Water Management Institute's groundwater station in Gujarat, says of India's water situation, "When the balloon bursts, untold anarchy will be the lot of rural India."[42]

Growth in India's grain harvest, squeezed both by water scarcity and the loss of cropland to non-farm uses, has slowed since 2000. A 2005 World Bank study reports that 15 percent of India's food supply is produced by mining groundwater. Stated otherwise, 175 million Indians are fed with grain produced by water mining.[43]

In the United States, the USDA reports that in parts of Texas, Oklahoma, and Kansas—three leading grain-producing states—the underground water table has dropped by more than 30 meters (100 feet). As a result, wells have gone dry on thousands of farms in the southern Great Plains, forcing farmers to return to lower-yielding dryland farming. Although the depletion of underground water is taking a toll on U.S. grain production, irrigated land accounts for only one fifth of the U.S. grain harvest, compared with close to three fifths of the harvest in India and four fifths in China.[44]

Pakistan, a country with 177 million people that is growing by 4 million per year, is also mining its underground water. In the Pakistani part of the fertile Punjab plain, the drop in water tables appears to be similar to that in India. Observation wells near the twin cities of Islamabad and Rawalpindi show a fall in the water table between 1982 and 2000 that ranges from 1 to nearly 2 meters a year.[45]

In the province of Balochistan, which borders Afghanistan, water tables around the capital, Quetta, are falling by 3.5 meters per year—pointing to the day when the city will run out of water. Sardar Riaz A. Khan, former director of Pakistan's Arid Zone Research Institute in Quetta, reports that six of Balochistan's basins have exhausted their groundwater supplies, leaving their irrigated lands barren.[46]

Iran is overpumping its aquifers by an average of 5 billion tons of water per year, the water equivalent of one fourth of its annual grain harvest. It too faces a day of reckoning.[47]

Israel, even though it is a pioneer in raising irrigation water productivity, is depleting both of its principal aquifers—the coastal aquifer and the mountain aquifer that it shares with Palestinians. In response, Israel has banned the irrigation of wheat, its staple food, and is now importing nearly all the wheat it consumes. Conflicts between Israelis and Palestinians over the allocation of water are ongoing.[48]

In Mexico—home to a population of 109 million that is projected to reach 129 million by 2050—the demand for water is outstripping supply. Mexico City's water problems are well known. Rural areas are also suffering. In the agricultural state of Guanajuato, the water table is falling by 2 meters or more a year. In the northwestern state of Sonora, farmers once pumped water from the Hermosillo aquifer at a depth of 10 meters (35 feet). Today they pump from more than 120 meters. At the national level, 51 percent of all water extraction is from aquifers that are being overpumped.[49]

Since the overpumping of aquifers is occurring in many countries more or less simultaneously, the depletion of aquifers and the resulting harvest cutbacks could come at roughly the same time. And the accelerating depletion of aquifers means this day may come soon, creating potentially unmanageable food scarcity.

Farmers Losing Water to Cities

The world's freshwater supplies are shrinking, and the world's farmers are getting a shrinking share of this shrinking supply. While water tensions among countries are more likely to make news headlines, it is the jousting for water between cities and farms within countries that preoccupies local political leaders. The economics of water use do not favor farmers in this competition, simply because it takes so much water to produce food. For example, while it takes only 14 tons of water to make a ton of steel, it takes 1,000 tons of water to grow a ton of wheat. In countries preoccupied with expanding the economy and creating jobs, agriculture becomes the residual claimant.[50]

Many of the world's largest cities, such as Los Angeles, Cairo, and New Delhi, can increase their water consumption only by taking it from agriculture. This rural-urban competition for underground water resources is intensifying throughout India. Nowhere is this more evident than in Chennai (formerly Madras), a city of 7 million in southern India. As a result of the city government's inability to supply water for some of the city's residents, a thriving tank-truck industry has emerged that buys water from farmers and hauls it to the city's thirsty residents.[51]

For farmers surrounding the city, the price of water far exceeds the value of the crops they can produce with it. Unfortunately, the 13,000 tankers hauling the water to Chennai are mining the region's underground water resources. Water tables are falling and shallow wells have gone dry. Eventually even the deeper wells will go dry, depriving these communities of both their food supply and their livelihood.[52]

Chinese farmers along the Juma River downstream from Beijing discovered in 2004 that the river had suddenly stopped flowing. A diversion dam had been built near the capital to take river water for Yanshan Petrochemical, a state-owned industry. Although the farmers protested bitterly, it was a losing battle. For the 120,000 villagers downstream from the diversion dam, the loss of water could cripple their ability to make a living from farming.[53]

In the U.S. southern Great Plains and the Southwest, where there is little unclaimed water, the growing water needs of cities and thousands of small towns can be satisfied only by taking water from agriculture. A monthly publication from California, *The Water Strategist*, devotes several pages each issue to a listing of water sales that took place in the western United States during the preceding month. Scarcely a working day goes by without another sale.[54]

Colorado has one of the world's most active water markets. Fast-growing cities and towns in a state with high immigration are buying irrigation water rights from farmers and ranchers. In the upper Arkansas River basin, which occupies the southeastern quarter of the state, Colorado Springs and Aurora (a suburb of Denver) have already bought water rights to one third of the basin's farmland.[55]

Far larger purchases are being made by cities in California. In 2003, San Diego bought annual rights to 247 million tons (200,000 acre-feet) of water from farmers in the nearby Imperial Valley—the largest farm-to-city water transfer in U.S. history. This agreement covers the next 75 years. And in 2004, the Metropolitan Water District, which supplies water to 18 million southern Californians in several cities, negotiated the purchase of 137 million tons of water per year from farmers for the next 35 years. Without irrigation water, and with sparse rainfall, the highly productive land owned by these farmers is wasteland. The farmers who are selling their water rights would like to continue farming, but city officials are offering far more for the water than the farmers could possibly earn by irrigating crops. Irrigated area in California shrank 10 percent between 1997 and 2007 as farmers sold their irrigation water to cities.[56]

Whether it is outright government expropriation, farmers being outbid by cities, or cities simply drilling deeper wells than farmers can afford, tillers of the land are losing the water war.

Historically, water scarcity was a local issue. It was up to national governments to balance water supply and demand. Now this is changing as scarcity crosses national boundaries via the international grain trade. Since it takes so much water to produce grain, importing grain is the most efficient way to import water. Countries are, in effect, using grain to balance their water books. Similarly, trading in grain futures is in a sense trading in water futures. To the extent there is a world water market, it is embodied in the grain market.[57]

The Middle East and North Africa—from Morocco in the west through Iran in the east—has become the world's fastest-growing grain import market. With virtually every country in the region pressing against its water limits, the growing urban demand for water can be satisfied only by taking irrigation water from agriculture. Egypt has become the leading importer of wheat in recent years. It now imports close to 40 percent of its total grain supply, a dependence that reflects a population that is outgrowing the grain harvest that can be produced with the Nile's water. Algeria, with 34 million people, imports more than 70 percent of its grain.[58]

Overall, the water required to produce the grain and other farm products imported into the Middle East and North Africa last year exceeded the annual flow of the Nile River at Aswan. In effect, the region's water deficit can be thought of as another Nile flowing into the region in the form of imported food.[59]

It is often said that future wars in the Middle East will more likely be fought over water than oil, but in reality the competition for water is taking place in world grain markets. Beyond this, several countries in the region are now attempting to acquire land in other countries and, what is more important, the water that comes with it.

Knowing where water deficits are developing today tells us where grain deficits will be concentrated tomorrow. Thus far, the countries importing much of their grain have been smaller ones. Now we are looking at the growing water deficits in both China and India, each with more than a billion people. At what point does water scarcity translate into food scarcity?[60]

Land and Water Conflicts

As land and water become scarce, competition for these vital resources intensifies within societies, particularly between the wealthy and those who are poor and dispossessed. The shrinkage of life-supporting resources per person that comes with population growth is threatening to drop the living standards of millions of people below the survival level, leading to potentially unmanageable social tensions.

Access to land is a prime source of social tension. Expanding world population has cut the grainland per person in half since 1950 to a mere quarter-acre, equal to half of a building lot in a U.S. suburb. The shrinkage in cropland per person not only threatens livelihoods; in largely subsistence societies, it threatens survival itself. Tensions within communities begin to build as landholdings shrink below that needed for survival.[61]

The Sahelian zone of Africa, with its fast-growing populations, is an area of spreading conflict. In troubled Sudan, 2 million people have died and over 4 million have been displaced in the long-standing conflict between the Muslim north and the Christian south. The more recent conflict in the Darfur region in western Sudan that began in 2003 illustrates the mounting tensions between two Muslim groups—camel herders and subsistence farmers. Government troops are backing the Arab herder militias, who are engaging in the wholesale slaughter of black Sudanese farmers in an effort to drive them off their land, sending them into refugee camps in neighboring Chad. An estimated 300,000 people have been killed in the conflict or died of hunger and disease in the refugee camps.[62]

Overgrazing and declining rainfall are combining to destroy the grasslands in this region. But well before the rainfall decline, the seeds of the conflict were being sown as Sudan's population climbed from 9 million in 1950 to 40 million in 2007, a fourfold rise. Meanwhile, the cattle population increased from 7 million to 41 million, an increase of nearly sixfold. The number of sheep and goats increased from 14 million to 94 million, a near sevenfold increase. No grassland can survive such rapid continuous growth in livestock populations.[63]

In Nigeria, where 151 million people are crammed into an area not much larger than Texas, overgrazing and overplowing are converting grassland and cropland into desert, putting farmers and herders in a war for survival. As Somini Sengupta reported in the *New York Times* in June 2004, "in recent years, as the desert has spread, trees have been felled and the populations of both herders and farmers have soared, the competition for land has only intensified."[64]

Unfortunately, the division between herders and farmers is also often the division between Muslims and Christians. The competition for land, amplified by religious differences and combined with a large number of frustrated young men with guns, has created what the *New York Times* described as a "combustible mix" that has "fueled a recent orgy of violence across this fertile central Nigerian state [Plateau]. Churches and mosques were razed. Neighbor turned against neighbor. Reprisal attacks spread until finally...the government imposed emergency rule."[65]

Similar divisions exist between herders and farmers in northern Mali, the *New York Times* noted, where "swords and sticks have been chucked for Kalashnikovs, as desertification and population growth have stiffened the competition between the largely black African farmers and the ethnic Tuareg and Fulani herders. Tempers are raw on both sides. The dispute, after all, is over livelihood and even more, about a way of life."[66]

Rwanda is a classic case study in how mounting population pressure can translate into political tension, conflict, and social tragedy. James Gasana, who was Rwanda's Minister of Agriculture and Environment in 1990–92, offers some insights. As the chair of a national agricultural commission in 1990, he had warned that without "profound transformations in its agriculture, [Rwanda] will not be capable of feeding adequately its population under the present growth rate." Although the country's demographers projected major future gains in population, Gasana said in 1990 that he did not see how Rwanda would reach 10 million inhabitants without social disorder "unless important progress in agriculture, as well as other sectors of the economy, were achieved."[67]

Gasana's warning of possible social disorder was prophetic. He further described how siblings inherited land from their parents and how, with an average of seven children per family, plots that were already small were fragmented further. Many farmers tried to find new land, moving onto steeply sloping mountains. By 1989, almost half of Rwanda's cultivated land was on slopes of 10 to 35 degrees, land that is universally considered uncultivable.[68]

In 1950, Rwanda's population was 2.4 million. By 1993, it had tripled to 7.5 million, making it the most densely populated country in Africa. As population grew, so did the demand for firewood. By 1991, the demand was more than double the sustainable yield of local forests. As trees disappeared, straw and other crop residues were used for cooking fuel. With less organic matter in the soil, land fertility declined.[69]

As the health of the land deteriorated, so did that of the people dependent on it. Eventually there was simply not enough food to go around. A quiet desperation developed. Like a drought-afflicted countryside, it could be ignited with a single match. That ignition came with the crash of a plane on April 6, 1994, shot down as it approached the capital Kigali, killing President Juvenal Habyarimana, a Hutu. The crash unleashed an organized attack by Hutus, leading to an estimated 800,000 deaths of Tutsis and moderate Hutus in 100 days. In some villages, whole families were slaughtered lest there be survivors to claim the family plot of land.[70]

Africa is not alone. In India, tension between Hindus and Muslims is never far below the surface. As each successive generation further subdivides already small plots, pressure on the land is intense. The pressure on water resources is even greater.

With India's population projected to grow from 1.2 billion in 2008 to 1.6 billion in 2050, a collision between rising human numbers and shrinking water supplies seems inevitable. The risk is that India could face social conflicts that would dwarf those in Rwanda. As James Gasana notes, the relationship between population and natural systems is a national security issue, one that can spawn conflicts along geographic, tribal, ethnic, or religious lines.[71]

Disagreements over the allocation of water among countries that share river systems is a common source of international political conflict, especially where populations are outgrowing the flow of the river. Nowhere is this potential conflict more stark than among Egypt, Sudan, and Ethiopia in the Nile River valley. Agriculture in Egypt, where it rarely rains, is wholly dependent on water from the Nile. Egypt now gets the lion's share of the Nile's water, but its current population of 82 million is projected to reach 130 million by 2050, thus greatly expanding the demand for grain and water. Sudan, whose 41 million people also depend heavily on food produced with Nile water, is expected to have 76 million by 2050. And the number of people in Ethiopia, the country that controls 85 percent of the river's headwaters, is projected to expand from 81 million to 174 million. Beyond this, recent acquisitions of vast tracts of land in Sudan by other countries for farming will further boost demands on the Nile.[72]

Since there is little water left in the Nile when it reaches the Mediterranean, if either Sudan or Ethiopia takes more water, Egypt will get less, making it increasingly difficult to feed an additional 48 million people. Although there is an existing water rights agreement among the three countries, Ethiopia receives only a minuscule share of water. Given its aspirations for a better life, and with the headwaters of the Nile being one of its few natural resources, Ethiopia will undoubtedly be taking more.[73]

To the north, Turkey, Syria, and Iraq share the waters of the Tigris and Euphrates river system. Turkey, controlling the headwaters, is developing a massive project on the Tigris to increase the water used for irrigation and power. Both Syria, which is expected to grow from 21 million people to 37 million by mid-century, and Iraq, which is projected to more than double its population of 30 million, are worried because they too will need more water.[74]

In the Aral Sea basin in Central Asia, there is an uneasy arrangement among five countries to share two rivers, the Amu Darya and the Syr Darya, that drain into the sea. The demand for water in Kazakhstan, Kyrgyzstan, Tajikistan, Turkmenistan, and Uzbekistan already exceeds the flow of the two rivers by 25 percent. Turkmenistan, which is upstream on the Amu Darya, is planning to develop still further its irrigated area. Racked by insurgencies, the region lacks the cooperation needed to manage its scarce water resources. On top of this, Afghanistan, which controls the headwaters of the Amu Darya, plans to use some of the water for its development. Geographer Sarah O'Hara of the University of Nottingham, who studies the region's water problems, says, "We talk about the developing world and the developed world, but this is the deteriorating world."[75]

Cars and People Compete for Grain

At a time when excessive pressures on the earth's land and water resources are of growing concern, there is a massive new demand emerging for cropland to produce fuel for cars—one that threatens world food security. Although this situation had been developing for a few decades, it was not until Hurricane Katrina in 2005, when oil prices jumped above $60 a barrel and U.S. gasoline prices climbed to $3 a gallon, that the situation came into focus. Suddenly investments in U.S. corn-based ethanol distilleries became hugely profitable, unleashing an investment frenzy that will convert one fourth of the 2009 U.S. grain harvest into fuel for cars.[76]

The United States quickly came to dominate the crop-based production of fuel for cars. In 2005, it eclipsed Brazil, formerly the world's leading ethanol producer. In Europe, where the emphasis is on producing biodiesel, mostly from rapeseed, some 2.1 billion gallons were set to be produced in 2009. To meet its biodiesel goal, the European Union, under cropland constraints, is increasingly turning to palm oil imported from Indonesia and Malaysia, a trend that depends on clearing rainforests for oil palm plantations.[77]

The price of grain is now tied to the price of oil. Historically the food and energy economies were separate, but now with the massive U.S. capacity to convert grain into ethanol, that is changing. In this new situation, when the price of oil climbs, the world price of grain moves up toward its oil-equivalent value. If the fuel value of grain exceeds its food value, the market will simply move the commodity into the energy economy. If the price of oil jumps to $100 a barrel, the price of grain will follow it upward. If oil goes to $200, grain will follow.

From 1990 to 2005, world grain consumption, driven largely by population growth and rising consumption of grain-based animal products, climbed by an average of 21 million tons per year. Then came the explosion in grain used in U.S. ethanol distilleries, which jumped from 54 million tons in 2006 to 95 million tons in 2008. This 41-million-ton jump doubled the annual growth in world demand for grain almost overnight, helping to triple world prices for wheat, rice, corn, and soybeans from mid-2006 to mid-2008. A World Bank analyst attributes 70 percent of the food price rise to this diversion of food to produce fuel for cars. Since then prices have subsided somewhat as a result of the global economic downturn, but as of mid-2009 they are still well above historical levels.[78]

From an agricultural vantage point, the world's appetite for crop-based fuels is insatiable. The grain required to fill an SUV's 25-gallon tank with ethanol just once will feed one person for a whole year. If the entire U.S. grain harvest were to be converted to ethanol, it would satisfy at most 18 percent of U.S. automotive fuel needs.[79]

Projections by Professors C. Ford Runge and Benjamin Senauer of the University of Minnesota in 2003 showed the number of hungry and malnourished people decreasing steadily to 2025. But their early 2007 update of these projections, which took into account the biofuel effect on world food prices, showed the number climbing rapidly in the years ahead. Millions of people living on the lower rungs of the global economic ladder, who are barely hanging on, are losing their grip and beginning to fall off.[80]

Since the budgets of international food aid agencies are set well in advance, a rise in food prices shrinks food assistance. The WFP, which is now supplying emergency food aid to more than 30 countries, cut shipments as prices soared. Hunger is on the rise, with 18,000 children dying each day from hunger and related illnesses.[81]

The emerging competition between the owners of the world's 910 million automobiles and the 2 billion poorest people is taking the world into uncharted territory. Suddenly the world is facing an epic moral and political issue: Should grain be used to fuel cars or feed people? The average income of the world's automobile owners is roughly $30,000 a year; the 2 billion poorest people earn on average less than $3,000 a year. The market says, let's fuel the cars.[82]

For every additional acre planted to corn to produce fuel, an acre of land must be cleared for cropping elsewhere. But there is little new land to be brought under the plow unless it comes from clearing tropical rainforests in the Amazon and Congo basins and in Indonesia or from clearing land in the Brazilian *cerrado*. Unfortunately, this has heavy environmental costs: a massive release of sequestered carbon, the loss of plant and animal species, and increased rainfall runoff and soil erosion.

While it makes little sense to use food crops to fuel cars if it drives up food prices, there is the option of producing automotive fuel from fast-growing trees, switchgrass, prairie grass mixtures, or other cellulosic materials, which can be grown on wasteland. The technologies to convert these cellulosic materials into ethanol exist, but the cost of producing cellulosic ethanol is close to double that of grain-based ethanol. Whether it will ever be cost-competitive with ethanol from grain is unclear.[83]

There are alternatives to this grim scenario. The decision in May 2009 to raise U.S. auto fuel efficiency standards 40 percent by 2016 will reduce U.S. dependence on oil far more than converting the country's entire grain harvest into ethanol could. The next step is a comprehensive shift to gas-electric plug-in hybrid cars that can be recharged at night, allowing most short-distance driving—daily commuting and grocery shopping, for example—to be done with electricity.[84]

As the leading grain exporter and ethanol producer, the United States is in the driver's seat. It needs to make sure that efforts to reduce its heavy dependence on imported oil do not create a far more serious problem: chaos in the world food economy. The choice is between a future of rising world food prices, spreading hunger, and growing political instability and one of more stable food prices, sharply reduced dependence on oil, and much lower carbon emissions.[85]

The Rising Tide of Environmental Refugees

Our early twenty-first century civilization is being squeezed between advancing deserts and rising seas. Measured by the biologically productive land area that can support human habitation, the earth is shrinking. Mounting population densities, once generated solely by population growth, are now also fueled by the relentless advance of deserts and may soon be affected by the projected rise in sea level. As overpumping depletes aquifers, millions more are forced to relocate in search of water.

Desert expansion in sub-Saharan Africa, principally in the Sahelian countries, is displacing millions of people—forcing them to either move southward or migrate to North Africa. A 2006 U.N. conference on desertification in Tunisia projected that by 2020 up to 60 million people could migrate from sub-Saharan Africa to North Africa and Europe. This flow of migrants has been under way for many years.[86]

In mid-October 2003, Italian authorities discovered a boat bound for Italy carrying refugees from Africa. After being adrift for more than two weeks and having run out of fuel, food, and water, many of the passengers had died. At first the dead were tossed overboard. But after a point, the remaining survivors lacked the strength to hoist the bodies over the side. The dead and the living shared the boat, resembling what a rescuer described as "a scene from Dante's *Inferno*."[87]

The refugees were believed to be Somalis who had embarked from Libya, but the survivors would not reveal their country of origin, lest they be sent home. We do not know whether they were political, economic, or environmental refugees. Failed states like Somalia produce all three. We do know that Somalia is an ecological disaster, with overpopulation, overgrazing, and the resulting desertification destroying its pastoral economy.[88]

Perhaps the largest flow of Somali migrants is into Yemen, another failing state. In 2008 an estimated 50,000 migrants and asylum seekers reached Yemen, 70 percent more than in 2007. And during the first three months of 2009 the migrant flow was up 30 percent over the same period in 2008. These numbers simply add to the already unsustainable pressures on Yemen's land and water resources, hastening its decline.[89]

On April 30, 2006, a man fishing off the coast of Barbados discovered a 20-foot boat adrift with the bodies of 11 young men on board, bodies that were "virtually mummified" by the sun and salty ocean spray. As the end drew near, one passenger left a note tucked between two bodies: "I would like to send my family in Basada [Senegal] a sum of money. Please excuse me and goodbye." The author of the note was apparently one of a group of 52 who had left Senegal on Christmas Eve aboard a boat destined for the Canary Islands, a jumping off point for Europe. They must have drifted for some 2,000 miles, ending their trip in the Caribbean. This boat was not unique. During the first weekend of September 2006, police intercepted boats from Mauritania with a record total of nearly 1,200 people on board.[90]

For those living in Central American countries, including Honduras, Guatemala, Nicaragua, and El Salvador, Mexico is often the gateway to the United States. In 2008, Mexican immigration authorities reported some 39,000 detentions and 89,000 deportations.[91]

In the city of Tapachula on the Guatemala-Mexico border, young men in search of jobs wait along the tracks for a slow-moving freight train passing through the city en route to the north. Some make it onto the train. Others do not. The Jesús el Buen Pastor refuge is home to 25 amputees who lost their grip and fell under a train while trying to board. For these young men, says Olga Sánchez Martínez, the director of the refuge, this is the "end of their American dream." A local priest, Flor María Rigoni, calls the migrants attempting to board the trains "the kamikazes of poverty."[92]

Today, bodies washing ashore in Italy, Spain, and Turkey are a daily occurrence, the result of desperate acts by desperate people. And each day Mexicans risk their lives in the Arizona desert trying to reach jobs in the United States. On average, some 100,000 or more Mexicans leave rural areas every year, abandoning plots of land too small or too eroded to make a living. They either head for Mexican cities or try to cross illegally into the United States. Many of those who try to cross the Arizona desert perish in its punishing heat. Since 2001, some 200 bodies have been found along the Arizona border each year.[93]

With the vast majority of the 2.4 billion people to be added to the world by 2050 coming in countries where water tables are already falling, water refugees are likely to become commonplace. They will be most common in arid and semiarid regions where populations are outgrowing the water supply and sinking into hydrological poverty. Villages in northwestern India are being abandoned as aquifers are depleted and people can no longer find water. Millions of villagers in northern and western China and in parts of Mexico may have to move because of a lack of water.[94]

Advancing deserts are squeezing expanding populations into an ever smaller geographic area. Whereas the U.S. Dust Bowl displaced 3 million people, the advancing desert in China's Dust Bowl provinces could displace tens of millions.[95]

Africa, too, is facing this problem. The Sahara Desert is pushing the populations of Morocco, Tunisia, and Algeria northward toward the Mediterranean. In a desperate effort to deal with drought and desertification, Morocco is geographically restructuring its agriculture, replacing grain with less thirsty orchards and vineyards.[96]

In Iran, villages abandoned because of spreading deserts or a lack of water already number in the thousands. In the vicinity of Damavand, a small town within an hour's drive of Tehran, 88 villages have been abandoned. And as the desert takes over in Nigeria, farmers and herders are forced to move, squeezed into a shrinking area of productive land. Desertification refugees typically end up in cities, many in squatter settlements. Others migrate abroad.[97]

In Latin America, deserts are expanding and forcing people to move in both Brazil and Mexico. In Brazil, some 66 million hectares of land are affected, much of it concentrated in the country's northeast. In Mexico, with a much larger share of arid and semiarid land, the degradation of cropland now extends over 59 million hectares.[98]

While desert expansion and water shortages are now displacing millions of people, rising seas promise to displace far greater numbers in the future, given the concentration of the world's population in low-lying coastal cities and rice-growing river deltas. The numbers could eventually reach the hundreds of millions, offering yet another powerful reason for stabilizing both climate and population.[99]

In the end, the issue with rising seas is whether governments are strong enough to withstand the political and economic stress of relocating large numbers of people while suffering heavy coastal losses of housing and industrial facilities.

During this century we must deal with the effects of trends—rapid population growth, advancing deserts, and rising seas—that we set in motion during the last century. Our choice is a simple one: reverse these trends or risk being overwhelmed by them.

3

Climate Change and the Energy Transition

Ever since civilization began, each generation has left the next a planet similar to the one it inherited. Our generation may be the first to abandon that tradition.

The earth's temperature is rising. It has gone up 0.6 degrees Celsius (1 degree Fahrenheit) since 1970, and it is projected to rise by up to 6 degrees Celsius (11 degrees Fahrenheit) by the end of this century. This rise will be uneven. It will be much greater at the higher latitudes than in the equatorial regions, greater over land than over oceans, and greater in continental interiors than in coastal regions.[1]

Sea level is rising too, as a result of the thermal expansion that takes place as ocean water warms and as ice sheets melt. Recent studies project a rise of 3–6 feet by the end of the century. During the entire twentieth century, sea level rose by 7 inches, but if it rises 6 feet by 2100, it will have risen an average of 7 inches per decade.[2]

Geographically, the oceans will expand and the continents will shrink. Low-lying island countries will disappear beneath the waves. Rising seas will inundate low-lying cities and rice-growing river deltas, generating hundreds of millions of refugees.

The rapidly rising temperature that is projected for this century with business as usual will alter every ecosystem on earth. Up to one third of all plant and animal species could be lost. Despite the fences we have built around parks and wildlife preserves, the ecosystems within them will not survive the thermal stress.[3]

Agriculture as we know it today evolved in a climate that was remarkably stable during its 11,000-year experience. As climate changes, agriculture will be increasingly out of sync with it.

At the same time that rising temperatures are reshaping the earth's ecology and geography, declining oil production will be reshaping the global economy. The twentieth century was the oil century. In 1900, the world produced 150 million barrels of oil. In 2000, it produced 28 billion barrels—a 185-fold jump. This was the century in which oil overtook coal to become the world's leading source of energy. It was also the century in which oil totally reshaped life for much of humanity.[4]

The rapidly expanding supply of cheap oil led to an explosive worldwide growth in food production, population, urbanization, and human mobility. But today's oil-based civilization is heavily dependent on a resource whose production will soon be falling. Since 1981, oil extraction has exceeded new discoveries by an ever-widening margin. In 2008, the world pumped nearly 31 billion barrels of oil but discovered only 7 billion barrels. World oil reserves are now in decline, dropping every year.[5]

As we look at the future of oil in a Plan B context, it is not only geological constraints but also escalating climate concerns that will reduce its use. Today roughly 43 percent of carbon dioxide (CO_2) emissions from burning fossil fuels comes from coal and 38 percent from oil. The remaining 19 percent comes from natural gas. Because coal is the most carbon-intensive fossil fuel, any effort to quickly cut CO_2 emissions means quickly cutting coal use[6]

Rising Temperature and Its Effects

We are entering a new era, one of rapid and often unpredictable climate change. In fact, the new climate norm is change. The 25 warmest years on record have come since 1980. And the 10 warmest years since global recordkeeping began in 1880 have come since 1996.[7]

The warming is caused by the accumulation of heat-trap-ping "greenhouse" gases and other pollutants in the atmosphere. Of the greenhouse gases, CO_2 accounts for 63 percent of the recent warming trend, methane 18 percent, and nitrous oxide 6 percent, with several lesser gases accounting for the remaining 13 percent. Carbon dioxide comes mostly from electricity generation, heating, transportation, and industry. In contrast, human-caused methane and nitrous oxide emissions come largely from agriculture—methane from rice paddies and cattle and nitrous oxide from the use of nitrogenous fertilizer.[8]

Atmospheric concentrations of CO_2, the principal driver of climate change, have climbed from nearly 280 parts per million (ppm) when the Industrial Revolution began around 1760 to 386 ppm in 2008. The annual rise in atmospheric CO_2 level, now one of the world's most predictable environmental trends, results from emissions on a scale that is overwhelming nature's capacity to absorb carbon. In 2008, some 7.9 billion tons of carbon were emitted from the burning of fossil fuels and 1.5 billion tons were emitted from deforestation, for a total of 9.4 billion tons. But since nature has been absorbing only about 5 billion tons per year in oceans, soils, and vegetation, the remainder stays in the atmosphere, pushing up CO_2 levels.[9]

Methane, a potent greenhouse gas, is produced when organic matter is broken down under anaerobic conditions, including the decomposition of plant material in bogs, organic materials in landfills, or forage in a cow's stomach. Methane can also be released with the thawing of permafrost, the frozen ground underlying the tundra that covers nearly 9 million square miles in the northern latitudes. All together, Arctic soils contain more carbon than currently resides in the atmosphere, which is a worry considering that permafrost is now melting in Alaska, northern Canada, and Siberia, creating lakes and releasing methane. Once they get under way, permafrost melting, the release of methane and CO_2, and a rising temperature create a self-reinforcing trend, what scientists call a "positive feedback loop." The risk is that the release of a massive amount of methane into the atmosphere from melting permafrost could simply overwhelm efforts to stabilize climate.[10]

Another unsettling development is the effect on climate of atmospheric brown clouds (ABCs) consisting of soot particles from burning coal, diesel fuel, or wood. These particles affect climate in three ways. First, by intercepting sunlight, they heat the upper atmosphere. Second, because they also reflect sunlight, they have a dimming effect, lowering the earth's surface temperature. And third, if particles from these brown clouds are deposited on snow and ice, they darken the surface and accelerate melting.[11]

These effects are of particular concern in India and China, where a large ABC over the Tibetan Plateau is contributing to the melting of high-altitude glaciers that supply the major rivers of Asia. Soot deposition causes earlier seasonal melting of mountain snow in ranges as different as the Himalayas of Asia and the Sierra Nevada of California, and it is also believed to be accelerating the melting of Arctic sea ice. Soot particles have even been found in snow in Antarctica, a region once thought to be pristine and untouched by pollution.[12]

In contrast to CO_2, which may remain in the atmosphere for a century or more, soot particles in these clouds are typically airborne for only a matter of weeks. Thus, once coal-fired power plants are closed or wood cooking stoves in villages are replaced with solar cookers, atmospheric soot disappears rapidly.[13]

If we continue with business as usual, the projected rise in the earth's average temperature of 1.1–6.4 degrees Celsius (2–11 degrees Fahrenheit) during this century seems all too possible. These projections are the latest from the Intergovernmental Panel on Climate Change (IPCC), the world body of more than 2,500 leading climate scientists that in 2007 released a consensus report affirming humanity's role in climate change. Unfortunately, during the several years since the study was completed, both global CO_2 emissions and atmospheric CO_2 concentrations have exceeded those in the IPCC's worst-case scenario.[14]

With each passing year the chorus of urgency from the scientific community intensifies. Each new report indicates that we are running out of time. For instance, a landmark 2009 study by a team of scientists from the Massachusetts Institute of Technology concluded that the effects of climate change will be twice as severe as those they projected as recently as six years ago. Instead of a likely global temperature rise of 2.4 degrees Celsius, they now see a rise of 5.2 degrees.[15]

Another report, this one prepared independently as a background document for the December 2009 international climate negotiations in Copenhagen, indicated that every effort should be made to hold the temperature rise to 2 degrees Celsius above pre-industrial levels. Beyond this, dangerous climate change is considered inevitable. To hold the temperature rise to 2 degrees, the scientists note that CO_2 emissions should be reduced by 60–80 percent immediately, but since this is not possible, they note that, "To limit the extent of the overshoot, emissions should peak in the near future."[16]

The effects of rising temperature are pervasive. Higher temperatures diminish crop yields, melt the mountain glaciers that feed rivers, generate more-destructive storms, increase the severity of flooding, intensify drought, cause more-frequent and destructive wildfires, and alter ecosystems everywhere.

What we can anticipate with a warmer climate is more extreme weather events. The insurance industry is painfully aware of the relationship between higher temperatures and storm intensity. Soaring weather-related damage claims have brought a drop in earnings and a flurry of lowered credit ratings for insurance companies as well as the reinsurance companies that back them up.[17]

Companies using historical records as a basis for calculating insurance rates for future storm damage are realizing that the past is no longer a reliable guide to the future. This is a challenge not only for the insurance industry but for all of us. We are altering the earth's climate, setting in motion trends we do not always understand with consequences we cannot anticipate.

Crop-withering heat waves have lowered grain harvests in key food-producing regions in recent years. In 2002, record-high temperatures and drought-reduced grain harvests in India, the United States, and Canada dropped the world harvest 90 million tons, or 5 percent below consumption. The record-setting 2003 European heat wave contributed to a world harvest that again fell short of consumption by 90 million tons. Intense heat and drought in the U.S. Corn Belt in 2005 contributed to a world grain shortfall of 34 million tons.[18]

Such intense heat waves also take a direct human toll. In 2003, the searing heat wave that broke temperature records across Europe claimed more than 52,000 lives in nine countries. Italy alone lost more than 18,000 people, while 14,800 died in

France. More than 18 times as many people died in Europe in this 2003 heat wave as died during the terrorist attacks on the World Trade Center in 2001.[19]

There has also been a dramatic increase in the land area affected by drought in recent decades. A team of scientists at the National Center for Atmospheric Research (NCAR) reports that the area experiencing very dry conditions expanded from less than 15 percent in the 1970s to roughly 30 percent by 2002. The scientists attribute part of the change to a rise in temperature and part to reduced precipitation, with high temperatures becoming progressively more important during the latter part of the period. Most of the drying was concentrated in Europe, Asia, Canada, western and southern Africa, and eastern Australia.[20]

A 2009 report published by the U.S. National Academy of Sciences and led by Susan Solomon of the National Oceanic and Atmospheric Administration reinforces these findings. It concludes that if atmospheric CO_2 climbs from 385 ppm to 450–600 ppm, the world will face irreversible dry-season rainfall reductions in several regions of the world. The study likened the conditions to those of the U.S. Dust Bowl era of the 1930s.[21]

Researchers with the U.S. Department of Agriculture's Forest Service, drawing on 85 years of fire and temperature records, projected that a 1.6-degree-Celsius rise in summer temperature could double the area of wildfires in the 11 western states.[22]

The Pew Center on Global Climate Change sponsored an analysis of some 40 scientific studies that link rising temperature with changes in ecosystems. Among the many changes reported are spring arriving nearly two weeks earlier in the United States, tree swallows nesting nine days earlier than they did 40 years ago, and a northward shift of red fox habitat that has it encroaching on the Arctic fox's range. Inuits have been surprised by the appearance of robins, a bird they have never seen before. Indeed, there is no word in Inuit for "robin."[23]

The National Wildlife Federation (NWF) reports that if temperatures continue to rise, by 2040 one out of five of the Pacific Northwest's rivers will be too hot for salmon, steelhead, and trout. Paula Del Giudice, Director of NWF's Northwest Natural Resource Center, notes that "global warming will add an enormous amount of pressure onto what's left of the region's prime cold-water fish habitat."[24]

Douglas Inkley, NWF senior science advisor and senior author of a report to The Wildlife Society, notes, "We face the prospect that the world of wildlife that we now know—and many of the places we have invested decades of work in conserving as refuges and habitats for wildlife—will cease to exist as we know them, unless we change this forecast."[25]

Melting Ice, Rising Seas

Ice is melting so fast that even climate scientists are scrambling to keep up with the shrinkage of ice sheets and glaciers. The melting of the earth's largest ice sheets—Greenland and West Antarctica—would raise sea level dramatically. If the Greenland ice sheet were to melt entirely, it would raise sea level 23 feet. Melting of the West Antarctic ice sheet, the most vulnerable portion of the Antarctic ice because of its exposure to both warming air and warming ocean water, would eventually raise sea level 16 feet. Many of the world's coastal cities would be under water; over 600 million coastal dwellers would be forced to move.[26]

Assessing the prospects for the Greenland ice sheet begins with looking at the warming of the Arctic region. A 2005 study, *Impacts of a Warming Arctic*, concluded that the Arctic is warming almost twice as fast as the rest of the planet. Conducted by the Arctic Climate Impact Assessment (ACIA) team, an international group of 300 scientists, the study found that in the regions surrounding the Arctic, including Alaska, western Canada, and eastern Russia, winter temperatures have climbed by 3–4 degrees Celsius (5–7 degrees Fahrenheit) over the last half-century. Robert Corell, the ACIA chairman, says this region "is experiencing some of the most rapid and severe climate change on Earth."[27]

In testimony before the U.S. Senate Commerce Committee, Sheila Watt-Cloutier, speaking on behalf of the 155,000 Inuits who live in Alaska, Canada, Greenland, and the Russian Federation, described their struggle to survive in the rapidly changing Arctic climate as "a snapshot of what is happening to the planet." For example, as the sea ice shrinks it threatens the ice-dwelling seals, a basic food source for the Inuit. She called the warming of the Arctic "a defining event in the history of this planet."[28]

The ACIA report noted that the retreat of the sea ice has devastating consequences for polar bears, whose very survival may be at stake. A subsequent report indicated that polar bears, desperate for food, are turning to cannibalism. Two thirds of the polar bear population could be gone by 2050.[29]

There is new evidence that Arctic sea ice is melting faster than previously thought. Scientists from the National Snow and Ice Data Center and NCAR examining data on Arctic Ocean summer ice since 1953 concluded that the ice is melting much faster than climate models had predicted. They found that from 1979 to 2006 the summer sea ice shrinkage accelerated to 9.1 percent a decade. In the summer of 2007, a record melt year, Arctic sea ice shrank to an area some 20 percent smaller than the previous record set in 2005. Recent evidence that the multi-year sea ice is not recovering in winter and therefore thinning overall only adds to concern about the ice cap's future.[30]

Walt Meier, a researcher at the U.S. National Snow and Ice Data Center, views the winter shrinkage with alarm. He believes there is "a good chance" that the Arctic tipping point has been reached. Some scientists now think that the Arctic Ocean could be ice-free in summer as early as 2015, but in early 2009 Warwick Vincent, director of the Center for Northern Studies at Laval University in Quebec, reported that this could happen by 2013. Arctic scientist Julienne Stroeve observed that the shrinking Arctic sea ice may have reached "a tipping point that could trigger a cascade of climate change reaching into Earth's temperate regions."[31]

Scientists have long been concerned that a self-reinforcing trend may be starting to kick in as the sea ice shrinks. When incoming sunlight strikes the ice in the Arctic Ocean, up to 70 percent of it is reflected back into space. Only 30 percent is absorbed. As the Arctic sea ice melts, however, and the incoming sunlight hits the much darker open water, only 6 percent is reflected back into space and 94 percent is converted into heat. This albedo effect helps explain the accelerating shrinkage of the Arctic sea ice and the rapidly rising regional temperature.[32]

If all the ice in the Arctic Ocean melts, it will not affect sea level because the ice is already in the water. But it will lead to a much warmer Arctic region as more of the incoming sunlight is converted to heat. And since Greenland lies largely within the

Arctic Circle, its ice sheet—up to 1.6 kilometers (1 mile) thick in places—is beginning to show the effects.[33]

Several recent studies report accelerated melting of the Greenland ice sheet. In September 2006, a University of Colorado team study published in *Nature* indicated that between April 2004 and April 2006 Greenland lost ice 2.5 times faster than during the preceding two years. In October 2006, a team of NASA scientists reported that the flow of glaciers into the sea was accelerating. Eric Rignot, a glaciologist at NASA's Jet Propulsion Laboratory, said that "none of this has been predicted by numerical models, and therefore all projections of the contribution of Greenland to sea level [rise] are way below reality."[34]

In late summer 2007 scientists at a symposium in Ilulissat, Greenland, said that the Greenland icecap is melting so fast that it is triggering minor earthquakes as pieces of ice weighing millions of tons break off and slide into the sea. ACIA chairman Corell reported that "we have seen a massive acceleration of the speed with which these glaciers are moving into the sea." The Ilulissat (Jakobshavn Isbrae) glacier, a large outlet glacier on Greenland's southwest coast, is moving at 2 meters per hour on a front 8 kilometers (5 miles) wide and 900 meters deep.[35]

Data gathered by NASA satellites indicated that Greenland's floating ice shelves shrank by 24 square miles in 2007. In the summer of 2008 this loss jumped to 71 square miles, nearly tripling. Part of this loss was observed directly by an Ohio State University research team, which saw a massive 11-square-mile chunk of ice break off from the Petermann Glacier in northern Greenland. An upstream crack in the glacier suggested an even larger chunk would be breaking off soon.[36]

What scientists once thought was a simple linear process—that at the surface an ice sheet melts a fixed amount each year, depending on the temperature—is now seen to be much more complex. As the surface ice begins to melt, some of the water filters down through cracks in the glacier, lubricating the surface between the glacier and the rock beneath it. This accelerates the glacial flow and the calving of icebergs into the surrounding ocean. The relatively warm water flowing through the moulins (deep holes) and cracks in the ice sheet also carries surface heat deep inside it far faster than it would otherwise penetrate by simple conduction.[37]

At the other end of the earth, the 2-kilometer-thick Antarctic ice sheet, which covers an area one and a half times the size of the United States and contains 70 percent of the world's fresh water, is also beginning to melt. Ice shelves formed by the flow of glaciers from the continent into the surrounding seas are breaking up at an alarming rate.[38]

The flow of ice, fed by the continuous formation of new ice on land and culminating in the breakup of the shelves on the outer fringe and the calving of icebergs, is not new. What is new is the pace of this process. Even veteran ice watchers are amazed at how quickly the disintegration is occurring. "The speed of it is staggering," said David Vaughan, a glaciologist at the British Antarctic Survey, which has been monitoring the Larsen ice shelf closely. Along the Antarctic Peninsula, in the vicinity of Larsen, the average temperature has risen 2.5 degrees Celsius over the last five decades.[39]

When Larsen A, a huge ice shelf on the eastern side of the Antarctic Peninsula, broke up in 1995, it was a signal that all was not well in the region. Then in 2000, a huge iceberg nearly the size of Connecticut—11,000 square kilometers (4,250 square miles)—broke off the Ross Ice Shelf on the south side of the continent.[40]

After Larsen A broke up, it was only a matter of time, given the rise in temperature in the region, before neighboring Larsen B would do the same. So when the northern part of the Larsen B Ice Shelf collapsed into the sea in March 2002, it was not a total surprise. At about the same time, a Rhode Island–sized chunk of ice broke off the Thwaites Glacier.[41]

In May 2007, a team of scientists from NASA and the University of Colorado reported satellite data showing widespread snow-melt on the interior of the Antarctic ice sheet over an area the size of California. This melting in 2005 was 900 kilometers inland, only about 500 kilometers from the South Pole. Team member Konrad Steffen observed, "Antarctica has shown little to no warming in the recent past with the exception of the Antarctic Peninsula, but now large regions are showing the first signs of the impacts of warming."[42]

Ice sheets are now breaking up at a remarkable rate. At the end of February 2008, a NASA satellite caught a Manhattan-sized piece of the Wilkins ice shelf breaking up. Within 10 days, the 5,000-square-mile ice shelf lost 160 square miles of ice.[43]

Just over a year later, a NASA satellite image showed the collapse of an ice bridge that signaled the final demise of the Wilkins ice shelf. Yet another chunk of the West Antarctic ice sheet is disappearing. NASA reports that the Wilkins breakup is the tenth major Antarctic ice sheet to collapse in recent times.[44]

When ice shelves already largely in the water break off from the continental ice mass, this does not have much direct effect on sea level per se. But without the ice shelves to impede the flow of glacial ice, typically moving 400–900 meters a year, the flow of ice from the continent can accelerate, leading to a thinning of the ice sheet on the edges of the Antarctic continent, thus contributing to sea level rise.[45]

The accelerated melting of both the Greenland and West Antarctic ice sheets is leading to much higher projected rises in sea level for this century. The IPCC projections of 18–59 centimeters during this century do not fully include the dynamic processes accelerating ice melt on the Greenland and West Antarctic ice sheets. As scientists take these into account, they are revising their projections. In 2008, a report by the U.S. Climate Change Science Program indicated that the IPCC sea level rise is likely an underestimate. A team led by W. Tad Pfeffer of the Institute of Arctic and Alpine Research at the University of Colorado concluded in September 2008 that with melting continuing to accelerate, the world could see a sea level rise of 0.8–2 meters (3–6 feet) by 2100.[46]

The International Institute for Environment and Development (IIED) has analyzed the effect of a 10-meter rise in sea level, providing a sense of how humanity would be affected if the two ice sheets started to disappear. The IIED study begins by pointing out that 634 million people currently live along coasts at or below 10 meters above sea level, most of them in cities and rice-growing river deltas.[47]

One of the most vulnerable countries is China, with 144 million potential climate refugees. India and Bangladesh are next, with 63 million and 62 million respectively. Viet Nam has 43 million vulnerable people, and Indonesia 42 million. Others in the top 10 include Japan with 30 million, Egypt with 26 million, and the United States with 23 million.[48]

It is difficult to imagine the displacement of so many people.

Some of the refugees could simply retreat to higher ground within their own country. Others—facing extreme crowding in the interior regions of their homeland or a total inundation of their low-lying island countries—would seek refuge elsewhere. Rising-sea refugees in already crowded Bangladesh would likely try to do this, which helps explain why neighboring India has built a fence along its border.

Not only would some of the world's largest cities, such as Shanghai, Kolkata, London, and New York, be partly or entirely inundated, but vast areas of productive farmland would also be lost. The rice-growing river deltas and floodplains of Asia, including the Gangetic and Mekong deltas, would be covered with salt water, depriving Asia of part of its food supply.

Melting Glaciers, Shrinking Harvests

If all the earth's mountain glaciers melted, they would raise sea level only a matter of inches. But it is the summer ice melt from these glaciers that sustains so many of the world's rivers during the dry season. Thus, as temperature rises there will be a shrinkage of river-based irrigation water supplies. In early 2009 the University of Zurich's World Glacier Monitoring Service reported that 2007 marked the eighteenth consecutive year of glacier retreat. And glaciers are melting at double the rate of a decade ago.[49]

Mountain glaciers are melting in the Andes, the Rocky Mountains, the Alps, and elsewhere, but nowhere does this melting threaten world food security more than in the Himalayas and on the Tibet-Qinghai Plateau, where the melting of glaciers could soon deprive the major rivers of India and China of the ice melt needed to sustain them during the dry season. In the Indus, Ganges, Yellow, and Yangtze River basins, where irrigated agriculture depends heavily on rivers, this loss of dry-season flow will shrink harvests and could create unmanageable food shortages.[50]

The world has never faced such a predictably massive threat to food production as that posed by the melting mountain glaciers of Asia. As noted in Chapter 1, China and India are the world's leading wheat producers, and they totally dominate the rice harvest.[51]

The IPCC reports that Himalayan glaciers are receding rapidly and that many could melt entirely by 2035. If the giant Gangotri Glacier—whose ice melt supplies 70 percent of the Ganges flow during the dry season—disappears, the Ganges could become a seasonal river, flowing during the rainy season but not during the dry season when irrigation needs are greatest.[52]

In China, which is even more dependent than India on river water for irrigation, the situation is particularly challenging. Chinese government data show that the glaciers on the Tibet-Qinghai Plateau that feed the Yellow and Yangtze Rivers are melting at a torrid pace. The Yellow River, whose basin is home to 147 million people, could experience a large dry-season flow reduction. The Yangtze River, by far the larger of the two, is threatened by the disappearance of glaciers as well. The basin's 369 million people rely heavily on rice from fields irrigated with its water.[53]

Yao Tandong, one of China's leading glaciologists, predicts that two thirds of China's glaciers could be gone by 2050. "The full-scale glacier shrinkage in the plateau region," Yao says, "will eventually lead to an ecological catastrophe."[54]

Agriculture in the Central Asian countries of Afghanistan, Kazakhstan, Kyrgyzstan, Tajikistan, Turkmenistan, and Uzbekistan depends heavily on snowmelt from the Hindu Kush, Pamir, and Tien Shan mountain ranges for irrigation water. Nearby Iran gets much of its water from the snowmelt in the 5,700-meter-high Alborz Mountains between Tehran and the Caspian Sea.[55]

In Africa, Tanzania's snow-capped Kilimanjaro may soon be snow- and ice-free. Ohio State University glaciologist Lonnie Thompson's studies of Kilimanjaro show that Africa's tallest mountain lost 84 percent of its ice field between 1912 and 2007. He projects that its snowcap could disappear entirely by 2015. Nearby Mount Kenya has lost 7 of its 18 glaciers. Local rivers fed by these glaciers are becoming seasonal rivers, generating conflict among the 2 million people who depend on them for water supplies during the dry season.[56]

Bernard Francou, research director for the French government's Institute of Research and Development, believes that 80 percent of South American glaciers could disappear within the next decade. For countries like Bolivia, Ecuador, and Peru, which rely on glacial melt for household and irrigation use, this is not good news.[57]

Peru, which stretches some 1,600 kilometers along the vast Andean mountain range and is the site of 70 percent of the earth's tropical glaciers, is in trouble. Some 22 percent of its glacial endowment, which feeds the many Peruvian rivers that supply water to the cities in the semi-arid coastal regions, has disappeared. Lonnie Thompson reported in 2007 that the Quelccaya Glacier in southern Peru, which was retreating by 6 meters per year in the 1960s, was then retreating by 60 meters annually. In an interview with *Science News* in early 2009, he said, "It's now retreating up the mountainside by about 18 inches a day, which means you can almost sit there and watch it lose ground."[58]

Many of Peru's farmers irrigate their wheat and potatoes with the river water from these disappearing glaciers. During the dry season, farmers are totally dependent on irrigation water. For Peru's 29 million people, shrinking glaciers will eventually mean a shrinking food supply.[59]

Lima's 8 million residents get most of their water from three rivers high in the Andes, rivers that are fed partly by glacial melt. While the glaciers are melting, the rivers swell, but once they are gone, the river flows will drop sharply, leaving Lima with a swelling population and a shrinking water supply.[60]

In early 2009 Wilfried Haeberli, head of the World Glacier Monitoring Service, reported that some 90 percent of the glacial ice in Spain's Pyrenees Mountains has disappeared over the last century. These glaciers feed the Gállego, Cinca, and Garona Rivers that flow southward, supplying summertime water in the region's foothills and plains.[61]

The story is the same everywhere. Daniel Fagre, U.S Geological Survey ecologist at Glacier National Park, reported in 2009 that the park's glaciers, which had been projected to disappear by 2030, may in fact be gone by 2020.[62]

In the southwestern United States, the Colorado River—the region's primary source of irrigation water—depends on snowfields in the Rockies for much of its flow. California, in addition to depending heavily on the Colorado, also relies on snowmelt from the Sierra Nevada range in the eastern part of the state. Both the Sierra Nevada and the coastal range supply irrigation water to California's Central Valley, the country's fruit and vegetable basket.[63]

With a business-as-usual energy policy, global climate models project a 70-percent reduction in the amount of snow pack for the western United States by mid-century. A detailed study of the Yakima River Valley, a vast fruit-growing region in Washington State, conducted by the Pacific Northwest National Laboratory of the U.S. Department of Energy shows progressively heavier harvest losses as the snow pack shrinks, reducing irrigation water flows.[64]

The snow and ice masses in the world's leading mountain ranges and the water they store are taken for granted simply because they have been there since agriculture began. As the earth gets hotter, we risk losing these "reservoirs in the sky" on which both farmers and cities depend.

Rising Temperatures, Falling Yields

Since farming began thousands of years ago, crops have been developed to maximize yields in a relatively stable climatic regime. Now that regime is changing.

Since crops typically are grown at or near their thermal optimum, even a relatively minor increase during the growing season of 1 or 2 degrees Celsius can shrink the grain harvest in major food-producing regions, such as the North China Plain, the Gangetic Plain of India, or the U.S. Corn Belt.[65]

Higher temperatures can halt photosynthesis, prevent pollination, and lead to crop dehydration. Although the elevated concentrations of atmospheric CO_2 that raise temperature can also raise crop yields, after a certain point the detrimental effect of higher temperatures on yields overrides the CO_2 fertilization effect for the major crops.

Two scientists in India, K. S. Kavi Kumar and Jyoti Parikh, assessed the effect of higher temperatures on wheat and rice yields. Basing their model on data from 10 sites, they concluded that in north India a 1-degree Celsius rise in mean temperature did not meaningfully reduce wheat yields, but a 2-degree rise lowered yields at almost all sites. When they looked at temperature change alone, a 2-degree Celsius rise led to a decline in irrigated wheat yields ranging from 37 percent to 58 percent. When they combined the negative effects of higher temperature with the positive effects of CO_2 fertilization, the decline in yields among the various sites ranged from 8 percent to 38 percent. For a country projected to add 400 million people by mid-century, rising temperatures are a troubling prospect.[66]

In a study of local ecosystem sustainability, Mohan Wali and his colleagues at Ohio State University noted that as temperature rises, photosynthetic activity in plants increases until the temperature reaches 20 degrees Celsius (68 degrees Fahrenheit). The rate of photosynthesis then plateaus as the temperature climbs until it hits 35 degrees Celsius (95 degrees Fahrenheit), whereupon it begins to decline, until at 40 degrees Celsius (104 degrees Fahrenheit), photosynthesis ceases entirely.[67]

Within the last few years, crop ecologists in several countries have been focusing on the precise relationship between temperature and crop yields. One of the most comprehensive of these studies was conducted at the International Rice Research Institute (IRRI) in the Philippines. A team of eminent crop scientists using crop yield data from experimental field plots of irrigated rice confirmed the rule of thumb emerging among crop ecologists—that a 1-degree Celsius rise in temperature above the norm lowers wheat, rice, and corn yields by 10 percent. The IRRI finding was consistent with those of other recent research projects. The scientists concluded that "temperature increases due to global warming will make it increasingly difficult to feed Earth's growing population."[68]

The most vulnerable part of a plant's life cycle is the pollination period. Of the world's three food staples—rice, wheat, and corn—corn is particularly vulnerable. In order for corn to reproduce, pollen must fall from the tassel to the strands of silk that emerge from the end of each ear of corn. Each of these silk strands is attached to a kernel site on the cob. If the kernel is to develop, a grain of pollen must fall on the silk strand and then journey to the kernel site. When temperatures are uncommonly high, the silk strands quickly dry out and turn brown, unable to play their role in the fertilization process.

The effects of temperature on rice pollination have been studied in detail in the Philippines. Scientists there report that the pollination of rice falls from 100 percent at 34 degrees Celsius to near zero at 40 degrees Celsius, leading to crop failure.[69]

High temperatures can also dehydrate plants. When a corn plant curls its leaves to reduce exposure to the sun, photosynthesis is reduced. And when the stomata on the underside of the leaves close to reduce moisture loss, CO_2 intake is also reduced, thereby restricting photosynthesis. At elevated temperatures, the corn plant, which under ideal conditions is so extraordinarily productive, goes into thermal shock.

Countless global climate models show that as temperature rises, some parts of the world will become more vulnerable to drought. Among these are the southwestern United States and the Sahelian region of Africa, where heat plus drought can be deadly. The Sahel, a wide savannah-like region that stretches across Africa from Mauritania and Senegal in the west to Sudan, Ethiopia, and Somalia in the east, already suffers devastating periodic droughts and high temperatures. Now the low rainfall in this region is becoming even more sparse.[70]

For tens of millions in this region across Africa, lower rainfall and higher temperatures threaten their survival. For them time is running out. Cary Fowler, head of the Global Crop Diversity Trust, says, "If we wait until it's too hot to grow maize in Chad and Mali, then it will be too late to avoid a disaster that could easily destabilize an entire region and beyond."[71]

The Decline of Oil and Coal

Climate change poses a threat to our civilization that has no precedent. A business-as-usual energy policy is no longer an option. At issue is whether we can quickly transition from fossil fuels to renewables. If we wait until massive climate change forces us to make the shift, it may be too late.

For oil, geological constraints are leading to production declines in many oil-producing countries. Paralleling the oil field depletions are security concerns in oil-importing countries, since so much oil comes from the politically volatile Persian Gulf region. For the United States, which imports 60 percent of its oil and where 88 percent of the labor force travels to work by car, this is not a trivial matter.[72]

Reducing oil use is not at all farfetched. For several reasons, including record high gasoline prices, consumption of oil in the United States—the world's leading oil consumer—dropped 6 percent in 2008. This decline appears to be continuing in 2009 as motorists turn to public transit, bicycles, and more fuel-efficient cars.[73]

With oil supply, the geological handwriting on the wall is clearly visible. Discoveries of conventional oil total roughly 2 trillion barrels, of which 1 trillion have been extracted so far. By themselves, however, these numbers miss a central point. As security analyst Michael Klare notes, the first trillion barrels was easy oil: "oil that's found on shore or near to shore; oil close to the surface and concentrated in large reservoirs; oil produced in friendly, safe, and welcoming places." The other half, Klare notes, is tough oil: "oil that's buried far offshore or deep underground; oil scattered in small, hard-to-find reservoirs; oil that must be obtained from unfriendly, politically dangerous, or hazardous places."[74]

Another clue to the oil production prospect is the actions of the major oil companies themselves. To begin with, the collective production of the eight leading independents has peaked and is declining. This decline notwithstanding, there have not been any dramatic increases in exploration and development, suggesting that the companies agree with the petroleum geologists who say that 95 percent of all the oil in the earth has already been discovered. "The whole world has now been seismically searched and picked over," says independent geologist Colin Campbell. "Geological knowledge has improved enormously in the past 30 years and it is almost inconceivable now that major fields remain to be found."[75]

Matt Simmons, a prominent oil investment banker, says in reference to new oil fields: "We've run out of good projects. This is not a money issue...if these oil companies had fantastic projects, they'd be out there [developing new fields]." Both Walter Youngquist, author of *GeoDestinies*, and the late A.M. Samsam Bakhtiari of the Iranian National Oil Company projected that oil production would peak in 2007.[76]

Yet another way of gauging the oil prospect is simply to look at the age of the major oil fields. Of the 20 largest oil fields ever found, 18 were discovered between 1917 (Bolivar in Venezuela) and 1968 (Shaybah in Saudi Arabia). The two most recent large ones, Cantarell in Mexico and East Baghdad Field in Iraq, were discovered during the 1970s, but none have been found since then. Neither Kazakhstan's discovery of the Kashagan oil field in the Caspian Sea in 2000 nor Brazil's discovery of the Tupi oil field in 2006—both good-sized finds—make the all-time top 20. With so many of the largest oil fields aging and in decline, offsetting this with new discoveries or more-advanced extraction technologies is increasingly difficult.[77]

The big news in 2008 was the announcement by Russia, the world's leading oil producer in recent years, that its oil output had peaked in the late 2007 and would henceforth be declining. Data through mid-2009 confirm the decline, supporting those who think world oil production has already peaked.[78]

Aside from conventional petroleum, which can easily be pumped to the surface, vast amounts of oil are stored in tar sands and in oil shale. The Athabasca tar sand deposits in Alberta, Canada, total an estimated 1.8 trillion barrels, but only about 300 billion barrels of this may be recoverable. Venezuela also has a large deposit of extra heavy oil, estimated at 1.2 trillion barrels. Perhaps a third of it could be recovered.[79]

Oil shale concentrated in Colorado, Wyoming, and Utah in the United States holds large quantities of kerogen, an organic material that can be converted into oil and gas. In the late 1970s the United States launched a major effort to develop the oil shale on the western slope of the Rocky Mountains in Colorado. When oil prices dropped in 1982, the oil shale industry collapsed. Exxon quickly pulled out of its $5-billion Colorado project, and the remaining companies soon followed suit.[80]

The one large-scale project that is moving ahead is the tar sands project in Canada. Launched in the early 1980s, it was producing 1.3 million barrels of oil a day in 2008, an amount equivalent to nearly 7 percent of current U.S. oil consumption. This tar sand oil is not cheap, becoming economical only when oil is priced at $70 per barrel. Some think it may take $90 oil to spur new investments.[81]

There is growing doubt as to whether oil in tar sands and shale should be tapped at all because of the many damaging effects, including climate disruption. Since getting oil out of tar sands requires "cooking" the sands to separate the oil, the carbon emissions from producing a barrel of tar sands oil are at least three times those from pumping a barrel of conventional oil. As oil analyst Richard Heinberg notes, "Currently, two tons of sand must be mined in order to yield one barrel of oil." Beyond this, the quantity of water needed to extract oil from shale or tar sands can be prohibitive, particularly in the western United States, where virtually all water is spoken for. Considering carbon emissions, water requirements, local water pollution, and the overall environmental devastation from processing billions of tons of tar sands or oil shale, civilization would be better off if this oil were simply left in the ground.[82]

With coal, worldwide supply depletion is not imminent, but any strategy to stabilize climate must have the phaseout of coal as its centerpiece. Coal is carbon-intensive, with CO_2 emissions per unit of energy produced double those from natural gas and half again those from oil.[83]

Coal is also the most damaging to human health. Black lung disease among coal miners is all too common. Beyond this, an estimated 3 million people die each year, more than 8,000 a day, from breathing polluted air—much of it from burning coal. Coal burning is also the leading source of mercury pollution, a potent neurotoxin, one that is particularly dangerous to children.[84]

Mercury emitted from coal smokestacks literally blankets the earth's land and water surfaces. In the United States, virtually every state warns against eating too much fish taken from fresh water, lakes, and streams because of dangerously high mercury content.[85]

In China, where cancer is now the leading source of death, coal pollution is a growing concern. A Ministry of Health survey of 30 cities and 78 counties that was released in 2007 reveals a rising tide of cancer. Populations of some "cancer villages" are being decimated by the disease.[86]

Coal is only part of the problem, but in a country that was building a new coal-fired power plant every week, it is a large part. The new reality is that each year China grows richer and sicker. The Chinese leadership is becoming increasingly concerned not only with the cancer epidemic but with the sharp rise in birth defects. Concern about the health effects of coal burning may help explain why China is making a massive push with wind and solar energy, planning to soon be the world leader in both.[87]

A sign of the emerging changes in China came when the *New York Times* reported in July 2009 that the Ministry of Environmental Protection has temporarily prohibited three of the country's five biggest power companies from building coal-fired power plants because they had not complied with environmental regulations on their existing plants. This is a major step for China, and one that would not have been made without approval at the highest level.[88]

In addition to coal's disproportionate contribution to climate disruption and damage to human health, it also is the most easily replaced of the three fossil fuels. Electricity is electricity, whether it comes from coal-fired power plants or wind farms, solar thermal power plants, and geothermal power plants. In contrast, replacing oil is more complicated because it is so pervasive in the economy.

The third fossil fuel, natural gas, accounts for only 19 percent of CO_2 emissions from fossil fuels. Because it is so much less carbon-intensive than coal and cleaner-burning than oil, it is emerging as the transition fuel as the world shifts from fossil fuels to renewable sources of energy. Its use, too, will be reduced, although not nearly as fast as that of coal.[89]

A Challenge Without Precedent

Given the need to simultaneously stabilize climate, stabilize population, eradicate poverty, and restore the earth's natural systems, our early twenty-first-century civilization is facing challenges that have no precedent. Rising to any one of these challenges would be taxing, but we have gotten ourselves into a situation where we have to effectively respond to each of them at the same time, given their mutual interdependence. And food security depends on reaching all four goals. There is no middle ground with Plan B.

As political stresses from oil shortages, food shortages, and climate change intensify, the number of failing states is growing. Beyond this, there are dangerous signs that the strong system of international cooperation that evolved after World War II, and on which global economic progress is based, is weakening. For example, concern about access to oil led the United States to convert part of its grain harvest to fuel for cars regardless of its effect on world food prices and low-income consumers.

More recently, we have seen how grain-exporting countries faced with soaring food prices restricted or banned exports in order to control internal food price rises, thereby creating a growing sense of insecurity in food-importing countries. As importing countries lost confidence in the market to supply their needs, the more affluent among them began buying or leasing massive tracts of land in other countries, many of them land-scarce, hunger-ridden countries. How do we reverse this trend toward each country fending for itself rather than working together for the common good?

Plan B is shaped by the urgent need to halt the rise in atmospheric CO_2 concentrations, to reverse the decline in world food security, and to shorten the list of failing states. In setting the climate goal of cutting net carbon emissions 80 percent by 2020, we did not ask what sort of cut was politically feasible. Instead we asked how much and how fast do we have to cut carbon emissions if we want to have a decent chance of saving the Greenland ice sheet and avoiding a politically destabilizing sea level rise. How fast do we have to cut carbon emissions if we want to save at least the larger glaciers in the Himalayas and on the Tibetan Plateau, the glaciers whose ice melt irrigates wheat and rice fields in China and India?

With energy, our goal is to close all coal-fired power plants by 2020, replacing them largely with wind farms. In the Plan B economy the transportation system will be electrified with a broad-based shift to plug-in hybrids, all-electric cars, and high-speed intercity rail. And in the Plan B world, cities are designed for people, not for cars.

Plan B is shaped not by what we have done in the past but by what we need to do for the future. We are offering a vision of what that future might look like, a road map of how to get from here to there, and a timetable for doing so. Plan B is not based on conventional thinking. That is what got us into this mess. It takes a different kind of thinking, a new mindset, to get us out.

Plan B is obviously ambitious and, to some, impossibly so. Recognizing the enormity of the challenge the world faces, Paul Hawken, corporate entrepreneur and environmentalist, counseled the graduates at the University of Portland in May 2009: "Don't be put off by people who know what is not possible. Do what needs to be done, and check to see if it was impossible only after you are done."[90]

II

THE RESPONSE

4

Stabilizing Climate: An Energy Efficiency Revolution

The world is in the early stages of two energy revolutions. The first is a shift to new energy-efficient technologies across the board. The larger energy savings potentials include shifting from century-old technologies such as incandescent light bulbs and internal combustion engines to far more efficient technologies. Incandescents are being replaced by compact fluorescent bulbs that use one fourth as much electricity. This in turn will be cut in half by the light-emitting diodes (LEDs) coming on the market. And the most advanced plug-in hybrid car prototypes use only one fifth as much gasoline per mile as the average U.S. car on the road today.

The second energy revolution—the shift from an economy powered by oil, coal, and natural gas to one powered by wind, solar, and geothermal energy—is under way and moving fast. In Europe, new electrical generating capacity from wind, solar, and other renewables now exceeds that from fossil fuels by a wide margin. In the United States, new wind-generating capacity of 8,400 megawatts in 2008 dwarfed the 1,400 megawatts from coal. Nuclear power is fading, too. Worldwide, nuclear power generation actually declined in 2008 while wind electric generating capacity increased by 27,000 megawatts, enough to supply 8 million American homes. The world is changing fast.[1]

This chapter begins with a brief description of Plan B's goal of cutting net carbon emissions and then describes in detail the components of the first revolution—the push to raise energy efficiency worldwide. Chapter 5 describes the transition to an economy powered largely by wind, solar, and geothermal energy.

Implementing Plan B entails cutting net carbon dioxide (CO_2) emissions 80 percent by 2020. This would keep atmospheric CO_2 levels from exceeding 400 parts per million (ppm), up only modestly from 386 ppm in 2008.[2]

This sets the stage for reducing CO_2 concentrations to the 350 ppm that James Hansen and other climate scientists think is needed to avoid runaway climate change. It will also help keep future temperature rise to a minimum. Such a basic economic restructuring in time to avoid catastrophic climate disruption will be challenging, but how can we face the next generation if we do not try?[3]

This restructuring of the world energy economy is being driven by some traditional concerns and some newer ones. Among the former are mounting concerns over climate change, a growing sense of oil insecurity, the rising level and volatility of fossil fuel prices, and financial outlays for importing oil.

The recent global economic downturn and the record number of young people entering job markets in developing countries has also made labor intensity a goal of energy policymaking. Improving energy efficiency and developing renewable sources of energy are both much more labor-intensive than burning fossil fuels. Closely associated with this is the realization that the countries and companies that are at the forefront of developing new energy technologies will have a strong competitive advantage in world markets.[4]

The energy component of Plan B is straightforward. We raise world energy efficiency enough to at least offset all projected growth in energy use from now until 2020. We also turn to wind, solar, geothermal, and other renewable sources to largely replace oil, coal, and natural gas. In effect, Plan B outlines the transition from fossil fuels to renewable sources of energy by 2020. Difficult? Yes. Impossible? No!

Stephen Pacala and Robert Socolow at Princeton University set the stage for Plan B in 2004 when they published an article in *Science* that showed how annual carbon emissions from burning fossil fuels could be held at 7 billion tons instead of rising to 14 billion tons over the next 50 years, as would occur with business as usual. Their goal was to prevent atmospheric CO_2 concentrations, then near 375 ppm, from rising above 500 ppm.[5]

Pacala and Socolow described 15 proven technologies, including efficiency gains and new energy from various renewables, that could each cut carbon emissions 1 billion tons per year by 2054. Any 7 of these options could be combined to prevent an increase in carbon emissions from now through 2054. They further theorized that advancing technology would allow annual carbon emissions to be cut to 2 billion tons by 2104, a level that could likely be absorbed by natural carbon sinks on land and in the oceans.[6]

The Pacala/Socolow exercise was neither a plan nor a projection but a conceptualization, one that has been extraordinarily useful in helping analysts think about the future relationship between energy and climate. Now it is time to select the most promising energy technologies and structure an actual plan to cut carbon emissions. And since climate is changing much faster than anticipated even a few years ago, we believe the world needs to halt the rise in CO_2 levels not at 500 ppm in 2054 but at 400 ppm in 2020. First we look at the enormous potential for raising energy efficiency in the lighting sector.[7]

A Revolution in Lighting Technology

Since the lighting sector is on the edge of a spectacular revolution based on new technologies, perhaps the quickest, most profitable way to reduce electricity use worldwide is simply to change light bulbs.

The first advance in this field came with compact fluorescent lamps (CFLs), which use 75 percent less electricity than old-fashioned incandescents. Replacing inefficient incandescent bulbs that are still widely used today with new CFLs can reduce the electricity used for lighting by three fourths. Over its lifetime, each standard (13 watt) CFL will reduce electricity bills by roughly $30. And though a CFL may cost twice as much as an incandescent, it lasts 10 times as long. Each one reduces energy use compared with an incandescent by the equivalent of 200 pounds of coal over its lifetime. For perspective, the energy saved by replacing a 100-watt incandescent bulb with an equivalent CFL over its lifetime is sufficient to drive a Toyota Prius hybrid car from New York to San Francisco.[8]

CFL production in China, which accounts for 85 percent of the world total, climbed from 750 million units in 2001 to 2.4 billion units in 2006. Sales in the United States climbed from 21 million CFLs in 2000 to 397 million in 2007. Of the estimated 4.7 billion light sockets in the United States, close to 1 billion now have CFLs.[9]

The world may be moving toward a political tipping point to replace inefficient light bulbs across the board. In February 2007 Australia announced it would phase out the sale of incandescents by 2010, replacing them with CFLs. Canada soon followed with a 2012 phaseout goal. In early 2009, the European Union (EU) approved a phaseout of incandescent bulbs, one that will save the average EU consumer 25–50 euros each year.[10]

Brazil, hit by a nationwide electricity shortage in 2000–02, responded with an ambitious program to replace incandescents with CFLs. As a result, an estimated half of the light sockets there now contain these efficient bulbs. In 2007, China—working with the Global Environment Facility—announced a plan to replace all its incandescents with more-efficient lighting within a decade. And India is planning to phase out incandescent bulbs by 2012.[11]

Retailers are joining the switch too. Wal-Mart, the world's largest retailer, began an ambitious marketing campaign in 2007 to boost its cumulative U.S. sales of compact fluorescents to over 260 million. Currys, Britain's largest electrical retail chain, went further—discontinuing sales of incandescent light bulbs in 2007.[12]

For office buildings, commercial outlets, and factories, where linear (tubular) fluorescents are widely used, the key to cutting electricity use is shifting to the most advanced models, which are even more efficient than CFLs. However, since linear fluorescents are long-lasting, many of those now in use rely on an earlier, less energy-efficient technology.

The second major advance in lighting technology is the light-emitting diode, which uses up to 85 percent less electricity than incandescents. Although LEDs are the ultimate in lighting efficiency, they are still too costly for most uses. They are rapidly taking over several niche markets, however, such as traffic lights, where they now have 52 percent of the U.S. market, and exit signs in buildings, where they hold 88 percent of U.S. sales. New York City has replaced traditional bulbs with LEDs in many of its traffic lights, cutting its annual bill for maintenance and electricity by $6 million. In early 2009, Los Angeles Mayor Antonio Villaraigosa said the city would replace its 140,000 street lights with LEDs, saving taxpayers $48 million over the next seven years. The resulting reduction in carbon emissions would be like taking 7,000 cars off the road.[13]

Universities are also getting involved. In California, the University of California-Davis has a Smart Lighting Initiative. One of its first projects was to replace all the light bulbs in a campus parking garage with LEDs, dramatically reducing electricity use. This success has evolved into LED University, a project to disseminate this technology. Early adopters include the University of California-Santa Barbara, Tianjin Polytechnic University in China, and the University of Arkansas.[14]

LEDs offer another strong economic advantage. While CFLs last 10 times as long as incandescents, LEDs last 50 times as long. Indeed, a typical LED installed at the time of a child's birth will still be working when the youngster graduates from college. The savings in commercial situations from both lower electricity costs and the virtual elimination of replacement maintenance often more than offsets the higher initial cost.[15]

In addition to switching bulbs, energy can be saved just by turning lights off when they are not in use. There are numerous technologies for doing this, including motion sensors that turn lights off in unoccupied offices, living rooms, washrooms, hallways, and stairwells. Sensors and dimmers can also be used to take advantage of daylighting to reduce the intensity of interior lighting when sunlight is bright. In cities, dimmers can be used to reduce streetlight intensity. In fact, these smart lighting technologies can cut the electricity use of LEDs to less than 10 percent of that with incandescents.[16]

In summary, shifting to CFLs in homes, to the most advanced linear fluorescents in office buildings, commercial outlets, and factories, and to LEDs in traffic lights would cut the world share of electricity used for lighting from 19 percent to 7 percent. This would save enough electricity to close 705 of the world's 2,670 coal-fired plants. If the high cost of LEDs drops faster than we have assumed, making widespread use feasible, lighting efficiency gains will come even faster than we have projected.[17]

In a world facing almost daily new evidence of climate change and its consequences, a quick and decisive victory is needed in the battle to cut carbon emissions and stabilize climate. A rapid shift to the most energy-efficient lighting technologies would provide just such a victory—generating momentum for even greater advances in climate stabilization.

Energy-Efficient Appliances

Just as CFLs offer great electricity savings over incandescent light bulbs, a similar range of efficiencies is available for many household appliances, such as refrigerators. The U.S. Energy Policy Act of 2005 was designed to exploit some of these potential savings by raising appliance efficiency standards enough to close 29 coal-fired power plants. Other provisions in the act—such as tax incentives that encourage the adoption of energy-efficient technologies, a shift to more combined heat and power generation, and the adoption of real-time pricing of electricity (a measure to discourage optional electricity use during peak demand periods)—would cut electricity demand enough to close an additional 37 coal-fired power plants. Appliance efficiency standards and other measures in the bill would also reduce natural gas consumption substantially. Altogether, these measures are projected to reduce consumer electricity and gas bills in 2020 by more than \$20 billion.[18]

Although the U.S. Congress passed legislation raising efficiency for some 30 categories of household and industrial appliances—from refrigerators to industrial-scale electric motors—the U.S. Department of Energy (DOE) has for many years failed to write the standards needed to actually implement the legislation. To remedy this, just days after taking office President Barack Obama ordered the DOE to write regulations to translate law into policy.[19]

With appliances, the big challenge is China. In 1980 its appliance manufacturers produced only 50,000 refrigerators, virtually all for domestic use. In 2008 they produced 48 million refrigerators, 90 million color TVs, and 42 million clothes washers, many of which were for export.[20]

Market penetration of these modern appliances in urban China today is already similar to that in industrial countries. For every 100 urban households there are 138 color TV sets, 97 washing machines, and 88 room air conditioners. Even in rural areas there are 95 color TVs and 46 washing machines for every 100 households. This phenomenal growth in household appliance use in China, along with the extraordinary growth of industry, raised China's electricity use 11-fold from 1980 to 2007. Although China established standards for most appliances by 2005, these are not strictly enforced.[21]

The other major concentration of home appliances is in the European Union, home to 495 million people. Greenpeace notes that even though Europeans on average use half as much electricity as Americans do, they still have a large potential for reducing their usage. A refrigerator in Europe uses scarcely half as much electricity as one in the United States, for example, but the most efficient refrigerators on the market today use only one fourth as much electricity as the average refrigerator in Europe, suggesting a huge potential for cutting electricity use.[22]

But this is not the end of the efficiency trail, since advancing technology keeps raising the potential. Japan's Top Runner Program is the world's most dynamic system for upgrading appliance efficiency standards. In this system, the most efficient appliances marketed today set the standard for those sold tomorrow. Using this program, between the late 1990s and the end of 2007 Japan raised efficiency standards for individual appliances by anywhere from 15 to 83 percent, depending on the appliance. This is an ongoing process that continually exploits advances in efficiency technologies. A 2008 report indicates that the Top Runner Program for all appliances is running ahead of the ambitious initial expectations—and often by a wide margin.[23]

In an analysis of potential energy savings by 2030 by type of appliance, the Organisation for Economic Co-operation and Development (OECD) put the potential savings from reducing electricity for standby use—the power consumed when an appliance is not being used—at the top of the list. The electricity used by appliances in standby mode worldwide accounts for up to 10 percent of total electricity consumption. In OECD countries, individual household standby power ranged from a low of perhaps 30 watts to a high of over 100 watts in both U.S. and

New Zealand households. Since this power is used around the clock, even though the wattage is relatively low, the cumulative use is substantial.[24]

Some governments are capping standby power use by TV sets, computers, microwaves, DVD players, and so on at 1 watt per appliance. South Korea, for example, is mandating a 1-watt limit on standby for many appliances by 2010. Australia is doing the same for nearly all appliances by 2012.[25]

A U.S. study estimates that roughly 5 percent of U.S. residential electricity use is from appliances in standby mode. If this figure dropped to 1 percent, which could be done easily, 17 coal-fired power plants could be closed. If China were to lower its standby losses to 1 percent, it could close a far larger number of power plants.[26]

A more recent efficiency challenge has come with the market invasion of large, flat-screen televisions. The screens now on the market use easily twice as much electricity as a traditional cathode ray tube television. If the flat screen is a large-screen plasma model, it can use four times as much electricity. In the United Kingdom, some Cabinet members are proposing to ban the energy-guzzling flat-screen plasma televisions. California is proposing that all new televisions draw one third less electricity than current sets by 2011 and 49 percent less by 2013.[27]

Consumers often do not buy the most energy-efficient appliances because the initial purchase price is higher, even though this is more than offset by lower appliance lifetime operating costs. If, however, societies adopt a carbon tax reflecting the costs of climate change, the more efficient appliances would be economically much more attractive. Energy use labeling requirements would help consumers choose more wisely.

A worldwide set of appliance efficiency standards keyed to the most efficient models on the market would lead to energy savings in the appliance sector approaching or exceeding the 12 percent of world electricity savings from more-efficient lighting. Thus the combined gains in lighting and appliance efficiencies alone would enable the world to avoid building 1,410 coal-fired power plants—more than the 1,283 new coal-fired power plants that the International Energy Agency (IEA) projects will be built by 2020.[28]

Zero-Carbon Buildings

The building sector is responsible for a large share of world electricity consumption and raw materials use. In the United States, buildings—commercial and residential—account for 72 percent of electricity use and 38 percent of CO_2 emissions. Worldwide, building construction accounts for 40 percent of materials use.[29]

Because buildings last for 50–100 years or longer, it is often assumed that cutting carbon emissions in the building sector is a long-term process. But that is not the case. An energy retrofit of an older inefficient building can cut energy use and energy bills by 20–50 percent. The next step, shifting entirely to carbon-free electricity, either generated onsite or purchased, to heat, cool, and light the building completes the job. Presto! A zero-carbon operating building.[30]

The building construction and real estate industries are recognizing what an Australian firm, Davis Langdon, calls "the looming obsolescence of non-green buildings"—one that is driving a wave of reform in both construction and real estate. Further, Davis Langdon says, "going green is future-proofing your asset."[31]

Some countries are taking bold steps. Notable among them is Germany, which as of January 2009 requires that all new buildings either get at least 15 percent of space and water heating from renewable energy or dramatically improve energy efficiency. Government financial support is available for owners of both new and existing buildings for installing renewable energy systems or making efficiency improvements. In reality, once builders or home owners start to plan these installations, they will quickly see that in most cases it makes economic sense to go far beyond the minimal requirements.[32]

There are already signs of progress in the United States. In February 2009, the U.S. Congress passed—and the President signed—the American Recovery and Reinvestment Act, legislation designed to stimulate the U.S. economy. Among other items, it provides for the weatherization of more than a million homes, beginning with an energy audit to identify the measures that would quickly reduce energy use. A second part calls for the weatherization and retrofitting of a large share of the nation's stock of public housing. A third component is the greening of government buildings by making them more energy-efficient and, wherever possible, installing devices such as rooftop solar water and space heaters and rooftop solar electric arrays. The combination of these initiatives is intended to help build a vigorous new industry that would play an active role in raising U.S. energy efficiency and cutting carbon emissions.[33]

In the private sector, the U.S. Green Building Council (USGBC)—well known for its Leadership in Energy and Environmental Design (LEED) certification and rating program—heads the field. This voluntary program, which sets standards well above those of the U.S. government Energy Star building certification program, has four certification levels—certified, silver, gold, and platinum. A LEED-certified building must meet minimal standards in environmental quality, materials use, energy efficiency, and water efficiency. LEED-certified buildings are attractive to buyers because they have lower operating costs, higher lease rates, and typically happier, healthier occupants than traditional buildings do.[34]

The LEED certification standards for construction of new buildings were issued in 2000. Any builder who wants a structure to be rated must request and pay for certification. In 2004 the USGBC also began certifying the interiors of commercial buildings and tenant improvements of existing buildings. And in 2007 it began issuing certification standards for home builders.[35]

Looking at the LEED criteria provides insight into the many ways buildings can become more energy-efficient. The certification process for new buildings begins with site selection, and then moves on to energy efficiency, water efficiency, materials use, and indoor environmental quality. In site selection, points are awarded for proximity to public transport, such as subway, light rail, or bus lines. Beyond this, a higher rating depends on provision of bicycle racks and shower facilities for employees. New buildings must also maximize the exposure to daylight, with minimum daylight illumination for 75 percent of the occupied space.[36]

With energy, exceeding the high level of efficiency required for basic certification earns additional points. Further points are awarded for the use of renewable energy, including rooftop solar cells to generate electricity, rooftop solar water and space heaters, and the purchase of green power.[37]

Thus far LEED has certified 1,600 new buildings in the United States, with some 11,600 planned or under construction that have applied for certification. The commercial building space that has been certified or registered for certification approval totals 5 billion square feet of floor space, or some 115,000 acres (the equivalent of 115,000 football fields).[38]

The Chesapeake Bay Foundation's office building for its 100 staff members near Annapolis, Maryland, was the first to earn a LEED platinum rating. Among its features are a ground-source heat pump for heating and cooling, a rooftop solar water heater, and sleekly designed composting toilets that produce a rich humus used to fertilize the landscape surrounding the building.[39]

Toyota's North American headquarters in Torrance, California, which houses 2,000 employees, has a LEED gold rating and is distinguished by a large solar-electric generating facility that provides much of its electricity. Waterless urinals and rainwater recycling enable it to operate with 94 percent less water than a conventionally designed building of the same size. Less water use also means less energy use.[40]

The 54-story Bank of America tower in New York is the first large skyscraper expected to earn a platinum rating. It has its own co-generation power plant and collects rainwater, reuses waste water, and used recycled materials in construction.[41]

A 60-story office building with a gold rating being built in Chicago will use river water to cool the building in summer, and the rooftop will be covered with plants to reduce runoff and heat loss. Energy-conserving measures will save the owner $800,000 a year in energy bills. The principal tenant, Kirkland and Ellis LLP, a Chicago-based law firm, insisted that the building be gold-certified and that this be incorporated into the lease.[42]

The state of California commissioned Capital E, a green building consulting firm, to analyze the economics of 33 LEED-certified buildings in the state. The study concluded that certification raised construction costs by $4 per square foot but that because operating costs as well as employee absenteeism and turnover were lower and productivity was higher than in other buildings, the standard- and silver-certified buildings earned a profit over the first 20 years of $49 per square foot, and the gold- and platinum-certified buildings earned $67 per square foot.[43]

In 2002 a global version of the USGBC, the World Green Building Council, was formed. As of spring 2009 it included Green Building Councils in 14 countries, including Brazil, India, and the United Arab Emirates. Eight other countries—ranging from Spain to Viet Nam—are working to meet the prerequisites for membership. Among the current members, India ranks second in certification after the United States, with 292 million square feet of LEED-certified floor space, followed by China (287 million) and Canada (257 million).[44]

Beyond greening new buildings, there are numerous efforts to make older structures more efficient. In 2007, the Clinton Foundation announced an Energy Efficiency Building Retrofit Program, a project of the Clinton Climate Initiative. In cooperation with C40, a large-cities climate leadership group, this program brings together five of the world's largest banks and four leading energy service companies to work with an initial group of 16 cities to retrofit buildings, reducing their energy use by 20–50 percent. Among the cities are some of the world's largest: Bangkok, Berlin, Karachi, London, Mexico City, Mumbai, New York, Rome, and Tokyo. Each of the banks involved—ABN AMRO, Citi, Deutsche Bank, JP Morgan Chase, and UBS—is committed to investing up to $1 billion in this effort, enough to easily double the current worldwide level of energy saving retrofits.[45]

The energy service companies—Honeywell, Johnson Controls, Siemens, and Trane—committed not only to do the actual retrofitting but also to provide "performance guarantees," thus ensuring that all the retrofits will be profitable. At the launch of this program, former President Bill Clinton pointed out that banks and energy service companies would make money, building owners would save money, and carbon emissions would fall. As of February 2009, the Clinton Climate Initiative had been involved with 250 retrofit projects and over 500 million square feet of floor space.[46]

In April 2009, the owners of New York's Empire State Building announced plans to retrofit the 2.6 million square feet of office space in the nearly 80-year-old 102-story building, thereby reducing its energy use by nearly 40 percent. The resulting energy savings of $4.4 million a year is expected to recover the retrofitting costs in three years.[47]

Beyond these voluntary measures, the government-designed

building codes, which set minimal standards for building energy efficiency, are highly effective. In the United States this has been dramatically demonstrated in differences between California and the country as a whole in housing energy efficiency. Between 1975 and 2002, residential energy use per person dropped 16 percent in the country as a whole. But in California, which has stringent building codes, it dropped by 40 percent. The bottom line is that there is an enormous potential for reducing energy use in buildings in the United States and, indeed, the world.[48]

One firm believer in that potential is Edward Mazria, a climate-conscious architect from New Mexico. He has launched the 2030 Challenge. Its principal goal is for U.S. architects to be designing buildings in 2030 that use no fossil fuels. Mazria observes that the buildings sector is the leading source of carbon emissions, easily eclipsing transportation. Therefore, he says, "it's the architects who hold the key to turning down the global thermostat." To reach his goal, Mazria has organized a coalition of several organizations, including the American Institute of Architects, the USGBC, and the U.S. Conference of Mayors.[49]

Mazria also recognizes the need for faculty retraining in the country's 124 architectural schools to "transform architecture from its mindless and passive reliance on fossil fuels to an architecture intimately linked to the natural world in which we live."[50]

Today's architectural concepts and construction technologies enable architects to easily design new buildings with half the energy requirements of existing ones. Among the design technologies they can use are natural daylighting, rooftop solar-electric cells, rooftop solar water and space heaters, ultra insulation, natural ventilation, ground source heat pumps, glazed windows, waterless urinals, more-efficient lighting technologies, and motion sensors for lighting. Designing and constructing energy-efficient buildings, combined with a massive harnessing of renewable energy, makes it not only possible but also profitable for buildings to operate without fossil fuels.[51]

Electrifying the Transport System

Among the keys to cutting carbon emissions are redesigning urban transport (see Chapter 6) and the overall electrification of transportation. The last century witnessed the evolution of an oil-powered transport system: gasoline for cars and diesel fuel for trucks and trains. Now that is changing. With both cars and rail systems, oil will be replaced by electricity. And the power will come increasingly from wind farms and from solar and geothermal power plants.

With peak oil on our doorstep, the world desperately needs a new automotive energy economy. Fortunately, the foundation for this has been laid with two new technologies: gas-electric hybrid plug-in cars and all-electric cars.

The Toyota Prius—the world's top-selling hybrid car—gets an impressive 50 miles per gallon (mpg) in combined city/highway driving, nearly double that of the average new U.S. passenger vehicle. The United States could easily cut its gasoline use in half simply by converting the entire American automobile fleet to highly efficient hybrid cars. But this is only the beginning.[52]

Now that hybrid cars are well established, it is a relatively small additional step to manufacture plug-in hybrids that run largely on electricity. By shifting to lithium ion batteries to boost electricity storage capacity and by adding an extension cord so the battery can be recharged from the grid, drivers can do their commuting, grocery shopping, and other short-distance travel almost entirely with electricity, using gasoline only for the occasional long trip. Even more exciting, recharging batteries with off-peak wind-generated electricity costs the equivalent of less than $1 per gallon of gasoline.[53]

As of mid-2009, nearly all major car makers have announced plans to bring either plug-in hybrids or all-electric cars to market. The world's first commercially available plug-in hybrid car reached the market in December 2008 in China. While the world was focusing on the race between Toyota and GM, China's BYD (Build Your Dreams) had quietly forged ahead, bringing its plug-in hybrid car to market. Already in mass production and selling for a highly competitive $22,000, it is scheduled to appear in U.S. and European markets in 2010.[54]

Meanwhile, Toyota apparently has gotten the jump on GM by announcing it would start to market a limited number of plug-in hybrids for selected use by the end of 2009. The Chevrolet Volt, GM's entry, is expected to average 150 mpg, largely because of a stronger battery and greater all-electric range. It is this prospect of triple-digit gasoline mileage that is selling customers on plug-in hybrids.[55]

Nissan has been emphasizing the development of an all-electric car, which it plans to market in 2010. Chrysler plans to produce an electric version of several of its models, effectively offering customers a choice between gasoline and electrically powered vehicles. Think, an entrepreneurial Norwegian firm, already producing an all-electric car in Norway, is planning an assembly plant in the United States in 2010 to produce up to 60,000 electric cars per year.[56]

Shifting to plug-in electric hybrids and all-electric cars does not require a costly new infrastructure, since the network of gasoline service stations and the electricity grid are already in place. A 2006 study by the U.S. Pacific Northwest National Laboratory estimated that over 80 percent of the electricity needs of a national fleet of all plug-in cars could be satisfied with the existing electrical infrastructure since the recharging would take place largely at night, when there is an excess of generating capacity. What will be needed is the installation of electrical outlets in parking garages, parking lots, and street-side parking meters, along with a credit card access device to identify the user for billing purposes.[57]

Silicon Valley entrepreneur Shai Agassi is working with Nissan and the governments of Israel, Denmark, Australia, and Canada's Ontario Province, as well as the San Francisco Bay area of California and Hawaii in the United States, to set up networks of electric-car service stations. These stations would replace depleted batteries with freshly charged ones, thus eliminating the need for time-consuming recharges. Whether the typical daily driving distance will warrant investment in battery replacement on this scale remains to be seen.[58]

While the future of transportation in cities lies with a mix of light rail, buses, bicycles, some cars, and walking, the future of intercity travel belongs to high-speed trains. Japan, with its bullet trains, pioneered this mode of travel. Operating at speeds up to 190 miles per hour, Japan's bullet trains carry almost a million passengers a day. On some of the heavily used intercity high-speed lines, trains depart every three minutes.[59]

Beginning in 1964 with the 322-mile line from Tokyo to Osaka, Japan's high-speed rail network now stretches for 1,360 miles, linking nearly all its major cities. One of the most heavily traveled links is the original line, where the bullet trains carry 413,000 passengers a day. The transit time of two-and-a-half hours between Tokyo and Osaka compares with a driving time of eight hours. High-speed trains save time as well as energy.[60]

Although Japan's bullet trains have carried billions of passengers in great comfort over 40 years at high speeds, there has not been a single casualty. Late arrivals average 6 seconds. If we were selecting seven wonders of the modern world, Japan's high-speed rail system surely would be among them.[61]

Although the first European high-speed line, from Paris to Lyon, did not begin operation until 1981, Europe has made enormous strides since then. As of 2009 there were 3,100 miles (5,000 kilometers) of high-speed rail operating in Europe. The goal is to triple this track length by 2020 and eventually to integrate the eastern countries, including Poland, the Czech Republic, and Hungary, into a continental network.[62]

While France and Germany were the early European leaders in intercity rail, Spain is fast building a high-speed intercity rail network as well. Within a year of opening the Barcelona-to-Madrid connection, domestic airlines lost roughly a fifth of their passengers to these high-speed intercity trains. Spain plans to link with high-speed systems in France to become firmly integrated into the European network.[63]

Existing international links, such as the one between Paris and Brussels, are being joined by connections between Paris and Stuttgart, Frankfurt and Paris, and London and Paris (the latter via the Channel Tunnel). On the newer lines, trains are operating at up to 200 miles per hour. As *The Economist* notes, "Europe is in the grip of a high speed rail revolution."[64]

High-speed links between cities dramatically raise rail travel. For example, when the Paris-to-Brussels link opened—the 194 miles is covered by train in just 85 minutes—the share of those traveling between the two cities by train rose from 24 percent to 50 percent. The car share dropped from 61 to 43 percent, and plane travel virtually disappeared.[65]

Carbon dioxide emissions per passenger mile on electric high-speed trains are roughly one third those of cars and one fourth those of planes. In the Plan B economy, carbon emissions from trains will essentially be zero, since they will be powered almost entirely by renewable electricity. In addition to being comfortable and convenient, these rail links reduce air pollution, congestion, noise, and accidents. They also free travelers from the frustrations of traffic congestion and long airport security check lines.[66]

There is a huge gap in high-speed rail between Japan and Europe on the one hand and the rest of the world on the other. But China is beginning to develop high-speed trains linking some of its major cities. A high-speed link between Beijing and Shanghai scheduled for completion by 2013 will slice train travel time in half, from 10 to 5 hours. China now has 3,890 miles of track that can handle train speeds of up to 125 miles per hour. The plan is to triple the length of high-speed track by 2020.[67]

The United States has a "high speed" Acela Express that links Washington, New York, and Boston, but unfortunately neither its rail bed and speed nor its reliability come close to the trains in Japan and Europe. The good news is that the U.S. economic stimulus plan signed into law in February 2009 contained some $8 billion to help launch a new era of high-speed rail construction in the United States.[68]

In the United States, the need to cut carbon emissions and prepare for shrinking oil supplies calls for this shift in investment from roads and highways to railways. In 1956 U.S. President Dwight Eisenhower launched the interstate highway system, justifying it on national security grounds. Today the threat of climate change and the insecurity of oil supplies argue for the construction of a high-speed electrified rail system, for both passenger and freight traffic. The additional electricity needed could easily be supplied from renewable sources, mainly wind energy.[69]

The passenger rail system would be modeled after those of Japan and Europe. A high-speed transcontinental line that averaged 170 miles per hour would mean traveling coast-to-coast in 15 hours, even with stops in major cities along the way. There is a parallel need to develop an electrified national rail freight network that would greatly reduce the need for long-haul trucks.

Voters in California approved a bond referendum in November 2008 of nearly $10 billion to build a high-speed rail system to link northern and southern California. This would reduce the use of cars and eliminate many of the fuel-guzzling short-distance flights linking California's major cities.[70]

Any meaningful global effort to cut transport carbon emissions begins with the United States, which consumes more gasoline than the next 20 countries combined (including Japan, China, Russia, Germany, and Brazil). The United States—with 249 million passenger vehicles out of the global 912 million—not only has the largest fleet but it is near the top in miles driven per car and near the bottom in fuel efficiency.[71]

The first step to reduce this massive U.S. consumption of gasoline is to raise fuel efficiency standards. The 40-percent increase in these standards by 2016 announced by the Obama administration in May 2009 will greatly reduce U.S. gasoline use and bring the country closer to the fuel economy levels prevailing in Europe and China. A crash program to shift the U.S. fleet to plug-in hybrids and all-electric cars would make an even greater contribution. And shifting public funds from highway construction to public transit would reduce the number of cars needed, bringing us close to our goal of cutting carbon emissions 80 percent by 2020.[72]

A New Materials Economy

The production, processing, and disposal of materials in our modern throwaway economy wastes not only materials but energy as well. In nature, one-way linear flows do not survive long. Nor, by extension, can they survive long in the expanding global economy. The throwaway economy that has evolved over the last half-century is an aberration, now itself headed for the junk heap of history.

The potential for sharply reducing materials use was first identified in Germany, initially by Friedrich Schmidt-Bleek in the early 1990s and then by Ernst von Weizsäcker, an environmental leader in the German Bundestag. They argued that modern industrial economies could function very effectively using only one fourth the virgin raw materials prevailing at the time. A few years later, Schmidt-Bleek, who founded the Factor Ten Institute in France, showed that raising resource productivity even more—by a factor of 10—was well within the reach of existing technology and management, given the right policy incentives.[73]

In their book *Cradle to Cradle: Remaking the Way We Make Things*, American architect William McDonough and German chemist Michael Braungart conclude that waste and pollution are to be avoided entirely. "Pollution," says McDonough, "is a symbol of design failure."[74]

Beyond reducing materials use, the energy savings from recycling are huge. Steel made from recycled scrap takes only 26 percent as much energy as that from iron ore. For aluminum, the figure is just 4 percent. Recycled plastic uses only 20 percent as much energy. Recycled paper uses 64 percent as much—and with far fewer chemicals during processing. If the world recycling rates of these basic materials were raised to those already attained in the most efficient economies, carbon emissions would drop precipitously.[75]

Industry, including the production of plastics, fertilizers, steel, cement, and paper, accounts for more than 30 percent of world energy consumption. The petrochemical industry, which produces such things as plastics, fertilizer, and detergents, is the biggest consumer of energy in the manufacturing sector, accounting for about a third of worldwide industrial energy use. Since a large part of industry fossil fuel use is for feedstock to manufacture plastics and other materials, increased recycling can reduce feedstock needs. Worldwide, increasing recycling rates and moving to the most efficient manufacturing systems in use today could easily reduce energy use in the petrochemical industry by 32 percent.[76]

The global steel industry, producing over 1.3 billion tons in 2008, accounts for 19 percent of industrial energy use. Efficiency measures, such as adopting the most efficient blast furnace systems in use today and the complete recovery of used steel, could reduce energy use in the steel industry by 23 percent.[77]

Reducing materials use begins with recycling steel, the use of which dwarfs that of all other metals combined. Steel use is dominated by three industries—automobile, household appliances, and construction. In the United States, virtually all cars are recycled. They are simply too valuable to be left to rust in out-of-the-way junkyards. The U.S. recycling rate for household appliances is estimated at 90 percent. For steel cans it is 63 percent, and for construction steel the figures are 98 percent for steel beams and girders but only 65 percent for reinforcement steel. Still, the steel discarded each year in various forms is enough to meet the needs of the U.S. automobile industry.[78]

Steel recycling started climbing more than a generation ago with the advent of the electric arc furnace, a technology that produces steel from scrap using only one fourth the energy required to produce it from virgin ore. Electric arc furnaces using scrap now account for half or more of steel production in more than 20 countries. A few countries, including Venezuela and Saudi Arabia, use electric arc furnaces exclusively. If three fourths of steel production were to switch to electric arc furnaces using scrap, energy use in the steel industry could be cut by almost 40 percent.[79]

The cement industry, turning out 2.9 billion tons in 2008, is another major energy consumer. China, accounting for half of world production, manufactures more cement than the next 20 countries combined, yet it does so with extraordinary inefficiency. If China used the same kiln technologies as Japan, it could reduce its cement production energy use by 45 percent. Worldwide, if all cement producers used the most efficient dry kiln process, energy use in the industry could drop 42 percent.[80]

Restructuring the transportation system also has a huge potential for reducing materials use as light rail and buses replace cars. For example, improving urban transit means that one 12-ton bus can easily replace 60 cars weighing 1.5 tons each, or a total of 90 tons, reducing material use 87 percent. And every time someone replaces a car with a bike, material use is reduced 99 percent.[81]

The big challenge for cities in saving energy is to recycle as many components of the urban waste flow as possible. Virtually all paper products can now be recycled, including cereal boxes, junk mail, and paper bags in addition to newspapers and magazines. So too can metals, glass, and most plastics. Kitchen and yard waste can be composted to recycle plant nutrients.

Advanced industrial economies with stable populations, such as those in Europe and Japan, can rely primarily on the stock of materials already in the economy rather than using virgin raw materials. Metals such as steel and aluminum can be used and reused indefinitely.[82]

In the United States, the latest *State of Garbage in America* report shows that 29 percent of garbage is recycled, 7 percent is burned, and 64 percent goes to landfills. Recycling rates among U.S. cities vary from less than 30 percent in some cities to more than 70 percent in San Francisco, the highest in the country. When San Francisco hit 70 percent in 2008, Mayor Gavin Newsom immediately announced a plan to reach 75 percent. Among the largest U.S. cities, recycling rates vary from 34 percent in New York to 55 percent in Chicago and 60 percent in Los Angeles. At the state level, Florida has boldly set a goal of recycling 75 percent of waste by 2020.[83]

One of the most effective ways to encourage recycling is to adopt a landfill tax. For example, when the state of New Hampshire adopted a "pay-as-you-throw" program that encourages municipalities to charge residents for each bag of garbage, it dramatically reduced the flow of materials to landfills. In the small town of Lyme, with nearly 2,000 people, adoption of a landfill tax raised the share of garbage recycled from 13 to 52 percent in one year.[84]

The recycled material in Lyme, which jumped from 89 tons in 2005 to 334 tons in 2006, included corrugated cardboard, which sold for $90 a ton, mixed paper at $45 a ton, and aluminum at $1,500 a ton. This program simultaneously reduced the town's landfill fees while generating a cash flow from the sale of recycled material.[85]

In addition to measures that encourage recycling, there are those that encourage or mandate the reuse of products such as beverage containers. Finland, for example, has banned the use of one-way soft drink containers. Canada's east coast province, Prince Edward Island, has adopted a similar ban on all nonrefillable beverage containers. The result in both cases is a sharply reduced flow of garbage to landfills. A refillable glass bottle used over and over requires about 10 percent as much energy per use as an aluminum can that is recycled. Cleaning, sterilizing, and relabeling a used bottle requires little energy compared with recycling cans made from aluminum, which has a melting point of 1,220 degrees Fahrenheit. Banning nonrefillables is a quintuple win option—cutting material use, carbon emissions, air pollution, water pollution, and landfill costs simultaneously. There are also substantial transport fuel savings, since the refillable containers are simply back-hauled by delivery trucks to the original bottling plants or breweries for refilling.[86]

San José, California, already diverting 62 percent of its municipal waste from landfills for reuse and recycling, is now focusing on the large flow of trash from construction and demolition sites. This material is trucked to one of two dozen specialist recycling firms in the city. For example, at Premier Recycle up to 300 tons of building debris are delivered each day. This is skillfully separated into recyclable piles of concrete, scrap metal, wood, and plastics. Some materials the company sells, some it gives away, and some it just pays someone to take.[87]

Before the program began, only about 100,000 tons per year of San José's mixed construction and demolition materials were reused or recycled. Now it is nearly 500,000 tons. The scrap metal that is salvaged goes to recycling plants, wood can be converted into gardening mulch or into wood chips for fueling power plants, and concrete can be recycled to build road banks. By deconstructing a building instead of simply demolishing it, most of the material in it can be reused or recycled, thus dramatically reducing energy use and carbon emissions. San José is becoming a model for cities everywhere.[88]

Germany and, more recently, Japan are requiring that products such as automobiles, household appliances, and office equipment be designed for easy disassembly and recycling. In May 1998, the Japanese Diet enacted a tough appliance recycling law, one that prohibits discarding household appliances, such as washing machines, TV sets, or air conditioners. With consumers bearing the cost of disassembling appliances in the form of a disposal fee to recycling firms, which can come to $60 for a refrigerator or $35 for a washing machine, there is strong pressure to design appliances so they can be more easily and cheaply disassembled.[89]

With computers becoming obsolete every few years as technology advances, the need to quickly disassemble and recycle them is another paramount challenge in building an eco-economy. In Europe, information technology (IT) firms are exploring the reuse of computer components. Because European law requires manufacturers to pay for the collection, disassembly, and recycling of toxic materials in IT equipment, they have begun to focus on how to disassemble everything from computers to cell phones. Finland-based Nokia, for example, has designed a cell phone that will virtually disassemble itself.[90]

On the clothing front, Patagonia, an outdoor gear retailer, has launched a garment recycling program beginning with its polyester fiber garments. Working with Teijin, a Japanese firm, Patagonia is taking back and recycling not only the polyester garments it sells but also those sold by its competitors. Patagonia estimates that making a garment from recycled polyester, which is indistinguishable from the initial polyester made from petroleum, uses less than one fourth as much energy. With this success behind it, Patagonia has broadened the program to recycle its cotton tee shirts as well as nylon and wool clothing.[91]

Remanufacturing is even more efficient. Within the heavy industry sector, Caterpillar has emerged as a leader. At a plant in Corinth, Mississippi, the company recycles some 17 truckloads of diesel engines a day. These engines, retrieved from Caterpillar's clients, are disassembled by hand by workers who do not throw away a single component, not even a bolt or screw. Once the engine is disassembled, it is reassembled with all worn parts repaired or replaced. The resulting engine is as good as new. In 2006, Caterpillar's remanufacturing division was racking up $1 billion a year in sales and growing at 15 percent annually, contributing impressively to the company's bottom line.[92]

Another emerging industry is airliner recycling. Daniel Michaels writes in the *Wall Street Journal* that Boeing and Airbus, which have been building jetliners in competition for nearly 40 years, are now vying to see who can dismantle planes most efficiently. The first step is to strip the plane of its marketable components, such as engines, landing gear, galley ovens, and hundreds of other items. For a jumbo jet, these key components can collectively sell for up to $4 million. Then comes the final dismantling and recycling of aluminum, copper, plastic, and other materials. The next time around the aluminum may show up in cars, bicycles, or another jetliner.[93]

The goal is to recycle 90 percent of the plane, and perhaps one day 95 percent or more. With more than 3,000 airliners already put out to pasture and many more to come, this retired fleet has become the equivalent of an aluminum mine.[94]

Another increasingly attractive option for cutting carbon emissions is to discourage energy-intensive but nonessential industries. The gold jewelry, bottled water, and plastic bag industries are prime examples. The annual world production of 2,380 tons of gold, the bulk of it used for jewelry, requires the processing of 500 million tons of ore. For comparison, while 1 ton of steel requires the processing of 2 tons of ore, 1 ton of gold involves processing an almost incomprehensible 200,000 tons of ore. Processing ore for gold consumes a vast amount of energy—and emits as much CO_2 as 5.5 million cars.[95]

In a world trying to stabilize climate, it is very difficult to justify bottling water (often tap water to begin with), hauling it over long distances, and then selling it for 1,000 times the price of tap water. Although clever marketing, designed to undermine public confidence in the safety and quality of municipal water supplies, has convinced many consumers that bottled water is safer and healthier than water from faucets, a detailed study by the World Wide Fund for Nature could not find any support for this claim. It notes that in the United States and Europe there are more standards regulating the quality of tap water than bottled water. For people in developing countries where water is unsafe, it is far cheaper to boil or filter water than to buy it in bottles.[96]

Manufacturing the nearly 28 billion plastic bottles used each year to package water in the United States alone requires the equivalent of 17 million barrels of oil. And whereas tap water is delivered through a highly energy-efficient infrastructure, bottled water is hauled by trucks, sometimes over hundreds of miles. Including the energy for hauling water from bottling plants to sales outlets and the energy needed for refrigeration, the U.S. bottled water industry consumes roughly 50 million barrels of oil per year, enough oil to fuel 3 million cars for one year.[97]

The good news is that people are beginning to see how wasteful and climate-disruptive this industry is. Mayors of U.S. cities are refusing to spend taxpayer dollars to buy bottled water for their employees at exorbitant prices when high-quality tap water is readily available. Mayor Rocky Anderson of Salt Lake City noted the "total absurdity and irresponsibility, both economic and environmental, of purchasing and using bottled water when we have perfectly good and safe sources of tap water."[98]

San Francisco Mayor Newsom has banned the use of city funds to purchase bottled water. Other cities following a similar strategy include Los Angeles, Salt Lake City, and St. Louis. New York City has launched a $5-million ad campaign to promote its tap water and thus to rid the city of bottled water and the fleets of delivery trucks that tie up traffic. In response to initiatives such as these, U.S. sales of bottled water began to decline in 2008.[99]

Like plastic water bottles, throwaway plastic shopping bags are also made from fossil fuels, can take centuries to decompose, and are almost always unnecessary. In addition to local initiatives, several national governments are moving to ban or severely restrict the use of plastic shopping bags, including China, Ireland, Eritrea, Tanzania, and the United Kingdom.[100]

In summary, there is a vast worldwide potential for cutting carbon emissions by reducing materials use. This begins with the major metals—steel, aluminum, and copper—where recycling requires only a fraction of the energy needed to produce these metals from virgin ore. It continues with the design of cars, household appliances, and electronic products so they are easily disassembled into their component parts for reuse or recycling. And it includes avoiding unnecessary products.

Smarter Grids, Appliances, and Consumers

More and more utilities are beginning to realize that building large power plants just to handle peak daily and seasonal demand is a very costly way of managing an electricity system. Existing electricity grids are typically a patchwork of local grids that are simultaneously inefficient, wasteful, and dysfunctional in that they often are unable, for example, to move electricity surpluses to areas of shortages. The U.S. electricity grid today resembles the roads and highways of the mid-twentieth century before the interstate highway system was built. What is needed today is the electricity equivalent of the interstate highway system.[101]

The inability to move low-cost electricity to consumers because of congestion on transmission lines brings with it costs similar to those associated with traffic congestion. The lack of transmission capacity in the eastern United States is estimated to cost consumers $16 billion a year in this region alone.[102]

In the United States, a strong national grid would permit power to be moved continuously from surplus to deficit regions, thus reducing the total generating capacity needed. Most important, the new grid would link regions rich in wind, solar, and geothermal energy with consumption centers. A national grid, drawing on a full range of renewable energy sources, would itself be a stabilizing factor.

Establishing strong national grids that can move electricity as needed and that link new energy sources with consumers is only half the battle, however. The grids and appliances need to become "smarter" as well. In the simplest terms, a smart grid is one that takes advantage of advances in information technology, integrating this technology into the electrical generating, delivery, and user system, enabling utilities to communicate directly with customers and, if the latter agree, with their household appliances.

Smart grid technologies can reduce power disruption and fluctuation that cost the U.S. economy close to $100 billion a year, according to the Electric Power Research Institute. In an excellent 2009 Center for American Progress study, *Wired for Progress 2.0: Building a National Clean-Energy Smart Grid*, Bracken Hendricks notes the vast potential for raising grid efficiency with several information technologies: "A case in point would be encouraging the widespread use of synchrophasors to monitor voltage and current in real time over the grid network. It has been estimated that better use of this sort of real-time information across the entire electrical grid could allow at least a 20 percent improvement in energy efficiency in the United States." This and many other examples give us a sense of the potential for increasing grid efficiency.[103]

A smart grid not only moves electricity more efficiently in geographic terms; it also enables electricity use to be shifted over time—for example, from periods of peak demand to those of off-peak demand. Achieving this goal means working with consumers who have "smart meters" to see exactly how much electricity is being used at any particular time. This facilitates two-way communication between utility and consumer so they can cooperate in reducing peak demand in a way that is advantageous to both. And it allows the use of two-way metering so that customers who have a rooftop solar electric panel or their own windmill can sell surplus electricity back to the utility.[104]

Smart meters coupled with smart appliances that can receive

signals from the grid allow electricity use to be shifted away from peak demand. Higher electricity prices during high demand periods also prod consumers to change their behavior, thus improving market efficiency. For example, a dishwasher can be programmed to run not at 8 p.m. but at 3 a.m., when electricity demand is much lower, or air conditioners can be turned off for a brief period to lighten the demand load.[105]

Another approach being pioneered in Europe achieves the same goal but uses a different technology. In any grid, there is a narrow range of fluctuation in the power being carried. An Italian research team is testing refrigerators that can monitor the grid flow and, when demand rises or supply drops, simply turn themselves off for as long as it is safe to do so. *New Scientist* reports that if this technology were used in the 30 million refrigerators in the United Kingdom, it would reduce national peak demand by 2,000 megawatts of generating capacity, allowing the country to close four coal-fired power plants.[106]

A similar approach could be used for air conditioning systems in both residential and commercial buildings. Karl Lewis, COO of GridPoint, a U.S. company that designs smart grids, says "we can turn off a compressor in somebody's air conditioning system for 15 minutes and the temperature really won't change in the house." The bottom line with a smart grid is that a modest investment in information technology can reduce peak power, yielding both savings in electricity and an accompanying reduction in carbon emissions.[107]

Some utilities are pioneers in using time-based pricing of electricity, when electricity used during off-peak hours is priced much lower than that used during peak hours. Similarly, in regions with high summer temperatures, there is often a costly seasonal peak demand. Baltimore Gas and Electric (BGE), for example, conducted a pilot program in 2008 in which participating customers who permitted the utility to turn off their air conditioners for selected intervals during the hottest days were credited generously for the electricity they saved. The going rate in the region is roughly 14¢ per kilowatt-hour. But for a kilowatt-hour saved during peak hours on peak days, customers were paid up to $1.75—more than 12 times as much. Thus if they saved 4 kilowatt-hours of electricity in one afternoon, they got a $7 credit on their electricity bill. Customers reduced their peak electricity consumption by as much as one third, encouraging BGE to design a similar program with even more "smart" technology for summer 2009.[108]

Within the United States the shift to smart meters is moving fast, with some 28 utilities planning to deploy smart meters in the years ahead. Among the leaders are California's two major utilities, Pacific Gas and Electric and Southern California Edison, which are planning on full deployment to their 5.1 million and 5.3 million customers by 2012. Both will offer variable rates to reduce peak electricity use. Among the many other utilities aiming for full deployment are American Electric Power in the Midwest (5 million customers) and Florida Power and Light (4.4 million customers).[109]

Europe, too, is installing smart meters, with Finland setting the pace. A Swedish research firm, Berg Insight, projects that Europe will have 80 million smart meters installed by 2013.[110]

Unfortunately, the term "smart meters" describes a wide variety of meters, ranging from those that simply provide consumers with real-time data on electricity use to those that facilitate two-way communication between the utility and customer or even between the utility and individual household appliances. The bottom line: the smarter the meter, the greater the savings.[111]

Taking advantage of information technology to increase the efficiency of the grid, the delivery system, and the use of electricity at the same time is itself a smart move. Simply put, a smart grid combined with smart meters enables both electrical utilities and consumers to be much more efficient.

The Energy Savings Potential

The goal for this chapter was to identify energy-saving measures that will offset the nearly 30 percent growth in global energy demand projected by the IEA between 2006 and 2020. My colleagues and I are confident that the measures proposed will more than offset the projected growth in energy use.[112]

Shifting to more energy-efficient lighting alone lowers world electricity use by 12 percent. With appliances, the key to raising energy efficiency is to establish international efficiency standards that reflect the most efficient models on the market today, regularly raising this level as technologies advance. This would in effect be the global version of Japan's Top Runner program to raise appliance efficiency.

Given the potential for raising appliance efficiency, the energy saved by 2020 should at least match the savings in the lighting sector. Combining more-efficient lights and appliances with a smart grid that uses time-of-day pricing, peak demand sensors, and the many other technologies described in this chapter shows a huge potential for reducing both overall electricity use and peak demand.[113]

It is easy to underestimate the potential for reducing electricity use. Within the United States, the Rocky Mountain Institute calculates that if the 40 least efficient states were to achieve the electrical efficiency of the 10 most efficient ones, national electricity use would be cut by one third. This would allow the equivalent of 62 percent of all U.S. coal-fired power plants to be closed down. But even the most efficient states have a substantial potential for further reducing electricity use and, indeed, are planning to keep cutting carbon emissions and saving money.[114]

In terms of transportation, the short-term keys to reducing oil use and carbon emissions involve shifting to highly fuel-efficient cars (including electric vehicles), diversifying urban transport systems, and building intercity rapid rail systems modeled on those in Japan and Europe. This shift from car-dominated transport systems to diversified systems is evident in the actions of hundreds of mayors worldwide who struggle daily with traffic congestion and air pollution. They are devising ingenious ways of limiting not only the use of cars but also the very need for them. As the urban car presence diminishes, the nature of the city itself will change.

Within the industrial sector, there is a hefty potential for reducing energy use. In the petrochemical industry, moving to the most efficient production technologies now available and recycling more plastic can cut energy use by 32 percent. Gains in manufacturing efficiency in steel can cut energy use by 23 percent. Even larger gains are within reach for cement, where simply shifting to the most efficient dry kiln technologies can reduce energy use by 42 percent.[115]

With buildings—even older buildings, where retrofitting can reduce energy use by 20–50 percent—there is a profitable potential for saving energy. As noted earlier, such a reduction in energy use, combined with the use of renewable electricity to heat, cool, and light the building, means that it will be easier to create carbon-neutral buildings than we may have thought.

One simple way to achieve all these gains is to adopt a carbon tax that would help reflect the full cost of burning fossil fuels. We recommend increasing this carbon tax by $20 per ton each year over the next 10 years, for a total of $200 ($55 per ton of CO_2), offsetting it with a reduction in income taxes. High though this may seem, it does not come close to covering all the indirect costs of burning fossil fuels. It does, however, encourage investment in both efficiency and carbon-free sources of energy.

In seeking to raise energy efficiency as described in this chapter, there have been some exciting surprises in the vast potential for doing so. We now turn to developing the earth's renewable sources of energy, where there are equally exciting possibilities.

5

Stabilizing Climate: Shifting to Renewable Energy

As fossil fuel prices rise, as oil insecurity deepens, and as concerns about climate change cast a shadow over the future of coal, a new energy economy is emerging. The old energy economy, fueled by oil, coal, and natural gas, is being replaced by one powered by wind, solar, and geothermal energy. Despite the global economic crisis, this energy transition is moving at a pace and on a scale that we could not have imagined even two years ago. And it is a worldwide phenomenon.

Consider Texas. Long the leading U.S. oil-producing state, it is now also the leading generator of electricity from wind, having overtaken California three years ago. Texas now has 7,900 megawatts of wind generating capacity online, 1,100 more in the construction stage, and a huge amount in the development stage. When all of these wind farms are completed, Texas will have 53,000 megawatts of wind generating capacity—the equivalent of 53 coal-fired power plants. This will more than satisfy the residential needs of the state's 24 million people, enabling Texas to export electricity, just as it has long exported oil.[1]

Texas is not alone. In South Dakota, a wind-rich, sparsely populated state, development has begun on a vast 5,050-

megawatt wind farm (1 megawatt of wind capacity supplies 300 U.S. homes) that when completed will produce nearly five times as much electricity as the 796,000 people living in the state need. Altogether, some 10 states in the United States, most of them in the Great Plains, and several Canadian provinces are planning to export wind energy.[2]

Across the Atlantic, the government of Scotland is negotiating with two sovereign wealth funds in the Middle East to invest $7 billion in a grid in the North Sea off its eastern coast. This grid will enable Scotland to develop nearly 60,000 megawatts of off-shore wind generating capacity, close to the 79,000 megawatts of current electrical generating capacity for the United Kingdom.[3]

We are witnessing an embrace of renewable energy on a scale we've never seen for fossil fuels or nuclear power. And not only in industrial countries. Algeria, which knows it will not be exporting oil forever, is planning to build 6,000 megawatts of solar thermal generating capacity for export to Europe via undersea cable. The Algerians note that they have enough harnessable solar energy in their vast desert to power the entire world economy. This is not a mathematical error. A similarly striking fact is that the sunlight striking the earth in just one hour is enough to power the world economy for one year.[4]

Turkey, which now has 39,000 megawatts of total electrical generating capacity, issued a request for proposals in 2007 to build wind farms. It received bids from both domestic and international wind development firms to build a staggering 78,000 megawatts of wind generating capacity. Having selected 15,000 megawatts of the most promising proposals, the government is now issuing construction permits.[5]

In mid-2008, Indonesia—a country with 128 active volcanoes and therefore rich in geothermal energy—announced that it would develop 6,900 megawatts of geothermal generating capacity, with Pertamina, the state oil company, responsible for developing the lion's share. Indonesia's oil production has been declining for the last decade, and in each of the last four years the country has been an oil importer. As Pertamina shifts resources from oil into the development of geothermal energy, it could become the first oil company—state-owned or independent—to make the transition from oil to renewable energy.[6]

These are only a few of the visionary initiatives to tap the earth's renewable energy. The resources are vast. In the United States, three states—North Dakota, Kansas, and Texas—have enough harnessable wind energy to run the entire economy. In China, wind will likely become the dominant power source. Indonesia could one day get all its power from geothermal energy alone. Europe will be powered largely by wind farms in the North Sea and solar thermal power plants in the North African desert.[7]

The Plan B goals for developing renewable sources of energy by 2020 that are laid out in this chapter are based not on what is conventionally believed to be politically feasible but on what we think is needed. This is not Plan A, business as usual. This is Plan B—a wartime mobilization, an all-out response that is designed to avoid destabilizing economic and political stresses that will come with unmanageable climate change.

To reduce worldwide net carbon dioxide (CO_2) emissions by 80 percent by 2020, the first priority is to replace all coal- and oil-fired electricity generation with renewable sources. Whereas the twentieth century was marked by the globalization of the world energy economy as countries everywhere turned to oil, much of it coming from the Middle East, this century will see the localization of energy production as the world turns to wind, solar, and geothermal energy.

This century will also see the electrification of the economy. The transport sector will shift from gasoline-powered automobiles to plug-in gas-electric hybrids, all-electric cars, light rail transit, and high-speed intercity rail. And for long-distance freight, the shift will be from diesel-powered trucks to electrically powered rail freight systems. The movement of people and goods will be powered largely by electricity. In this new energy economy, buildings will rely on renewable electricity almost exclusively for heating, cooling, and lighting.

In the electrification of the economy, we do not count on a buildup in nuclear power. Our assumption is that the limited number of nuclear power plants now under construction worldwide will simply offset the closing of aging plants, with no overall growth in capacity by 2020. If we use full-cost pricing—requiring utilities to absorb the costs of disposing of nuclear waste, of decommissioning a plant when it wears out, and of insuring reactors against possible accidents and terrorist attacks—building nuclear plants in a competitive electricity market is simply not economical.[8]

Beyond the costs of nuclear power are the political questions. If we say that expanding nuclear power is an important part of our energy future, do we mean for all countries or only for some countries? If the latter, who makes the A-list and the B-list of countries? And who enforces the listings?

In laying out the climate component of Plan B, we also exclude the oft-discussed option of carbon sequestration at coal-fired power plants. Given the costs and the lack of investor interest within the coal community itself, this technology is not likely to be economically viable on a meaningful scale by 2020.

Can we expand renewable energy use fast enough? We think so. Recent trends in the adoption of mobile phones and personal computers give a sense of how quickly new technologies can spread. Once cumulative mobile phone sales reached 1 million units in 1986, the stage was set for explosive growth, and the number of cell phone subscribers doubled in each of the next three years. Over the next 12 years the number doubled every two years. By 2001 there were 961 million cell phones—nearly a 1,000-fold increase in just 15 years. And now there are more than 4 billion cell phone subscribers worldwide.[9]

Sales of personal computers followed a similar trajectory. In 1980 roughly a million were sold, but by 2008 the figure was an estimated 270 million—a 270-fold jump in 28 years. We are now seeing similar growth figures for renewable energy technologies. Installations of solar cells are doubling every two years, and the annual growth in wind generating capacity is not far behind. Just as the communications and information economies have changed beyond recognition over the past two decades, so too will the energy economy over the next decade.[10]

There is one outstanding difference. Whereas the restructuring of the information economy was shaped only by advancing technology and market forces, the restructuring of the energy economy will be driven also by the realization that the fate of civilization may depend not only on doing so, but on doing it at wartime speed.

Turning to the Wind

Wind is the centerpiece of the Plan B energy economy. It is abundant, low cost, and widely distributed; it scales up easily and can be developed quickly. Oil wells go dry and coal seams run out, but the earth's wind resources cannot be depleted.

A worldwide survey of wind energy by the Stanford University team of Cristina Archer and Mark Jacobson concluded that harnessing one fifth of the earth's available wind energy would provide seven times as much electricity as the world currently uses. For example, China—with vast wind-swept plains in the north and west, countless mountain ridges, and a long coastline, all rich with wind—has enough readily harnessable wind energy to easily double its current electrical generating capacity.[11]

The United States is also richly endowed. In addition to having enough land-based wind energy to satisfy national electricity needs several times over, the National Renewable Energy Lab has identified 1,000 gigawatts (1 gigawatt equals 1,000 megawatts) of wind energy waiting to be tapped off the East Coast and 900 gigawatts off the West Coast. This offshore capacity alone is sufficient to power the U.S. economy.[12]

Europe is already tapping its off-shore wind. An assessment by the Garrad Hassan wind energy consulting group concluded that if governments aggressively develop their vast off-shore resources, wind could supply all of Europe's residential electricity by 2020.[13]

For many years, a small handful of countries dominated growth in the industry, but this is changing as the industry goes global, with some 70 countries now harnessing wind resources. World wind electric generation is growing at a frenetic pace. From 2000 to 2008, generating capacity increased from 17,000 megawatts to an estimated 121,000 megawatts. The world leader in total capacity is now the United States, followed by Germany (until recently the leader), Spain, China, and India. But with China's wind generation doubling each year, the U.S. lead may be short-lived.[14]

Measured by share of national electricity supplied by wind, Denmark is the leader, at 21 percent. Four north German states now get one third or more of their electricity from wind. For Germany as a whole, the figure is 8 percent—and climbing.[15]

Denmark is now looking to push the wind share of its electricity to 50 percent, with most of the additional power coming from off-shore. In contemplating this prospect, Danish planners have turned energy policy upside down. They are looking at using wind as the mainstay of their electrical generating system and fossil-fuel-generated power to fill in when the wind ebbs.[16]

In Spain, which already has nearly 17,000 megawatts of capacity, the government is shooting for 20,000 megawatts by 2010. France, a relative newcomer to wind energy, is looking to develop 25,000 megawatts of wind by 2020; out of this, 6,000 megawatts would be off-shore.[17]

As of early 2009 the United States had just over 28,000 megawatts of wind generating capacity, with an additional 38 wind farms under construction. Beyond this, proposed wind farms that can generate some 300,000 megawatts are on hold, awaiting grid construction.[18]

In addition to Texas and California, which is planning a 4,500-megawatt wind farm complex in the southern end of the state, several other states are emerging as wind superpowers. As noted earlier, Clipper Windpower and BP are teaming up to build the 5,050-megawatt Titan wind farm in eastern South Dakota. Colorado billionaire Philip Anschutz is developing a 2,000-megawatt wind farm in south central Wyoming to generate electricity for transmission to California, Arizona, and Nevada.[19]

In the east, Maine—a wind energy newcomer—is planning to develop 3,000 megawatts of wind generating capacity, far more than the state's 1.3 million residents need. New York State, which has 1,300 megawatts of wind generating capacity, plans to add another 8,000 megawatts, with most of the power being generated by winds coming off Lake Erie and Lake Ontario. And soon Oregon will nearly double its wind generating capacity with the 900-megawatt wind farm planned for the windy Columbia River Gorge.[20]

While U.S. attention has focused on the wind-rich Great Plains, and rightly so, another area is now gathering attention. For years, the only off-shore wind project in the east that was moving through the permitting stage was a 400-megawatt project off the coast of Cape Cod, Massachusetts. Now Massachusetts has been joined by Rhode Island, New York, New Jersey, and Delaware. Delaware is planning an off-shore wind farm of up to 600 megawatts, an installation that could satisfy half the state's residential electricity needs.[21]

East Coast off-shore wind is attractive for three reasons. One, it is strong and reliable. The off-shore region stretching from Massachusetts southward to North Carolina has a potential wind generating capacity that exceeds the requirement of the states in the region. Two, the East Coast has an extensive, rather shallow off-shore area, which makes off-shore wind construction less costly. And three, this electricity source is close to consumers.[22]

To the north, Canada, with its vast area and only 33 million people, has one of the highest wind-to-population ratios of any country. Ontario, Quebec, and Alberta are far and away the leaders in installed capacity at this point. But in recent months three of Canada's four Atlantic provinces—New Brunswick, Prince Edward Island, and Nova Scotia—have begun discussions to jointly develop and export some of their wealth of wind energy to the densely populated U.S. Northeast.[23]

Impressive though the U.S. growth is, the expansion now under way in China is even more so. China has some 12,000 megawatts of wind generating capacity, mostly in the 50- to 100-megawatt wind farm category, with many more medium-size wind farms coming. Beyond this, its Wind Base program is creating six mega-complexes of wind farms of at least 10 gigawatts each. These are located in Gansu Province (15 gigawatts), Western Inner Mongolia (20 gigawatts), Eastern Inner Mongolia (30 gigawatts), Hebei Province (10 gigawatts), Xinjiang Hami (20 gigawatts), and along the coast north of Shanghai in Jiangsu Province (10 gigawatts). When completed, these complexes will have a generating capacity of 105 gigawatts—as much wind power as the entire world had in early 2008.[24]

In considering the land requirements to produce energy, wind turbines are extraordinarily efficient. For example, an acre of corn land in northern Iowa used to site a wind turbine can produce $300,000 worth of electricity per year. This same acre of land planted in corn would yield 480 gallons of ethanol worth $960. This extraordinary energy yield of land used for wind turbines helps explain why investors find wind farms so attractive.[25]

And since wind turbines occupy only 1 percent of the land covered by a wind farm, farmers and ranchers continue to grow grain and graze cattle. In effect, they can double crop their land, simultaneously harvesting a food crop—wheat, corn, or cattle—and energy. With no investment on their part, farmers and ranchers typically receive $3,000–10,000 a year in royalties for each wind turbine erected on their land. For thousands of ranchers in the U.S. Great Plains, the value of electricity produced on their land in the years ahead will dwarf their cattle sales.[26]

One of the early concerns with wind energy was the risk it posed to birds, but this can be managed by careful siting to avoid risky migration and breeding areas. The most recent research indicates that bird fatalities from wind farms are minuscule compared with the number of birds that die flying into skyscrapers, colliding with cars, or being captured by cats.[27]

Other critics are concerned about the visual effect. When some people see a wind farm they see a blight on the landscape. Others see a civilization-saving source of energy. Although there are NIMBY problems ("not in my backyard"), the PIMBY response ("put it in my backyard") is much more pervasive. Within rural communities, competition for wind farms—whether in ranch country in Colorado or dairy country in upstate New York—is intense. This is not surprising, since the jobs, the royalties from wind turbines, and the additional tax revenue are welcomed by local communities.

At the heart of Plan B is a crash program to develop 3,000 gigawatts (3 million megawatts) of wind generating capacity by 2020, enough to satisfy 40 percent of world electricity needs. This will require a near doubling of capacity every two years, up from a doubling every three years over the last decade.[28]

This climate-stabilizing initiative would require the installation of 1.5 million wind turbines of 2 megawatts each. Manufacturing such a huge number of wind turbines over the next 11 years sounds intimidating until it is compared with the 70 million automobiles the world produces each year. At $3 million per installed turbine, this would mean investing $4.5 trillion by 2020, or $409 billion per year. This compares with world oil and gas capital expenditures that are projected to reach $1 trillion per year by 2016.[29]

Wind turbines can be mass-produced on assembly lines, much as B-24 bombers were in World War II at Ford's massive Willow Run assembly plant in Michigan. Indeed, the idled capacity in the U.S. automobile industry is sufficient to produce all the wind turbines the world needs to reach the Plan B global goal. Not only do the idle plants exist, but there are skilled workers in these communities eager to return to work. The state of Michigan, for example, in the heart of the wind-rich Great Lakes region, has more than its share of idled auto assembly plants.[30]

Wind has many attractions. For utilities, being able to sign long-term fixed-price contracts is a godsend for them and their customers. When they look at natural gas, they look at a fuel source with a volatile price. When they look at coal-fired power, they face the uncertainty of future carbon costs.

The appeal of wind energy can be seen in its growth relative to other energy sources. In 2008, for example, wind accounted for 36 percent of new generating capacity in the European Union compared with 29 percent for natural gas, 18 percent for photovoltaics, 10 percent for oil, and only 3 percent for coal. In the United States, new wind generating capacity has exceeded coal by a wide margin each year since 2005. Worldwide, no new nuclear-generating capacity came online in 2008, while new wind generating capacity totaled 27,000 megawatts. The structure of the world energy economy is not just changing, it is changing fast.[31]

Solar Cells and Thermal Collectors

Energy from the sun can be harnessed with solar photovoltaics (PV) and solar thermal collectors. Solar PV cells—both often silicon-based semiconductors and thin films—convert sunlight directly into electricity. Solar thermal collectors convert sunlight into heat that can be used, for example, to warm water, as in rooftop solar water heaters. Alternatively, collectors can be used to concentrate sunlight on a vessel containing water to produce steam and generate electricity.

Worldwide, photovoltaic installations jumped by some 5,600 megawatts in 2008, pushing total installations to nearly 15,000 megawatts. One of the world's fastest-growing energy sources, solar PV production is growing by 45 percent annually, doubling every two years. In 2006, when Germany installed 1,100 megawatts of solar cell generating capacity, it became the first country to add over 1 gigawatt (1,000 megawatts) in a year.[32]

Until recently PV production was concentrated in Japan, Germany, and the United States. But several energetic new players have entered the field, with companies in China, Taiwan, the Philippines, South Korea, and the United Arab Emirates. China overtook the United States in PV production in 2006. Taiwan did so in 2007. Today there are scores of firms competing in the world market, driving investments in both research and manufacturing.[33]

For the nearly 1.6 billion people living in communities not yet connected to an electrical grid, it is now often cheaper to install PV panels rooftop-by-rooftop than to build a central power plant and a grid to reach potential consumers. For Andean villagers, for example, who have depended on tallow-based candles for their lighting, the monthly payment for a solar cell installation over 30 months is less than the monthly outlay for candles.[34]

When a villager buys a solar PV system, that person is in effect buying a 25-year supply of electricity. With no fuel cost and very little maintenance, it is the upfront outlay that requires financing. Recognizing this, the World Bank and the U.N. Environment Programme have stepped in with programs to help local lenders set up credit systems to finance this cheap source of electricity. An initial World Bank loan has helped 50,000 homeowners in Bangladesh obtain solar cell systems. A second, much larger round of funding will enable 200,000 more families to do the same.[35]

Villagers in India who lack electricity and who depend on kerosene lamps face a similar cost calculation. Installing a home solar electric system in India, including batteries, costs roughly $400. Such systems will power two, three, or four small appliances or lights and are widely used in homes and shops in lieu of polluting and increasingly costly kerosene lamps. In one year a kerosene lamp burns nearly 20 gallons of kerosene, which at $3 a gallon means $60 per lamp. A solar PV lighting system that replaces two lamps would pay for itself within four years and then become essentially a free source of electricity.[36]

Switching from kerosene to solar cells is particularly helpful in fighting climate change. Although the estimated 1.5 billion kerosene lamps used worldwide provide less than 1 percent of all residential lighting, they account for 29 percent of that sector's CO_2 emissions. They use the equivalent of 1.3 million barrels of oil per day, equal to roughly half the oil production of Kuwait.[37]

The cost of solar energy is falling fast in industrial countries. Michael Rogol and his PHOTON consulting firm estimate that by 2010 fully integrated companies that encompass all phases of solar PV manufacturing will be installing systems that produce electricity for 12¢ a kilowatt-hour in sun-drenched Spain and 18¢ a kilowatt-hour in southern Germany. Although these costs will be dropping below those of conventional electricity in many locations, this will not automatically translate into a wholesale conversion to solar PV. But as one energy industry analyst observes, the "big bang" is under way.[38]

After starting with relatively small residential rooftop installations, investors are now turning to utility-scale solar cell complexes. A 20-megawatt facility completed in Spain in 2007 was the largest ever built—but not for long. A 60-megawatt facility, also in Spain, came online in 2008 and tripled the ante. Even larger solar cell installations are being planned, including 80-megawatt facilities in California and Israel.[39]

In mid-2008, Pacific Gas and Electric (PG&E), one of two large utilities in California, announced a contract with two firms to build solar PV installations with a combined generating capacity of 800 megawatts. Covering 12 square miles, this complex will generate as much electricity at peak power as a nuclear power plant. The bar has been raised yet again.[40]

And in early 2009, China Technology Development Group Corporation and Qinghai New Energy Group announced they were joining forces to build a 30-megawatt solar PV power facility in remote Qinghai Province. This is the first stage in what is eventually expected to become a 1,000-megawatt generating facility. For a country that ended 2008 with only 145 megawatts of installed solar cell capacity, this is a huge leap into the future.[41]

More and more countries, states, and provinces are setting solar installation goals. Italy's solar industry group is projecting 16,000 megawatts of installed capacity by 2020. Japan is planning 14,000 megawatts by 2020. The state of California has set a goal of 3,000 megawatts by 2017. New Jersey has a goal of 2,300 megawatts of solar installations by 2021, and Maryland is aiming for 1,500 megawatts by 2022.[42]

With installations of solar PV now doubling every two years and likely to continue doing so at least until 2020, annual installations, at nearly 5,600 megawatts in 2008, will climb to 500,000 megawatts in 2020. By this time the cumulative installed capacity would exceed 1.5 million megawatts (1,500 gigawatts). Although this may seem overly ambitious, it could in fact turn out to be a conservative goal. For one thing, if most of the nearly 1.6 billion people who lack electricity today get it by 2020, it will likely be because they have installed home solar systems.[43]

A second, very promising way to harness solar energy on a massive scale is simply to use reflectors to concentrate sunlight on a closed vessel containing water or some other liquid, heating the liquid to produce steam that drives a turbine. This solar thermal technology, often referred to as concentrating solar power (CSP), first came on the scene with the construction of a 350-megawatt solar thermal power plant complex in California. Completed in 1991, it remained the world's only utility-scale solar thermal generating facility until the completion of a 64-megawatt power plant in Nevada in 2007. As of early 2009, the United States has 6,100 megawatts of solar thermal power plants under development, all with signed long-term power purchase agreements.[44]

In mid-2009 Lockheed Martin, an aerospace defense and information technology contractor, announced that it was building a 290-megawatt CSP plant in Arizona. This plant, like many other CSP plants, will have six hours of storage, enabling it to generate electricity until midnight or beyond. The entry into the solar field of a company with annual sales of $43 billion and vast engineering skills signals a major new commitment to harnessing the earth's abundance of solar energy.[45]

As noted earlier, the government of Algeria plans to produce 6,000 megawatts of solar thermal electrical capacity for transmission to Europe via undersea cable. The German government was quick to respond to the Algerian initiative. The plan is to build a 1,900-mile high-voltage transmission line from Adrar deep in the Algerian desert to Aachen, a town on Germany's border with the Netherlands.[46]

The first plant under construction in Algeria is a solar/natural-gas hybrid, with the natural gas taking over power generation entirely after the sun goes down. Although the first few plants in this massive new project will be hybrids, New Energy Algeria, the government firm specifically created to encourage renewable energy development, plans soon to switch exclusively to solar thermal power. These plants will likely use molten salt or some other medium for storing heat in order to extend generation several hours beyond sundown and through the high-demand evening hours.[47]

The U.S. plants under development and this announcement by the Algerians were the early indications that the world is entering the utility-scale solar thermal power era. By the end of 2008, there were some 60 commercial-scale solar thermal power plants in the pipeline, most of them in the United States and Spain. Among the 10 largest proposed plants, 8 are to be built in the United States. Ranging in size from 250 to 900 megawatts, most of them will be in California. The early months of 2009 brought many more announcements. BrightSource Energy announced a blockbuster package with Southern California Edison of seven projects with a collective total of 1,300 megawatts of generating capacity. Shortly thereafter, it announced an identical package with PG&E's. NRG, a New Jersey–based firm, and eSolar announced that together they would develop 500 megawatts of CSP at sites in the southwestern United States.[48]

Spain, another solar superpower, has 50 or so plants, each close to 50 megawatts in size, in various phases of development. There are a scattering of proposed CSP plants in other countries, including Israel, Australia, South Africa, the United Arab Emirates, and Egypt. At least a dozen other sun-drenched countries now recognize the potential of this inexhaustible, low-cost source of electricity and are mobilizing to tap it.[49]

One of the countries for which CSP plants are ideally suited is India. Although this nation is not nearly as richly endowed with wind energy as, say, China or the United States, the Great Indian Desert in the northwest offers a huge opportunity for building solar thermal power plants. Hundreds of plants in the desert could satisfy most of India's electricity needs. And because it is such a compact country, the distance for building transmission lines to connect with major population centers is relatively short.

Solar thermal electricity costs are falling fast. Today it costs roughly 12–18¢ per kilowatt-hour. The U.S. Department of Energy goal is to invest in research that will lower the cost to 5–7¢ per kilowatt-hour by 2020.[50]

We know solar energy is abundant. The American Solar Energy Society notes there are enough solar thermal resources in the U.S. Southwest to satisfy current U.S. electricity needs nearly four times over. The U.S. Bureau of Land Management, the agency that manages public lands, has received requests for the land rights to develop solar thermal power plants or photovoltaic complexes with a total of 23,000 megawatts of generating capacity in Nevada, 40,000 megawatts in Arizona, and over 54,000 megawatts in the desert region of southern California.[51]

At the global level, Greenpeace, the European Solar Thermal Electricity Association, and the International Energy Agency's SolarPACES program have outlined a plan to develop 1.5 million megawatts of solar thermal power plant capacity by 2050. For Plan B we suggest a more immediate world goal of 200,000 megawatts by 2020, a goal that may well be exceeded as the economic potential becomes clearer.[52]

The pace of solar energy development is accelerating as solar water heaters—the other use of solar collectors—take off. China, for example, is now home to 27 million rooftop solar water heaters. With nearly 4,000 Chinese companies manufacturing these devices, this relatively simple low-cost technology has leapfrogged into villages that do not yet have electricity. For as little as $200, villagers can have a rooftop solar collector installed and take their first hot shower. This technology is sweeping China like wildfire, already approaching market saturation in some communities. Beijing plans to boost the current 114 million square meters of rooftop solar collectors for heating water to 300 million by 2020.[53]

The energy harnessed by these installations in China is equal to the electricity generated by 49 coal-fired power plants. Other developing countries such as India and Brazil may also soon see millions of households turning to this inexpensive water heating technology. This leapfrogging into rural areas without an electricity grid is similar to the way cell phones bypassed the traditional fixed-line grid, providing services to millions of people who would still be on waiting lists if they had relied on traditional phone lines. Once the initial installment cost of rooftop solar water heaters is paid, the hot water is essentially free.[54]

In Europe, where energy costs are relatively high, rooftop solar water heaters are also spreading fast. In Austria, 15 percent of all households now rely on them for hot water. And, as in China, in some Austrian villages nearly all homes have rooftop collectors. Germany is also forging ahead. Janet Sawin of the Worldwatch Institute notes that some 2 million Germans are now living in homes where water and space are both heated by rooftop solar systems.[55]

Inspired by the rapid adoption of rooftop water and space heaters in Europe in recent years, the European Solar Thermal Industry Federation (ESTIF) has established an ambitious goal of 500 million square meters, or 1 square meter of rooftop collector for every European by 2020—a goal slightly greater than the 0.93 square meters per person found today in Cyprus, the world leader. Most installations are projected to be Solar-Combi systems that are engineered to heat both water and space.[56]

Europe's solar collectors are concentrated in Germany, Austria, and Greece, with France and Spain also beginning to mobilize. Spain's initiative was boosted by a March 2006 mandate requiring installation of collectors on all new or renovated buildings. Portugal followed quickly with its own mandate. ESTIF estimates that the European Union has a long-term potential of developing 1,200 thermal gigawatts of solar water and space heating, which means that the sun could meet most of Europe's low-temperature heating needs.[57]

The U.S. rooftop solar water heating industry has historically concentrated on a niche market—selling and marketing 10 million square meters of solar water heaters for swimming pools between 1995 and 2005. Given this base, however, the industry was poised to mass-market residential solar water and space heating systems when federal tax credits were introduced in 2006. Led by Hawaii, California, and Florida, U.S. installation of these systems tripled in 2006 and has continued at a rapid pace since then.[58]

We now have the data to make some global projections. With

China setting a goal of 300 million square meters of solar water heating capacity by 2020, and ESTIF's goal of 500 million square meters for Europe by 2020, a U.S. installation of 300 million square meters by 2020 is certainly within reach given the recently adopted tax incentives. Japan, which now has 7 million square meters of rooftop solar collectors heating water but which imports virtually all its fossil fuels, could easily reach 80 million square meters by 2020.[59]

If China and the European Union achieve their goals and Japan and the United States reach the projected adoptions, they will have a combined total of 1,180 million square meters of water and space heating capacity by 2020. With appropriate assumptions for developing countries other than China, the global total in 2020 could exceed 1.5 billion square meters. This would give the world a solar thermal capacity by 2020 of 1,100 thermal gigawatts, the equivalent of 690 coal-fired power plants.[60]

The huge projected expansion in solar water and space heating in industrial countries could close some existing coal-fired power plants and reduce natural gas use, as solar water heaters replace electric and gas water heaters. In countries such as China and India, however, solar water heaters will simply reduce the need for new coal-fired power plants.

Solar water and space heaters in Europe and China have a strong economic appeal. On average, in industrial countries these systems pay for themselves from electricity savings in fewer than 10 years. They are also responsive to energy security and climate change concerns.[61]

With the cost of rooftop heating systems declining, particularly in China, many other countries will likely join Israel, Spain, and Portugal in mandating that all new buildings incorporate rooftop solar water heaters. No longer a passing fad, these rooftop appliances are fast entering the mainstream.[62]

Thus the harnessing of solar energy is expanding on every front as concerns about climate change and energy security escalate, as government incentives for harnessing solar energy expand, and as these costs decline while those of fossil fuels rise. In 2009, new U.S. generating capacity from solar sources could exceed that from coal for the first time.[63]

Energy from the Earth

The heat in the upper six miles of the earth's crust contains 50,000 times as much energy as found in all the world's oil and gas reserves combined—a startling statistic that few people are aware of. Despite this abundance, only 10,500 megawatts of geothermal generating capacity have been harnessed worldwide.[64]

Partly because of the dominance of the oil, gas, and coal industries, which have been providing cheap fuel by omitting the costs of climate change and air pollution from fuel prices, relatively little has been invested in developing the earth's geothermal heat resources. Over the last decade, geothermal energy has been growing at scarcely 3 percent a year.[65]

Half the world's existing generating capacity is in the United States and the Philippines. Mexico, Indonesia, Italy, and Japan account for most of the remainder. Altogether some 24 countries now convert geothermal energy into electricity. Iceland, the Philippines, and El Salvador respectively get 27, 26, and 23 percent of their electricity from geothermal power plants.[66]

The potential of geothermal energy to provide electricity, to heat homes, and to supply process heat for industry is vast. Among the countries rich in geothermal energy are those bordering the Pacific in the so-called Ring of Fire, including Chile, Peru, Colombia, Mexico, the United States, Canada, Russia, China, Japan, the Philippines, Indonesia, and Australia. Other geothermally rich countries include those along the Great Rift Valley of Africa, such as Kenya and Ethiopia, and those around the Eastern Mediterranean.[67]

Beyond geothermal electrical generation, an estimated 100,000 thermal megawatts of geothermal energy are used directly—without conversion into electricity—to heat homes and greenhouses and as process heat in industry. This includes, for example, the energy used in hot baths in Japan and to heat homes in Iceland and greenhouses in Russia.[68]

An interdisciplinary team of 13 scientists and engineers assembled by the Massachusetts Institute of Technology (MIT) in 2006 assessed U.S. geothermal electrical generating potential. Drawing on the latest technologies, including those used by oil and gas companies in drilling and in enhanced oil recovery, the team estimated that enhanced geothermal systems could be used to massively develop geothermal energy. This technology involves drilling down to the hot rock layer, fracturing the rock and pumping water into the cracked rock, then extracting the superheated water to drive a steam turbine. The MIT team notes that with this technology the United States has enough geothermal energy to meet its energy needs 2,000 times over.[69]

Though it is still costly, this technology can be used almost anywhere to convert geothermal heat into electricity. Australia is currently the leader in developing pilot plants using this technology, followed by Germany and France. To fully realize this potential for the United States, the MIT team estimated that the government would need to invest $1 billion in geothermal research and development in the years immediately ahead, roughly the cost of one coal-fired power plant.[70]

Even before this exciting new technology is widely deployed, investors are moving ahead with existing technologies. For many years, U.S. geothermal energy was confined largely to the Geysers project north of San Francisco, easily the world's largest geothermal generating complex, with 850 megawatts of generating capacity. Now the United States, which has more than 3,000 megawatts of geothermal generation, is experiencing a geothermal renaissance. Some 126 power plants under development in 12 states are expected to nearly triple U.S. geothermal generating capacity. With California, Nevada, Oregon, Idaho, and Utah leading the way, and with many new companies in the field, the stage is set for massive U.S. geothermal development.[71]

Indonesia, richly endowed with geothermal energy, stole the spotlight in 2008 when it announced a plan to develop 6,900 megawatts of geothermal generating capacity. The Philippines, currently the world's number two generator of electricity from geothermal sources, is planning a number of new projects.[72]

Among the Great Rift countries in Africa—including Tanzania, Kenya, Uganda, Eritrea, Ethiopia, and Djibouti—Kenya is the early leader. It now has over 100 megawatts of geothermal generating capacity and is planning 1,200 more megawatts by 2015. This would double its current electrical generating capacity of 1,200 megawatts from all sources.[73]

Japan, which has 18 geothermal power plants with a total of 535 megawatts of generating capacity, was an early leader in this field. Now, following nearly two decades of inactivity, this geothermally rich country—long known for its thousands of hot baths—is again beginning to build geothermal power plants.[74]

In Europe, Germany has 4 small geothermal power plants in operation and some 180 plants in the pipeline. Werner Bussmann, head of the German Geothermal Association, says, "Geothermal sources could supply Germany's electricity needs 600 times over." Monique Barbut, head of the Global Environment Facility, expects the number of countries tapping geothermal energy for electricity to rise from roughly 20 when the century began to close to 50 by 2010.[75]

Beyond geothermal power plants, geothermal (ground source) heat pumps are now being widely used for both heating and cooling. These take advantage of the remarkable stability of the earth's temperature near the surface and then use that as a source of heat in the winter when the air temperature is low and a source of cooling in the summer when the temperature is high. The great attraction of this technology is that it can provide both heating and cooling and do so with 25–50 percent less electricity than would be needed with conventional systems. In Germany, for example, there are now 130,000 geothermal heat pumps operating in residential or commercial buildings. This base is growing steadily, as at least 25,000 new pumps are installed each year.[76]

In the direct use of geothermal heat, Iceland and France are among the leaders. Iceland's use of geothermal energy to heat almost 90 percent of its homes has largely eliminated coal for this use. Geothermal energy accounts for more than one third of Iceland's total energy use. Following the two oil price hikes in the 1970s, some 70 geothermal heating facilities were constructed in France, providing both heat and hot water for an estimated 200,000 residences. In the United States, individual homes are supplied directly with geothermal heat in Reno, Nevada, and in Klamath Falls, Oregon. Other countries that have extensive geothermally based district-heating systems include China, Japan, and Turkey.[77]

Geothermal heat is ideal for greenhouses in northern countries. Russia, Hungary, Iceland, and the United States are among the many countries that use it to produce fresh vegetables in the winter. With rising oil prices boosting fresh produce transport costs, this practice will likely become far more common in the years ahead.[78]

Among the 16 countries using geothermal energy for aquaculture are China, Israel, and the United States. In California, for example, 15 fish farms annually produce some 10 million pounds of tilapia, striped bass, and catfish using warm water from underground.[79]

The number of countries turning to geothermal energy for both electricity and heat is rising fast. So, too, is the range of uses. Romania, for instance, uses geothermal energy for district heating, for greenhouses, and to supply hot water for homes and factories.[80]

Hot underground water is widely used for both bathing and swimming. Japan has 2,800 spas, 5,500 public bathhouses, and 15,600 hotels and inns that use geothermal hot water. Iceland uses geothermal energy to heat some 100 public swimming pools, most of them year-round open-air pools. Hungary heats 1,200 swimming pools with geothermal energy.[81]

If the four most populous countries located on the Pacific Ring of Fire—the United States, Japan, China, and Indonesia—were to seriously invest in developing their geothermal resources, they could easily make this a leading world energy source. With a conservatively estimated potential in the United States and Japan alone of 240,000 megawatts of generation, it is easy to envisage a world with thousands of geothermal power plants generating some 200,000 megawatts of electricity, the Plan B goal, by 2020.[82]

Plant-Based Sources of Energy

As oil and natural gas reserves are being depleted, the world's attention is also turning to plant-based energy sources. In addition to the energy crops discussed in Chapter 2, these include forest industry byproducts, sugar industry byproducts, urban waste, livestock waste, plantations of fast-growing trees, crop residues, and urban tree and yard wastes—all of which can be used for electrical generation, heating, or the production of automotive fuels.

The potential use of plant-based sources of energy is limited because even corn—the most efficient of the grain crops—can convert just 0.5 percent of solar energy into a usable form. In contrast, solar PV or solar thermal power plants convert roughly 15 percent of sunlight into a usable form, namely electricity. In a land–scarce world, energy crops cannot compete with solar electricity, much less with the far more land-efficient wind power.[83]

In the forest products industry, including both sawmills and paper mills, waste has long been used to generate electricity. U.S. companies burn forest wastes both to produce process heat for their own use and to generate electricity for sale to local utilities. The nearly 11,000 megawatts in U.S. plant-based electrical generation comes primarily from burning forest waste.[84]

Wood waste is also widely used in urban areas for combined heat and power production, with the heat typically used in district heating systems. In Sweden, nearly half of all residential and commercial buildings are served with district heating systems. As recently as 1980, imported oil supplied over 90 percent of the heat for these systems, but by 2007 oil had been largely replaced by wood chips and urban waste.[85]

In the United States, St. Paul, Minnesota—a city of 275,000 people—began to develop district heating more than 20 years ago. It built a combined heat and power plant to use tree waste from the city's parks, industrial wood waste, and wood from other sources. The plant, using 250,000 tons or more of waste wood per year, now supplies district heating to some 80 percent of the downtown area, or more than 1 square mile of residential and commercial floor space. This shift to wood waste largely replaced coal, thus simultaneously cutting carbon emissions by 76,000 tons per year, disposing of waste wood, and providing a sustainable source of heat and electricity.[86]

Oglethorpe Power, a large group of utilities in the state of Georgia, has announced plans to build up to three 100-megawatt biomass-fueled power plants. The principal feedstocks will be wood chips, sawmill wood waste, forest harvest residue, and, when available, pecan hulls and peanut shells.[87]

The sugar industry recently has begun to burn cane waste to cogenerate heat and power. This received a big boost in Brazil, when companies with cane-based ethanol distilleries realized that burning bagasse, the fibrous material left after the sugar syrup is extracted, could simultaneously produce heat for their fermentation process and generate electricity that they could sell to the local utility. This system, now well established, is spreading to sugar mills in other countries that produce the remaining four fifths of the world's sugar harvest.[88]

Within cities, garbage is also burned to produce heat and power after, it is hoped, any recyclable materials have been removed. In Europe, waste-to-energy plants supply 20 million consumers with heat. France, with 128 plants, and Germany, with 67 plants, are the European leaders. In the United States, some 89 waste-to-energy plants convert 20 million tons of waste into power for 6 million consumers. It would, however, be preferable to work toward a zero-garbage economy where the energy invested in the paper, cardboard, plastic, and other combustible materials could largely be recovered by recycling. Burning garbage is not a smart way to deal with the waste problem.[89]

Until we get zero waste, however, the methane (natural gas) produced in existing landfills as organic materials in buried garbage decompose can also be tapped to produce industrial process heat or to generate electricity in combined heat and power plants. The 35-megawatt landfill-gas power plant planned by Puget Sound Energy and slated to draw methane from Seattle's landfill will join more than 100 other such power plants in operation in the United States.[90]

Near Atlanta, Interface—the world's largest manufacturer of industrial carpet—convinced the city to invest $3 million in capturing methane from the municipal landfill and to build a nine-mile pipeline to an Interface factory. The natural gas in this pipeline, priced 30 percent below the world market price, meets 20 percent of the factory's needs. The landfill is projected to supply methane for 40 years, earning the city $35 million on its original $3 million investment while reducing operating costs for Interface.[91]

As discussed in Chapter 2, crops are also used to produce automotive fuels, including both ethanol and biodiesel. In 2009 the world was on track to produce 19 billion gallons of fuel ethanol and nearly 4 billion gallons of biodiesel. Half of the ethanol will come from the United States, a third from Brazil, and the remainder from a dozen or so other countries, led by China and Canada. Germany and France are each responsible for 15 percent of the world's biodiesel output; the other major producers are the United States, Brazil, and Italy.[92]

Once widely heralded as the alternative to oil, crop-based fuels have come under closer scrutiny in recent years, raising serious doubts about their feasibility. In the United States, which surged ahead of Brazil in ethanol production in 2005, the near doubling of output during 2007 and 2008 helped to drive world food prices to all-time highs. In Europe, with its high goals for biodiesel use and low potential for expanding oilseed production, biodiesel refiners are turning to palm oil from Malaysia and Indonesia, driving the clearing of rainforests for palm plantations.[93]

In a world that no longer has excess cropland capacity, every acre planted in corn for ethanol means another acre must be cleared somewhere for crop production. An early 2008 study led by Tim Searchinger of Princeton University that was published in *Science* used a global agricultural model to show that when including the land clearing in the tropics, expanding U.S. biofuel production increased annual greenhouse gas emissions dramatically instead of reducing them, as more narrowly based studies claimed.[94]

Another study published in *Science*, this one by a team from the University of Minnesota, reached a similar conclusion. Focusing on the carbon emissions associated with tropical deforestation, it showed that converting rainforests or grasslands to corn, soybean, or palm oil biofuel production led to a carbon emissions increase—a "biofuel carbon debt"—that was at least 37 times greater than the annual reduction in greenhouse gases resulting from the shift from fossil fuels to biofuels.[95]

The case for crop-based biofuels was further undermined when a team led by Paul Crutzen, a Nobel Prize–winning chemist at the Max Planck Institute for Chemistry in Germany, concluded that emissions of nitrous oxide, a potent greenhouse gas, from the synthetic nitrogen fertilizer used to grow crops such as corn and rapeseed for biofuel production can negate any net reductions of CO_2 emissions from replacing fossil fuels with biofuels, thus making biofuels a threat to climate stability. Although the U.S. ethanol industry rejected these findings, the results were confirmed in a 2009 report from the International Council for Science, a worldwide federation of scientific associations.[96]

The more research is done on liquid biofuels, the less attractive they become. Fuel ethanol production today relies almost entirely on sugar and starch feedstocks, but work is now under way to develop efficient technologies to convert cellulosic materials into ethanol. Several studies indicate that switchgrass and hybrid poplars could produce relatively high ethanol yields on marginal lands, but there is no low-cost technology for converting cellulose into ethanol available today or in immediate prospect.[97]

A third report published in *Science* indicates that burning cellulosic crops directly to generate electricity to power electric cars yields 81 percent more transport miles than converting the crops into liquid fuel. The question is how much could plant materials contribute to the world's energy supply. Based on a study from the U.S. Departments of Energy and Agriculture, we estimate that using forest and urban wood waste, as well as some perennial crops such as switchgrass and fast-growing trees on nonagricultural land, the United States could develop more than 40 gigawatts of electrical generating capacity by 2020, roughly four times the current level. For Plan B, we estimate that the worldwide use of plant materials to generate electricity could contribute 200 gigawatts of capacity by 2020.[98]

Hydropower: Rivers, Tides, and Waves

The term hydropower has traditionally referred to dams that harnessed the energy in river flows, but today it also includes harnessing the energy in tides and waves as well as using smaller "in-stream" turbines to capture the energy in rivers and tides without building dams.[99]

Roughly 16 percent of the world's electricity comes from hydropower, most of it from large dams. Some countries such as Brazil and the Democratic Republic of the Congo get the bulk of their electricity from river power. Large dam building flourished during the third quarter of the last century, but then slowed as the remaining good sites for dam building dwindled and as the costs of displacing people, ecological damage, and land inundation became more visible.[100]

Small-scale projects, which are not nearly as disruptive, are still in favor. In 2006, small dams with a combined 6,000 megawatts of generating capacity were built in rural areas of China. For many rural communities these are currently the only source of electricity. Though China leads in new construction, many other countries are also building small-scale structures, as the economics of generation increasingly favor renewable sources over fossil fuels. And there is growing interest in in-stream turbines that do not need a dam and are less environ-mentally intrusive.[101]

Tidal power (actually, lunar power) holds a certain fascina-tion because of its sheer potential scale. Canada's Bay of Fundy, for example, has a potential generating capacity of more than 4,000 megawatts. Other countries are looking at possible proj-ects in the 7,000- to 15,000-megawatt range.[102]

The first large tidal generating facility—La Rance barrage, with a maximum generating capacity of 240 megawatts—was built 40 years ago in France and is still operating today. Within the last few years interest in tidal power has spread rapidly. South Korea, for example, is building a 254-megawatt project on its west coast. Scheduled for completion in 2009, this facility will provide enough electricity for the half-million people living in the nearby city of Ansan. At another site 30 miles to the north, engineers are planning an 812-megawatt tidal facility near Incheon. In March 2008, Lunar Energy of the United King-dom reached agreement with Korea Midland Power to develop a turbine field off the coast of South Korea that would generate 300 megawatts of power. China is planning a 300-megawatt tidal facility at the mouth of the Yalu River near North Korea. Far to the south, New Zealand is planning a 200-megawatt proj-ect in the Kaipara Harbour on the country's northwest coast.[103]

Giant projects are under consideration in several countries, including India, Russia, and the United Kingdom. India is plan-ning to build a 39-mile barrage across the Gulf of Khambhat on the country's northwest coast with a 7,000-megawatt generating capacity. In the United Kingdom, several political leaders are pushing for an 8,600-megawatt tidal facility in the Severn Estu-ary on the country's southwest coast. This is equal to 11 percent of U.K. electrical generating capacity. Russian planners are talk-ing in terms of a 15,000-megawatt tidal barrage in the White Sea in northwestern Russia, near Finland. Part of this power would likely be exported to Europe. A facility under discussion for Tugurski Bay on the country's Far Eastern coast would provide 8,000 megawatts to power local industry.[104]

In the United States, the focus is on smaller tidal facilities. Since 2007 the Federal Energy Regulatory Commission has issued more than 30 preliminary permits, including those for projects in Puget Sound, San Francisco Bay, and New York's East River. The San Francisco Bay project by Oceana Energy Company will have at least 20 megawatts of generating capacity.[105]

Wave power, though it is a few years behind tidal power, is now attracting the attention of both engineers and investors. In the United States, the northern Californian utility PG&E has filed a plan to develop a 40-megawatt wave farm off the state's north coast. GreenWave Energy Solutions has been issued preliminary permits for two projects of up to 100 megawatts each off California's coast, one in the north and one in the south. And San Francisco is seeking a permit to develop a 10–30 megawatt wave power project off its coast.[106]

The world's first wave farm, a 2-megawatt facility built by Pelamis Wave Power of the United Kingdom, is operating off the coast of Portugal. The project's second phase would expand this to 22 megawatts. Scottish firms Aquamarine Power and Airtricity are teaming up to build 1,000 megawatts of wave and tidal power off the coast of Ireland and the United Kingdom. Ireland as a whole has the most ambitious wave power development goal, planning 500 megawatts of wave generating capacity by 2020, enough to supply 7 percent of its electricity. Worldwide, the harnessing of wave power could generate a staggering 10,000 gigawatts of electricity, more than double current world electricity generation of 4,000 gigawatts from all sources.[107]

We project that the 945 gigawatts (945,000 megawatts) of hydroelectric power in operation worldwide in 2008 will expand to 1,350 gigawatts by 2020. According to China's official projections, 270 gigawatts will be added there, mostly from large dams in the country's southwest. The remaining 135 gigawatts in our projected growth of hydropower would come from a scattering of large dams still being built in countries like Brazil and Turkey, a large number of small hydro facilities, a fast-growing number of tidal projects, and numerous smaller wave power projects.[108]

Within the United States, where there is little interest in new dams, there is a resurgence of interest in installing generating facilities in non-powered dams and in expanding existing hydro facilities. If the worldwide interest in tidal and wave energy continues to escalate, the additional capacity from hydro, tidal, and wave power by 2020 could easily exceed the 400 gigawatts needed to reach the Plan B goal.[109]

The World Energy Economy of 2020

As this chapter has described, the transition from coal, oil, and gas to wind, solar, and geothermal energy is well under way. In the old economy, energy was produced by burning something— oil, coal, or natural gas—leading to the carbon emissions that have come to define our economy. The new energy economy harnesses the energy in wind, the energy coming from the sun, and heat from within the earth itself. It will be largely electrically driven. In addition to its use for lighting and for household appliances, electricity will be widely used in the new economy both in transport and to heat and cool buildings. Climate-disrupting fossil fuels will fade into the past as countries turn to clean, climate-stabilizing, nondepletable sources of energy.

Backing away from fossil fuels begins with the electricity sector, where the development of 5,300 gigawatts of new renewable generating capacity worldwide by 2020—over half of it from wind—would be more than enough to replace all the coal and oil and 70 percent of the natural gas now used to generate electricity. The addition of close to 1,500 gigawatts of thermal heating capacity by 2020, roughly two thirds of it from rooftop solar water and space heaters, will sharply reduce the use of both oil and gas for heating buildings and water. (See Table 5–1.)[110]

In looking at the broad shifts from 2008 to the Plan B energy economy of 2020, fossil-fuel-generated electricity drops by 90 percent worldwide. This is more than offset by the fivefold growth in renewably generated electricity. In the transportation sector, energy use from fossil fuels drops by some 70 percent. This comes first from shifting to all-electric and highly efficient plug-in hybrids cars that will run almost entirely on electricity, nearly all of it from renewable sources. And it also comes from shifting to electric trains, which are much more efficient than diesel-powered ones. Many buildings will be all-electric—heated, cooled, and illuminated entirely with carbon-free renewable electricity.

At the country and regional level, each energy profile will be shaped by the locally unique endowment of renewable sources of energy. Some countries, such as the United States, Turkey,

Table 5–1. *World Renewable Energy Capacity in 2008
and Plan B Goals for 2020*

Source	2008	Goal for 2020
Electricity Generating Capacity	(electrical gigawatts)	
Wind	121	3,000
Rooftop solar electric systems	13	1,400
Solar electric power plants	2	100
Solar thermal power plants	0	200
Geothermal	10	200
Biomass	52	200
Hydropower	945	1,350
Total	1,143	6,450
Thermal Energy Capacity	(thermal gigawatts)	
Solar rooftop water and space heaters	120	1,100
Geothermal	100	500
Biomass	250	350
Total	470	1,950

Source: See endnote 110.

and China, will likely rely on the broad base of renewables—wind, solar, and geothermal power—for their energy. But wind, including both onshore and offshore, is likely to emerge as the leading energy source in each of these countries.

In June 2009, Xiao Ziniu, director of China's National Climate Center, said that China had up to 1,200 gigawatts of wind generating potential. This compares with the country's current total electricity generating capacity of 790 gigawatts. Xiao said the new assessment he was citing "assures us that the country's entire electricity demand can be met by wind power alone." In addition, the study identified 250 gigawatts of offshore wind power potential. A senior Chinese official had earlier announced that wind generating capacity would reach 100 megawatts by 2020, which means it would overtake nuclear power well before then.[111]

Other countries, including Spain, Algeria, Egypt, India, and Mexico, will turn primarily to solar thermal power plants and solar PV arrays to power their economies. For Iceland, Indonesia, Japan, and the Philippines, geothermal energy will likely be their mother lode. Still others will likely rely heavily on hydro, including Norway, the Democratic Republic of the Congo, and Nepal. Some technologies, such as rooftop solar water heaters, will be used virtually everywhere.

With the Plan B energy economy of 2020, the United States will get 44 percent of its electricity from wind farms. Geothermal power plants will supply another 11 percent. Photovoltaic cells, most of them on rooftops, will supply 8 percent of electricity, with solar thermal power plants providing 5 percent. Roughly 7 percent will come from hydropower. The remaining 25 percent comes from nuclear power, biomass, and natural gas, in that order. (See capacity figures in Table 5–2.)[112]

As the energy transition progresses, the system for transporting energy from source to consumers will change beyond recognition. In the old energy economy, pipelines carried oil from fields to consumers or to ports, where it was loaded on tankers. A huge fleet of tankers moved oil from the Persian Gulf to markets on every continent.

Texas offers a model of how to build a grid to harness renewable energy. After a survey showed that the state had two strong concentrations of wind energy, one in West Texas and the other in the Panhandle, the Public Utility Commission coordinated the design of a network of high-voltage transmission lines to link these regions with consumption centers such as Dallas/Ft. Worth and San Antonio. With a $5-billion investment and up to 2,900 miles of transmission lines, the stage has been set to harness 18,500 megawatts of wind generating capacity from these two regions alone, enough to supply half of the state's 24 million residents.[113]

Already, major utilities and private investors are proposing to build highly efficient high-voltage direct-current (HVDC) lines to link wind-rich regions with consumption centers. For example, TransCanada is proposing to develop two high-voltage lines: the Zephyr Line, which will link wind-rich Wyoming with the California market, and the Chinook Line, which will do the same for wind-rich Montana. These lines of roughly

Table 5–2. *U.S. Electricity Generating Capacity in 2008 and Plan B Goals for 2020*

Source	2008	Goal for 2020
	(electrical gigawatts)	
Fossil Fuels and Nuclear		
Coal	337	0
Oil	62	0
Natural Gas	459	140
Nuclear	106	106
Total	965	246
Renewables		
Wind	25	710
Rooftop solar electric systems	1	190
Solar electric power plants	0	30
Solar thermal power plants	0	120
Geothermal	3	70
Biomass	11	40
Hydropower	78	100
Total	119	1,260

Note: Columns may not add to totals due to rounding.
Source: See endnote 112.

1,000 miles each are both designed to accommodate 3,000 megawatts of wind-generated electricity.[114]

In the Northern Plains and the Midwest, ITC Holdings Corporation is proposing what it calls the Green Power Express. This investment in 3,000 miles of high-voltage transmission lines is intended to link 12,000 megawatts of wind capacity from North Dakota, South Dakota, Iowa, and Minnesota with the more densely populated industrial Midwest. These initial heavy-duty transmission lines can eventually become part of the national grid that U.S. Energy Secretary Steven Chu wants to build.[115]

A strong, efficient national grid will reduce generating capacity needs, lower consumer costs, and cut carbon emissions. Since no two wind farms have identical wind profiles, each one added to the grid makes wind a more stable source of electricity. With thousands of wind farms spread from coast to coast, wind becomes a stable source of energy, part of baseload power. This, coupled with the capacity to forecast wind speeds and solar intensity throughout the country at least a day in advance, makes it possible to manage the diversity of renewable energy resources efficiently.[116]

For India, a national grid would enable it to harness the vast solar resources of the Great Indian Desert. Europe, too, is beginning to think seriously of investing in a continental super-grid. Stretching from Norway to Egypt and from Morocco to western Siberia, it would enable the region to harness vast amounts of wind energy, particularly in offshore Western Europe, and the almost unlimited solar energy in the northern Sahara and on Europe's southern coast. Like the proposed U.S. national grid, the Europe-wide grid would use high-voltage direct-current lines that transmit electricity far more efficiently than existing lines do.[117]

An Irish firm, Mainstream Renewable Power, is proposing to use HVDC undersea cables to build the European supergrid off-shore. The grid would stretch from the Baltic Sea to the North Sea then south through the English Channel to southern Europe. The company notes that this could avoid the time-consuming acquisition of land to build a continental land-based system. The Swedish firm ABB Group, which has just completed a 400-mile HVDC undersea cable linking Norway and the Netherlands, is partnering with Mainstream Renewable Power in proposing to build the first stages of the supergrid.[118]

A long-standing proposal by the Club of Rome, called DESERTEC, goes further, with plans to connect Europe to the abundant solar energy of North Africa and the Middle East. In July 2009, 11 leading European firms—including Munich Re, Deutsche Bank, ABB, and Siemens—and an Algerian company, Cevital, announced a plan to create the DESERTEC Industrial Initiative. This firm's goal will be to craft a concrete plan and funding proposal to develop enough solar thermal generating capacity in North Africa and the Middle East to export electricity to Europe and to meet the needs of producer countries. This energy proposal, which could exceed 300,000 megawatts of solar thermal generating capacity, is huge by any standard. It is being driven by concerns about disruptive climate change and by the depletion of oil and gas reserves. Caio Koch-Weser, Deutsche Bank vice chairman, said, "The Initiative shows in what dimensions and on what scale we must think if we are to master the challenges from climate change."[119]

The twentieth century witnessed the globalization of the world energy economy as the entire world came to depend heavily on a handful of countries for oil, many of them in one region of the world. This century will witness the localization of the world energy economy as countries begin to tap their indigenous resources of renewable energy.

The localization of the energy economy will lead to the localization of the food economy. For example, as the cost of shipping fresh produce from distant markets rises with the price of oil, there will be more local farmers' markets. Diets will be more locally based and seasonally sensitive than they are today. The combination of moving down the food chain and reducing the food miles in our diets will dramatically reduce energy use in the food economy.

As agriculture localizes, livestock production will likely start to shift from mega-sized cattle, hog, and poultry feeding operations. There will be fewer specialized farms and more mixed crop-livestock operations. Feeding operations will become smaller as the pressure to recycle nutrients mounts with the depletion of the world's finite phosphate reserves and as fertilizer prices rise. The recent growth in the number of small farms in the United States will likely continue. As world food insecurity mounts, more and more people will be looking to produce some of their own food in backyards, in front yards, on rooftops, in community gardens, and elsewhere, further contributing to the localization of agriculture.

The new energy economy will be highly visible from the air. A few years ago on a flight from Helsinki to London I counted 22 wind farms when crossing Denmark, long a wind power leader. Is this a glimpse of the future, I wondered? One day U.S. air travelers will see thousands of wind farms in the Great Plains, stretching from the Gulf Coast of Texas to the Canadian border, where ranchers and farmers will be double cropping wind with cattle, corn, and wheat.

The deserts of the U.S. Southwest will feature clusters of solar thermal power plants, with vast arrays of mirrors, covering several square miles each. Wind farms and solar thermal power plants will be among the more visible features of the new energy economy. The roofs of millions of homes and commercial buildings will sport solar cell arrays as rooftops become a source of electricity. How much more local can you get? There will also be millions of rooftops with solar water and space heaters.

Governments are using a variety of policy instruments to help drive this energy restructuring. These include tax restructuring—raising the tax on carbon emissions and lowering the tax on income—and carbon cap-and-trade systems. The former approach is more transparent and easily administered and not so readily manipulated as the latter.[120]

For restructuring the electricity sector, feed-in tariffs, in which utilities are required to pay more for electricity generated from renewable sources, have been remarkably successful. Germany's impressive early success with this measure has led to its adoption by more than 40 other countries, including most of those in the European Union. In the United States, at least 33 states have adopted renewable portfolio standards requiring utilities to get a certain share of their electricity from renewable sources. The United States has also used tax credits for wind, geothermal, solar photovoltaics, solar water and space heating, and geothermal heat pumps.[121]

To achieve some goals, governments are simply using mandates, such as those requiring rooftop solar water heaters on all new buildings, higher efficiency standards for cars and appliances, or a ban on the sale of incandescent light bulbs. Each government has to select the policy instruments that work best in its particular economic and cultural settings.

In the new energy economy, our cities will be unlike any we have known during our lifetime. The air will be clean and the streets will be quiet, with only the scarcely audible hum of electric motors. Air pollution alerts will be a thing of the past as coal-fired power plants are dismantled and recycled and as gasoline- and-diesel-burning engines largely disappear.

This transition is now building its own momentum, driven by an intense excitement from the realization that we are tapping energy sources that can last as long as the earth itself. Oil wells go dry and coal seams run out, but for the first time since the Industrial Revolution began we are investing in energy sources that can last forever.

6

Designing Cities for People

As I was being driven through Tel Aviv from my hotel to a conference center in 1998, I could not help but note the overwhelming presence of cars and parking lots. It was obvious that Tel Aviv, expanding from a small settlement a half-century ago to a city of some 3 million today, had evolved during the automobile era. It occurred to me that the ratio of parks to parking lots may be the best single indicator of the livability of a city—an indication of whether the city is designed for people or for cars.[1]

Tel Aviv is not the world's only fast-growing city. Urbanization is the second dominant demographic trend of our time, after population growth itself. In 1900, some 150 million people lived in cities. By 2000, it was 2.8 billion people, a 19-fold increase. As of 2008, more than half of us live in cities—making humans, for the first time, an urban species.[2]

In 1900 only a handful of cities had a million people. Today 431 cities have at least that many inhabitants. And there are 19 megacities with 10 million or more residents. Greater Tokyo, with 36 million residents, has more people than all of Canada. The New York metropolitan area's population of 19 million is nearly equal to that of Australia. Mexico City, Mumbai (formerly Bombay), São Paulo, Delhi, Shanghai, Kolkata (Calcutta), and Dhaka follow close behind.[3]

The world's cities are facing unprecedented challenges. In Mexico City, Tehran, Kolkata, Bangkok, Beijing, and hundreds of other cities, the air is no longer safe to breathe. In some cities the air is so polluted that breathing is equivalent to smoking two packs of cigarettes a day. Respiratory illnesses are rampant. In many places, the number of hours commuters spend sitting in traffic-congested streets and highways climbs higher each year, raising frustration levels.[4]

In response to these conditions, we are seeing the emergence of a new urbanism, a planning philosophy that environmentalist Francesca Lyman says "seeks to revive the traditional city planning of an era when cities were designed around human beings instead of automobiles." One of the most remarkable modern urban transformations has occurred in Bogotá, Colombia, where Enrique Peñalosa served as mayor for three years. When he took office in 1998 he did not ask how life could be improved for the 30 percent who owned cars; he wanted to know what could be done for the 70 percent—the majority—who did not own cars.[5]

Peñalosa realized that a city with a pleasant environment for children and the elderly would work for everyone. In just a few years, he transformed the quality of urban life with his vision of a city designed for people. Under his leadership, the city banned the parking of cars on sidewalks, created or renovated 1,200 parks, introduced a highly successful bus-based rapid transit (BRT) system, built hundreds of kilometers of bicycle paths and pedestrian streets, reduced rush hour traffic by 40 percent, planted 100,000 trees, and involved local citizens directly in the improvement of their neighborhoods. In doing this, he created a sense of civic pride among the city's 8 million residents, making the streets of Bogotá in this strife-torn country safer than those in Washington, D.C.[6]

Peñalosa observes that "high quality public pedestrian space in general and parks in particular are evidence of a true democracy at work." He further observes: "Parks and public space are also important to a democratic society because they are the only places where people meet as equals.... In a city, parks are as essential to the physical and emotional health of a city as the water supply." He notes this is not obvious from most city budgets, where parks are deemed a luxury. By contrast, "roads, the public space for cars, receive infinitely more resources and less budget cuts than parks, the public space for children. Why," he asks, "are the public spaces for cars deemed more important than the public spaces for children?"[7]

In espousing this new urban philosophy, Peñalosa is not alone. Some cities in industrial and developing countries alike are dramatically increasing urban mobility by moving away from the car. Jaime Lerner, when he was mayor of Curitiba, Brazil, pioneered the design and adoption of an alternative transportation system that is inexpensive and commuter-friendly. Since 1974 Curitiba's transportation system has been totally restructured. Although 60 percent of the people own cars, busing, biking, and walking totally dominate, accounting for 80 percent of all trips in the city.[8]

Now planners everywhere are experimenting, seeking ways to design cities for people, not cars. Cars promise mobility, and in a largely rural setting they provide it. But in an urbanizing world there is an inherent conflict between the automobile and the city. After a point, as their numbers multiply, automobiles provide not mobility but immobility.[9]

The Ecology of Cities

The evolution of modern cities was tied to advances in transport, initially for ships and trains. But it was the internal combustion engine combined with cheap oil that provided mobility for people and freight that fueled the phenomenal urban growth of the twentieth century.

Cities require a concentration of food, water, energy, and materials that nature cannot provide. Collecting these masses of materials and later dispersing them in the form of garbage, sewage, and pollutants in air and water is challenging city managers everywhere.

Early cities relied on food and water from the surrounding countryside, but today cities often depend on distant sources for basic amenities. Los Angeles, for example, draws much of its water from the Colorado River, some 600 miles away. Mexico City's burgeoning population, living at an altitude of over 9,000 feet, depends on the costly pumping of water from 100 miles away that must be lifted over 3,000 feet to augment inadequate water supplies. Beijing is planning to draw water from the Yangtze River basin some 800 miles away.[10]

Food comes from even greater distances, as illustrated by Tokyo. While the city still gets its rice from the highly productive farmers in Japan, with their land carefully protected by government policy, its wheat comes largely from the Great Plains of North America and from Australia. Its corn supply comes largely from the U.S. Midwest. Soybeans come from the U.S. Midwest and the Brazilian *cerrado*.[11]

The oil used to move resources into and out of cities often comes from distant oil fields. Rising oil prices will affect cities, but they will affect even more the suburbs that surround them. The growing scarcity of water and the high energy cost of transporting it over long distances may begin to constrain the growth of some cities.

Against this backdrop, Richard Register, author of *Ecocities: Rebuilding Cities in Balance with Nature*, says it is time to fundamentally rethink the design of cities. He agrees with Peñalosa that cities should be designed for people, not for cars. He goes even further, talking about pedestrian cities—communities designed so that people do not need cars because they can walk or take public transportation wherever they need to go. Register says that a city should be seen as a functioning system not in terms of its parts but in terms of its whole. He also makes a convincing case that cities should be integrated into local ecosystems rather than imposed on them.[12]

He describes with pride an after-the-fact integration into the local ecosystem of San Luis Obispo, a California town of 43,000 residents north of Los Angeles: "[It] has a beautiful creek restoration project with several streets and through-building passageways lined with shops that connect to the town's main commercial street, and people love it. Before closing a street, turning a small parking lot into a park, restoring the creek and making the main street easily accessible to the 'nature' corridor, that is, the creek, the downtown had a 40 percent vacancy rate in the storefronts, and now it has zero. Of course it's popular. You sit at your restaurant by the creek...where fresh breezes rustle the trees in a world undisturbed by car noise and blasting exhaust."[13]

For Register, the design of the city and its buildings become a part of the local landscape, capitalizing on the local ecology. For example, buildings can be designed to be heated and cooled partly by nature. As oil prices rise, urban fruit and vegetable production will expand into vacant lots and onto rooftops. Cities can largely live on recycled water that is cleaned and used again and again. The "flush and forget" water system will become too costly for many water-short cities after oil production peaks.[14]

Redesigning Urban Transport

Urban transport systems based on a combination of rail lines, bus lines, bicycle pathways, and pedestrian walkways offer the best of all possible worlds in providing mobility, low-cost transportation, and a healthy urban environment.

A rail system provides the foundation for a city's transportation. Rails are geographically fixed, providing a permanent means of transport that people can count on. Once in place, the nodes on such a system become the obvious places to concentrate office buildings, high-rise apartment buildings, and shops.

Whether the best fit is underground rail, light-rail surface systems, or both depends in part on city size and geography. Berlin, for example, has both. Megacities regularly turn to underground rail systems to provide mobility. For cities of intermediate size, light rail is often an attractive option.[15]

As noted earlier, some of the most innovative public transportation systems, those that shift huge numbers of people from cars into buses, have been developed in Curitiba and Bogotá. The success of Bogotá's BRT system, TransMilenio, which uses special express lanes to move people quickly through the city, is being replicated not only in six other Colombian cities but in scores elsewhere too, including Mexico City, São Paulo, Hanoi, Seoul, Istanbul, and Quito. In China, Beijing is one of eight cities with BRT systems in operation.[16]

In Mexico City, the latest extension of the Insurgentes Avenue BRT corridor from 13 miles to 19 miles and the addition of 26 new articulated buses enables this line to carry 260,000 passengers daily. By 2012, the city plans to have 10 BRT lines in operation. And in southern China, by the end of 2009 Guangzhou will put into operation its BRT, which is designed to carry more than 600,000 passengers each day. In addition to linking with the city's underground Metro in three places, it will be paralleled throughout its entirety with a bike lane. Guangzhou will also have 5,500 bike parking spaces for those using a bike-BRT travel combination.[17]

In Iran, Tehran launched its first BRT line in early 2008. Several more lines are in the development stage, and all will be integrated with the city's new subway lines. Several cities in Africa are also planning BRT systems. Even industrial-country cities such as Ottawa, Toronto, New York, Minneapolis, Chicago, Las Vegas, and—much to everyone's delight—Los Angeles have launched or are now considering BRT systems.[18]

Some cities are reducing traffic congestion and air pollution by charging cars to enter the city. Singapore, long a leader in urban transport innovation, was one of the first to tax vehicles entering the city center. Electronic sensors identify each car and then debit the owner's credit card. This system has reduced the number of automobiles in Singapore, providing its residents with both more mobility and cleaner air.[19]

Singapore has been joined by three Norwegian cities—Oslo, Bergen, and Trondheim—as well as London and Stockholm. In London—where until recently the average speed of an automobile was comparable to that of a horse-drawn carriage a century ago—a congestion fee was adopted in early 2003. The initial £5 (about $8 at the time) charge on all motorists driving into the center city between 7 a.m. and 6:30 p.m. immediately reduced the number of vehicles, permitting traffic to flow more freely while cutting pollution and noise.[20]

In the first year after the new tax was introduced, the number of people using buses to travel into central London climbed by 38 percent and vehicle speeds on key thoroughfares increased by 21 percent. In July 2005, the congestion fee was raised to £8. Then in February 2007, the charging zone was extended westward. With the revenue from the congestion fee being used to upgrade and expand public transit, Londoners are steadily shifting from cars to buses, the subway, and bicycles. Since the congestion charge was adopted, the daily flow of cars and minicabs into central London during peak hours has dropped by 36 percent while the number of bicycles has increased by 66 percent.[21]

In January 2008, Milan adopted a "pollution charge" of $14 on vehicles entering its historic center in daytime hours during the week. Other cities now considering similar measures include San Francisco, Turin, Genoa, Kiev, Dublin, and Auckland.[22]

Paris Mayor Bertrand Delanoë, who was elected in 2001, inherited some of Europe's worst traffic congestion and air pollution. He decided traffic would have to be cut 40 percent by 2020. The first step was to invest in better transit in outlying regions to ensure that everyone in the greater Paris area had access to high-quality public transit. The next step was to create express lanes on main thoroughfares for buses and bicycles, thus reducing the number of lanes for cars. As the speed of buses increased, more people used them.[23]

A third innovative initiative in Paris was the establishment of a city bicycle rental program that has 20,600 bikes available at 1,450 docking stations throughout the city. Access to the bikes is by credit card, with a choice of daily, weekly, or annual rates ranging from just over $1 per day to $40 per year. If the bike is used for fewer than 30 minutes, the ride is free. Based on the first two years, the bicycles are proving to be immensely popular—with 48 million trips taken. Patrick Allin, a Parisian and an enthusiastic user of the bikes, says they are great for conversation: "We are no longer all alone in our cars—we are sharing. It's really changed the atmosphere here; people chat at the stations and even at traffic lights."[24]

In writing about the program in the *New York Times*, Serge Schmemann draws a "lesson for all big cities: this is an idea whose time has come." At this point Mayor Delanoë is working hard to realize his goal of cutting car traffic by 40 percent and carbon emissions by a similar amount by 2020. The popularity of this bike sharing program has led to its extension into 30 of the city's suburbs and has inspired cities such as London to also introduce bike sharing.[25]

The United States, which has lagged far behind Europe in developing diversified urban transport systems, is being swept by a "complete streets" movement, an effort to ensure that streets are friendly to pedestrians and bicycles as well as to cars. Many American communities lack sidewalks and bike lanes, making it difficult for pedestrians and cyclists to get around safely, particularly where streets are heavily traveled. In Charlotte, North Carolina, transportation planning manager Norm Steinman says: "We didn't build sidewalks here for 50 years. Streets designed by traffic engineers in the '60s, '70s, '80s, and '90s were mostly for autos."[26]

This cars-only model is being challenged by the National Complete Streets Coalition, a powerful assemblage of citizen groups, including the Natural Resources Defense Council, AARP (an organization of 40 million older Americans), and numerous local and national cycling organizations. The complete streets movement is the product of a "perfect storm of issues coming together," says Randy Neufeld, Chief Strategy Officer for the Active Transportation Alliance. Among these issues are the obesity epidemic, rising gasoline prices, the urgent need to cut carbon emissions, air pollution, and mobility constraints on aging baby boomers. The elderly who live in urban areas without sidewalks and who no longer drive are effectively imprisoned in their own homes.[27]

The National Complete Streets Coalition, headed by Barbara McCann, reports that as of July 2009, complete streets policies are in place in 18 states, including California and Illinois, and in 46 cities. One reason states have become interested in passing such legislation is that integrating bike paths and sidewalks into a project from the beginning is much less costly than adding them later. As McCann notes, it is "cheaper to do it right the first time." A national complete streets bill was introduced in both houses of Congress in early 2009.[28]

Closely related to this approach is a movement that encourages and facilitates walking to school. Beginning in the United Kingdom in 1994, it has now spread to some 40 countries, including the United States. Forty years ago, more than 40 percent of all U.S. children walked or biked to school, but now the figure is under 15 percent. Today 60 percent are driven or drive to school. Not only does this contribute to childhood obesity, but the American Academy of Pediatrics reports fatalities and injuries are much higher among children going to school in cars than among those who walk or ride in school buses. Among the potential benefits of the Walk to School movement is a reduction in obesity and early onset diabetes.[29]

Countries with well-developed urban transit systems and a mature bicycle infrastructure are much better positioned to withstand the stresses of a downturn in world oil production than those that depend heavily on cars. With a full array of walking and biking options, the number of trips by car can easily be cut by 10–20 percent.[30]

The Return of Bicycles

The bicycle has many attractions as a form of personal transportation. It alleviates congestion, lowers air pollution, reduces obesity, increases physical fitness, does not emit climate-disrupting carbon dioxide, and is priced within the reach of billions of people who cannot afford a car. Bicycles increase mobility while reducing congestion and the area of land paved over. Six bicycles can typically fit into the road space used by one car. For parking, the advantage is even greater, with 20 bicycles occupying the space required to park a car.[31]

World bicycle production, averaging 94 million per year from 1990 to 2002, climbed to 130 million in 2007, far outstripping automobile production of 70 million. Bicycle sales in some markets are surging as governments devise a myriad of incentives to encourage bicycle use in order to reduce air pollution and traffic congestion. For example, in 2009 the Italian government began a hefty incentive program to encourage the purchase of bicycles or electric bikes in order to improve urban air quality and reduce the number of cars on the road. The direct payments will cover up to 30 percent of the cost of the bicycle.[32]

China, with 430 million bikes, has the largest fleet, but ownership rates are higher in Europe. The Netherlands has more than one bike per person, while Denmark and Germany have just under one bike per person.[33]

The bicycle is not only a flexible means of transportation; it is an ideal way of restoring a balance between caloric intake and expenditure. Regular exercise of the sort provided by cycling to work reduces cardiovascular disease, osteoporosis, and arthritis, and it strengthens the immune system.

Few methods of reducing carbon emissions are as effective as substituting a bicycle for a car on short trips. A bicycle is a marvel of engineering efficiency, one where an investment in 22 pounds of metal and rubber boosts the efficiency of individual mobility by a factor of three. On my bike I estimate that I get easily 7 miles per potato. An automobile, which requires at least a ton of material to transport one person, is extraordinarily inefficient by comparison.

The capacity of the bicycle to provide mobility for low-income populations was dramatically demonstrated in China. In 1976, this country produced 6 million bicycles. After the reforms in 1978 that led to an open market economy and rapidly rising incomes, bicycle production started climbing, reaching nearly 90 million in 2007. The surge to 430 million bicycle owners in China since 1978 has provided the greatest increase in mobility in history. Bicycles took over rural roads and city streets. Although China's 14 million passenger cars and the urban congestion they cause get a lot of attention, it is bicycles that provide personal mobility for hundreds of millions of Chinese.[34]

In the United States, nearly 75 percent of police departments serving populations of 50,000 or more now have routine patrols by bicycle. Officers on bikes are more productive in cities partly because they are more mobile and can reach the scene of an accident or crime more quickly and more quietly than officers in cars. They typically make 50 percent more arrests per day than officers in squad cars. Fiscally, the cost of operating a bicycle is trivial compared with that of a police car.[35]

Colleges and universities are also turning to bicycles. As campuses are overwhelmed by cars, traffic congestion, and the need to build more residential facilities, they are being forced to take innovative measures to discourage cars. Chicago's St. Xavier University launched a bike-sharing program in the fall of 2008. This program is patterned after the one in Paris, except that students use their ID cards instead of credit cards. Emory University in Atlanta, Georgia, has introduced a free bike-sharing system, also based on ID cards. Jamie Smith, who manages the program, says, "We like the idea of bolstering the cycling culture here."[36]

Ripon College in Wisconsin and the University of New England in Maine have gone even further. They find it cheaper to give each incoming freshman a bike if they agree to leave their cars at home. Replacing cars with bikes on campus is not only reducing air pollution and traffic congestion, it is also creating a sense of community.[37]

Bicycle messenger services are common in the world's larger cities simply because they deliver small parcels more quickly than cars can and at a lower cost. As e-commerce expands, the need for quick, reliable, urban delivery services is escalating. For companies that market over the Internet, quick delivery wins more customers.[38]

The key to realizing the potential of the bicycle is to create a bicycle-friendly transport system. This means providing both bicycle trails and designated street lanes for bicycles. Among the industrial-country leaders in designing bicycle-friendly transport systems are the Netherlands, where 27 percent of all trips are by bike, Denmark with 18 percent, and Germany, 10 percent. By contrast, the United States and the United Kingdom are each at 1 percent.[39]

An excellent study by John Pucher and Ralph Buehler at Rutgers University analyzed the reasons for these wide disparities among countries. They note that "extensive cycling rights-of-way in the Netherlands, Denmark, and Germany are complemented by ample bike parking, full integration with public transport, comprehensive traffic education and training of both cyclists and motorists." These countries, they point out, "make driving expensive as well as inconvenient in central cities through a host of taxes and restrictions on car ownership, use and parking.... It is the coordinated implementation of this multi-faceted, mutually reinforcing set of policies that best explains the success of these three countries in promoting cycling." And it is the lack of these policies, they note, that explains "the marginal status of cycling in the UK and USA."[40]

Fortunately, many Americans are working to change this. Prominent among them is Congressman Earl Blumenauer of Oregon. An avid cyclist, he is the founder and coordinator of the 180-member Congressional Bicycle Caucus.[41]

The Netherlands, the unquestioned leader among industrial countries in encouraging bicycle use, has incorporated a vision of the role of bicycles into a Bicycle Master Plan. In addition to creating bike lanes and trails in all its cities, the system also often gives cyclists the advantage over motorists in right-of-way and at traffic lights. Some traffic signals permit cyclists to move out before cars. By 2007, Amsterdam had become the first western industrial city where the number of trips taken by bicycle exceeded those taken by car.[42]

Within the Netherlands, a nongovernmental group called

Interface for Cycling Expertise (I-ce) has been formed to share the Dutch experience in designing a modern transport system that prominently features bicycles. It is working with groups in Botswana, Brazil, Chile, Colombia, Ecuador, Ghana, India, Kenya, Peru, South Africa, and Uganda to facilitate bicycle use. Roelof Wittink, head of I-ce, observes: "If you plan only for cars then drivers will feel like the King of the Road. This reinforces the attitude that the bicycle is backward and used only by the poor. But if you plan for bicycles it changes the public attitude."[43]

Both the Netherlands and Japan have made a concerted effort to integrate bicycles and rail commuter services by providing bicycle parking at rail stations, making it easier for cyclists to commute by train. In Japan, the use of bicycles for commuting to rail transportation has reached the point where some stations have invested in vertical, multi-level parking garages for bicycles, much as is often done for automobiles.[44]

Sales of electric bicycles, a relatively new genre of transport vehicles, have taken off. They are similar to plug-in hybrid cars in that they are powered by two sources—in this case muscle and battery power—and can be plugged into the grid for recharging as needed. Sales in China, where this technology came into its own, climbed from 40,000 e-bikes in 1998 to 21 million in 2008. China now has close to 100 million electric bicycles on the road, compared with 14 million cars. These e-bikes are now attracting attention in other Asian countries similarly plagued with air pollution and in the United States and Europe, where combined sales now exceed 300,000 per year.[45]

In contrast to plug-in hybrid cars, electric bikes do not directly use any fossil fuel. If we can make the transition from coal-fired power plants to wind, solar, and geothermal power, then electrically powered bicycles can also be fossil-fuel-free.

The integration of walkways and bikeways into urban transport systems makes a city eminently more livable than one that relies almost exclusively on private automobiles. Noise, pollution, congestion, and frustration are all lessened. And we and the earth are both healthier.

Reducing Urban Water Use

The one-time use of water to disperse human and industrial wastes is an outmoded practice, made obsolete by new technologies and water shortages. Water enters a city, becomes contaminated with human and industrial wastes, and leaves the city dangerously polluted. Toxic industrial wastes discharged into rivers and lakes or into wells also permeate aquifers, making water—both surface and underground—unsafe for drinking.

The current engineering concept for dealing with human waste is to use vast quantities of water to wash it away, preferably into a sewer system, where it may or may not be treated before being discharged into the local river. The "flush and forget" system takes nutrients originating in the soil and typically dumps them into the nearest body of water. Not only are the nutrients lost from agriculture, but the nutrient overload has contributed to the death of many rivers and to the formation of some 405 "dead zones" in ocean coastal regions. This outdated system is expensive and water-intensive, disrupts the nutrient cycle, and can be a major source of disease and death. Worldwide, poor sanitation and personal hygiene claim the lives of some 2 million children per year, a toll that is one third the size of the 6 million lives claimed by hunger and malnutrition.[46]

Sunita Narain of the Centre for Science and Environment in India argues convincingly that a water-based disposal system with sewage treatment facilities is neither environmentally nor economically viable for India. She notes that an Indian family of five, producing 250 liters of excrement in a year and using a water flush toilet, contaminates 150,000 liters of water when washing away its wastes.[47]

As currently designed, India's sewer system is actually a pathogen-dispersal system. It takes a small quantity of contaminated material and uses it to make vast quantities of water unfit for human use. With this system, Narain says, both "our rivers and our children are dying." India's government, like that of many developing countries, is hopelessly chasing the goal of universal water-based sewage systems and sewage treatment facilities—unable to close the huge gap between services needed and provided, but unwilling to admit that it is not an economically viable option.[48]

Fortunately, there is a low-cost alternative: the composting toilet. This is a simple, waterless, odorless toilet linked to a small compost facility and sometimes a separate urine collecting facility. Collected urine can be trucked to nearby farms, much as fertilizer is. The dry composting converts human fecal material into a soil-like humus, which is essentially odorless and is scarcely 10 percent of the original volume. These compost facilities need to be emptied every year or so, depending on design and size. Vendors periodically collect the humus and market it as a soil supplement, thus ensuring that the nutrients and organic matter return to the soil, reducing the need for energy-intensive fertilizer.[49]

This technology sharply reduces residential water use compared with flush toilets, thus cutting water bills and lowering the energy needed to pump and purify water. As a bonus, it also reduces garbage flow if table wastes are incorporated, eliminates the sewage water disposal problem, and restores the nutrient cycle. The U.S. Environmental Protection Agency now lists several brands of dry compost toilets approved for use. Pioneered in Sweden, these toilets work well under the widely varying conditions in which they are now used, including Swedish apartment buildings, U.S. private residences, and Chinese villages. For many of the 2.5 billion people who lack improved sanitation facilities, composting toilets may be the answer.[50]

As Rose George, author of *The Big Necessity: The Unmentionable World of Human Waste and Why It Matters*, reminds us, the "flush and forget" system is an energy guzzler. There are two reasons for this. One, it takes energy to deliver large quantities of drinking-quality water (up to 30 percent of household water usage is for flushing). Two, it takes energy—and lots of it—to operate a sewage treatment facility. Many years ago U.S. President Theodore Roosevelt noted, "civilized people ought to know how to dispose of the sewage in some other way than putting it into the drinking water."[51]

In summary, there are several reasons why the advanced design composting toilets deserve top priority: spreading water shortages, rising energy prices, rising carbon emissions, shrinking phosphate reserves, a growing number of sewage-fed oceanic dead zones, the rising health care costs of sewage-dispersed intestinal diseases, and the rising capital costs of "flush and forget" sewage disposal systems.

Once a toilet is separated from the water use system, recycling household water becomes a much simpler process. For cities, the most effective single step to raise water productivity is to adopt a comprehensive water treatment/recycling system, reusing the same water continuously. With this system, which is much simpler if sewage is not included in the waste water, only a small percentage of water is lost to evaporation each time it cycles through. Given the technologies that are available today, it is quite possible to recycle the urban water supply indefinitely, largely removing cities as a claimant on scarce water resources.

Some cities faced with shrinking water supplies and rising water costs are beginning to recycle their water. Singapore, for example, which buys water from Malaysia at a high price, is already recycling water, reducing the amount it imports. Windhoek, capital of Namibia and one of the most arid locations in Africa, recycles waste water for drinking water. In water stressed California, Orange County invested in a $481-million treatment facility that opened in early 2008 to convert sewage into safe clean water, which is used to replenish the local aquifer. Los Angeles is planning to do the same. South Florida approved a plan in late 2007 to recycle waste water as drinking water. For more and more cities, water recycling is becoming a condition of survival.[52]

Individual industries facing water shortages are also moving away from the use of water to disperse waste. Some companies segregate effluent streams, treating each individually with the appropriate chemicals and membrane filtration, preparing the water for reuse. Peter Gleick, lead author of the biennial report *The World's Water*, writes: "Some industries, such as paper and pulp, industrial laundries, and metal finishing, are beginning to develop 'closed-loop' systems where all the wastewater is reused internally, with only small amounts of fresh water needed to make up for water incorporated into the product or lost in evaporation." Industries are moving faster than cities, but the technologies they are developing can also be used in urban water recycling.[53]

At the household level, water can also be saved by using more water-efficient showerheads, flush toilets, dishwashers, and clothes washers. Some countries are adopting water efficiency standards and labeling for appliances, much as has been done for energy efficiency. When water costs rise, as they inevitably will, investments in composting toilets and more water-efficient household appliances will become increasingly attractive to individual homeowners.

Two household appliances—toilets and showers—together account for over half of indoor water use. Whereas traditional flush toilets used 6 gallons (or 22.7 liters) per flush, the legal U.S. maximum for new toilets is 1.6 gallons (6 liters). New toilets with a dual-flush technology use only 1 gallon for a liquid waste flush and 1.6 gallons for a solid waste flush. Shifting from a showerhead flowing at 5 gallons per minute to a 2.5 gallons-per-minute model cuts water use in half. With washing machines, a horizontal axis design developed in Europe uses 40 percent less water than the traditional top-loading models.[54]

The existing water-based waste disposal economy is not viable. There are too many households, factories, and feedlots to simply try and wash waste away on our crowded planet. To do so is ecologically mindless and outdated—an approach that belongs to a time when there were far fewer people and far less economic activity.

Farming in the City

While attending a conference on the outskirts of Stockholm in the fall of 1974, I walked past a community garden near a high-rise apartment building. It was an idyllic Indian summer afternoon, with many people tending gardens a short walk from their residences. Some 35 years later I can still recall the setting because of the aura of contentment surrounding those working in their gardens. They were absorbed in producing not only vegetables, but in some cases flowers as well. I remember thinking, "This is the mark of a civilized society."

In 2005, the U.N. Food and Agriculture Organization (FAO) reported that urban and peri-urban farms—those within or immediately adjacent to a city—supply food to some 700 million urban residents worldwide. These are mostly small plots—vacant lots, yards, even rooftops.[55]

Within and near the city of Dar es Salaam, the capital of Tanzania, some 650 hectares of land produce vegetables. This land supplies not only the city's fresh produce but a livelihood for 4,000 farmers who intensively farm their small plots year-round. On the far side of the continent, an FAO project has urban residents in Dakar, Senegal, producing up to 30 kilograms (66 pounds) of tomatoes per square meter each year with continuous cropping in rooftop gardens.[56]

In Hanoi, Viet Nam, 80 percent of the fresh vegetables come from farms in or immediately adjacent to the city. Farms in the city or its shadow also produce 50 percent of the pork and the poultry consumed there. Half of the city's freshwater fish are produced by enterprising urban fish farmers. Forty percent of the egg supply is produced within the city or nearby. Urban farmers ingeniously recycle human and animal waste to nourish plants and to fertilize fish ponds.[57]

Fish farmers near Kolkata in India manage wastewater fish ponds that cover nearly 4,000 hectares and produce 18,000 tons of fish each year. Bacteria in the ponds break down the organic waste in the city's sewage. This, in turn, supports the rapid growth of algae that feed the local strains of herbivorous fish. This system provides the city with a steady supply of fresh fish that are consistently of better quality than any others entering the Kolkata market.[58]

The magazine *Urban Agriculture* describes how Shanghai has in effect created a nutrient recycling zone around the city. The municipal government manages 300,000 hectares of farmland to recycle the city's "night soil"—human wastes collected in areas without modern sanitation facilities. Half of Shanghai's pork and poultry, 60 percent of its vegetables, and 90 percent of its milk and eggs come from the city and the immediately surrounding region.[59]

In Caracas, Venezuela, a government-sponsored, FAO-assisted project has created 8,000 microgardens of 1 square meter each in the city's *barrios*, many of them within a few steps of family kitchens. As soon as one crop is mature, it is harvested and immediately replaced with new seedlings. Each square meter, continuously cropped, can produce 330 heads of lettuce, 18 kilograms of tomatoes, or 16 kilograms of cabbage per year. Venezuela's goal is to have 100,000 microgardens in the country's urban areas and 1,000 hectares of urban compost-based gardens nationwide.[60]

There is a long tradition of community gardens in European cities. As a visitor flies into Paris, numerous community gardens can be seen on its outskirts. The Community Food Security Coalition (CFSC) reports that 14 percent of London's residents produce some of their own food. For Vancouver, Canada's largest West Coast city, the comparable figure is an impressive 44 percent.[61]

In some countries, such as the United States, there is a huge unrealized potential for urban gardening. A survey indicated that Chicago has 70,000 vacant lots, and Philadelphia, 31,000. Nationwide, vacant lots in cities would total in the hundreds of thousands. The CFSC report summarizes why urban gardening is so desirable. It has "a regenerative effect...when vacant lots are transformed from eyesores—weedy, trash-ridden dangerous gathering places—into bountiful, beautiful, and safe gardens that feed people's bodies and souls."[62]

In Philadelphia, community gardeners were asked why they gardened. Some 20 percent did it for recreational reasons, 19 percent said it improved their mental health, and 17 percent their physical health. Another 14 percent did it because they wanted the higher-quality fresh produce that a garden could provide. Others said it was mostly cost and convenience.[63]

A parallel trend to urban gardening is the growing number of local farmers' markets, where farmers near a city produce fresh fruits and vegetables, pork, poultry, eggs, and cheese for direct marketing to consumers in urban markets.

Given the near inevitable rise in long-term oil prices, the economic benefits of expanding both urban agriculture and local farmers' markets will become more obvious. Aside from supplying more fresh produce, this will help millions discover the social benefits and the psychological well-being that urban gardening and locally produced food can bring.

Upgrading Squatter Settlements

Between 2000 and 2050, world population is projected to grow by 3 billion, but little of this growth is projected for industrial countries or for the rural developing world. Nearly all of it will take place in cities in developing countries, with much of the urban growth taking place in squatter settlements.[64]

Squatter settlements—whether the *favelas* in Brazil, *barriadas* in Peru, or *gecekondu* in Turkey—typically consist of an urban residential area inhabited by very poor people who do not own any land. They simply "squat" on vacant land, either private or public.[65]

Life in these settlements is characterized by grossly inadequate housing and a lack of access to urban services. As Hari Srinivas, coordinator of the Global Development Research Center, writes, these rural-urban migrants undertake the "drastic option of illegally occupying a vacant piece of land to build a rudimentary shelter" simply because it is their only option. They are often treated either with apathy or with outright antipathy by government agencies, who view them as invaders and trouble. Some see squatter settlements as a social "evil," something that needs to be eradicated.[66]

One of the best ways to make rural/urban migration manageable is to improve conditions in the countryside. This means not only providing basic social services, such as health care and education for children, as outlined in Chapter 7, but also encouraging industrial investment in small towns throughout the country rather than just in prime cities, such as Mexico City or Bangkok. Such policies will slow the flow into cities to a more orderly pace.

The evolution of cities in developing countries is often shaped by the unplanned nature of squatter settlements. Letting squatters settle wherever they can—on steep slopes, on river floodplains, or in other high-risk areas—makes it difficult to provide basic services such as transport, water, and sanitation. Curitiba, on the cutting edge of the new urbanism, has designated tracts of land for squatter settlements. By setting aside these planned tracts, the process can at least be structured in a way that is consistent with the development plan of the city.[67]

Among the simplest services that can be provided in a squatter settlement are taps that provide safe running water and community composting toilets. This combination can go a long way toward controlling disease in overcrowded settlements. And regular bus service enables workers living in the settlements to travel to their place of work. If the Curitiba approach is widely followed, parks and other commons areas can be incorporated into the community from the beginning.

Some political elites simply want to bulldoze squatter settlements out of existence, but this treats the symptoms of urban poverty, not the cause. People who lose what little they have been able to invest in housing are not richer as a result of the demolition, but poorer, as is the city itself. The preferred option by far is in situ upgrading of housing. The key to this is providing security of tenure and small loans to squatters, enabling them to make incremental improvements over time.[68]

Upgrading squatter settlements depends on local governments that respond to the problems in these areas rather than ignore them. Progress in eradicating poverty and creating stable, progressive communities depends on establishing constructive links with governments. Government-supported micro-credit lending facilities, for example, can help not only establish a link between the city government and the squatter communities but also offer hope to the residents.[69]

Although political leaders might hope that these settlements will one day be abandoned, the reality is that they will continue expanding. The challenge is to integrate them into urban life in a humane and organized way that provides hope through the potential for upgrading. The alternative is mounting resentment, social friction, and violence.

Cities for People

A growing body of evidence indicates there is an innate human need for contact with nature. Ecologists and psychologists have both been aware of this for some time. Ecologists, led by Harvard University biologist E. O. Wilson, have formulated the "biophilia hypothesis," which argues that those who are deprived of contact with nature suffer psychologically and that this deprivation leads to a measurable decline in well-being.[70]

Meanwhile, psychologists have coined their own term—ecopsychology—in which they make the same argument. Theodore Roszak, a leader in this field, cites a study of varying rates of patient recovery in a hospital in Pennsylvania. Those whose rooms overlooked gardens with grass, trees, flowers, and birds recovered from illnesses more quickly than those who were in rooms overlooking the parking lot.[71]

Creating more livable cities thus involves getting people out of their cars and more in touch with nature. The exciting news is that there are signs of change, daily indications of an interest in redesigning cities for people. That U.S. public transit ridership nationwide has risen by 2.5 percent a year since 1996 indicates that people are gradually abandoning their cars for buses, subways, and light rail. Higher gasoline prices encourage commuters to take the bus or subway or get on their bicycles.[72]

Mayors and city planners the world over are beginning to rethink the role of the car in urban transport systems. A group of eminent scientists in China challenged Beijing's decision to promote an automobile-centered transport system. They noted a simple fact: China does not have enough land to accommodate the automobile and to feed its people. This is also true for India and dozens of other densely populated developing countries.[73]

When 95 percent of a city's workers depend on cars for commuting, as in Atlanta, Georgia, the city is in trouble. By contrast, in Amsterdam 35 percent of all residents bike or walk to work, while one fourth use public transit and 40 percent drive. In Paris, fewer than half of commuters rely on cars, and even this share is shrinking thanks to the efforts of Mayor Delanoë. Even though these European cities are older, often with narrow streets, they have far less congestion than Atlanta.[74]

There are many ways to restructure the transportation system so that it satisfies the needs of all people, not just the affluent, it provides mobility, not immobility, and it improves health rather than running up health care costs. One way is to eliminate the subsidies, often indirect, that many employers provide for parking. In his book *The High Cost of Free Parking*, Donald Shoup estimates that off-street parking subsidies in the United States are worth at least $127 billion a year, obviously encouraging people to drive.[75]

In 1992, California mandated that employers match parking subsidies with cash that can be used by the recipient either to pay public transport fares or to buy a bicycle. In firms where data were collected, this shift in policy reduced automobile use by some 17 percent. At the national level, a provision was incorporated into the 1998 Transportation Equity Act for the 21st Century to change the tax code so that those who used public transit or vanpools would enjoy the same tax-exempt subsidies as those who received free parking. What societies should be striving for is not parking subsidies, but parking fees—fees that reflect the costs of traffic congestion and the deteriorating quality of life as cities are taken over by cars and parking lots.[76]

Scores of cities are declaring car-free areas, among them New York, Stockholm, Vienna, Prague, and Rome. Paris enjoys a total ban on cars along stretches of the Seine River on Sundays and holidays and is looking to make much of the central city traffic-free starting in 2012.[77]

In addition to ensuring that subways are functional and affordable, the idea of making them attractive, even cultural centers, is gaining support. In Moscow, with works of art in the stations, the subway system is justifiably referred to as Russia's crown jewel. In Washington, D.C., Union Station, which links the city's subway system with intercity rail lines, is an architectural delight. Since its restoration was completed in 1988, it has become a social gathering place, with shops, conference rooms, and a rich array of restaurants.

There is much more happening with cities and the reshaping of urban transport than meets the eye. Initial efforts to reverse the growth of urban car populations were based on specific measures, such as charging fees for cars entering the city during rush hour (Singapore, London, and Milan), investing in BRT lines (Curitiba, Bogotá, and Guangzhou), or fostering the bicycle alternative (Amsterdam and Copenhagen). One of the consequences of these and many other measures is that car sales have peaked and are declining in several countries in Europe and in Japan. Total vehicle sales in Japan peaked at 7.8 million in 1990, an economic boom year, and may drop below 5 million in 2009. Similar sales declines have occurred in several European countries and may be starting in the United States. For example, in mid-2008, U.S. automobile scrappage rates exceeded new car sales, a trend that promises to continue through 2009. Adverse economic conditions are a recent factor, but there is a more fundamental set of forces at work.[78]

Owning a car, once an almost universal status symbol, is beginning to lose its appeal. An early 2009 article in The Japan Times reports that many young Japanese no longer want to own a car. They see them as wasteful and, particularly in cities like Tokyo, far more trouble than they are worth.[79]

The attitude of young people in Japan appears to be mirrored by growing numbers in other countries, where interest in digital devices may be eclipsing that in cars. Young people are often more interested in their computers, Blackberries, and iPods and in electronic socialization than in "going for a spin" in a car. They have less interest in the latest model cars than their parents' generation had.

There are two ways of dealing with the environmental challenges facing cities. One is to modify existing cities. On Earth Day 2007, New York mayor Michael Bloomberg announced PlaNYC, a comprehensive plan to improve the city's environment, strengthen its economy, and make it a better place to live. At the heart of the plan is a 30-percent reduction in the city's greenhouse gas emissions by 2030. By 2009, PlaNYC—with nearly 130 initiatives—was showing some progress. For example, 15 percent of the taxicab fleet had been converted to fuel-efficient gas-electric hybrids. Nearly 200,000 trees had been planted. Raising the energy efficiency of buildings, a central goal, was under way in dozens of city buildings and many more in the private sector, including the iconic Empire State Building.[80]

The other way is to build new cities from scratch. For example, developer Sydney Kitson has acquired the 91,000-acre Babcock Ranch in southern Florida on which to build a new city. The first step was to help sell more than 73,000 acres of the land to the state government to maintain as a permanent preserve, thus ensuring an abundance of public green space. The heart of the city, intended to be home to 45,000 people, will include a business and commercial center and a high-density residential development. Several satellite communities, part of the overall development plan, will be linked to the downtown by public transportation.[81]

The purpose of the city is to both be a model green community and a center, a national focal point, for renewable energy research and development firms. Among the distinguishing features of this new community are that it will be powered entirely by solar electricity, all residential and commercial buildings will meet standards set by the Florida Green Buildings Coalition, and it will have more than 40 miles of greenways, allowing residents to walk or cycle to work.[82]

Half a world away, in oil-rich Abu Dhabi, construction has begun on another new development, Masdar City, designed for 50,000 people. The government's goal here is to create an international renewable energy research and development center, a sort of Silicon Valley East, that would house up to 1,500 firms, including start-ups and the research arms of major corporations.[83]

Masdar City has several important features. In addition to being powered largely by solar energy, this town of well-insulated buildings plans to be carless, relying on a rail-based, electrically powered, computer-controlled network of individual passenger vehicles. Resembling an enclosed golf cart, these vehicles will be clustered at stations throughout the city to provide direct delivery to each destination. In this water-scarce part of the world, the plan is to continuously recycle water used in the city. And nothing will go to a landfill; everything will be recycled, composted, or gasified to provide energy. How well these pre-engineered cities will perform and whether they will be attractive places to live and work in remains to be seen.[84]

We are only beginning to glimpse where we want to end up. Until now, changes in urban transport systems have been the result of a negative reaction to the growing number of cars in cities. But thinking is starting to change. In 2006, the History Channel sponsored a City of the Future Competition in which architectural firms were given one week to outline a vision of New York in 2106. Terreform, a design studio headed by architect Michael Sorkin, proposed gradually eliminating automobiles and converting half the city's street space into parks, farms, and gardens. The designers envisioned that by 2038, some 60 percent of New Yorkers would walk to work and that the city would eventually be transformed into a "paradise for people on foot."[85]

At this point, Terreform's proposal may seem a little far-fetched, but Manhattan's daily gridlock must be addressed simply because it has become both a financial burden and a public health threat. The Partnership for New York City, representing New York's leading corporate and investment firms, estimates conservatively that traffic congestion in and around the city costs the region more than $13 billion a year in lost time and productivity, wasted fuel, and lost business revenue.[86]

As the new century advances, the world is reconsidering the urban role of automobiles in one of the most fundamental shifts in transportation thinking in a century. The challenge is to redesign communities so that public transportation is the centerpiece of urban transport and streets are pedestrian- and bicycle-friendly. This also means planting trees and gardens and replacing parking lots with parks, playgrounds, and playing fields. We can design an urban lifestyle that systematically restores health by incorporating exercise into daily routines while reducing carbon emissions and eliminating health-damaging air pollution.

7

Eradicating Poverty and Stabilizing Population

The new century began on an inspiring note: the United Nations set a goal of reducing the share of the world's population living in extreme poverty by half by 2015. By early 2007 the world looked to be on track to meet this goal, but as the economic crisis unfolds and the outlook darkens, the world will have to intensify its poverty reduction effort.[1]

Among countries, China is the big success story in reducing poverty. The number of Chinese living in extreme poverty dropped from 685 million in 1990 to 213 million in 2007. With little growth in its population, the share of people living in poverty in China dropped from 60 percent to 16 percent, an amazing achievement by any standard.[2]

India's progress is mixed. Between 1990 and 2007, the number of Indians living in poverty actually increased slightly from 466 million to 489 million while the share living in poverty dropped from 51 percent to 42 percent. Despite its economic growth, averaging 9 percent a year for the last four years, and strong support by Prime Minister Manmohan Singh of a grassroots effort to eradicate poverty, India still has a long way to go.[3]

Brazil, on the other hand, has succeeded in reducing poverty with its Bolsa Familia program, an effort strongly supported by President Luiz Inácio Lula da Silva. This program is a conditional assistance program that offers poor mothers up to $35 a month if they keep their children in school, have them vaccinated, and make sure they get regular physical checkups. Between 1990 and 2007, the share of the population living in extreme poverty dropped from 15 to 5 percent. Serving 11 million families, nearly one fourth of the country's population, it has in the last five years raised incomes among the poor by 22 percent. By comparison, incomes among the rich rose by only 5 percent. Rosani Cunha, the program's director in Brasilia, observes, "There are very few countries that reduce inequality and poverty at the same time."[4]

Several countries in Southeast Asia have made impressive gains as well, including Thailand, Viet Nam, and Indonesia. Barring any major economic setbacks, these gains in Asia seemed to ensure that the U.N. Millennium Development Goal (MDG) of halving poverty by 2015 would be reached. Indeed, in a 2008 assessment of progress in reaching the MDGs, the World Bank reported that all regions of the developing world with the notable exception of sub-Saharan Africa were on track to cut the proportion of people living in extreme poverty in half by 2015.[5]

This upbeat assessment was soon modified, however. At the beginning of 2009, the World Bank reported that between 2005 and 2008 the incidence of poverty increased in East Asia, the Middle East, South Asia, and sub-Saharan Africa largely because of higher food prices, which hit the poor hard. This was compounded by the global economic crisis that dramatically expanded the ranks of the unemployed at home and reduced the flow of remittances from family members working abroad. The number the Bank classifies as extremely poor—people living on less than $1.25 a day—increased by at least 130 million. The Bank observed that "higher food prices during 2008 may have increased the number of children suffering permanent cognitive and physical injury caused by malnutrition by 44 million."[6]

Sub-Saharan Africa, with 820 million people, is sliding deeper into poverty. Hunger, illiteracy, and disease are on the march, partly offsetting the gains in countries like China and Brazil. The failing states as a group are also backsliding; an interregional tally of the Bank's fragile states is not encouraging since extreme poverty in these countries is over 50 percent—higher than in 1990.[7]

In addition to attacking poverty, other MDGs adopted in 2000 include reducing the share of those who are hungry by half, achieving universal primary school education, halving the share of people without access to safe drinking water, and reversing the spread of infectious diseases, especially HIV and malaria. Closely related to these are the goals of reducing maternal mortality by three fourths and under-five child mortality by two thirds.[8]

On the food front, the number of hungry is climbing. The long-term decline in the number of hungry and malnourished that characterized the last half of the twentieth century was reversed in the mid-1990s—rising from 825 million to roughly 850 million in 2000 and to over 1 billion in 2009. A number of factors contributed to this, but none more important than the massive diversion of grain to fuel ethanol distilleries in the United States. The U.S. grain used to produce fuel for cars in 2009 would feed 340 million people for one year.[9]

The goal of halving the share of hungry by 2015 is not within reach if we continue with business as usual. In contrast, the number of children with a primary school education does appear to be on the rise, but with much of the progress concentrated in a handful of larger countries, including India, Bangladesh, and Brazil.[10]

When the United Nations set the MDGs, it unaccountably omitted any population or family planning goals, even though as a January 2007 report from a U.K. All Party Parliamentary Group pointed out, "the MDGs are difficult or impossible to achieve with current levels of population growth in the least developed countries and regions." Although it came belatedly, the United Nations has since approved a new target that calls for universal access to reproductive health care by 2015.[11]

Countries everywhere have little choice but to strive for an average of two children per couple. There is no feasible alternative. Any population that increases indefinitely will eventually outgrow its natural life support systems. Any that decreases continually over the long term will eventually disappear.

In an increasingly integrated world with a lengthening list of failing states, eradicating poverty and stabilizing population have become national security issues. Slowing population growth helps eradicate poverty and its distressing symptoms, and, conversely, eradicating poverty helps slow population growth. With little time left to arrest the deterioration of the economy's natural support systems, the urgency of moving simultaneously on both fronts is clear.

Educating Everyone

One way of narrowing the gap between rich and poor segments of society is through universal education. This means making sure that the 75 million children currently not enrolled in school are able to attend. Children without any formal education start life with a severe handicap, one that almost ensures they will remain in abject poverty and that the gap between the poor and the rich will continue to widen. In an increasingly integrated world, this widening gap itself becomes a source of instability. As Nobel Prize–winning economist Amartya Sen points out: "Illiteracy and innumeracy are a greater threat to humanity than terrorism."[12]

In seeking universal primary education, the World Bank has taken the lead with its Education for All plan, where any country with a well-designed plan to achieve universal primary education is eligible for Bank financial support. The three principal requirements are that the country submit a sensible plan to reach universal basic education, commit a meaningful share of its own resources to the plan, and have transparent budgeting and accounting practices. If fully implemented, all children in poor countries would get a primary school education by 2015, helping them to break out of poverty.[13]

Some progress toward this goal has been made. In 2000, some 78 percent of children in developing countries were completing primary school; by 2006, this figure reached 85 percent. Gains have been strong but uneven, leaving the World Bank to conclude that only 58 of the 128 developing countries for which data are available will reach the goal of universal primary school education by 2015.[14]

The overwhelming majority of those living in poverty today are the children of people who lived in poverty. In effect, poverty is largely inherited. The key to breaking out of the culture of poverty is education—particularly of girls. As female educational levels rise, fertility falls. And mothers with at least five years of school lose fewer infants during childbirth or to early illnesses than their less well educated peers do. Economist Gene Sperling concluded in a study of 72 countries that "the expansion of female secondary education may be the single best lever for achieving substantial reductions in fertility."[15]

Basic education tends to increase agricultural productivity. Agricultural extension services that can use printed materials to disseminate information have an obvious advantage. So too do farmers who can read the instructions on a bag of fertilizer. The ability to read instructions on a pesticide container can be life-saving.

At a time when HIV is spreading, schools provide the institutional means to educate young people about the risks of infection. The time to inform and educate children about how the virus is spread is when they are young, not after they are infected. Young people can also be mobilized to conduct educational campaigns among their peers.

One great need in developing countries, particularly those where the ranks of teachers are being decimated by AIDS, is more teacher training. Providing scholarships for promising students from poor families to attend training institutes in exchange for a commitment to teach for, say, five years could be a highly profitable investment. It would help ensure that the teaching resources are available to reach universal primary education, and it would also foster an upwelling of talent from the poorest segments of society.

Gene Sperling believes that every plan should provide a way to get to the hardest-to-reach segments of society, especially poor girls in rural areas. He notes that Ethiopia has pioneered this with Girls Advisory Committees. Representatives of these groups go to the parents who are seeking early marriage for their daughters and encourage them to keep their girls in school. Some countries, Brazil and Bangladesh among them, actually provide small scholarships for girls or stipends to their parents where needed, thus helping those from poor families get a basic education.[16]

An estimated $10 billion in external funding, beyond what is being spent today, is needed for the world to achieve universal primary education. Having children who never go to school is no longer acceptable.[17]

As the world becomes ever more integrated economically, its nearly 800 million illiterate adults are severely handicapped. This deficit can best be overcome by launching adult literacy programs, relying heavily on volunteers. The international community could support this by offering seed money to provide educational materials and outside advisors where needed. Bangladesh and Iran, both of which have successful adult literacy programs, can serve as models. An adult literacy program would add $4 billion per year.[18]

Few incentives to get children in school are as effective as a school lunch program, especially in the poorest countries. Since 1946, every American child in public school has had access to a school lunch program, ensuring at least one good meal each day. There is no denying the benefits of this national program.[19]

Children who are ill or hungry miss many days of school. And even when they can attend, they do not learn as well. Jeffrey Sachs at Columbia University's Earth Institute notes, "Sick children often face a lifetime of diminished productivity because of interruptions in schooling together with cognitive and physical impairment." But when school lunch programs are launched in low-income countries, school enrollment jumps, the children's academic performance goes up, and children spend more years in school.[20]

Girls benefit especially. Drawn to school by the lunch, they stay in school longer, marry later, and have fewer children. This is a win-win-win situation. Launching school lunch programs in the 44 lowest-income countries would cost an estimated $6 billion per year beyond what the United Nations is now spending to reduce hunger.[21]

Greater efforts are also needed to improve nutrition before children even get to school age, so they can benefit from school lunches later. Former Senator George McGovern notes that "a women, infants and children (WIC) program, which offers nutritious food supplements to needy pregnant and nursing mothers," should also be available in the poor countries. Based on 33 years of experience, it is clear that the U.S. WIC program has been enormously successful in improving nutrition, health, and the development of preschool children from low-income families. If this were expanded to reach pregnant women, nursing mothers, and small children in the 44 poorest countries, it would help eradicate hunger among millions of small children at a time when it could make a huge difference.[22]

These efforts, though costly, are not expensive compared with the annual losses in productivity from hunger. McGovern thinks that this initiative can help "dry up the swamplands of hunger and despair that serve as potential recruiting grounds for terrorists." In a world where vast wealth is accumulating among the rich, it makes little sense for children anywhere to go to school hungry.[23]

Toward a Healthy Future

While heart disease, cancer, obesity, and smoking dominate health concerns in industrial countries, in developing countries infectious diseases are the overriding health threat. The principal diseases of concern are diarrhea, respiratory illnesses, tuberculosis, malaria, measles, and AIDS. Child mortality is high because childhood diseases such as measles, easily prevented by vaccination, take such a heavy toll.

Progress in reaching the MDG of reducing child mortality by two thirds between 1990 and 2015 is lagging badly. As of 2007 only 33 of 142 developing countries were on track to reach this goal. No country in sub-Saharan Africa was on that list; in fact, child mortality rates in seven sub-Saharan African countries have actually increased since 1990. And only 1 of the World Bank's 34 fragile states is likely to meet this goal by 2015.[24]

Along with the eradication of hunger, ensuring access to a safe and reliable supply of water for the estimated 1.1 billion people who lack it is essential to better health for all. The realistic option in many cities may be to bypass efforts to build costly water-based sewage removal and treatment systems and to opt instead for water-free waste disposal systems that do not disperse disease pathogens. (See the description of dry compost toilets in Chapter 6.) This switch would simultaneously help alleviate water scarcity, reduce the dissemination of disease agents in water systems, and help close the nutrient cycle—another win-win-win situation.[25]

One of the most impressive health gains has come from a campaign initiated by a little-heralded nongovernmental group in Bangladesh, BRAC, that taught every mother in the country how to prepare oral rehydration solution to treat diarrhea at home by simply adding a measured amount of salt and sugar to water. Founded by Fazle Hasan Abed, BRAC succeeded in dramatically reducing infant and child deaths from diarrhea in a country that was densely populated, poverty-stricken, and poorly educated.[26]

Seeing this great success, UNICEF used BRAC's model for its worldwide diarrheal disease treatment program. This global use of a remarkably simple oral rehydration technique has been extremely effective—reducing deaths from diarrhea among children from 4.6 million in 1980 to 1.6 million in 2006. Egypt alone used oral rehydration therapy to cut infant deaths from diarrhea by 82 percent between 1982 and 1989. Few investments have saved so many lives at such a low cost.[27]

Perhaps the leading privately funded life-saving activity in the world today is the childhood immunization program. In an effort to fill a gap in this global program, the Bill and Melinda Gates Foundation has invested more than $1.5 billion to protect children from infectious diseases like measles.[28]

Additional investments can help the many countries that cannot afford vaccines for childhood diseases and are falling behind in their vaccination programs. Lacking the funds to invest today, these countries pay a far higher price tomorrow. There are not many situations where just a few pennies spent per youngster can make as much difference as vaccination programs can.[29]

Similarly with AIDS, an ounce of prevention is worth a pound of cure. More than 25 million people have died from HIV-related causes thus far. Although progress is being made in curbing the spread of HIV, 2.7 million people were newly infected in 2007 and 2 million died of AIDS during that year. Two thirds of those living with HIV are in sub-Saharan Africa.[30]

The key to curbing the AIDS epidemic, which has so disrupted economic and social progress in Africa, is education about prevention. We know how the disease is transmitted; it is not a medical mystery. Where once there was a stigma associated with even mentioning the disease, governments are beginning to design effective prevention education programs. The first goal is to reduce quickly the number of new infections, dropping it below the number of deaths from the disease and thereby shrinking the number of those who are capable of infecting others.

Concentrating on the groups that are most likely to spread the disease is particularly effective. In Africa, infected truck drivers who travel far from home for extended periods often engage in commercial sex, spreading HIV from one country to another. Sex workers are also centrally involved in spreading the disease. In India, for example, educating the country's 2 million female sex workers, who have an average of two encounters per day, about HIV risks and the life-saving value of using a condom pays huge dividends.[31]

Another target group is the military. After soldiers become infected, usually from engaging in commercial sex, they return to their home communities and spread the virus further. In Nigeria, where the adult HIV infection rate is 3 percent, President Olusegun Obasanjo introduced free distribution of condoms to all military personnel. A fourth target group, intravenous drug users who share needles, figures prominently in the spread of the virus in the former Soviet republics.[32]

At the most fundamental level, dealing with the HIV threat requires roughly 13.5 billion condoms a year in the developing world and Eastern Europe. Including those needed for contraception adds another 4.4 billion. But of the 17.9 billion condoms needed, only 3.2 billion are being distributed, leaving a shortfall of 14.7 billion. At only 3¢ each, or $441 million, the cost of saved lives by supplying condoms is minuscule.[33]

In the excellent study *Condoms Count: Meeting the Need in the Era of HIV/AIDS*, Population Action International notes that "the costs of getting condoms into the hands of users—which involves improving access, logistics and distribution capacity, raising awareness, and promoting use—is many times that of the supplies themselves." If we assume that these costs are six times the price of the condoms, filling this gap would still cost less than $3 billion.[34]

The financial resources and medical personnel currently available to treat people who are already HIV-positive are severely limited compared with the need. For example, of the 7 million people who needed anti-retroviral therapy in sub-Saharan Africa at the end of 2007, just over 2 million were receiving the treatment that is widely available in industrial countries.

Although the number getting treatment was only one third of those who need it, it was still nearly double the number treated during the preceding year.[35]

Treating HIV-infected individuals is costly, but ignoring the need for treatment is a strategic mistake simply because treatment strengthens prevention efforts by giving people a reason to be tested. Africa is paying a heavy cost for its delayed response to the epidemic. It is a window on the future of other countries, such as India and China, if they do not move quickly to contain the virus, already well established within their borders.[36]

One of the United Nations' finest hours came with the eradication of smallpox, an effort led by the World Health Organization (WHO). This successful elimination of a feared disease, which required a worldwide immunization program, saves not only millions of lives each year but also hundreds of millions of dollars in smallpox vaccination programs and billions of dollars in health care expenditures.[37]

In an initiative patterned after the smallpox eradication, a WHO-led international coalition—including Rotary International, UNICEF, the U.S. Centers for Disease Control and Prevention (CDC), Ted Turner's U.N. Foundation, and, more recently, the Bill and Melinda Gates Foundation—has waged a worldwide campaign to wipe out polio, a disease that has crippled millions of children. Since 1988, Rotary International has contributed an extraordinary $800 million to this effort. Under this coalition-sponsored Global Polio Eradication Initiative, the number of polio cases worldwide dropped from some 350,000 per year in 1988 to fewer than 700 in 2003.[38]

By 2003, pockets of polio remained largely in Nigeria, India, Pakistan, Niger, Chad, and Burkina Faso, but then some of the predominantly Muslim states of northern Nigeria stopped vaccination because of a rumor that the vaccine would render people sterile or cause AIDS. By the end of 2004, after the misinformation was corrected, polio vaccinations were resumed in northern Nigeria. But during the interim, polio had become reestablished in several countries, apparently aided by the annual pilgrimage of Nigerian Muslims to Mecca. New infections appeared in the Central African Republic, Côte d'Ivoire, Indonesia, Mali, Saudi Arabia, Somalia, Sudan, and Yemen, which by 2006 allowed the global total of infections to rebound to nearly 2,000.[39]

By 2007, the number of reported new cases of polio was again shrinking when another roadblock emerged. In early 2007 violent opposition to vaccinations arose in Pakistan's North West Frontier Province, where a doctor and a health worker in the polio eradication program were killed. More recently, the Taliban have refused to let health officials administer polio vaccinations in the province's Swat Valley, further delaying the campaign.[40]

Despite these setbacks, in early 2009 the international community launched another major push to eradicate polio. This $630-million effort is being underwritten by the Gates Foundation, Rotary International, and the U.K. and German governments. But this was not all. In June 2009, President Obama announced in Cairo a new global effort working with the Organisation of the Islamic Conference to eradicate polio. Since so many of the remaining pockets of polio are in Muslim countries, this enhances the prospect of finally eradicating this disease.[41]

One of the more remarkable health success stories is the near eradication of guinea worm disease (dracunculiasis), a campaign led by former U.S. President Jimmy Carter and the Carter Center. These worms, whose larvae are ingested by drinking unfiltered water from lakes and rivers, mature in a person's body, sometimes reaching more than two feet in length. They then exit slowly through the skin in a very painful and debilitating ordeal that can last several weeks.[42]

With no vaccine to prevent infection and no drug for treatment, eradication depends on filtering drinking water to prevent larvae ingestion, thus eradicating the worm, which can survive only in a human host. Six years after the CDC launched a global campaign in 1980, the Carter Center took the reins and has since led the effort with additional support from partners like WHO, UNICEF, and the Gates Foundation. The number of people infected by the worm has been reduced from 3.5 million in 1986 to under 5,000 cases in 2008—an astounding drop of 99 percent. In the three countries where the worm existed outside Africa— India, Pakistan, and Yemen—eradication is complete. The remaining cases are found mainly in Sudan, Ghana, and Mali.[43]

Some leading sources of premature death are lifestyle-related, such as smoking. WHO estimates that 5.4 million people died in 2005 of tobacco-related illnesses, more than from any infectious disease including AIDS. Today there are some 25 known health threats that are linked to tobacco use, including heart disease, stroke, respiratory illness, many forms of cancer, and male impotence. Cigarette smoke kills more people each year than all other air pollutants combined—more than 5 million versus 3 million.[44]

Impressive progress is being made in reducing cigarette smoking. After a century-long buildup of the tobacco habit, the world is turning away from cigarettes, led by WHO's Tobacco Free Initiative. This gained further momentum when the Framework Convention on Tobacco Control, the first international accord to deal entirely with a health issue, was adopted unanimously in Geneva in May 2003. Among other things, the treaty calls for raising taxes on cigarettes, limiting smoking in public places, and strong health warnings on cigarette packages. In addition to WHO's initiative, the Bloomberg Global Initiative to Reduce Tobacco Use, funded by New York City Mayor Michael Bloomberg, is working to reduce smoking in lower- and middle-income countries, including China.[45]

Ironically, the country where tobacco originated is now the leader in moving away from cigarettes. In the United States, the average number of cigarettes smoked per person has dropped from its peak of 2,814 in 1976 to 1,225 in 2006—a decline of 56 percent. Worldwide, where the downturn lags that of the United States by roughly a dozen years, usage has dropped from the historical high of 1,027 cigarettes smoked per person in 1988 to 859 in 2004, a fall of 16 percent. Media coverage of the health effects of smoking, mandatory health warnings on cigarette packs, and sharp increases in cigarette sales taxes have all contributed to this encouraging development.[46]

The prospect of further reducing smoking in the United States got a major boost in April 2009 when the federal tax per pack of cigarettes was increased from 39¢ to $1.01 to reduce the fiscal deficit. Many states were contemplating a raise in state cigarette taxes for the same reason.[47]

Indeed, smoking is on the decline in nearly all the major countries where it is found, including such strongholds as France, China, and Japan. By 2007, the number of cigarettes smoked per person had dropped 20 percent in France after peaking in 1991, 5 percent in China since its peak in 1990, and 20 percent in Japan since 1992.[48]

Following approval of the Framework Convention, a number of countries took strong steps in 2004 to reduce smoking. Ireland imposed a nationwide ban on smoking in workplaces, bars, and restaurants; India banned smoking in public places; Norway and New Zealand banned smoking in bars and restaurants; and Scotland banned smoking in public buildings. Bhutan, a small Himalayan country, has prohibited tobacco sales entirely.[49]

In 2005, smoking was banned in public places in Bangladesh, and Italy banned it in all enclosed public spaces, including bars and restaurants. More recently, England has forbidden it in workplaces and enclosed public spaces, and France imposed a similar ban in 2008. Both Bulgaria and Croatia have since followed.[50]

Another disease that is often lifestyle-related, diabetes, is on the rise, reaching near epidemic levels in, for example, the United States and cities in India. Reversing the rising incidence of diabetes, an illness that appears to enhance the likelihood of Alzheimer's disease, depends heavily on lifestyle adjustments—fewer calories and more exercise.[51]

Effective responses to many emerging health problems often lie outside the purview of the Ministry of Health. For example, in China deaths from cancer have reached epidemic levels. Birth defects jumped by 40 percent between 2001 and 2006, with the biggest jumps coming in coal-producing provinces such as Shanxi and Inner Mongolia. The ability to reverse these trends lies not in the Ministry of Health but in altering the country's energy and environmental policies. On their own, doctors cannot halt the fast-rising number of deaths from cancer, now the leading cause of death in China.[52]

More broadly, a 2001 WHO study analyzing the economics of health care in developing countries concluded that providing the most basic health care services, the sort that could be supplied by a village-level clinic, would yield enormous economic benefits for developing countries and for the world as a whole. The authors estimate that providing basic universal health care in developing countries will require donor grants totaling on average $33 billion a year through 2015. In addition to basic services, this figure includes funding for the Global Fund to Fight AIDS, Tuberculosis and Malaria and for universal childhood vaccinations.[53]

Stabilizing Population

There are now two groups of countries where populations are projected to shrink, one because of falling fertility and the other because of rising mortality. In the first group, some 33 countries with roughly 674 million people have populations that are either essentially stable or declining slowly as a result of declining fertility. In countries with the lowest fertility rates—including Japan, Russia, and Germany—populations will likely decline measurably over the next half-century.[54]

The second group—countries with population declining due to a rising death rate—is a new one. Projections by the Washington-based Population Reference Bureau in 2008 show two countries in this group—Lesotho and Swaziland—both with high HIV infection rates and widespread hunger. Unfortunately, the number of countries in this group could expand in the years ahead as populations in low-income countries outgrow their land and water resources.[55]

In addition to 33 countries with essentially stable or declining populations, another group of countries, including China and the United States, have reduced fertility to replacement level or just below. But because of inordinately large numbers of young people moving into their reproductive years, their populations are still expanding. Once this group of young people moves through their high-fertility years, however, these countries too will be reaching population stability. The 29 countries in this category contain some 2.5 billion people.[56]

In stark contrast to these situations, a large group of countries are projected to continue expanding their populations in the years ahead—with some of them, including Ethiopia, the Democratic Republic of the Congo, and Uganda, projected to more than double in size by 2050.[57]

U.N. projections show world population growth under three different assumptions about fertility levels. The medium projection, the one most commonly used, has world population reaching 9.2 billion by 2050. The high one reaches 10.5 billion. The low projection, which assumes that the world will quickly move below replacement-level fertility, reaching 1.5 children per couple by 2050, has population peaking at just over 8 billion in 2042 and then declining. If the goal is to eradicate poverty, hunger, and illiteracy, then we have little choice but to strive for the lower projection.[58]

Slowing world population growth means that all women who want to plan their families should have access to the family planning services they need to do so. Unfortunately, this is currently not the case for 201 million women. Former U.S. Agency for International Development official J. Joseph Speidel notes that "if you ask anthropologists who live and work with poor people at the village level...they often say that women live in fear of their next pregnancy. They just do not want to get pregnant."[59]

The good news is that countries that want to help couples reduce family size can do so quickly. My colleague Janet Larsen writes that in just one decade Iran dropped its near-record population growth rate to one of the lowest in the developing world. When Ayatollah Khomeini assumed leadership in Iran in 1979, he immediately dismantled the well-established family planning programs and instead advocated large families. At war with Iraq between 1980 and 1988, Khomeini wanted large families to increase the ranks of soldiers for Islam. His goal was an army of 20 million.[60]

In response to his pleas, fertility levels climbed, pushing Iran's annual population growth to a peak of 4.2 percent in the early 1980s, a level approaching the biological maximum. As this enormous growth began to burden the economy and the environment, the country's leaders realized that overcrowding, environmental degradation, and unemployment were undermining Iran's future.[61]

In 1989 the government did an about-face and restored its family planning program. In May 1993, a national family planning law was passed. The resources of several government ministries, including education, culture, and health, were mobilized to encourage smaller families. Iran Broadcasting was given responsibility for raising awareness of population issues and of the availability of family planning services. Some 15,000 "health houses" or clinics were established to provide rural populations with health and family planning services.[62]

Religious leaders were directly involved in what amounted to a crusade for smaller families. Iran introduced a full panoply of contraceptive measures, including the option of male sterilization—a first among Muslim countries. All forms of birth control, including contraceptives such as the pill and sterilization, were free of charge. In fact, Iran became a pioneer—the only country to require couples to take a class on modern contraception before receiving a marriage license.[63]

In addition to the direct health care interventions, a broad-based effort was launched to raise female literacy, boosting it from 25 percent in 1970 to more than 70 percent in 2000. Female school enrollment increased from 60 to 90 percent. Television was used to disseminate information on family planning throughout the country, taking advantage of the 70 percent of rural households with TV sets. As a result of this initiative, family size in Iran dropped from seven children to fewer than three. From 1987 to 1994, Iran cut its population growth rate by half—an impressive achievement.[64]

While the attention of researchers has focused on the role of formal education in reducing fertility, soap operas on radio and television can even more quickly change people's attitudes about reproductive health, gender equity, family size, and environmental protection. A well-written soap opera can have a profound near-term effect on population growth. It costs relatively little and can proceed even while formal educational systems are being expanded.

The power of this approach was pioneered by Miguel Sabido, a vice president of Televisa, Mexico's national television network, when he did a series of soap opera segments on illiteracy. The day after one of the characters in his soap opera visited a literacy office wanting to learn how to read and write, a quarter-million people showed up at these offices in Mexico City. Eventually 840,000 Mexicans enrolled in literacy courses after watching the series.[65]

Sabido dealt with contraception in a soap opera entitled *Acompáñame*, which translates as *Come With Me*. Over the span of a decade this drama series helped reduce Mexico's birth rate by 34 percent.[66]

Other groups outside Mexico quickly picked up this

approach. The U.S.-based Population Media Center (PMC), headed by William Ryerson, has initiated projects in some 15 countries and is planning launches in several others. The PMC's work in Ethiopia over the last several years provides a telling example. Their radio serial dramas broadcast in Amharic and Oromiffa have addressed issues of reproductive health and gender equity, such as HIV/AIDS, family planning, and the education of girls. A survey two years after the broadcasts began in 2002 found that 63 percent of new clients seeking reproductive health care at Ethiopia's 48 service centers had listened to one of PMC's dramas.[67]

Among married women in the Amhara region of Ethiopia who listened to the dramas, there was a 55-percent increase in those using family planning. Male listeners sought HIV tests at a rate four times that of non-listeners, while female listeners were tested at three times the rate of female non-listeners. The average number of children per woman in the region dropped from 5.4 to 4.3. And demand for contraceptives increased 157 percent.[68]

The costs of providing reproductive health and family planning services are small compared with the benefits. Joseph Speidel estimates that expanding these services to reach all women in developing countries would take close to $17 billion in additional funding from industrial and developing countries.[69]

The United Nations estimates that meeting the needs of the 201 million women who do not have access to effective contraception could each year prevent 52 million unwanted pregnancies, 22 million induced abortions, and 1.4 million infant deaths. Put simply, filling the family planning gap may be the most urgent item on the global agenda. The costs to society of not doing so may be greater than we can afford.[70]

Shifting to smaller families brings generous economic dividends. In Bangladesh, for example, analysts concluded that $62 spent by the government to prevent an unwanted birth saved $615 in expenditures on other social services. Investing in reproductive health and family planning services leaves more fiscal resources per child for education and health care, thus accelerating the escape from poverty. For donor countries, ensuring that couples everywhere have access to the services they need would yield strong social returns in improved education and health care.[71]

Helping countries that want to slow their population growth brings with it what economists call the demographic bonus. When countries move quickly to smaller families, growth in the number of young dependents—those who need nurturing and educating—declines relative to the number of working adults. In this situation, productivity surges, savings and investment climb, and economic growth accelerates.[72]

Japan, which cut its population growth in half between 1951 and 1958, was one of the first countries to benefit from the demographic bonus. South Korea and Taiwan followed, and more recently China, Thailand, and Viet Nam have benefited from earlier sharp reductions in birth rates. This effect lasts for only a few decades, but it is usually enough to launch a country into the modern era. Indeed, except for a few oil-rich countries, no developing country has successfully modernized without slowing population growth.[73]

Rescuing Failing States

One of the leading challenges facing the international community is how to rescue failing states. Continuing with business as usual in international assistance programs is not working. The stakes could not be higher. If the number of failing states continues to increase, at some point this trend will translate into a failing global civilization. Somehow we must turn the tide of state decline.

Thus far the process of state failure has largely been a one-way street with few countries reversing the process. Among the few who have turned the tide are Liberia and Colombia.

Foreign Policy's annual ranking of failing states showed Liberia ranking ninth on the list in 2005, with number one being the worst case. But after 14 years of cruel civil war that took 200,000 lives, things began to turn around in 2005 with the election of Ellen Johnson-Sirleaf, a graduate of Harvard's Kennedy School of Government and an official at the World Bank, as president. A fierce effort to root out corruption and a multinational U.N. Peacekeeping Force of 15,000 troops who maintain the peace, repair roads, schools, and hospitals, and train police have brought progress to this war-torn country. In 2009, Liberia had dropped to thirty-third on the list of failing states.[74]

In Colombia, an improving economy—partly because of

strong coffee prices and partly because the government is steadily gaining in legitimacy—has helped turn things around.
Ranked fourteenth in 2005, Colombia in 2009 was forty-first on
the *Foreign Policy* list. Neither Liberia nor Colombia are out of
the woods yet, but both are moving in the right direction.[75]

Failing states are a relatively new phenomenon, and they
require a new response. The traditional project-based assistance
program is no longer adequate. State failure is a systemic failure
that requires a systemic response.

The United Kingdom and Norway have recognized that failing states need special attention and have each set up inter-
agency funds to provide a response mechanism. Whether they
are adequately addressing systemic state failure is not yet clear,
but they do at least recognize the need to devise a specific institutional response.[76]

In contrast, U.S. efforts to deal with weak and failing states
are fragmented. Several U.S. government departments are
involved, including State, Treasury, and Agriculture, to name a
few. And within the State Department, several different offices
are concerned with this issue. This lack of focus was recognized
by the Hart-Rudman U.S. Commission on National Security in
the Twenty-first Century: "Responsibility today for crisis prevention and response is dispersed in multiple AID [U.S. Agency
for International Development] and State bureaus, and among
State's Under Secretaries and the AID Administrator. In practice, therefore, no one is in charge."[77]

What is needed now is a new cabinet-level agency—a
Department of Global Security (DGS)—that would fashion a
coherent policy toward each weak and failing state. This rec-
ommendation, initially set forth in a report of the Commission
on Weak States and U.S. National Security, recognizes that the
threats to security are now coming less from military power and
more from the trends that undermine states, such as rapid population growth, poverty, deteriorating environmental support
systems, and spreading water shortages. The new agency would
incorporate AID (now part of the State Department) and all the
various foreign assistance programs that are currently in other
government departments, thereby assuming responsibility for
U.S. development assistance across the board. The State Department would provide diplomatic support for this new agency,

helping in the overall effort to reverse the process of state failure.[78]

The new Department of Global Security would be funded by shifting fiscal resources from the Department of Defense. In effect, the DGS budget would be the new defense budget. It would focus on the central sources of state failure by helping to stabilize population, restore environmental support systems, eradicate poverty, provide universal primary school education, and strengthen the rule of law through bolstering police forces, court systems, and, where needed, the military.

The DGS would deal with the production of and international trafficking in drugs. It would make such issues as debt relief and market access an integral part of U.S. policy. It would also provide a forum to coordinate domestic and foreign policy, ensuring that domestic policies, such as cotton export subsidies or subsidies to convert grain into fuel for cars, do not contribute to the failure of other countries. The department would provide a focus for the United States to help lead a growing international effort to reduce the number of failing states. This agency would also encourage private investment in failing states by providing loan guarantees to spur development.

As part of this effort the United States could rejuvenate the Peace Corps to assist with grassroots programs, including teaching in schools and helping to organize family planning, tree planting, and micro-lending programs. This program would involve young people while developing their sense of civic pride and social responsibility.

At a more senior level, the United States has a fast-growing reservoir of retired people who are highly skilled in such fields as management, accounting, law, education, and medicine and who are eager to be of use. Their talents could be mobilized through a voluntary Senior Service Corps. The enormous reservoir of management skills in this age group could be tapped to augment the skills so lacking in failing-state governments.

There are already, of course, a number of volunteer organizations that rely on the talents, energy, and enthusiasm of both U.S. young people and seniors, including the Peace Corps, Teach for America, and the Senior Corps. But conditions now require a more ambitious, systematic effort to tap this talent pool.

The world has quietly entered a new era, one where there is

no national security without global security. We need to recognize this and to restructure and refocus our efforts to respond to this new reality.

A Poverty Eradication Agenda and Budget

As indicated earlier, eradicating poverty involves much more than international aid programs. It also includes the debt relief that the poorest countries need in order to escape from poverty. For many developing countries, the reform of farm subsidies in aid-giving industrial countries and debt relief may be equally important. A successful export-oriented farm sector often offers a path out of poverty for a poor country. Sadly, for many developing countries this path is blocked by the self-serving farm subsidies of affluent countries. Overall, industrial-country farm subsidies of $258 billion are roughly double the development assistance from these governments.[79]

These subsidies encourage overproduction of some farm commodities, which then are sent abroad with another boost from export subsidies. The result is depressed world market prices, particularly for sugar and cotton, commodities where developing countries have the most to lose.[80]

Although the European Union (EU) accounts for more than half of the $120 billion in development assistance from all countries, much of the economic gain from this assistance in the past was offset by the EU's annual dumping of some 6 million tons of sugar on the world market. Fortunately, in 2005 the EU announced that it would reduce its sugar support price to farmers by 40 percent, thus reducing the amount of sugar exports to 1.3 million tons in 2008.[81]

Similarly, subsidies to U.S. farmers have historically enabled them to export cotton at low prices. And since the United States is the world's leading cotton exporter, its subsidies depress prices for all cotton exporters. As a result, U.S. cotton subsidies have faced a spirited challenge from four cotton-producing countries in Central Africa: Benin, Burkina Faso, Chad, and Mali. In addition, Brazil challenged U.S. cotton subsidies within the framework of the World Trade Organization (WTO), convincing a WTO panel that U.S. cotton subsidies were depressing world prices and harming their cotton producers.[82]

After the WTO ruled in Brazil's favor in 2004, the United

States made some token efforts to comply, but the WTO again ruled in Brazil's favor in December 2007, concluding that U.S. cotton subsidies were still depressing the world market price for cotton. The affluent world can no longer afford farm policies that permanently trap millions in poverty in aid-recipient countries by cutting off their main avenue of escape.[83]

Whereas most U.S. farm subsidies depress prices of exports from developing countries, the subsidy for converting grain into ethanol raises the price of grain, which most low-income countries import. In effect, U.S. taxpayers are subsidizing an increase in world hunger.[84]

Debt forgiveness is another essential component of the broader effort to eradicate poverty. A few years ago, for example, when sub-Saharan Africa was spending four times as much on debt servicing as it spent on health care, debt forgiveness was the key to boosting living standards in this last major bastion of poverty.[85]

In July 2005, heads of the G-8 industrial countries, meeting in Gleneagles, Scotland, agreed to cancel the multilateral debt that a number of the poorest countries owed to the World Bank, the International Monetary Fund (IMF), and the African Development Bank. Among other things, this initiative was intended to help the poorest countries reach the Millennium Development Goals. It immediately affected 18 of the poorest debt-ridden countries (14 in Africa and 4 in Latin America), offering these countries a new lease on life.[86]

The year after the Gleneagles meeting, Oxfam International reported that the IMF had eliminated the debts owed by 19 countries, the first major step toward the debt relief goal set at the G-8 meeting. For Zambia, the $6 billion of debt relief enabled President Levy Mwanawasa to announce that basic health care would be now free. In Oxfam's words, "the privilege of the few became the right of all." In East Africa, Burundi announced it would cancel school fees, permitting 300,000 children from poor families to enroll in school. In Nigeria, debt relief has been used to set up a poverty action fund, part of which will go to training thousands of new teachers.[87]

Even as debt was being reduced, development aid as a percentage of gross national income from donor countries decreased in 2006 and 2007. Although it rose in 2008, aid is still

$29 billion a year short of meeting the 2010 target of $130 billion that governments agreed on in 2005. The bad news is that
many of these same countries burdened by foreign debt were
being hit hard when the global economic crisis brought falling
prices for their mineral exports, falling remittances from
abroad, and rising prices for their grain imports.[88]

As noted earlier, the Bank estimates that increases in fuel and
food prices have pushed 130 million people below the poverty
line. And the Bank projected that another 53 million would be
pushed below the line in 2009. In referring to the difficulty many
developing countries were already experiencing in trying to
reach the MDGs, Bank president Robert Zoellick said in March
2009, "These targets now look even more distant."[89]

The steps needed to eradicate poverty and accelerate the
shift to smaller families are clear. They include filling several
funding gaps, including those needed to reach universal primary
education, to fight childhood and other infectious diseases, to
provide reproductive health care and family planning services,
and to contain the HIV epidemic. Collectively, the initiatives
discussed in this chapter are estimated to cost another $77 bil-

Table 7–1. *Plan B Budget: Additional Annual Funding Needed
to Reach Basic Social Goals*

Goal	Funding
	(billion dollars)
Universal primary education	10
Eradication of adult illiteracy	4
School lunch programs for 44 poorest countries	6
Assistance to preschool children and pregnant women in 44 poorest countries	4
Reproductive health and family planning	17
Universal basic health care	33
Closing the condom gap	3
Total	77

Source: See endnote 90.

lion a year. (See Table 7–1.)[90]

The heaviest investments in this effort center on education and health, which are the cornerstones of both human capital development and population stabilization. Education includes universal primary education and a global campaign to eradicate adult illiteracy. Health care includes the basic interventions to control infectious diseases, beginning with childhood vaccinations.[91]

As Columbia University economist Jeffrey Sachs regularly reminds us, for the first time in history we have the technologies and financial resources to eradicate poverty. Industrial-country investments in education, health, and school lunches are in a sense a humanitarian response to the plight of the world's poorest countries. But more fundamentally, they are investments that will help reverse the demographic and environmental trends that are undermining civilization.[92]

8

Restoring the Earth

We depend on the earth's natural systems for goods, ranging from building materials to water, as well as for services—everything from flood control to crop pollination. Thus if croplands are eroding and harvests are shrinking, if water tables are falling and wells are going dry, if grasslands are turning to desert and livestock are dying, we are in trouble. If civilization's environmental support systems continue to decline, eventually civilization itself will follow.

The devastation caused by deforestation and the soil erosion that results is exemplified by Haiti, where more than 90 percent of the original tree cover is gone, logged for firewood and cleared for crops. When hurricanes whip through the island shared by Haiti and the Dominican Republic, the carnage is often more severe for Haiti simply because there are no trees there to stabilize the soil and prevent landslides and flooding.[1]

Reflecting on this desperate situation, Craig Cox, executive director of the U.S.-based Soil and Water Conservation Society, wrote: "I was reminded recently that the benefits of resource conservation—at the most basic level—are still out of reach for many. Ecological and social collapses have reinforced each other in a downward spiral into poverty, environmental degradation, social injustice, disease, and violence." Unfortunately, the situation Cox describes is what lies ahead for more and more countries if we do not quickly take steps to reverse the damage we have caused.[2]

Restoring the earth will take an enormous international effort, one far larger and more demanding than the Marshall Plan that helped rebuild war-torn Europe and Japan. And such an initiative must be undertaken at wartime speed before environmental deterioration translates into economic decline, just as it did for earlier civilizations that violated nature's thresholds and ignored its deadlines.

Protecting and Restoring Forests

Since 1990, the earth's forest cover has shrunk by more than 7 million hectares each year, with annual losses of 13 million hectares in developing countries and regrowth of almost 6 million hectares in industrial countries. Protecting the earth's nearly 4 billion hectares of remaining forests and replanting those already lost are both essential for restoring the earth's health—the foundation for the new economy. Reducing rainfall runoff and the associated soil erosion and flooding, recycling rainfall inland, and restoring aquifer recharge depend on both forest protection and reforestation.[3]

There is a vast unrealized potential in all countries to lessen the demands that are shrinking the earth's forest cover. In industrial nations the greatest opportunity lies in reducing the quantity of wood used to make paper; in developing countries, it depends on reducing fuelwood use.

The use of paper, perhaps more than any other single product, reflects the throwaway mentality that evolved during the last century. There is an enormous possibility for reducing paper use simply by replacing facial tissues, paper napkins, disposable diapers, and paper shopping bags with reusable cloth alternatives.

First we reduce paper use, then we recycle as much as possible. The rates of paper recycling in the top 10 paper-producing countries range widely, from Canada and China on the low end, recycling just over a third of the paper they use, to Japan and Germany on the higher end, each at close to 70 percent, and

South Korea recycling an impressive 85 percent. The United States, the world's largest paper consumer, is far behind the leaders, but it has raised the share of paper recycled from roughly one fifth in 1980 to 55 percent in 2007. If every country recycled as much of its paper as South Korea does, the amount of wood pulp used to produce paper worldwide would drop by one third.[4]

The largest single demand on trees—fuelwood—accounts for just over half of all wood removed from the world's forests. Some international aid agencies, including the U.S. Agency for International Development (AID), are sponsoring fuelwood efficiency projects. One of AID's more promising projects is the distribution of 780,000 highly efficient cookstoves in Kenya that not only use far less wood than a traditional stove but also pollute less.[5]

Kenya is also the site of a project sponsored by Solar Cookers International, whose inexpensive cookers, made from cardboard and aluminum foil, cost $10 each. Requiring less than two hours of sunshine to cook a complete meal, they can greatly reduce firewood use at little cost and save women valuable time by freeing them from traveling long distances to gather wood. The cookers can also be used to pasteurize water, thus saving lives.[6]

Over the longer term, developing alternative energy sources is the key to reducing forest pressure in developing countries. Replacing firewood with solar thermal cookers or even with electric hotplates powered by wind, geothermal, or solar thermal energy will lighten the load on forests.

Despite the high ecological and economic value to society of intact forests, only about 290 million hectares of global forest area are legally protected from logging. An additional 1.4 billion hectares are economically unavailable for harvesting because of geographic inaccessibility or low-value wood. Of the remaining area thus far not protected, 665 million hectares are virtually undisturbed by humans and nearly 900 million hectares are semi-natural and not in plantations.[7]

There are two basic approaches to timber harvesting. One is clearcutting. This practice, often preferred by logging companies, is environmentally devastating, leaving eroded soil and silted streams, rivers, and irrigation reservoirs in its wake. The alternative is simply to cut only mature trees on a selective basis, leaving the forest intact. This ensures that forest productivity can be maintained in perpetuity. The World Bank has recently begun to systematically consider funding sustainable forestry projects. In 1997 the Bank joined forces with the World Wide Fund for Nature to form the Alliance for Forest Conservation and Sustainable Use. By the end of 2005 they had helped designate 56 million hectares of new forest protected areas and certify 32 million hectares of forest as being harvested sustainably. That year the Alliance also announced a goal of reducing global net deforestation to zero by 2020.[8]

Several forest product certification programs let environmentally conscious consumers know about the management practices in the forest where wood products originate. The most rigorous international program, certified by a group of nongovernmental organizations, is the Forest Stewardship Council (FSC). Some 114 million hectares of forests in 82 countries are certified by FSC-accredited bodies as responsibly managed. Among the leaders in FSC-certified forest area are Canada, with 27 million hectares, followed by Russia, the United States, Sweden, Poland, and Brazil.[9]

Forest plantations can reduce pressures on the earth's remaining forests as long as they do not replace old-growth forest. As of 2005, the world had 205 million hectares in forest plantations, almost one third as much as the 700 million hectares planted in grain. Tree plantations produce mostly wood for paper mills or for wood reconstitution mills. Increasingly, reconstituted wood is substituted for natural wood as the world lumber and construction industries adapt to a shrinking supply of large logs from natural forests.[10]

Production of roundwood (logs) on plantations is estimated at 432 million cubic meters per year, accounting for 12 percent of world wood production. Six countries account for 60 percent of tree plantations. China, which has little original forest remaining, is by far the largest, with 54 million hectares. India and the United States follow, with 17 million hectares each. Russia, Canada, and Sweden are close behind. As tree farming expands, it is starting to shift geographically to the moist tropics. In contrast to grain yields, which tend to rise with distance from the equator and with longer summer growing days, yields from tree plantations are higher with the year-round growing conditions found closer to the equator.[11]

In eastern Canada, for example, the average hectare of forest plantation produces 4 cubic meters of wood per year. In the southeastern United States, the yield is 10 cubic meters. But in Brazil, newer plantations may be getting close to 40 cubic meters. While corn yields in the United States are nearly triple those in Brazil, timber yields are the reverse, favoring Brazil by nearly four to one.[12]

Plantations can sometimes be profitably established on already deforested and often degraded land. But they can also come at the expense of existing forests. And there is competition with agriculture, since land that is suitable for crops is also good for growing trees. Since fast-growing plantations require abundant moisture, water scarcity is another constraint.

Nonetheless, the U.N. Food and Agriculture Organization (FAO) projects that as plantation area expands and yields rise, the harvest could more than double during the next three decades. It is entirely conceivable that plantations could one day satisfy most of the world's demand for industrial wood, thus helping protect the world's remaining forests.[13]

Historically, some highly erodible agricultural land in industrial countries was reforested by natural regrowth. Such is the case for New England in the United States. Settled early and cleared by Europeans, this geographically rugged region suffered from cropland productivity losses because soils were thin and the land was rocky, sloping, and vulnerable to erosion. As highly productive farmland opened up in the Midwest and the Great Plains during the nineteenth century, pressures on New England farmland lessened, permitting cropped land to return to forest. New England's forest cover has increased from a low of roughly one third two centuries ago to four fifths today, slowly regaining its original health and diversity.[14]

A somewhat similar situation exists now in parts of the former Soviet Union and in several East European countries. As centrally planned agriculture was replaced by market-based agriculture in the early 1990s, unprofitable marginal land was abandoned. Precise figures are difficult to come by, but millions of hectares of low-quality farmland there are now returning to forest.[15]

South Korea is in many ways a reforestation model for the rest of the world. When the Korean War ended, half a century ago, the mountainous country was largely deforested. Beginning around 1960, under the dedicated leadership of President Park Chung Hee, the South Korean government launched a national reforestation effort. Relying on the formation of village cooperatives, hundreds of thousands of people were mobilized to dig trenches and to create terraces for supporting trees on barren mountains. Se-Kyung Chong, researcher at the Korea Forest Research Institute, writes, "The result was a seemingly miraculous rebirth of forests from barren land."[16]

Today forests cover 65 percent of the country, an area of roughly 6 million hectares. While driving across South Korea in November 2000, it was gratifying to see the luxuriant stands of trees on mountains that a generation ago were bare. We can reforest the earth![17]

In Turkey, a mountainous country largely deforested over the millennia, a leading environmental group, TEMA (Türkiye Erozyonla Mücadele, Agaclandirma), has made reforestation its principal activity. Founded by two prominent Turkish businessmen, Hayrettin Karaca and Nihat Gökyigit, TEMA launched in 1998 a 10-billion-acorn campaign to restore tree cover and reduce runoff and soil erosion. Since then, 850 million oak acorns have been planted. The program is also raising national awareness of the services that forests provide.[18]

Reed Funk, professor of plant biology at Rutgers University, believes the vast areas of deforested land can be used to grow trillions of trees bred for food (mostly nuts), fuel, and other purposes. Funk sees nuts used to supplement meat as a source of high-quality protein in developing-country diets.[19]

In Niger, farmers faced with severe drought and desertification in the 1980s began leaving some emerging acacia tree seedlings in their fields as they prepared the land for crops. As the trees matured they slowed wind speeds, thus reducing soil erosion. The acacia, a legume, fixes nitrogen, thereby enriching the soil and helping to raise crop yields. During the dry season, the leaves and pods provide fodder for livestock. The trees also supply firewood.[20]

This approach of leaving 20–150 tree seedlings per hectare to mature on some 3 million hectares has revitalized farming communities in Niger. Assuming an average of 40 trees per hectare reaching maturity, this comes to 120 million trees. This practice also has been central to reclaiming 250,000 hectares of abandoned cropland. The key to this success story was the shift in tree ownership from the state to individual farmers, giving them the responsibility for protecting the trees.[21]

Shifting subsidies from building logging roads to planting trees would help protect forest cover worldwide. The World Bank has the administrative capacity to lead an international program that would emulate South Korea's success in blanketing mountains and hills with trees.

In addition, FAO and the bilateral aid agencies can work with individual farmers in national agroforestry programs to integrate trees wherever possible into agricultural operations. Well-chosen, well-placed trees provide shade, serve as windbreaks to check soil erosion, and can fix nitrogen, which reduces the need for fertilizer.

Reducing wood use by developing more-efficient wood stoves and alternative cooking fuels, systematically recycling paper, and banning the use of throwaway paper products all lighten pressure on the earth's forests. But a global reforestation effort is unlikely to succeed unless it is accompanied by the stabilization of population. With such an integrated plan, coordinated country by country, the earth's forests can be restored.

Planting Trees to Sequester Carbon

In recent years the shrinkage of forests in tropical regions has released 2.2 billion tons of carbon into the atmosphere annually. Meanwhile, expanding forests in the temperate regions are absorbing close to 700 million tons of carbon. On balance, therefore, some 1.5 billion tons of carbon are being released into the atmosphere each year from forest loss, contributing to climate change.[22]

Tropical deforestation in Asia is driven primarily by the fast-growing demand for timber and, increasingly, by the soaring use of palm oil for fuel. In Latin America, by contrast, the growing market for soybeans, beef, and sugarcane ethanol is deforesting the Amazon. In Africa, it is mostly the gathering of fuelwood and the clearing of new land for agriculture as existing cropland is degraded and abandoned. Two countries, Indonesia and

Brazil, account for more than half of all deforestation and thus have the highest potential for avoiding emissions from clearing forests. The Democratic Republic of the Congo, also high on the list, is considered a failing state, making forest management there particularly difficult.[23]

The Plan B goals are to end net deforestation worldwide and to sequester carbon through a variety of tree planting initiatives and the adoption of improved agricultural land management practices. Today, because the earth's forests are shrinking, they are a major source of carbon dioxide (CO_2). The goal is to expand the earth's tree cover, growing more trees to soak up CO_2.

Although banning deforestation may seem farfetched, environmental reasons have pushed three countries—Thailand, the Philippines, and China—to implement complete or partial bans on logging. All three bans were imposed following devastating floods and mudslides resulting from the loss of forest cover. The Philippines, for example, has banned logging in most remaining old-growth and virgin forests largely because the country has become so vulnerable to flooding, erosion, and landslides. The country was once covered by rich stands of tropical hardwood forests, but after years of massive clearcutting, it lost the forest's products as well as its services and became a net importer of forest products.[24]

In China, after suffering record losses from several weeks of nonstop flooding in the Yangtze River basin in 1998, the government noted that when forest policy was viewed not through the eyes of the individual logger but through those of society as a whole, it simply did not make economic sense to continue deforesting. The flood control service of trees standing, they said, was three times as valuable as the timber from trees cut. With this in mind, Beijing then took the unusual step of paying the loggers to become tree planters—to reforest instead of deforest.[25]

Other countries cutting down large areas of trees will also face the environmental effects of deforestation, including flooding. If Brazil's Amazon rainforest continues to shrink, it may also continue to dry out, becoming vulnerable to fire. If the Amazon rainforest were to disappear, it would be replaced largely by desert and scrub forestland. The capacity of the rainforest to cycle water to the interior of the continent, including to the agricultural areas in the west and to the south, would be lost. At this point, a fast-unfolding local environmental calamity would become a global economic disaster, and, because the burning Amazon would release billions of tons of carbon into the atmosphere, it would become a global climate disaster.[26]

Just as national concerns about the effects of continuing deforestation eventually eclipsed local interests, deforestation has become a global challenge. It is no longer just a matter of local flooding. Because it drives climate change, deforestation is a matter of melting mountain glaciers, crop-shrinking heat waves, rising seas, and the many other effects of climate change worldwide. Nature has just raised the ante on protecting forests.

Reaching a goal of zero net deforestation will require reducing the pressures that come from population growth, rising affluence, growing biofuel consumption, and the fast-growing use of paper and wood products. Protecting the earth's forests means halting population growth as soon as possible. And for the earth's affluent residents who are responsible for the growing demand for beef and soybeans that is deforesting the Amazon basin, it means moving down the food chain and eating less meat. Ending deforestation may require a ban on the construction of additional biodiesel refineries and ethanol distilleries.

Because of the importance of forests in modulating climate, the Intergovernmental Panel on Climate Change (IPCC) has examined the potential for tree planting and improved forest management to sequester CO_2. Since every newly planted tree seedling in the tropics removes an average of 50 kilograms of CO_2 from the atmosphere each year during its growth period of 20–50 years, compared with 13 kilograms of CO_2 per year for a tree in the temperate regions, much of the afforestation and reforestation opportunity is found in tropical countries.[27]

Estimates vary widely on the full potential for tree planting to sequester carbon. Looking at global models, the IPCC notes that on the high end, tree planting and improved forest management could sequester some 2.7 billion tons of carbon (9.8 billion tons CO_2) per year by 2030 at a carbon price of less than $367 per ton ($100 per ton of CO_2). Nearly two thirds of that potential—or roughly 1.7 billion tons per year—is thought to be achievable at half that carbon price. Plan B, with its 2020 timeline, cuts the IPCC sequestration figure in half, to get 860 million tons of carbon sequestered per year by 2020 at a carbon price below $200 per ton.[28]

To achieve this goal, billions of trees would need to be planted on millions of hectares of degraded lands that had lost their tree cover and on marginal cropland and pastureland that was no longer productive. Spread over a decade, to reach annual sequestration rates of 860 million tons of carbon by 2020, this would mean investing $17 billion a year to give climate stabilization a large and potentially decisive boost.

This global forestation plan to remove atmospheric CO_2, most of it put there by industrial countries, would need to be funded by them. In comparison with other mitigation strategies, stopping deforestation and planting trees are relatively inexpensive. They pay for themselves many times over. An independent body could be set up to administer and monitor the vast tree planting initiative. The key is moving quickly to stabilize climate before temperature rises too high, thus giving these trees the best possible chance of survival.[29]

There are already many tree planting initiatives proposed or under way that are driven by a range of concerns, from climate change and desert expansion to soil conservation and making cities more habitable.

Kenyan Nobel laureate Wangari Maathai, who years ago organized women in Kenya and several nearby countries to plant 30 million trees, inspired the Billion Tree Campaign that is managed by the United Nations Environment Programme (UNEP). The initial goal was to plant 1 billion trees in 2007. If half of those survive, they will sequester 5.6 million tons of carbon per year. As soon as this goal was reached, UNEP set a new goal of planting 7 billion trees by the end of 2009—which would mean planting a tree for every person on earth in three years. As of July 2009, pledges toward the 7 billion plantings had passed 6.2 billion, with 4.1 billion trees already in the ground.[30]

Among the leaders in this initiative are Ethiopia and Turkey, each with over 700 million trees planted. Mexico is a strong third, with some 537 million trees. Kenya, Cuba, and Indonesia have each planted 100 million or more seedlings. Some state and provincial governments have also joined in. In Brazil, the state of Paraná, which launched an effort to plant 90 million trees in 2003 to restore its riparian zones, committed to planting 20 million trees in 2007. Uttar Pradesh, India's most populous state, mobilized 600,000 people to plant 10.5 million trees in a single day in July 2007, putting the trees on farmland, in state forests, and on school grounds.[31]

Many of the world's cities are also planting trees. Tokyo, for example, has been planting trees and shrubs on the rooftops of buildings to help offset the urban heat island effect and cool the city. Washington, D.C., is in the early stages of an ambitious campaign to restore its tree canopy.[32]

An analysis of the value of planting trees on the streets and in the parks of five western U.S. cities—from Cheyenne in Wyoming to Berkeley in California—concluded that for every $1 spent on planting and caring for trees, the benefits to the community exceeded $2. A mature tree canopy in a city shades buildings and can reduce air temperatures by 5–10 degrees Fahrenheit, thus reducing the energy needed for air conditioning. In cities with severe winters like Cheyenne, the reduction of winter wind speed by evergreen trees cuts heating costs. Real estate values on tree-lined streets are typically 3–6 percent higher than where there are few or no trees.[33]

Planting trees is just one of many activities that will remove meaningful quantities of carbon from the atmosphere. Improved grazing practices and land management practices that increase the organic matter content in soil also sequester carbon.

Conserving and Rebuilding Soils

The literature on soil erosion contains countless references to the "loss of protective vegetation." Over the last half-century, people have removed so much of that protective cover by clearcutting, overgrazing, and overplowing that the world is quickly losing soil accumulated over long stretches of geological time. Preserving the biological productivity of highly erodible cropland depends on planting it in grass or trees before it becomes wasteland.

The 1930s Dust Bowl that threatened to turn the U.S. Great Plains into a vast desert was a traumatic experience that led to revolutionary changes in American agricultural practices, including the planting of tree shelterbelts (rows of trees planted beside fields to slow wind and thus reduce wind erosion) and strip cropping (the planting of wheat on alternate strips with fallowed land each year). Strip cropping permits soil moisture to accumulate on the fallowed strips, while the alternating planted strips reduce wind speed and hence erosion on the idled land.[34]

In 1985, the U.S. Congress, with strong support from the environmental community, created the Conservation Reserve Program (CRP) to reduce soil erosion and control overproduction of basic commodities. By 1990 there were some 14 million hectares (35 million acres) of highly erodible land with permanent vegetative cover under 10-year contracts. Under this program, farmers were paid to plant fragile cropland to grass or trees. The retirement of those 14 million hectares under the CRP, together with the use of conservation practices on 37 percent of all cropland, reduced U.S. soil erosion from 3.1 billion tons to 1.9 billion tons between 1982 and 1997. The U.S. approach offers a model for the rest of the world.[35]

Another tool in the soil conservation toolkit—and a relatively new one—is conservation tillage, which includes both no-till and minimum tillage. Instead of the traditional cultural practices of plowing land and discing or harrowing it to prepare the seedbed, and then using a mechanical cultivator to control weeds in row crops, farmers simply drill seeds directly through crop residues into undisturbed soil, controlling weeds with herbicides. The only soil disturbance is the narrow slit in the soil surface where the seeds are inserted, leaving the remainder of the soil undisturbed, covered by crop residues and thus resistant to both water and wind erosion. In addition to reducing erosion, this practice retains water, raises soil carbon content, and greatly reduces energy use for tillage.[36]

In the United States, where farmers during the 1990s were required to implement a soil conservation plan on erodible cropland in order to be eligible for commodity price supports, the no-till area went from 7 million hectares in 1990 to 27 million hectares (67 million acres) in 2007. Now widely used in the production of corn and soybeans, no-till has spread rapidly in the western hemisphere, covering 26 million hectares in Brazil, 20 million hectares in Argentina, and 13 million in Canada. Australia, with 12 million hectares, rounds out the five leading no-till countries.[37]

Once farmers master the practice of no-till, its use can spread rapidly, particularly if governments provide economic incentives or require farm soil conservation plans for farmers to be eligible for crop subsidies. Recent FAO reports describe the growth in no-till farming over the last few years in Europe, Africa, and Asia.[38]

A number of these agricultural practices can have the added benefit of increasing the carbon stored as organic matter in soils. Farming practices that reduce soil erosion and raise cropland productivity usually also lead to higher carbon content in the soil. Among these are the shift to minimum-till and no-till farming, the more extensive use of cover crops, the return of all livestock and poultry manure to the land, expansion of irrigated area, a return to more mixed crop-livestock farming, and the forestation of marginal farmlands.

Other approaches are being used to halt soil erosion and desert encroachment on cropland. In July 2005, the Moroccan government, responding to severe drought, announced that it was allocating $778 million to canceling farmers' debts and converting cereal-planted areas into less vulnerable olive and fruit orchards.[39]

Sub-Saharan Africa faces a similar situation, with the desert moving southward all across the Sahel, from Mauritania and Senegal in the west to the Sudan in the east. Countries are concerned about the growing displacement of people as grasslands and croplands turn to desert. As a result, the African Union has launched the Green Wall Sahara Initiative. This plan, originally proposed by Olusegun Obasanjo when he was president of Nigeria, calls for planting 300 million trees on 3 million hectares in a long band stretching across Africa. Senegal, which is currently losing 50,000 hectares of productive land each year, would anchor the green wall on the western end. Senegal's Environment Minister Modou Fada Diagne says, "Instead of waiting for the desert to come to us, we need to attack it." Since the initiative was launched, its scope has broadened to include improved land management practices such as rotational grazing.[40]

China is likewise planting a belt of trees to protect land from the expanding Gobi Desert. This green wall, a modern version of the Great Wall, is projected to extend some 4,480 kilometers

(2,800 miles), stretching from outer Beijing through Inner Mongolia (Nei Monggol). In addition to its Great Green Wall, China is paying farmers in the threatened provinces to plant their cropland in trees. The goal is to plant trees on 10 million hectares of grainland, easily one tenth of China's current grainland area. Unfortunately, recent pressures to expand food production appear to have slowed this tree planting initiative.[41]

In Inner Mongolia, efforts to halt the advancing desert and to reclaim the land for productive uses rely on planting desert shrubs to stabilize the sand dunes. And in many situations, sheep and goats have been banned entirely. In Helin County, south of the provincial capital of Hohhot, the planting of desert shrubs on abandoned cropland has now stabilized the soil on the county's first 7,000-hectare reclamation plot. Based on this success, the reclamation effort is being expanded.[42]

The Helin County strategy centers on replacing the large number of sheep and goats with dairy cattle. The dairy herds are kept within restricted areas, feeding on cornstalks, wheat straw, and the harvest from a drought-tolerant forage crop resembling alfalfa, which is used to reclaim land from the desert. Local officials estimate that this program will double incomes within the county during this decade.[43]

To relieve pressure on China's rangelands as a whole, Beijing is asking herders to reduce their flocks of sheep and goats by 40 percent. But in communities where wealth is measured in livestock numbers and where most families are living in poverty, such cuts are not easy or, indeed, likely, unless alternative livelihoods are offered to pastoralists along the lines proposed in Helin County.[44]

In the end, the only viable way to eliminate overgrazing on the two fifths of the earth's land surface classified as rangelands is to reduce the size of flocks and herds. Not only do the excessive numbers of cattle, and particularly sheep and goats, remove the vegetation, but their hoofs pulverize the protective crust of soil that is formed by rainfall and that naturally checks wind erosion. In some situations, the preferred option is to keep the animals in restricted areas, bringing the forage to them. India, which has successfully adopted this practice for its thriving dairy industry, is the model for other countries.[45]

Protecting the earth's soil also warrants a worldwide ban on the clearcutting of forests in favor of selective harvesting, simply because with each successive clearcut there are heavy soil losses until the forest regenerates. And with each subsequent cutting, more soil is lost and productivity declines further. Restoring the earth's tree and grass cover, as well as practicing conservation agriculture, protects soil from erosion, reduces flooding, and sequesters carbon.

Rattan Lal, a senior agronomist with the Carbon Management and Sequestration Center at Ohio State University, has calculated the range of potential carbon sequestration for many practices. For example, expanding the use of cover crops to protect soil during the off-season can store from 68 million to 338 million tons of carbon worldwide each year. Calculating the total carbon sequestration potential from this broad scope of practices, using the low end of the range for each, shows that 400 million tons of carbon could be sequestered each year. Aggregating the numbers from the more optimistic high end of the range for each practice yields a total of 1.2 billion tons of carbon per year. For our carbon budget we are assuming, perhaps conservatively, that 600 million tons of carbon can be sequestered as a result of adopting these carbon-sensitive farming and land management practices.[46]

Regenerating Fisheries

For decades governments have tried to save specific fisheries by restricting the catch of individual species. Sometimes this worked; sometimes it failed and fisheries collapsed. In recent years, support for another approach—the creation of marine reserves or marine parks—has been gaining momentum. These reserves, where fishing is banned, serve as natural hatcheries, helping to repopulate the surrounding area.[47]

In 2002, at the World Summit on Sustainable Development in Johannesburg, coastal nations pledged to create national networks of marine reserves or parks that would cover 10 percent of the world's oceans by 2012. Together these could constitute a global network of such parks.

Progress is slow. By 2006 there were 4,500 marine protected area (MPAs), most of them quite small, covering 2.2 million square kilometers, or less than 1 percent of the world's oceans. Of the area covered by MPAs, only 0.01 percent is covered by marine reserves where fishing is banned. And a survey of 255 marine reserves reported that only 12 were routinely patrolled to enforce the ban.[48]

Marine biologists are learning that there are biological hotspots that contain an unusual diversity of species in the oceans as well as on land. The challenge in marine conservation is first to identify these marine hotspots and breeding grounds and then to incorporate them into marine reserves.[49]

Among the more ambitious initiatives to create marine parks thus far are one by the United States and another by Kiribati. In 2006, President George W. Bush designated 140,000 square miles in the northwestern Hawaiian Islands as a marine park. Named the Papahānaumokuākea Marine National Monument, this one park is larger than all the U.S. land-based parks combined. It is home to over 7,000 marine species, one fourth of them found only in the Hawaiian archipelago. In early 2009, President Bush declared three more ecologically rich regions nearby also as national monuments, bringing the total protected area to 195,000 square miles, an area larger than the states of Washington and Oregon combined. Fishing is limited within these monument areas, and mining and oil drilling are prohibited.[50]

In early 2008, Kiribati, an island country of 98,000 people located in the South Pacific midway between Hawaii and New Zealand, announced what was at the time the world's largest marine protected area, covering some 158,000 square miles. Comparable in size to the state of California, it encompasses eight coral atolls, two submerged reefs, and a deep-sea tuna spawning ground.[51]

A U.K. team of scientists led by Dr. Andrew Balmford of the Conservation Science Group at Cambridge University has analyzed the costs of operating marine reserves on a large scale based on data from 83 relatively small, well-managed reserves. They concluded that managing reserves that covered 30 percent of the world's oceans would cost $12–14 billion a year. This did not take into account the likely additional income from recovering fisheries, which would reduce the actual cost.[52]

At stake in the creation of a global network of marine reserves is the protection and possible increase of an annual oceanic fish catch worth $70–80 billion. Balmford said, "Our study suggests that we could afford to conserve the seas and their resources in perpetuity, and for less than we are now spending on subsidies to exploit them unsustainably."[53]

Coauthor Callum Roberts of the University of York noted: "We have barely even begun the task of creating marine parks. Here in Britain a paltry one-fiftieth of one percent of our seas is encompassed by marine nature reserves and only one-fiftieth of their combined area is closed to fishing." Still the seas are being devastated by unsustainable fishing, pollution, and mineral exploitation. The creation of the global network of marine reserves—"Serengetis of the seas," as some have dubbed them— would also create more than 1 million jobs. Roberts went on to say, "If you put areas off limits to fishing, there is no more effective way of allowing things to live longer, grow larger, and produce more offspring."[54]

In 2001 Jane Lubchenco, former President of the American Association for the Advancement of Science and now head of the National Oceanic and Atmospheric Administration, released a statement signed by 161 leading marine scientists calling for urgent action to create the global network of marine reserves. Drawing on the research on scores of marine parks, she said: "All around the world there are different experiences, but the basic message is the same: marine reserves work, and they work fast. It is no longer a question of whether to set aside fully protected areas in the ocean, but where to establish them."[55]

The signatories noted how quickly sea life improves once the reserves are established. A case study of a snapper fishery off the coast of New England showed that fishers, though they violently opposed the establishment of the reserve, now champion it because they have seen the local population of snapper increase 40-fold. In a study in the Gulf of Maine, all fishing methods that put groundfish at risk were banned within three marine reserves totaling 17,000 square kilometers. Unexpectedly, scallops flourished in this undisturbed environment, and their populations increased by up to 14-fold within five years. This buildup within the reserves also greatly increased the scallop population outside the reserves. The 161 scientists noted that within a year or two of establishing a marine reserve, population densities increased 91 percent, average fish size went up 31 percent, and species diversity rose 20 percent.[56]

While the creation of marine reserves is clearly the overriding priority in the long-standing effort to protect marine ecosystems, other measures are also required. One is to reduce the nutrient flows from fertilizer runoff and sewage that create the world's 400 or so oceanic dead zones, in effect "deserts of the deep." Another needed measure is to reduce the discharge of toxic chemicals, heavy metals, and endocrine disrupters directly into the water or indirectly through discharge into the atmosphere. Each of these discharges that build up in the oceanic food chain threaten not only predatory marine mammals, such as seals, dolphins, and whales, but also the large predatory fish, such as tuna and swordfish, as well as the humans who eat them.[57]

On a broader level, the buildup of atmospheric CO_2 is leading to acidification of the oceans, which could endanger all sea life. Most immediately threatened are the coral reefs, whose carbonate structure makes them highly vulnerable to the acidification that is under way and that is gaining momentum as CO_2 emissions increase. Protecting shallow water reefs that are invariably hotspots of plant and animal diversity may now depend on quickly phasing out coal-fired power plants, as does the attainment of so many other environmental goals.

In the end, governments need to eliminate fishery subsidies. Partly as a result of these subsidies, there are now so many fishing trawlers that their catch potential is nearly double the sustainable fish catch. Managing a network of marine reserves governing 30 percent of the oceans would cost only $12–14 billion—less than the $22 billion in harmful subsidies that governments dole out today to fishers.[58]

Protecting Plant and Animal Diversity

The two steps essential to protecting the earth's extraordinary biological diversity are stabilization of the human population and the earth's climate. If our numbers rise above 9 billion by mid-century, as projected, countless more plant and animal species may be crowded off the planet. If temperatures continue to rise, every ecosystem on earth will change.[59]

One reason we need to stabilize population at 8 billion by 2040 is to protect this rich diversity of life. As it becomes more difficult to raise land productivity, continuing population growth will force farmers to clear ever more tropical forests in the Amazon and Congo basins and the outer islands of Indonesia.

Better water management, particularly at a time of growing water shortages, is a key to protecting freshwater and marine species. When rivers are drained dry to satisfy growing human needs for irrigation and for water in cities, fish and other aquatic species cannot survive.

Perhaps the best known and most popular way of trying to protect plant and animal species is to create reserves. Millions of square kilometers have been set aside as parks. Indeed, some 13 percent of the earth's land area is now included in parks and nature preserves. With more resources for enforced protection, some of these parks in developing countries that now exist only on paper could become a reality.[60]

Some 20 years ago, Norman Myers and other scientists conceived the idea of biodiversity "hotspots"—areas that were especially rich biologically and thus deserving of special protection. The 34 hotspots identified once covered nearly 16 percent of the earth's land surface, but largely because of habitat destruction they now cover less than 3 percent. Concentrating preservation efforts in these biologically rich regions is now a common strategy among conservation groups and governments.[61]

In 1973 the United States enacted the Endangered Species Act. This legislation prohibited any activities, such as clearing new land for agriculture and housing developments or draining wetlands, that would threaten an endangered species. Numerous species in the United States, such as the bald eagle, might now be extinct had it not been for this legislation.[62]

Another promising school of thought centers on the extension of species conservation into agriculture, urban landscapes, roadways, and other landscapes. Among other things, this protects and strengthens wildlife corridors. Wildlife action plans for individual states, developed by the U.S. Fish and Wildlife Service, could be a template for this approach.

The traditional approach to protecting biological diversity by building a fence around an area and calling it a park or nature preserve is no longer sufficient. If we cannot also stabilize population and the climate, there is not an ecosystem on earth that we can save.

The Earth Restoration Budget

We can roughly estimate how much it will cost to reforest the earth, protect topsoil, restore rangelands and fisheries, stabilize water tables, and protect biological diversity. The goal is not to offer a set of precise numbers but to provide a set of reasonable estimates for an earth restoration budget. (See Table 8–1.)[63]

Calculating the cost of reforestation is complicated by the range of approaches used. As noted, the extraordinary reforestation success of South Korea was based almost entirely on locally mobilized labor. Other countries, including China, have tried extensive reforestation, but mostly under more arid conditions and with less success.[64]

In calculating reforestation costs, the focus is on developing countries since forested area is already expanding in the northern hemisphere's industrial countries. Meeting the growing fuelwood demand in developing countries will require an estimated 55 million additional hectares of forested area. Conserving soils and restoring hydrological stability would require roughly another 100 million hectares located in thousands of watersheds in developing countries. Recognizing some overlap between these

Table 8–1. *Plan B Budget:*
Additional Annual Funding Needed to Restore the Earth

Activity	Funding (billion dollars)
Planting trees to reduce flooding and conserve soil	6
Planting trees to sequester carbon	17
Protecting topsoil on cropland	24
Restoring rangelands	9
Restoring fisheries	13
Protecting biological diversity	31
Stabilizing water tables	10
Total	110

Source: See endnote 63.

two, we will reduce the 155 million total to 150 million hectares. Beyond this, an additional 30 million hectares will be needed to produce lumber, paper, and other forest products.[65]

Only a small share of this tree planting will likely come from plantations. Much of the planting will be on the outskirts of villages, along field boundaries and roads, on small plots of marginal land, and on denuded hillsides. The labor for this will be local; some will be paid labor, some volunteer. Much of it will be rural off-season labor. In China, farmers now planting trees where they once planted grain are compensated with grain from state-held stocks over a five-year period while the trees are becoming established.[66]

If seedlings cost $40 per thousand, as the World Bank estimates, and if the typical planting rate is roughly 2,000 per hectare, then seedlings cost $80 per hectare. Labor costs for planting trees are high, but since much of the labor would consist of locally mobilized volunteers, we are assuming a total of $400 per hectare, including both seedlings and labor. With a total of 150 million hectares to be planted over the next decade, this will come to roughly 15 million hectares per year at $400 each for an annual expenditure of $6 billion.[67]

Planting trees to conserve soil, reduce flooding, and provide firewood sequesters carbon. But because climate stabilization is essential, we tally the cost of planting trees for carbon sequestration separately. Doing so would reforest or afforest hundreds of millions of hectares of marginal lands over 10 years. Because it would be a more commercialized undertaking focused exclusively on wasteland reclamation and carbon sequestration, it would be more costly. Using the value of sequestered carbon of $200 per ton, it would cost close to $17 billion per year.[68]

Conserving the earth's topsoil by reducing erosion to the rate of new soil formation or below involves two principal steps. One is to retire the highly erodible land that cannot sustain cultivation—the estimated one tenth of the world's cropland that accounts for perhaps half of all excess erosion. For the United States, that has meant retiring 14 million hectares (nearly 35 million acres). The cost of keeping this land out of production is close to $50 per acre or $125 per hectare. In total, annual payments to farmers to plant this land in grass or trees under 10-year contracts approached $2 billion.[69]

The second initiative consists of adopting conservation practices on the remaining land that is subject to excessive erosion—that is, erosion that exceeds the natural rate of new soil formation. This initiative includes incentives to encourage farmers to adopt conservation practices such as contour farming, strip cropping, and, increasingly, minimum-till or no-till farming. These expenditures in the United States total roughly $1 billion per year.[70]

In expanding these estimates to cover the world, it is assumed that roughly 10 percent of the world's cropland is highly erodible and should be planted in grass or trees before the topsoil is lost and it becomes barren land. In both the United States and China, the two leading food-producing countries that together account for over a third of the world grain harvest, the official goal is to retire one tenth of all cropland. In Europe, it likely would be much less than 10 percent, but in Africa and the Andean countries it could be substantially higher. For the world as a whole, converting 10 percent of cropland that is highly erodible to grass or trees seems like a reasonable goal. Since this costs roughly $2 billion in the United States, which represents one eighth of the world cropland area, the total for the world would be roughly $16 billion annually.[71]

Assuming that the need for erosion control practices for the rest of the world is similar to that in the United States, we again multiply the U.S. expenditure by eight to get a total of $8 billion for the world as a whole. The two components together—$16 billion for retiring highly erodible land and $8 billion for adopting conservation practices—give an annual total for the world of $24 billion.[72]

For cost data on rangeland protection and restoration, we turn to the United Nations Plan of Action to Combat Desertification. This plan, which focuses on the world's dryland regions, containing nearly 90 percent of all rangeland, estimates that it would cost roughly $183 billion over a 20-year restoration period—or $9 billion per year. The key restoration measures include improved rangeland management, financial incentives to eliminate overstocking, and revegetation with appropriate rest periods, during which grazing would be banned.[73]

This is a costly undertaking, but every $1 invested in rangeland restoration yields a return of $2.50 in income from the increased productivity of the rangeland ecosystem. From a societal point of view, countries with large pastoral populations where the rangeland deterioration is concentrated are invariably among the world's poorest. The alternative to action—ignoring the deterioration—brings a loss not only of land productivity but also of livelihood, and ultimately leads to millions of refugees. Though not quantified here, restoring this vulnerable land will also have carbon sequestration benefits.[74]

The restoration of oceanic fisheries centers primarily on the establishment of a worldwide network of marine reserves that would cover roughly 30 percent of the ocean's surface. For this exercise we use the detailed calculations by the U.K. team cited earlier in the chapter. Their estimated range of expenditures centers on $13 billion per year.[75]

For wildlife protection, the bill is somewhat higher. The World Parks Congress estimates that the annual shortfall in funding needed to manage and protect existing areas designated as parks comes to roughly $25 billion a year. Additional areas needed, including those encompassing the biologically diverse hotspots not yet included in designated parks, would cost perhaps another $6 billion a year, yielding a total of $31 billion.[76]

For stabilizing water tables, we have only a guess. The key to stabilizing water tables is raising water productivity, and for this we have the experience gained when the world started to systematically raise land productivity beginning a half-century ago. The elements needed in a comparable water model are research to develop more water-efficient irrigation practices and technologies, the dissemination of these research findings to farmers, and economic incentives that encourage farmers to adopt and use these improved irrigation practices and technologies.

The area to focus on for raising irrigation water productivity is much smaller than that for land productivity. Indeed, only about one fifth of the world's cropland is irrigated. In disseminating the results of irrigation research, there are actually two options today. One is to work through agricultural extension services, which were created to funnel new information to farmers on a broad range of issues, including irrigation. Another possibility is to work through the water users associations that have been formed in many countries. The advantage of the latter is that they are focused exclusively on water.[77]

Effectively managing underground water supplies requires knowledge of the amount of water pumped and aquifer recharge rates. In most countries this information is simply not available. Finding out how much is pumped may mean installing meters on irrigation well pumps, as has been done in Jordan and Mexico.[78]

In some countries, the capital needed to fund a program to raise water productivity can come from eliminating subsidies that often encourage the wasteful use of irrigation water. Sometimes these are energy subsidies, as in India; other times they are subsidies that provide water at prices well below costs, as in the United States. Removing these subsidies will effectively raise the price of water, thus encouraging its more efficient use. In terms of additional resources needed worldwide, including research needs and the economic incentives for farmers to use more water-efficient practices and technologies, we assume it will take an annual expenditure of $10 billion.[79]

Altogether, then, restoring the earth will require additional expenditures of just $110 billion per year. Many will ask, Can the world afford these investments? But the only appropriate question is, Can the world afford the cost of not making these investments?

9

Feeding Eight Billion People Well

As we prepare to feed a world population of 8 billion within the next two decades, we are entering a new food era. Early signs of this are the record-high grain prices of the last few years, the restriction on grain exports by exporting countries, and the acquisition of vast tracts of land abroad by grain-importing countries. And because some of the countries where land is being acquired do not have enough land to adequately feed their own people, the stage is being set for future conflicts between the so-called land grabbers and hungry local people.

The leaders in this land acquisition movement—Saudi Arabia, South Korea, and China—are all facing growing food insecurity. Saudi Arabia's wheat harvest is shrinking as it loses irrigation water to aquifer depletion. South Korea, heavily dependent on corn imports to sustain its livestock and poultry production, sees its principal supplier—the United States—diverting more corn to fuel production for cars than to exports. China is losing irrigation water as its aquifers are depleted and its mountain glaciers disappear.[1]

The growing competition for land across national boundaries is indirectly competition for water. In effect, land acquisitions are also water acquisitions. As Sudan sells or leases land to other countries, for example, the water to irrigate this land will likely come from the Nile, leaving less for Egypt.

Attention has focused on oil insecurity, and rightly so, but it is not the same as food insecurity. An empty gas tank is one thing, an empty stomach another. And while there are substitutes for oil, there are none for food.

In the world food economy, as in the energy economy, achieving an acceptable balance between supply and demand now includes reducing demand as well as expanding supply. It means accelerating the shift to smaller families to reduce future population size. For those in affluent countries, it means moving down the food chain. And for oil-insecure countries, it means finding substitutes for oil other than fuel from food crops.

As noted early on, securing future food supplies now goes far beyond agriculture. In our crowded, warming world, policies dealing with energy, population, water, climate, and transport all directly affect food security. That said, there are many things that can be done in agriculture to raise land and water productivity.

Raising Land Productivity

Investment in agriculture by international development agencies has lagged badly over the last two decades. Some of the stronger developing countries, such as China and Brazil, moved ahead on their own, but many suffered.[2]

Prior to 1950, expansion of the food supply came almost entirely from expanding cropland area. Then as frontiers disappeared and population growth accelerated after World War II, the world quickly shifted to raising land productivity. Between 1950 and 2008 grain yields nearly tripled, climbing from 1.1 to 3.2 tons per hectare. In one of the most spectacular achievements in world agricultural history, farmers doubled the grain harvest between 1950 and 1973. Stated otherwise, during this 23-year-span, growth in the grain harvest equaled that of the preceding 11,000 years.[3]

After several decades of rapid rise, however, it is now becoming more difficult to raise land productivity. From 1950 to 1990, world grainland productivity increased by 2.1 percent per year, but from 1990 until 2008 it went up by only 1.3 percent annually.[4]

Gains in land productivity have come primarily from three sources—the growing use of fertilizer, the spread of irrigation, and the development of higher-yielding varieties. As farmers attempted to remove nutrient constraints on crop yields, fertilizer use climbed from 14 million tons in 1950 to 175 million tons in 2008. In some countries, such as the United States, several in Western Europe, and Japan, fertilizer use has leveled off. It may do so soon in China and India as well, for each of them now uses more fertilizer than the United States does.[5]

Farmers remove soil moisture limits on crop yields by irrigating, using both surface water from rivers and underground water. World irrigated area increased from 94 million hectares in 1950 to 278 million hectares in 2000. Since then, it has increased very little. Future gains from irrigation will likely come more from raising irrigation efficiency than from expanding irrigation water supplies.[6]

The third source of higher land productivity is higher-yielding varieties. The initial breakthrough came when Japanese scientists succeeded in dwarfing both wheat and rice plants in the late nineteenth century. This decreased the share of photosynthate going into straw and increased that going into grain, often doubling yields.[7]

With corn, now the world's largest grain crop, the early breakthrough came with hybridization in the United States. As a result of the dramatic advances associated with hybrid corn, and the recent, much more modest gains associated with genetic modification, corn yields are still edging upward.[8]

Most recently, Chinese scientists have developed commercially viable hybrid rice strains. While they have raised yields, the gains have been small compared with the earlier gains from dwarfing the rice plant.[9]

There are distinct signs of yields leveling off in the higher-yield countries that are using all available technologies. With wheat, the first of the big three grains to be cultivated, it appears that once the yield reaches 7 tons per hectare it becomes difficult to go much higher. This is borne out by the plateauing of wheat yields at that level in France, Europe's largest wheat producer, and in Egypt, Africa's largest producer.[10]

In the Asian rice economy, the highest yields are in Japan, China, and South Korea. All three have moved above 4 tons per hectare, but moving above 5 tons is difficult. Japan reached 4 tons per hectare in 1967 but has yet to reach 5 tons. In China, rice yields appear to be plateauing as they approach the Japanese level. South Korea has leveled off right around 5 tons.[11]

Among the three grains, corn is the only one where the yield is continuing to rise in high-yield countries. In the United States, which accounts for 40 percent of the world corn harvest, yields are now approaching an astonishing 10 tons per hectare. Even though fertilizer use has not increased since 1980, corn yields continue to edge upward as seed companies invest huge sums in corn breeding. Iowa, with corn yields among the world's highest, now produces more grain than Canada does.[12]

Despite dramatic past leaps in grain yields, it is becoming more difficult to expand world food output. There is little productive new land to bring under the plow. Expanding the irrigated area is difficult. Returns on the use of additional fertilizer are diminishing in many countries.

Agricultural endowments vary widely by country. Achieving high grain yields means having an abundance of soil moisture, either from rainfall, as in the corn-growing U.S. Midwest and wheat-growing Western Europe, or from irrigation, as in Egypt, China, and Japan. Countries with chronically low soil moisture, as in Australia, much of Africa, and the Great Plains in North America, have not experienced dramatic grain yield advances. U.S. corn yields today are nearly four times wheat yields, partly because wheat is grown under low rainfall conditions. India's wheat yields are now close to double those of Australia not because India's farmers are better but because they have more water to work with.[13]

Some developing countries have dramatically boosted farm output. In India, after the monsoon failure of 1965 that required the import of a fifth of the U.S. wheat crop to avoid famine, a highly successful new agricultural strategy was adopted. It included replacing grain ceiling prices that catered to the cities with grain support prices to encourage farmers to invest in raising land productivity. The construction of fertilizer plants was moved from the government sector into the private sector, where the plants could be built quickly. The high-yielding wheats that were developed in Mexico and that had already been tested in India were introduced by the shipload. This combination of positive developments enabled India to double its wheat harvest in seven years. No major country before or since has managed to double the harvest of a staple food in such a short period of time.[14]

A similar situation developed in Malawi, a country of 15 million people, after the drought of 2005 that left many hungry and some starving. In response, the government issued coupons to small farmers, entitling them to 200 pounds of fertilizer at a greatly reduced price, and free packets of improved seed corn, the national food staple. Costing some $70 million per year and funded partly by outside donors, this fertilizer and seed subsidy program helped nearly double Malawi's corn harvest within two years, leading to an excess of grain. Fortunately this grain could be profitably exported to nearby Zimbabwe, which was experiencing acute grain shortages.[15]

Some years earlier, a similar initiative had been undertaken in Ethiopia. It too led to a dramatic growth in production. But because there was no way either to distribute the harvest to remote areas or to export the surplus, this led to a crash in prices—a major setback to the country's farmers and to Ethiopia's food security. This experience also underlines a major challenge to agricultural development in much of Africa, namely the lack of infrastructure, such as roads to get fertilizer to farmers and their products to market.[16]

In the more arid countries of Africa, such as Chad, Mali, Mauritania, and Namibia, there is not enough rainfall to raise yields dramatically. Modest yields are possible with improved agricultural practices, but in many of these countries there has not been a green revolution for the same reason there has not been one in Australia—namely, low soil moisture and the associated limit on fertilizer use.

The shrinking backlog of unused agricultural technology and the associated loss of momentum in raising yields is worldwide, signaling a need for fresh thinking on how to raise cropland productivity. One way is to breed crops that are more tolerant of drought and cold. U.S. corn breeders have developed corn varieties that are more drought-tolerant, enabling corn production to move westward into Kansas, Nebraska, and South Dakota. For example, Kansas, the leading U.S. wheat-producing state, now produces more corn than wheat. Similarly, corn production is moving northward in North Dakota and Minnesota.[17]

Another way to raise land productivity, where soil moisture permits, is to expand the area of land that produces more than one crop per year. Indeed, the tripling in the world grain harvest from 1950 to 2000 was due in part to widespread increases in multiple cropping in Asia. Some of the more common combinations are wheat and corn in northern China, wheat and rice in northern India, and the double or triple cropping of rice in southern China and southern India.[18]

The spread of double cropping of winter wheat and corn on the North China Plain helped boost China's grain production to where it now rivals that of the United States. Winter wheat grown there yields 5 tons per hectare. Corn also averages 5 tons. Together these two crops, grown in rotation, can yield 10 tons per hectare per year. China's double-cropped rice yields over 8 tons per hectare.[19]

Forty or so years ago, grain production in northern India was confined largely to wheat, but with the advent of the earlier maturing high-yielding wheats and rices, wheat could be harvested in time to plant rice. This combination is now widely used throughout the Punjab, Haryana, and parts of Uttar Pradesh. The wheat yield of 3 tons and rice yield of 2 tons combine for 5 tons of grain per hectare, helping to feed India's 1.2 billion people.[20]

In North America and Western Europe, which in the past have restricted cropped area to control surpluses, there may be some potential for double cropping that has not been fully exploited. In the United States, the end of idling cropland to control production in 1996 opened new opportunities for multiple cropping. The most common U.S. double cropping combination is winter wheat with soybeans in the summer. Since soybeans fix nitrogen in the soil, making it available to plants, this reduces the amount of fertilizer applied to wheat.[21]

A concerted U.S. effort to both breed earlier-maturing varieties and develop cultural practices that would facilitate multiple cropping could boost crop output. If China's farmers can extensively double crop wheat and corn, then U.S. farmers—at a similar latitude and with similar climate patterns—could do more if agricultural research and farm policy were reoriented to support it.

Western Europe, with its mild winters and high-yielding

winter wheat, might also be able to double crop more with a summer grain, such as corn, or an oilseed crop. Elsewhere, Brazil and Argentina, which have extensive frost-free growing seasons, commonly multicrop wheat or corn with soybeans.[22]

One encouraging effort to raise cropland productivity in Africa is the simultaneous planting of grain and leguminous trees. At first the trees grow slowly, permitting the grain crop to mature and be harvested; then the saplings grow quickly to several feet in height, dropping leaves that provide nitrogen and organic matter, both sorely needed in African soils. The wood is then cut and used for fuel. This simple, locally adapted technology, developed by scientists at the International Centre for Research in Agroforestry in Nairobi, has enabled farmers to double their grain yields within a matter of years as soil fertility builds.[23]

Another often overlooked issue is the effect of land tenure on productivity. In China, this issue was addressed in March 2007 when the National People's Congress passed legislation protecting property rights. Farmers who had previously occupied their land under 30-year leases would gain additional protection from land confiscation by local officials who, over the years, had seized land from some 40 million farmers, often for construction. Secure land ownership encourages farmers to invest in and improve their land. A survey by the Rural Development Institute revealed that farmers in China with documented land rights were twice as likely to make long-term investments in their land, such as adding greenhouses, orchards, or fishponds.[24]

In summary, while grain production is falling in some countries, either because of unfolding water shortages or spreading soil erosion, the overwhelming majority still have a substantial unrealized production potential. The challenge is for each country to fashion agricultural and economic policies in order to realize its unique potential. Countries like India in the late 1960s or Malawi in the last few years give a sense of how to exploit the possibilities for expanding food supplies.

Raising Water Productivity

With water shortages constraining food production growth, the world needs an effort to raise water productivity similar to the one that nearly tripled land productivity over the last half-century. Since it takes 1,000 tons of water to produce 1 ton of grain, it is not surprising that 70 percent of world water use is devoted to irrigation. Thus, raising irrigation efficiency is central to raising water productivity overall.[25]

Data on the efficiency of surface of water projects—that is, dams that deliver water to farmers through a network of canals—show that crop usage of irrigation water never reaches 100 percent simply because some irrigation water evaporates, some percolates downward, and some runs off. Water policy analysts Sandra Postel and Amy Vickers found that "surface water irrigation efficiency ranges between 25 and 40 percent in India, Mexico, Pakistan, the Philippines, and Thailand; between 40 and 45 percent in Malaysia and Morocco; and between 50 and 60 percent in Israel, Japan, and Taiwan."[26]

Irrigation water efficiency is affected not only by the type and condition of irrigation systems but also by soil type, temperature, and humidity. In hot arid regions, the evaporation of irrigation water is far higher than in cooler humid regions.

In a May 2004 meeting, China's Minister of Water Resources Wang Shucheng outlined for me in some detail the plans to raise China's irrigation efficiency from 43 percent in 2000 to 51 percent in 2010 and then to 55 percent in 2030. The steps he described included raising the price of water, providing incentives for adopting more irrigation-efficient technologies, and developing the local institutions to manage this process. Reaching these goals, he felt, would assure China's future food security.[27]

Raising irrigation efficiency typically means shifting from the less efficient flood or furrow systems to overhead sprinklers or drip irrigation, the gold standard of irrigation efficiency. Switching from flood or furrow to low-pressure sprinkler systems reduces water use by an estimated 30 percent, while switching to drip irrigation typically cuts water use in half.[28]

As an alternative to furrow irrigation, a drip system also raises yields because it provides a steady supply of water with minimal losses to evaporation. Since drip systems are both labor-intensive and water-efficient, they are well suited to countries with a surplus of labor and a shortage of water. A few small countries—Cyprus, Israel, and Jordan—rely heavily on drip irrigation. Among the big three agricultural producers, this more-efficient technology is used on 1–3 percent of irrigated land in India and China and on roughly 4 percent in the United States.[29]

In recent years, small-scale drip-irrigation systems—literally a bucket with flexible plastic tubing to distribute the water—have been developed to irrigate small vegetable gardens with roughly 100 plants (covering 25 square meters). Somewhat larger systems using drums irrigate 125 square meters. In both cases, the containers are elevated slightly, so that gravity distributes the water. Large-scale drip systems using plastic lines that can be moved easily are also becoming popular. These simple systems can pay for themselves in one year. By simultaneously reducing water costs and raising yields, they can dramatically raise incomes of smallholders.[30]

Sandra Postel estimates that drip technology has the potential to profitably irrigate 10 million hectares of India's cropland, nearly one tenth of the total. She sees a similar potential for China, which is now also expanding its drip irrigated area to save scarce water.[31]

In the Punjab, with its extensive double cropping of wheat and rice, fast-falling water tables led the state farmers' commission in 2007 to recommend a delay in transplanting rice from May to late June or early July. This would reduce irrigation water use by roughly one third, since transplanting would coincide with the arrival of the monsoon. The resulting reduction in groundwater use would help stabilize the water table, which has fallen from 5 meters below the surface down to 30 meters in parts of the state.[32]

Institutional shifts—specifically, moving the responsibility for managing irrigation systems from government agencies to local water users associations—can facilitate the more efficient use of water. In many countries farmers are organizing locally so they can assume this responsibility, and since they have an economic stake in good water management, they tend to do a better job than a distant government agency.

Mexico is a leader in developing water users associations. As of 2008, farmers associations managed more than 99 percent of the irrigated area held in public irrigation districts. One advantage of this shift for the government is that the cost of maintaining the irrigation system is assumed locally, reducing the drain on the treasury. This means that associations often need to charge more for irrigation water, but for farmers the production gains from managing their water supply themselves more than outweigh this additional outlay.[33]

In Tunisia, where water users associations manage both irrigation and residential water, the number of associations increased from 340 in 1987 to 2,575 in 1999, covering much of the country. As of 2009, China has more than 40,000 water users associations to locally manage water resources and to maximize water use efficiency. Many other countries now have similar bodies. Although the first groups were organized to deal with large publicly developed irrigation systems, some recent ones have been formed to manage local groundwater irrigation as well. Their goal is to stabilize the water table to avoid aquifer depletion and the economic disruption that it brings to the community.[34]

Low water productivity is often the result of low water prices. In many countries, subsidies lead to irrationally low water prices, creating the impression that water is abundant when in fact it is scarce. As water becomes scarce, it needs to be priced accordingly.

A new mindset is needed, a new way of thinking about water use. For example, shifting to more water-efficient crops wherever possible boosts water productivity. Rice production is being phased out around Beijing because rice is such a thirsty crop. Similarly, Egypt restricts rice production in favor of wheat.[35]

Any measures that raise crop yields on irrigated land also raise the productivity of irrigation water. For people consuming unhealthy amounts of livestock products, moving down the food chain reduces water use. In the United States, where the annual consumption of grain as food and feed averages some 800 kilograms (four fifths of a ton) per person, a modest reduction in the consumption of meat, milk, and eggs could easily cut grain use per person by 100 kilograms. For 300 million Americans, such a reduction would cut grain use by 30 million tons and the need for irrigation water by 30 billion tons.[36]

Bringing water use down to the sustainable yield of aquifers and rivers worldwide involves a wide range of measures not only in agriculture but throughout the economy. The more obvious steps, in addition to more water-efficient irrigation practices and water-efficient crops, include adopting more water-efficient industrial processes and using both more water-efficient household appliances and those such as the new odorless dry-compost toilets that use no water at all. Recycling urban water supplies is another obvious step in countries facing acute water shortages.

Producing Protein More Efficiently

Another way to raise both land and water productivity is to produce animal protein more efficiently. With some 36 percent (750 million tons) of the world grain harvest used to produce animal protein, even a modest gain in efficiency can save a large quantity of grain.[37]

World meat consumption increased from 44 million tons in 1950 to 260 million tons in 2007, more than doubling annual consumption per person from 17 kilograms to 39 kilograms (86 pounds). Consumption of milk and eggs has also risen. In every society where incomes have risen, so has meat consumption, reflecting a taste that evolved over 4 million years of hunting and gathering.[38]

As both the oceanic fish catch and the production of beef on rangelands have leveled off, the world has shifted to grain-based production of animal protein to expand output. Within the meat economy, both health concerns and price differences are shifting consumer demand from beef and pork to poultry and fish, sources that convert grain into protein most efficiently.

The efficiency with which various animals convert grain into protein varies widely. With cattle in feedlots, it takes roughly 7 kilograms of grain to produce a 1-kilogram gain in live weight. For pork, the figure is over 3 kilograms of grain per kilogram of weight gain, for poultry it is just over 2, and for herbivorous species of farmed fish (such as carp, tilapia, and catfish), it is less than 2. As the market shifts production to the more grain-efficient products, it raises the productivity of both land and water.[39]

Global beef production, most of which comes from rangelands, grew less than 1 percent a year from 1990 to 2007. Growth in the number of cattle feedlots was minimal. Pork production grew by 2 percent annually, and poultry by nearly 5 percent. World pork production, nearly half of it now in China, overtook beef production in 1979 and has continued to widen the lead since then. The growth in poultry production from 41 million tons in 1990 to 88 million tons in 2007 enabled poultry to eclipse beef in 1995, moving into second place behind pork.[40]

Fast-growing, highly grain-efficient world fish farm output may also overtake world beef production in the next few years. In fact, aquaculture has been the fastest-growing source of animal protein since 1990, largely because herbivorous fish convert feed into protein so efficiently. Aquacultural output expanded from 13 million tons in 1990 to 50 million tons in 2007, growing by more than 8 percent a year.[41]

Public attention has focused on aquacultural operations that are environmentally inefficient or disruptive, such as the farming of salmon, a carnivorous species, and shrimp. These operations account for slightly more than 10 percent of the world's farmed fish output. Salmon are inefficient in that they are fed other fish, usually as fishmeal, which comes either from fish processing wastes or from low-value fish caught specifically for this purpose. Shrimp farming often involves the destruction of coastal mangrove forests to create areas for the shrimp. Farming salmon and shrimp in offshore ponds concentrates waste, contributing to eutrophication and dead zone creation.[42]

Worldwide, however, aquaculture is dominated by herbivorous species—mainly carp in China and India, but also catfish in the United States and tilapia in several countries—and shellfish. This is where the great growth potential for efficient animal protein production lies.

China accounts for 62 percent of global fish farm production. Its output is dominated by finfish (mostly carp), which are grown in inland freshwater ponds, lakes, reservoirs, and rice paddies, and by shellfish (mostly oysters, clams, and mussels), which are produced mostly in coastal regions.[43]

Over time, China has developed a fish polyculture using four types of carp that feed at different levels of the food chain, in effect emulating natural aquatic ecosystems. Silver and bighead carp are filter feeders, eating phytoplankton and zooplankton respectively. The grass carp, as its name implies, feeds largely on vegetation, while the common carp is a bottom feeder, living on detritus. These four species thus form a small ecosystem, each filling a particular niche. This multi-species system, which converts feed into high-quality protein with remarkable efficiency, allowed China to produce some 14 million tons of carp in 2007.[44]

While poultry production has grown rapidly in China, as in other developing countries, it has been dwarfed by the phenomenal growth of aquaculture. Today aquacultural output in China—at 31 million tons—is double that of poultry, making it the first large country where fish farming has eclipsed poultry farming.[45]

China's aquaculture is often integrated with agriculture, enabling farmers to use agricultural wastes, such as pig or duck manure, to fertilize ponds, thus stimulating the growth of plankton on which the fish feed. Fish polyculture, which commonly boosts pond productivity over that of monocultures by at least half, is widely practiced in both China and India.[46]

With incomes now rising in densely populated Asia, other countries are following China's aquacultural lead. Among them are Thailand and Viet Nam. Viet Nam, for example, devised a plan in 2001 of developing 700,000 hectares of land in the Mekong Delta for aquaculture, which now produces more than 1 million tons of fish and shrimp.[47]

In the United States, catfish are the leading aquacultural product. U.S. annual catfish production of 515 million pounds (1.6 pounds per person) is concentrated in the South. Mississippi, with half the country's output, is the U.S. catfish capital.[48]

When we want high-quality protein, we typically look to soybeans, as either tofu, veggie burgers, or other meat substitutes. But most of the world's fast-growing soybean harvest is consumed indirectly in the beef, pork, poultry, milk, eggs, and farmed fish that we eat. Although not a visible part of our diets, the incorporation of soybean meal into feed rations has revolutionized the world feed industry.

In 2008, the world's farmers produced 213 million tons of soybeans—1 ton for every 10 tons of grain produced. Of this, some 20 million tons were consumed directly as tofu or meat substitutes. The bulk of the remaining 193 million tons, after some was saved for seed, was crushed in order to extract 36 million tons of soybean oil, separating it from the highly valued, high-protein meal.[49]

The 150 million or so tons of protein-rich soybean meal that remain after the oil is extracted are fed to cattle, pigs, chickens, and fish. Combining soybean meal with grain in roughly one part meal to four parts grain dramatically boosts the efficiency with which grain is converted into animal protein, sometimes nearly doubling it. The world's three largest meat producers—China, the United States, and Brazil—now all rely heavily on soybean meal as a protein supplement in feed rations.[50]

The heavy use of soybean meal to boost the efficiency of feed use helps explain why the share of the world grain harvest used for feed has not increased over the last 20 years even though production of meat, milk, eggs, and farmed fish has climbed. It also explains why world soybean production has increased 13-fold since 1950.[51]

Mounting pressures on land and water resources have led to the evolution of some promising new animal protein production systems that are based on roughage rather than grain, such as milk production in India. Since 1970, India's milk production has increased fivefold, jumping from 21 million to 106 million tons. In 1997 India overtook the United States to become the world's leading producer of milk and other dairy products.[52]

The spark for this explosive growth came in 1965 when an enterprising young Indian, Verghese Kurien, organized the National Dairy Development Board, an umbrella organization of dairy cooperatives. The dairy co-op's principal purpose was to market the milk from tiny herds that typically averaged two to three cows each, thus providing the link between the growing market for dairy products and the millions of village families who each had only a small marketable surplus.[53]

Creating the market for milk spurred the fivefold growth in output. In a country where protein shortages stunt the growth of so many children, expanding the milk supply from less than half a cup per person a day 30 years ago to nearly one cup today represents a major advance.[54]

What is so remarkable is that India has built the world's largest dairy industry almost entirely on crop residues—wheat straw, rice straw, and corn stalks—and grass gathered from the roadside. Even so, the value of the milk produced each year now exceeds that of the rice harvest.[55]

A second new protein production model, one that also relies on ruminants and roughage, has evolved in four provinces in eastern China—Hebei, Shangdong, Henan, and Anhui—where double cropping of winter wheat and corn is common. Although wheat straw and cornstalks are often used as fuel for cooking, villagers are shifting to other sources of energy for this, which lets them feed the straw and cornstalks to cattle.[56]

These four crop-producing provinces in China, dubbed the Beef Belt by officials, use crop residues to produce much more beef than the vast grazing provinces in the northwest do. The use of crop residues to produce milk in India and beef in China lets farmers reap a second harvest from the original grain crop, thus boosting both land and water productivity. Similar systems can be adopted in other countries as population pressures intensify, as demand for meat and milk increases, and as farmers seek new ways to convert plant products into animal protein.[57]

The world desperately needs new more-efficient protein production techniques such as these. Meat consumption is growing almost twice as fast as population, egg consumption is growing more than twice as fast, and growth in the demand for fish—both from the oceans and from fish farms—is also outpacing that of population.[58]

While the world has had decades of experience in feeding an additional 70 million people each year, it has no experience with some 3 billion people striving to move up the food chain. For a sense of what this translates into, consider what has happened in China, where record economic growth has in effect telescoped history, showing how rapidly diets change when incomes rise. As recently as 1978, meat consumption in China consisted mostly of modest amounts of pork. Since then, consumption of meat, including pork, beef, poultry, and mutton, has climbed severalfold, pushing China's total meat consumption far above that of the United States.[59]

The Localization of Agriculture

In the United States, there has been a surge of interest in eating fresh local foods, corresponding with mounting concerns about the climate effects of consuming food from distant places and about the obesity and other health problems associated with junk food diets. This is reflected in the rise in urban gardening, school gardening, and farmers' markets.[60]

With the fast-growing local foods movement, diets are

becoming more locally shaped and more seasonal. In a typical supermarket in an industrial country today it is often difficult to tell what season it is because the store tries to make everything available on a year-round basis. As oil prices rise, this will become less common. In essence, a reduction in the use of oil to transport food over long distances—whether by plane, truck, or ship—will also localize the food economy.

This trend toward localization is reflected in the recent rise in the number of farms in the United States, which may be the reversal of a century-long trend of farm consolidation. Between the agricultural census of 2002 and that of 2007, the number of farms in the United States increased by 4 percent to roughly 2.2 million. The new farms were mostly small, many of them operated by women, whose numbers in farming jumped from 238,000 in 2002 to 306,000 in 2007, a rise of nearly 30 percent.[61]

Many of the new farms cater to local markets. Some produce fresh fruits and vegetables exclusively for farmers' markets or for their own roadside stands. Others produce specialized products, such as the goat farms that produce milk, cheese, and meat or the farms that grow flowers or wood for fireplaces. Others specialize in organic food. The number of organic farms in the United States jumped from 12,000 in 2002 to 18,200 in 2007, increasing by half in five years.[62]

Gardening was given a big boost in the spring of 2009 when U.S. First Lady Michelle Obama worked with children from a local school to dig up a piece of lawn by the White House to start a vegetable garden. There was a precedent. Eleanor Roosevelt planted a White House victory garden during World War II. Her initiative encouraged millions of victory gardens that eventually grew 40 percent of the nation's fresh produce.[63]

Although it was much easier to expand home gardening during World War II, when the United States was largely a rural society, there is still a huge gardening potential—given that the grass lawns surrounding U.S. residences collectively cover some 18 million acres. Converting even a small share of this to fresh vegetables and fruit trees could make an important contribution to improving nutrition.[64]

Many cities and small towns in the United States and England are creating community gardens that can be used by those who would otherwise not have access to land for gardening.

Providing space for community gardens is seen by many local governments as an essential service, like providing playgrounds for children or tennis courts and other sport facilities.[65]

Many market outlets are opening up for local produce. Perhaps the best known of these are the farmers' markets where local farmers bring their produce for sale. In the United States, the number of these markets increased from 1,755 in 1994 to more than 4,700 in mid-2009, nearly tripling over 15 years. Farmers' markets reestablish personal ties between producers and consumers that do not exist in the impersonal confines of the supermarket. Many farmers' markets also now take food stamps, giving low-income consumers access to fresh produce that they might not otherwise be able to afford. With so many trends now boosting interest in these markets, their numbers may grow even faster in the future.[66]

In school gardens, children learn how food is produced, a skill often lacking in urban settings, and they may get their first taste of freshly picked peas or vine-ripened tomatoes. School gardens also provide fresh produce for school lunches. California, a leader in this area, has 6,000 school gardens.[67]

Many schools and universities are now making a point of buying local food because it is fresher, tastier, and more nutritious and it fits into new campus greening programs. Some universities compost kitchen and cafeteria food waste and make the compost available to the farmers who supply them with fresh produce.

Supermarkets are increasingly contracting with local farmers during the season when locally grown produce is available. Upscale restaurants emphasize locally grown food on their menus. In some cases, year-round food markets are evolving that market just locally produced foods, including not only fruit and vegetables but also meat, milk, cheese, eggs, and other farm products.[68]

Food from more distant locations boosts carbon emissions while losing flavor and nutrition. A survey of food consumed in Iowa showed conventional produce traveled on average 1,500 miles, not including food imported from other countries. In contrast, locally grown produce traveled on average 56 miles—a huge difference in fuel investment. And a study in Ontario, Canada, found that 58 imported foods traveled an average of 2,800 miles. Simply put, consumers are worried about food security in a long-distance food economy. This trend has led to a new term: locavore, complementing the better known terms herbivore, carnivore, and omnivore.[69]

Concerns about the climate effects of consuming food transported from distant locations has also led Tesco, the leading U.K. supermarket chain, to label products with their carbon footprint—indicating the greenhouse gas contribution of food items from the farm to supermarket shelf.[70]

The shift from factory farm production of milk, meat, and eggs by returning to mixed crop-livestock operations also facilitates nutrient recycling as local farmers return livestock manure to the land. The combination of high prices of natural gas, which is used to make nitrogen fertilizer, and of phosphate, as reserves are depleted, suggests a much greater future emphasis on nutrient recycling—an area where small farmers producing for local markets have a distinct advantage over massive feeding operations.[71]

Strategic Reductions in Demand

Despite impressive local advances, the global loss of momentum in expanding food production is forcing us to think more seriously about reducing demand by stabilizing population, moving down the food chain, and reducing the use of grain to fuel cars.

The Plan B goal is to halt world population growth at no more than 8 billion by 2040. This will require an all-out population education effort to help people everywhere understand how fast the relationship between us and our natural support systems is deteriorating. It also means that we need a crash program to get reproductive health care and birth control services to the 201 million women today who want to plan their families but lack access to the means to do so.[72]

While the effect of population growth on the demand for grain is rather clear, that of rising affluence is much less so. One of the questions I am often asked is, "How many people can the earth support?" I answer with another question: "At what level of food consumption?" Using round numbers, at the U.S. level of 800 kilograms of grain per person annually for food and feed, the 2-billion-ton annual world harvest of grain would support 2.5 billion people. At the Italian level of consumption of close to 400 kilograms, the current harvest would support 5 billion people. At the 200 kilograms of grain consumed by the average Indian, it would support 10 billion.[73]

Of the roughly 800 kilograms of grain consumed per person each year in the United States, about 100 kilograms is eaten directly as bread, pasta, and breakfast cereals, while the bulk of the grain is consumed indirectly in the form of livestock and poultry products. By contrast, in India, where people consume just under 200 kilograms of grain per year, or roughly a pound per day, nearly all grain is eaten directly to satisfy basic food energy needs. Little is available for conversion into livestock products.[74]

Among the United States, Italy, and India, life expectancy is highest in Italy even though U.S. medical expenditures per person are much higher. People who live very low or very high on the food chain do not live as long as those at an intermediate level. People consuming a Mediterranean-type diet that includes meat, cheese, and seafood, but all in moderation, are healthier and live longer. People living high on the food chain can improve their health by moving down the food chain. For those who live in low-income countries like India, where a starchy staple such as rice can supply 60 percent or more of total caloric intake, eating more protein-rich foods can improve health and raise life expectancy.[75]

Although we seldom consider the climate effect of various dietary options, they are substantial, to say the least. Gidon Eshel and Pamela A. Martin of the University of Chicago have studied this issue. They begin by noting that for Americans the energy used to provide the typical diet and that used for personal transportation are roughly the same. They calculate that the range between the more and less carbon-intensive transportation options and dietary options is each about four to one. The Toyota Prius, for instance, uses roughly one fourth as much fuel as a Chevrolet Suburban SUV. Similarly with diets, a plant-based diet requires roughly one fourth as much energy as a diet rich in red meat. Shifting from the latter to a plant-based diet cuts greenhouse gas emissions almost as much as shifting from a Suburban to a Prius would.[76]

Shifting from the more grain-intensive to the less grain-intensive forms of animal protein can also reduce pressure on the earth's land and water resources. For example, shifting from grain-fed beef that requires roughly 7 pounds of grain concentrate for each additional pound of live weight to poultry or catfish, which require roughly 2 pounds of grain per pound of live weight, substantially reduces grain use.[77]

When considering how much animal protein to consume, it is useful to distinguish between grass-fed and grain-fed products. For example, most of the world's beef is produced with grass. Even in the United States, with an abundance of feedlots, over half of all beef cattle weight gain comes from grass rather than grain. The global area of grasslands, which is easily double the world cropland area and which is usually too steeply sloping or too arid to plow, can contribute to the food supply only if it is used for grazing to produce meat, milk, and cheese.[78]

Beyond the role of grass in providing high-quality protein in our diets, it is sometimes assumed that we can increase the efficiency of land and water use by shifting from animal protein to high-quality plant protein, such as that from soybeans. It turns out, however, that since corn yields in the U.S. Midwest are three to four times those of soybeans, it may be more resource-efficient to produce corn and convert it into poultry or catfish at a ratio of two to one than to have everyone heavily reliant on soy.[79]

Although population growth has been a source of growing demand ever since agriculture began, the large-scale conversion of grain into animal protein emerged only after World War II. The massive conversion of grain into fuel for cars began just a few years ago. If we are to reverse the spread of hunger, we will almost certainly have to reduce the latter use of grain. Remember, the estimated 104 million tons of grain used to produce ethanol in 2009 in the United States is the food supply for 340 million people at average world grain consumption levels.[80]

Quickly shifting to smaller families, moving down the food chain either by consuming less animal protein or by turning to more grain-efficient animal protein sources, and removing the incentives for converting food into fuel will help ensure that everyone has enough to eat. It will also lessen the pressures that lead to overpumping of groundwater and the clearing of tropical rainforests, helping us to reach the Plan B goals.

Action on Many Fronts

In this new food era, ensuring future food security depends on elevating responsibility for it from the minister of agriculture's office to that of the head of state. The minister of agriculture, no matter how competent, can no longer be expected to secure food supplies. Policies in the ministry of energy may affect food security more than those in the ministry of agriculture do. Efforts by the minister of health and family planning to accelerate the shift to smaller families may have a greater effect on food security than efforts in the ministry of agriculture to raise crop yields.

If ministries of energy cannot quickly cut carbon emissions, as outlined earlier, the world will face crop-shrinking heat waves that can massively and unpredictably reduce harvests. A hotter world will mean melting ice sheets, rising sea level, and the inundation of the highly productive rice-growing river deltas of Asia. Saving the mountain glaciers whose ice melt irrigates much of the world's cropland is the responsibility of the ministry of energy, not the ministry of agriculture.

If the world's ministers of energy cannot collectively formulate policies to cut carbon emissions quickly, the loss of glaciers in the Himalayas and on the Tibetan Plateau will shrink wheat and rice harvests in both India and China. If ministries of water resources cannot quickly raise water productivity and arrest the depletion of aquifers, grain harvests will shrink not only in smaller countries like Saudi Arabia and Yemen but also in larger countries, such as India and China. If we continue with business as usual, these two countries, the world's most populous, will face water shortages driven by both aquifer depletion and melting glaciers.

If the ministries of forestry and agriculture cannot work together to restore tree cover and reduce floods and soil erosion, then we face a situation where grain harvests will shrink not only in smaller countries like Haiti and Mongolia, but also in larger countries, such as Russia and Argentina—both wheat exporters.

And where water is a more serious constraint on expanding food output than land, it will be up to ministries of water resources to do everything possible to raise the efficiency of water use. With water, as with energy, the principal opportunities now are in increasing efficiency on the demand side, not in expanding the supply side.

In a world where cropland is scarce and becoming more so, decisions made in ministries of transportation on whether to develop land-consuming, auto-centered transport systems or more-diversified systems, including light rail, buses, and bicycles that are much less land-intensive, will directly affect world food security.

Now in our overpopulated, climate-changing, water-scarce world, food security is a matter for the entire society and for all government ministries. Since hunger is almost always the result of poverty, eradicating hunger depends on eradicating poverty. And where populations are outrunning their land and water resources, this depends on stabilizing population.

And finally, if ministries of finance cannot reallocate resources in a way that recognizes the new threats to security posed by agriculture's deteriorating natural support systems, continuing population growth, human-driven climate change, and spreading water shortages, then food shortages could indeed bring down civilization.

Given that a handful of the more affluent grain-importing countries are reportedly investing some $20–30 billion in land acquisition, there is no shortage of capital to invest in agricultural development. Why not invest it across the board in helping low-income countries develop their unrealized potential for expanding food production, enabling them to export more grain?[81]

One way to quickly reverse this deteriorating political situation is for the United States to restrict the use of grain to produce fuel for cars. Given the turmoil in world grain markets over the last three years, it is time for the U.S. government to abolish the subsidies and mandates that are driving the conversion of grain into fuel. That would help stabilize grain prices and set the stage for relaxing the political tensions that have emerged within importing countries.

And finally, we have a role to play as individuals. Whether we bike, bus, or drive to work will affect carbon emissions, climate change, and food security. The size of the car we drive to the supermarket and its effect on climate may indirectly affect the size of the bill at the supermarket checkout counter. If we are living high on the food chain, we can move down, improving our health while helping to stabilize climate. Food security is something in which we all have a stake—and a responsibility.

III
THE GREAT MOBILIZATION

10

Can We Mobilize Fast Enough?

There is much that we do not know about the future. But one thing we do know is that business as usual will not continue for much longer. Massive change is inevitable. "The death of our civilization is no longer a theory or an academic possibility; it is the road we're on," says Peter Goldmark, former Rockefeller Foundation president and current director of the climate program at the Environmental Defense Fund (EDF). Can we find another road before time runs out?[1]

The notion that our civilization is approaching its demise is not an easy concept to grasp or accept. It is difficult to imagine something we have not previously experienced. We hardly have the vocabulary, much less the experience, to discuss this prospect. We know which economic indicators to watch for signs of an economic recession, such as declining industrial output, rising unemployment, or falling consumer confidence, but we do not follow a similar set of indicators that signal civilizational collapse.

Given the role of food shortages in earlier civilizational declines, we obviously should watch food price and hunger trends closely. The growing number of hungry people, the projected continuation of this trend, and the lack of a plan to reverse it should be a matter of concern to political leaders everywhere.[2]

Neither spreading hunger nor the threat of it unfolds in a political vacuum. Affluent grain-importing countries are buying large tracts of land in poorer countries in the emerging cross-border competition for control of land and water resources. This opens a new chapter in the geopolitics of food scarcity. Where ultimately does this lead? We do not know. We have not been here before.

In many ways, the most basic indicator of our plight is the number of failing states. Each year this list grows longer. How many states must fail before our global civilization begins to unravel? Again, we do not know the answer because we have not been here before.

Our future depends on reversing both the spread of hunger and the growing number of failing states, but this will not happen if we continue with business as usual. Turning this situation around will take a worldwide, wartime-like mobilization. We call it Plan B. This plan, or something similar to it, is our only way out.

Plan B embraces a massive mobilization to restructure the world economy—and at wartime speed. The closest analogy is the belated U.S. mobilization during World War II. But unlike that chapter in history, in which one country totally restructured its industrial economy in a matter of months, the Plan B mobilization requires decisive action on a global scale.

The four mutually dependent Plan B goals—stabilizing climate, stabilizing population, eradicating poverty, and restoring the economy's natural support systems—are all essential to restoring food security. It's unlikely that we can reach any one without reaching the others.

Eradicating poverty is not only the key to population stabilization, political stabilization, and a better life, it also provides hope. As Nobel laureate Mohammed Yunus, founder of the Grameen Bank for micro-credit in Bangladesh, has pointed out, "Poverty leads to hopelessness, which provokes people to desperate acts."[3]

Stabilizing population not only helps eradicate poverty, it makes it easier to reach almost every other goal that we seek. On a finite planet, where we are pushing the earth beyond its limits, every country should have a population stabilization policy.

As noted in Chapter 7, international assistance programs require a special initiative, a unique component, to rescue failing states. Just as hospitals have intensive care units that give special attention to the most seriously ill, so too international assistance programs need a special facility to deal with seriously ill nation states.

We know from our analysis of climate change, from the accelerating deterioration of the economy's ecological supports, and from our projections of future resource use that the western economic model—the fossil-fuel-based, automobile-centered, throwaway economy—will not last much longer. We need to build a new economy, one that will be powered by renewable sources of energy, that will have a diversified transport system, and that will reuse and recycle everything.

We can describe this new economy in some detail. The question is, How do we get from here to there before time runs out? In effect, we are in a race between political tipping points and natural tipping points. Can we reach the political tipping point that will enable us to cut carbon emissions before we reach the point where the melting of the Himalayan glaciers becomes irreversible? Will we be able to halt the deforestation of the Amazon before it dries out, becomes vulnerable to fire from natural causes, and turns into wasteland?

The key to building a global economy that can sustain economic progress is the creation of an honest market, one that tells the ecological truth. To create an honest market, we need to restructure the tax system by reducing taxes on work and raising those on carbon emissions and other environmentally destructive activities, thus incorporating indirect costs into the market price.

If we can get the market to tell the truth, then we can avoid being blindsided by a faulty accounting system that leads to bankruptcy. As Øystein Dahle, former Vice President of Exxon for Norway and the North Sea, has observed: "Socialism collapsed because it did not allow the market to tell the economic truth. Capitalism may collapse because it does not allow the market to tell the ecological truth."[4]

Some countries are recognizing the need for bold dramatic

change. Several governments have announced that they plan to become carbon-neutral, including Norway, Costa Rica, and the Maldives. They have formally joined the Climate Neutral Network launched by the U.N. Environment Programme (UNEP) in 2008. The Maldives, a low-lying island country of 385,000 people that is threatened by rising seas, is on a fast track, planning to systematically develop its wind and solar resources to replace fossil fuels and reach carbon neutrality by 2019. Costa Rica is shooting for 2021. The Maldives and Costa Rica are the first countries to adopt a carbon reduction goal more ambitious than that of Plan B.[5]

Achim Steiner, Executive Director of UNEP, describes climate neutrality as "an idea whose time has come, driven by the urgent need to address climate change but also the abundant economic opportunities emerging for those willing to embrace a transition to a Green Economy." By far the most effective policy tool in striving for carbon neutrality is restructuring taxes and subsidies.[6]

Shifting Taxes and Subsidies

The need for tax shifting—lowering taxes on income while raising those on environmentally destructive activities—has been widely endorsed by economists. For example, a tax on coal that incorporates the increased health care costs associated with mining it and breathing the air it pollutes, the costs of damage from acid rain, and the costs of climate disruption would encourage investment in clean renewable sources of energy such as wind and solar.[7]

A market that is allowed to ignore the indirect costs in pricing goods and services is irrational, wasteful, and self-destructive The first step in creating an honest market is to calculate indirect costs. Perhaps the best model for this is a U.S. government study on smoking from the Centers for Disease Control and Prevention (CDC). In 2006 the CDC calculated the cost to society of smoking cigarettes—including both the cost of treating smoking-related illnesses and the lost worker productivity from these illnesses—at $10.47 per pack.[8]

This calculation provides a framework for raising taxes on cigarettes. In New York City, smokers now pay $4.25 per pack in state and local cigarette taxes. Chicago is not far behind at

$3.66 per pack. Among states, Rhode Island has the highest tax at $3.46 per pack. Since a 10-percent price rise typically reduces smoking by 4 percent, the health benefits of tax increases are substantial.[9]

For a gasoline tax, the most detailed analysis available of indirect costs is found in *The Real Price of Gasoline* by the International Center for Technology Assessment. The many indirect costs to society—including climate change, oil industry tax breaks, oil supply protection, oil industry subsidies, and treatment of auto exhaust-related respiratory illnesses—total around $12 per gallon ($3.17 per liter), marginally more than the cost to society of smoking a pack of cigarettes. If this external or social cost is added to the roughly $3 per gallon average price of gasoline in the United States, a gallon would cost $15. These are real costs. Someone bears them. If not us, our children.[10]

Gasoline's indirect cost of $12 a gallon provides a reference point for raising taxes to where the price reflects the environmental truth. Gasoline taxes in Italy, France, Germany, and the United Kingdom—averaging $4 per gallon—are a good start. The average U.S. gas tax of 46¢ per gallon, scarcely one tenth that in Europe, helps explain why the United States uses more gasoline than the next 20 countries combined. The high gasoline taxes in Europe have contributed to an oil-efficient economy and to far greater investment in high-quality public transportation over the decades, making it less vulnerable to oil supply disruptions.[11]

Phasing in an incremental gasoline tax rising by 40¢ per gallon per year for the next 10 years and offsetting it with a reduction in income taxes would raise the U.S. gas tax to the $4 per gallon tax prevailing today in Europe. This will still fall short of the $12 of indirect costs currently associated with burning a gallon of gasoline, but combined with the rising price of producing gasoline and the far smaller carbon tax discussed earlier, it should be enough to encourage motorists to use improved public transport and to buy the plug-in hybrid and all-electric cars as they come to market, starting in 2010.

These carbon and gasoline taxes may seem high, but again we look to smoking for at least one dramatic precedent. A series of lawsuits led the U.S. tobacco industry in November of 1998 to agree to reimburse state governments with a cumulative sum of $251 billion for the Medicare costs of treating smoking-related illnesses—nearly $1,000 for every person in the United States. This landmark agreement was, in effect, a retroactive tax on cigarettes smoked in the past, one designed to cover indirect costs. To pay this enormous bill, companies raised cigarette prices, bringing them closer to their true costs and further discouraging smoking.[12]

Tax shifting is not new in Europe. A four-year plan adopted in Germany in 1999 systematically shifted taxes from labor to energy. By 2003, this plan had reduced annual carbon dioxide (CO_2) emissions by 20 million tons and helped to create approximately 250,000 additional jobs. It also accelerated growth in the renewable energy sector; by 2006 there were 82,100 jobs in the wind industry alone, a number that is projected to rise by another 60,000 jobs by 2010.[13]

Between 2001 and 2006, Sweden shifted an estimated $2 billion of taxes from income to environmentally destructive activities. Much of this shift of $500 or so per household was levied on road transport, including hikes in vehicle and fuel taxes. France, Italy, Norway, Spain, and the United Kingdom are among the countries also using this policy instrument. In Europe and the United States, polls indicate that at least 70 percent of voters support environmental tax shifting once it is explained to them.[14]

Some 2,500 economists, including nine Nobel Prize winners in economics, have endorsed the concept of tax shifts. Harvard economics professor and former chairman of George W. Bush's Council of Economic Advisors N. Gregory Mankiw wrote in *Fortune* magazine: "Cutting income taxes while increasing gasoline taxes would lead to more rapid economic growth, less traffic congestion, safer roads, and reduced risk of global warming—all without jeopardizing long-term fiscal solvency. This may be the closest thing to a free lunch that economics has to offer."[15]

Environmental taxes are now being used for several purposes. Landfill taxes that discourage waste and encourage recycling are becoming more common. A number of cities are now taxing cars that enter the city. Others are simply imposing a tax on automobile ownership. In Denmark, the registration tax on the purchase of a new car exceeds the price of the car by 180 percent. A new car that sells for $20,000 costs the buyer $56,000. In Singapore, the tax on a $14,200 Ford Focus, for example, more than triples the price, pushing it to $45,500. Other governments are moving in this direction. In Shanghai, the registration fee in 2009 averaged $4,500 per car.[16]

Cap-and-trade systems using tradable permits are sometimes an alternative to environmental tax restructuring. The principal difference between them is that with permits, governments set the amount of a given activity that is allowed, such as the harvest from a fishery, and let the market set the price of the permits as they are auctioned off. With environmental taxes, in contrast, the price of the environmentally destructive activity is incorporated in the tax rate, and the market determines the amount of the activity that will occur at that price. Both economic instruments can be used to discourage environmentally irresponsible behavior.

The use of cap-and-trade systems with marketable permits has been effective at the national level, ranging from restricting the catch in an Australian fishery to reducing sulfur emissions in the United States. For example, the government of Australia, concerned about lobster overharvesting, estimated the sustainable yield of lobsters and issued catch permits totaling that amount. Fishers could then bid for these permits. In effect, the government decided how many lobsters could be taken each year and let the market decide what the permits were worth. Since the permit trading system was adopted in 1992, the fishery has stabilized and appears to be operating on a sustainable basis.[17]

Although tradable permits are popular in the business community, permits are administratively more complicated and not as well understood as taxes. Edwin Clark, former senior economist with the White House Council on Environmental Quality, observes that tradable permits "require establishing complex regulatory frameworks, defining the permits, establishing the rules for trades, and preventing people from acting without permits." In contrast to paying taxes, something with which there is wide familiarity, tradable permits are a concept not widely understood by the public, making it more difficult to generate broad public support.[18]

The other side of the tax shifting coin is subsidy shifting. Each year the world's taxpayers provide an estimated $700 billion of subsidies for environmentally destructive activities, such as fossil fuel burning, overpumping aquifers, clearcutting forests, and overfishing. An Earth Council study, *Subsidizing Unsustainable Development*, observes that "there is something unbelievable about the world spending hundreds of billions of dollars annually to subsidize its own destruction."[19]

Carbon emissions could be cut in scores of countries by simply eliminating fossil fuel subsidies. Iran provides a classic example of extreme subsidies when it prices oil for internal use at one tenth the world price, strongly encouraging car ownership and gas consumption. If its $37-billion annual subsidy were phased out, the World Bank reports, Iran's carbon emissions would drop by a staggering 49 percent. This move would also strengthen the economy by freeing up public revenues for investment in the country's economic development. Iran is not alone. The Bank reports that removing energy subsidies would reduce carbon emissions in India by 14 percent, in Indonesia by 11 percent, in Russia by 17 percent, and in Venezuela by 26 percent.[20]

Some countries are already doing this. Belgium, France, and Japan have phased out all subsidies for coal. Germany reduced its coal subsidy from a high of 6.7 billion euros in 1996 to 2.5 billion euros in 2007. Coal use dropped by 34 percent between 1991 and 2006. Germany plans to phase out this support entirely by 2018. As oil prices have climbed, a number of countries have greatly reduced or eliminated subsidies that held fuel prices well below world market prices because of the heavy fiscal cost. Among these are China, Indonesia, and Nigeria.[21]

A study by the U.K. Green Party, *Aviation's Economic Downside*, describes subsidies to the U.K. airline industry. The giveaway begins with $18 billion in tax breaks, including a total exemption from the national tax. External or indirect costs that are not paid, such as treating illness from breathing the air polluted by planes, the costs of climate change, and so forth, add nearly $7.5 billion to the tab. The subsidy in the United Kingdom totals $426 per resident. This is also an inherently regressive tax policy simply because a part of the U.K. population cannot afford to fly, yet they help subsidize this high-cost travel for their more affluent compatriots.[22]

While some leading industrial countries have been reducing subsidies to fossil fuels—notably coal, the most climate-disrupting of all fuels—the United States has increased its support for the fossil fuel and nuclear industries. Doug Koplow, founder of Earth Track, calculated in a 2006 study that annual U.S. federal energy subsidies have a total value to the industry of $74 billion. Of this, the oil and gas industry gets $39 billion, coal $8 billion, and nuclear $9 billion. He notes that since 2006 these numbers "would likely be a good deal higher." At a time when there is a need to conserve oil resources, U.S. taxpayers are subsidizing their depletion.[23]

A world facing economically disruptive climate change can no longer justify subsidies to expand the burning of coal and oil. Shifting these subsidies to the development of climate-benign energy sources such as wind, solar, biomass, and geothermal power will help stabilize the earth's climate. Shifting subsidies from road construction to rail construction could increase mobility in many situations while reducing carbon emissions. And shifting the $22 billion in annual fishing industry subsidies, which encourage destructive overfishing, to the creation of marine parks to regenerate fisheries would be a giant step in restoring oceanic fisheries.[24]

In a troubled world economy, where many governments are facing fiscal deficits, these proposed tax and subsidy shifts can help balance the books, create additional jobs, and save the economy's eco-supports. Tax and subsidy shifting promises greater energy efficiency, cuts in carbon emissions, and reductions in environmental destruction—a win-win-win situation. A carbon tax on coal, for example, that fully incorporated the climate and health costs of burning it would lead to a quick phaseout.

Coal: The Beginning of the End

The past two years have witnessed the emergence of a powerful movement opposing the construction of new coal-fired power plants in the United States. Initially led by environmental groups, both national and local, it has since been joined by prominent national political leaders and many state governors. The principal reason for opposing coal plants is that they are changing the earth's climate. There is also the effect of mercury emissions on health and the 23,600 U.S. deaths each year from power plant air pollution.[25]

Over the last few years the coal industry has suffered one set-back after another. The Sierra Club, which has kept a tally of proposed coal-fired power plants and their fates since 2000, reports that 101 plants have been defeated, with another 59 facing opposition in the courts. Of the 229 plants being tracked, only 23 currently have a chance at gaining the permits necessary to begin construction and eventually come online. Building a coal plant may soon be impossible.[26]

What began as a few local ripples of resistance to coal-fired power quickly evolved into a national tidal wave of grassroots opposition from environmental, health, farm, and community organizations. In a national poll by the Opinion Research Corporation that asked which electricity source people would prefer, only 3 percent chose coal. Despite a heavily funded ad campaign to promote so-called clean coal (one reminiscent of the tobacco industry's earlier efforts to convince people that cigarettes were not unhealthy), the American public is turning against coal.[27]

One of the first major industry setbacks came in early 2007 when a grassroots movement took on Texas-based utility TXU. A coalition headed by the Environmental Defense Fund led a damaging public campaign against plans for 11 new coal-fired power plants. A quick drop in the utility's stock price caused by the media storm prompted a $45-billion buyout offer from the private equity firms Kohlberg Kravis Roberts and Company and Texas Pacific Group. Only after negotiating a ceasefire with EDF and the Natural Resources Defense Council and reducing the number of proposed plants from 11 to 3, thus preserving the value of the company, did the firms proceed with purchasing the utility. It was a major win for the environmental community, which mustered the public support necessary to stop 8 plants outright and impose stricter regulations on the remaining 3. Meanwhile, the energy focus in Texas has shifted to developing its vast resources of wind energy, pushing it ahead of California in wind-generated electricity.[28]

In May 2007, Florida's Public Service Commission refused to license a huge $5.7 billion, 1,960-megawatt coal plant because the utility could not prove that building the plant would be cheaper than investing in conservation, efficiency, and renewable energy sources. This point, made by Earthjustice, a non-profit environmental legal group, combined with widely expressed public opposition to any more coal-fired power plants in Florida, led to the quiet withdrawal of four other coal plant proposals in the state.[29]

Coal's future is also suffering as Wall Street turns its back on the industry. In July 2007, Citigroup downgraded coal company stocks across the board and recommended that its clients switch to other energy stocks. In January 2008, Merrill Lynch also downgraded coal stocks. In early February 2008, investment banks Morgan Stanley, Citi, and J.P. Morgan Chase announced that any future lending for coal-fired power would be contingent on the utilities demonstrating that the plants would be economically viable with the higher costs associated with future federal restrictions on carbon emissions. Later that month, Bank of America announced it would follow suit.[30]

In August 2007, coal took a heavy political hit when U.S. Senate Majority Leader Harry Reid of Nevada, who had been opposing three coal-fired power plants in his own state, announced that he was now against building coal-fired power plants anywhere in the world. Former Vice President Al Gore has also voiced strong opposition to building any coal-fired power plants. So too have many state governors, including those in California, Florida, Michigan, Washington, and Wisconsin.[31]

In her 2009 State of the State address, Governor Jennifer Granholm of Michigan argued that the state should not be importing coal from Montana and Wyoming but instead should be investing in technologies to improve energy efficiency and to tap the renewable resources within Michigan, including wind and solar. This, she said, would create thousands of jobs in the state, helping offset those lost in the automobile industry.[32]

December 2008 brought another major coal industry setback. One of the unresolved burdens haunting this sector, in addition to the emissions of CO_2, is what to do with the coal ash—the remnant of burning coal—that is accumulating in 194 landfills and 161 holding ponds in 47 states. This ash is not an easy material to dispose of since it is laced with arsenic, lead, mercury, and many other toxic materials. The industry's dirty secret came into full public view just before Christmas 2008 when the containment wall of a coal ash pond in eastern Tennessee released a billion gallons of toxic brew.[33]

Unfortunately, the industry does not have a plan for safely

disposing of the 130 million tons of ash produced each year, enough to fill 1 million railroad cars. The dangers are such that the Department of Homeland Security tried to put 44 of the most vulnerable storage facilities on a classified list lest they fall into the hands of terrorists. The spill of toxic coal ash in Tennessee drove another nail into the lid of the coal industry coffin.[34]

In April 2009, the chairman of the powerful U.S. Federal Energy Regulatory Commission, Jon Wellinghoff, observed that the United States may no longer need any additional coal or nuclear power plants. Regulators, investment banks, and political leaders are now beginning to see what has been obvious for some time to climate scientists such as NASA's James Hansen, who says that it makes no sense to build coal-fired power plants when we will have to bulldoze them in a few years.[35]

In April 2007, the U.S. Supreme Court ruled that the Environmental Protection Agency (EPA) is both authorized and obligated to regulate CO_2 emissions under the Clean Air Act. This watershed decision prompted the Environmental Appeals Board of the EPA in November 2008 to conclude that a regional EPA office must address CO_2 emissions before issuing air pollution permits for a new coal-fired power plant. This not only put the brakes on the plant in question but also set a precedent, stalling permits for all other proposed coal plants across the United States. Acting on the same Supreme Court decision, in March 2009 the EPA submitted an endangerment finding to the White House Office of Management and Budget. It confirmed that CO_2 emissions threaten human health and welfare and must be regulated, jeopardizing new coal plants everywhere.[36]

The bottom line is that the United States now has, in effect, a de facto moratorium on the building of new coal-fired power plants. This has led the Sierra Club, the national leader on this issue, to expand its campaign to reduce carbon emissions to include the closing of existing plants.[37]

Given the huge potential for reducing electricity use in the United States, as noted in Chapter 4, this may be much easier than it appears. If the efficiency level of the other 49 states were raised to that of New York, the most energy-efficient state, the energy saved would be sufficient to close 80 percent of the country's coal-fired power plants. The few remaining plants could be shut down by turning to renewable energy—wind farms, solar thermal power plants, solar cell rooftop arrays, and geothermal power and heat.[38]

The handwriting is on the wall. In 2008, only five small coal-fired power plants that were in the planning stage for years were completed, adding 1,400 megawatts of generating capacity to the grid. Meanwhile, nearly 100 new wind farms came online, adding 8,400 megawatts of generating capacity to the grid.[39]

With the likelihood that few, if any, new coal-fired power plants will be approved in the United States, this de facto moratorium will send a message to the world. Denmark and New Zealand have already banned new coal-fired power plants. Other countries are likely to join this effort to cut carbon emissions. Even China, which was building one new coal plant a week, is surging ahead with harnessing renewable energy development and will soon overtake the United States in wind electric generation. These and other developments suggest that the goal of cutting carbon emissions 80 percent by 2020 may be much more attainable than many would have thought.[40]

Stabilizing Climate

Earlier we outlined the need to cut net carbon dioxide emissions 80 percent by 2020 to minimize the future rise in temperature. Here we summarize the Plan B measures for doing so, including both reducing fossil fuel use and increasing biological sequestration.

After energy demand is stabilized by dramatically improving efficiency, replacing fossil fuels with renewable sources of energy for generating electricity and heat will reduce carbon emissions in 2020 by more than 3.2 billion tons. (See Table 10–1.) The biggest single cut in carbon emissions comes from phasing out the use of coal to generate electricity. Other cuts come from eliminating all the oil and 70 percent of the natural gas used to generate electricity.[41]

In the transport sector, the greatly reduced use of oil will eliminate 1.4 billion tons of carbon emissions. This reduction relies heavily on the shift to plug-in hybrid and all-electric cars that will run on carbon-free sources of electricity such as wind. The remainder comes largely from shifting long-haul freight from trucks to trains, electrifying freight and passenger trains, and using green electricity to power them.[42]

Table 10–1. *Plan B Carbon Dioxide Emissions Reductions and Sequestration in 2020*

Action	Amount
	(million tons carbon)
Energy Restructuring	
Replacing fossil fuels with renewables for electricity and heat	3,210
Restructuring the transport system	1,400
Reducing coal and oil use in industry	100
Biological Carbon Sequestration	
Ending net deforestation	1,500
Planting trees to sequester carbon	860
Managing soils to sequester carbon	600
Total Carbon Dioxide Reductions in 2020	7,670
Carbon Dioxide Emissions in 2006	9,350
Percent Reduction from 2006 Baseline	82.0

Source: See endnote 41.

At present, net deforestation of the earth is responsible for an estimated 1.5 billion tons of carbon emissions per year. The Plan B goal is to bring deforestation to a halt by 2020, thus totally eliminating this source of carbon emissions. But we are not content with just halting deforestation. We want to increase the number of trees in order to sequester carbon. Planting trees on deforested areas and marginal lands will sequester more than 860 million tons of carbon each year. The similarly ambitious planting of trees to control flooding, reduce rainfall runoff to recharge aquifers, and protect soils from erosion will take additional carbon out of the atmosphere.[43]

The other initiative to sequester carbon biologically is achieved through land use management. This includes expanding the area of minimum- or no-till cropland, planting more cover crops during the off-season, and using more perennials instead of annuals in cropping patterns. The latter would mean, for example, using less corn and more switchgrass to produce fuel ethanol. These practices can sequester an estimated 600 million tons of carbon per year.[44]

Together, replacing fossil fuels in electricity generation with renewable sources of energy, switching to plug-in hybrid and all-electric cars, shifting to all-electric railways, banning deforestation, and sequestering carbon by planting trees and improving soil management will drop net carbon dioxide emissions in 2020 more than 80 percent below today's levels. This reduction gives us the best chance of keeping atmospheric CO_2 concentrations from topping 400 parts per million, limiting the future rise in temperature.[45]

The most efficient means of restructuring the energy economy to stabilize atmospheric CO_2 levels is a carbon tax. As noted in Chapter 4, we propose a worldwide carbon tax of $200 per ton to be phased in at the rate of $20 per year between 2010 and 2020.

Paid by the primary producers—the oil and coal companies—this tax would permeate the entire fossil fuel energy economy. The tax on coal would be almost double that on natural gas simply because coal has a much higher carbon content. Once a schedule for phasing in the carbon tax and reducing the tax on income is in place, the new prices can be used by all economic decisionmakers to make more intelligent decisions. In contrast to a cap-and-trade approach, in which the price of carbon fluctuates, the price of carbon with tax restructuring is predictable. For investors, this reduction in risk is invaluable.

For countries everywhere, particularly developing ones, the economic good news is that the Plan B energy economy is much more labor-intensive than the fossil-fuel-based economy it is replacing. In Germany, for example, which is a leader in the energy transition, renewable energy industries already employ more workers than the long-standing fossil fuel and nuclear industries do. In a world where expanding employment is a universal goal, this is welcome news indeed.[46]

The restructuring of the energy economy outlined here will not only dramatically drop CO_2 emissions, helping to stabilize climate, it will also eliminate much of the air pollution that we know today. The idea of a pollution-free environment is difficult for us even to imagine, simply because none of us has ever known an energy economy that was not highly polluting. Working in coal mines will be history. Black lung disease will eventually disappear. So too will "code red" alerts warning us to avoid strenuous exercise because of dangerous levels of air pollution.

And, finally, in contrast to investments in oil fields and coal mines, where depletion and abandonment are inevitable, the new energy sources are inexhaustible. While wind turbines, solar cells, and solar thermal systems will all need repair and occasional replacement, to invest in these new energy sources is to invest in energy systems that can last forever. This well will not go dry.

Three Models of Social Change

Can we change fast enough? When thinking about the enormous need for social change as we attempt to move the world economy onto a sustainable path, I find it useful to look at various models of change. Three stand out. One is the catastrophic event model, which I call the Pearl Harbor model, where a dramatic event fundamentally changes how we think and behave. The second model is one where a society reaches a tipping point on a particular issue often after an extended period of gradual change in thinking and attitudes. This I call the Berlin Wall model. The third is the sandwich model of social change, where there is a strong grassroots movement pushing for change on a particular issue that is fully supported by strong political leadership at the top.

The surprise Japanese attack on Pearl Harbor on December 7, 1941, was a dramatic wakeup call. It totally changed how Americans thought about the war. If the American people had been asked on December 6th whether the country should enter World War II, probably 95 percent would have said no. By Monday morning, December 8th, perhaps 95 percent would have said yes.

The weakness of the Pearl Harbor model is that if we have to wait for a catastrophic event to change our behavior, it might be too late. It could lead to stresses that would themselves lead to social collapse. When scientists are asked to identify a possible "Pearl Harbor" scenario on the climate front, they frequently point to the possible breakup of the West Antarctic ice sheet. Relatively small blocks of it have been breaking off for more than a decade now, but huge parts of the sheet could break off, sliding into the ocean.

It is conceivable that this breakup could raise sea level a frightening two or three feet within a matter of years. Unfortunately, if we reach this point it may be too late to cut carbon emissions fast enough to save the remainder of the West Antarctic ice sheet or the Greenland ice sheet, whose melting is also accelerating. This is not the model we want to follow for social change on climate.

The Berlin Wall model is of interest because the wall's dismantling in November 1989 was a visual manifestation of a much more fundamental social change. At some point, the people living in Eastern Europe, buoyed by changes in Moscow, had rejected the great "socialist experiment" with its one-party political system and centrally planned economy. Although it was not anticipated, Eastern Europe experienced a political revolution, an essentially bloodless revolution, that changed the form of government in every country in the region. It had reached a tipping point, but it was not expected. You can search the political science journals of the 1980s in vain for an article warning that Eastern Europe was on the verge of a political revolution. In Washington the Central Intelligence Agency (CIA) "had no idea in January 1989 that a tidal wave of history was about to break upon us," reflected Robert Gates, formerly with the CIA and now U.S. Secretary of Defense, in a 1996 interview.[47]

Many social changes occur when societies reach tipping points or cross key thresholds. Once that happens, change comes rapidly and often unpredictably. One of the best known U.S. tipping points is the growing opposition to smoking that took place during the last half of the twentieth century. This anti-smoking movement was fueled by a steady flow of information on the health-damaging effects of smoking, a process that began with the Surgeon General's first report in 1964 on smoking and health. The tipping point came when this information flow finally overcame the heavily funded disinformation campaign funded by the tobacco industry.[48]

Published almost every year, the Surgeon General's report both drew attention to what was being learned about the effect of smoking on health and spawned countless new research projects on this relationship. There were times in the 1980s and 1990s when it seemed every few weeks another study was being released that had analyzed and documented one health effect or another associated with smoking. Eventually smoking was linked to more than 15 forms of cancer and to heart disease and strokes. As public awareness of the damaging effects of smoking on health accumulated, various measures were adopted that banned smoking on planes and in offices, restaurants, and other public places. As a result of these collective changes, cigarette smoking per person peaked around 1970 and began a long-term decline that continues today.[49]

One of the defining events in this social shift came when the tobacco industry agreed to compensate state governments for past Medicare costs of treating smoking victims. More recently, in June 2009 Congress passed by an overwhelming margin and President Obama signed a bill that gave the Food and Drug Administration the authority to regulate tobacco products, including advertising. It opened a new chapter in the effort to reduce the health toll from smoking.[50]

The sandwich model of social change is in many ways the most attractive one, partly because it brings a potential for rapid change. As of mid-2009, the strong grassroots interest in cutting carbon emissions and developing renewable sources of energy is merging with the interests of President Obama and his administration. One result, as noted earlier, is the de facto moratorium on building new coal plants.

There are many signs that the United States may be moving toward a tipping point on climate, much as it did on civil rights in the 1960s. Though some of the indicators also reflect the economic downturn, it now seems likely that carbon emissions in the United States peaked in 2007 and have begun what will be a long-term decline. The burning of coal and oil, the principal sources of carbon emissions, may both now be declining. And the automobile fleet may be shrinking. With the cars to be scrapped in 2009 likely to exceed sales, the U.S. automobile fleet may have peaked and also begun to decline.[51]

The shift to more fuel-efficient cars over the last two years, spurred in part by higher gasoline prices, was strongly reinforced by the new automobile fuel efficiency standards and by rescue package pressures on the automobile companies to improve fuel efficiency. Shifts within the energy sector, with rapid growth in wind and solar energy while coal and oil are declining, also signal a basic shift in values, one that could eventually alter every sector of the economy. If so, this combined with a national leadership that shares these emerging values, could lead to social and economic change on a scale and at a pace we cannot now easily imagine.[52]

It is quite possible that U.S. oil consumption, for example, has peaked. The combination of much more demanding automobile efficiency standards, a dramatic restoration of funding for public transit, and an encouraging shift not only to more fuel-efficient gas-electric hybrid cars but to both plug-in hybrids and electric cars could dramatically reduce gasoline sales. The U.S. Department of Energy in past years had projected substantial growth in U.S. oil consumption, but it has recently revised this downward. The question now is not will oil use decline, but how fast will it do so. Carbon emissions may also have peaked.[53]

Of the three models of social change, relying on the Pearl Harbor model is by far the riskiest, because by the time a society-changing catastrophic event occurs, it may be too late. The Berlin Wall model works, despite the lack of government support, but it does take time. Some 40 years elapsed after the communist takeover of the governments of Eastern Europe before the spreading opposition became strong enough to overcome repressive regimes and switch to democratically elected governments. The ideal situation for rapid, historic progress occurs when mounting grassroots pressure for change merges with a national leadership committed to the same change. This may help explain why the world has such high hopes for the new U.S. leadership as it faces the challenges described in earlier chapters.

A Wartime Mobilization

The U.S. entry into World War II offers an inspiring case study in rapid mobilization. Mobilizing to save civilization both parallels and contrasts with this earlier mobilization. For the war, the United States underwent a massive economic restructuring, but it was only intended to be temporary. Mobilizing to save civilization, in contrast, requires an economic restructuring that will endure.

Initially, the United States resisted involvement in the war and responded only after it was directly attacked at Pearl Harbor on December 7, 1941. But respond it did. After an all-out commitment, the U.S. engagement helped turn the tide of war, leading the Allied Forces to victory within three-and-a-half years.[54]

In his State of the Union address on January 6, 1942, one month after the bombing of Pearl Harbor, President Franklin D. Roosevelt announced the country's arms production goals. The United States, he said, was planning to produce 45,000 tanks, 60,000 planes, 20,000 anti-aircraft guns, and several thousand ships. He added, "Let no man say it cannot be done."[55]

No one had ever seen such huge arms production numbers. Public skepticism was widespread. But Roosevelt and his colleagues realized that the world's largest concentration of industrial power at that time was in the U.S. automobile industry. Even during the Depression, the United States was producing 3 million or more cars a year. After his State of the Union address, Roosevelt met with auto industry leaders and told them that the country would rely heavily on them to reach these arms production goals. Initially they wanted to continue making cars and simply add on the production of armaments. What they did not yet know was that the sale of new cars would soon be banned. From early February 1942 through the end of 1944, nearly three years, essentially no cars were produced in the United States.[56]

In addition to a ban on the production and sale of cars for private use, residential and highway construction was halted, and driving for pleasure was banned. Strategic goods—including tires, gasoline, fuel oil, and sugar—were rationed beginning in 1942. Cutting back on private consumption of these goods freed up material resources that were vital to the war effort.[57]

The year 1942 witnessed the greatest expansion of industrial output in the nation's history—all for military use. Wartime aircraft needs were enormous. They included not only fighters, bombers, and reconnaissance planes, but also the troop and cargo transports needed to fight a war on distant fronts. From the beginning of 1942 through 1944, the United States far exceeded the initial goal of 60,000 planes, turning out a staggering 229,600 aircraft, a fleet so vast it is hard today to even visualize it. Equally impressive, by the end of the war more than 5,000 ships were added to the 1,000 or so that made up the American Merchant Fleet in 1939.[58]

In her book *No Ordinary Time*, Doris Kearns Goodwin describes how various firms converted. A sparkplug factory was among the first to switch to the production of machine guns. Soon a manufacturer of stoves was producing lifeboats. A merry-go-round factory was making gun mounts; a toy company was turning out compasses; a corset manufacturer was producing grenade belts; and a pinball machine plant began to make armor-piercing shells.[59]

In retrospect, the speed of this conversion from a peacetime to a wartime economy is stunning. The harnessing of U.S. industrial power tipped the scales decisively toward the Allied Forces, reversing the tide of war. Germany and Japan, already fully extended, could not counter this effort. British Prime Minister Winston Churchill often quoted his foreign secretary, Sir Edward Grey: "The United States is like a giant boiler. Once the fire is lighted under it, there is no limit to the power it can generate."[60]

This mobilization of resources within a matter of months demonstrates that a country and, indeed, the world can restructure the economy quickly if convinced of the need to do so. Many people—although not yet the majority—are already convinced of the need for a wholesale economic restructuring. The purpose of this book is to convince more people of this need, helping to tip the balance toward the forces of change and hope.

Mobilizing to Save Civilization

Mobilizing to save civilization means fundamentally restructuring the global economy in order to stabilize climate, eradicate poverty, stabilize population, restore the economy's natural support systems, and, above all, restore hope. We have the technologies, economic instruments, and financial resources to do this. The United States, the wealthiest society that has ever existed, has the resources to lead this effort.

On the eradication of poverty, Jeffrey Sachs of Columbia University's Earth Institute sums it up well: "The tragic irony of this moment is that the rich countries are so rich and the poor so poor that a few added tenths of one percent of GNP from the rich ones ramped up over the coming decades could do what was never before possible in human history: ensure that the basic needs of health and education are met for all impoverished children in this world."[61]

We can calculate roughly the costs of the changes needed to move our twenty-first century civilization off the decline-and-collapse path and onto a path that will sustain civilization. What we cannot calculate is the cost of *not* adopting Plan B. How do you put a price tag on civilizational collapse and the massive suffering and death that typically accompanies it?

As noted in Chapter 7, the additional external funding needed to achieve universal primary education in developing countries that require help, for instance, is conservatively estimated at $10 billion per year. Funding for adult literacy programs based largely on volunteers will take an estimated additional $4 billion annually. Providing for the most basic health care in developing countries is estimated at $33 billion by the World Health Organization. The additional funding needed to provide reproductive health care and family planning services to all women in developing countries amounts to $17 billion a year.[62]

Closing the condom gap by providing the additional 14.7 billion condoms needed each year to control the spread of HIV in the developing world and Eastern Europe requires roughly $3 billion—$440 million for condoms and $2.2 billion for AIDS prevention education and condom distribution. The cost of extending school lunch programs to the 44 poorest countries is $6 billion. An estimated $4 billion per year would cover the cost of assistance to preschool children and pregnant women in these countries. Altogether, the cost of reaching basic social goals comes to $77 billion a year.[63]

As noted in Chapter 8, a poverty eradication effort that is not accompanied by an earth restoration effort is doomed to fail. Protecting topsoil, reforesting the earth, restoring oceanic fisheries, and other needed measures will cost an estimated $110 billion in additional expenditures per year. The most costly activities, protecting biological diversity at $31 billion and conserving soil on cropland at $24 billion, account for almost half of the earth restoration annual outlay.[64]

Combining social goals and earth restoration components into a Plan B budget yields an additional annual expenditure of

$187 billion, roughly one third of the current U.S. military budget or 13 percent of the global military budget. (See Tables 10–2 and 10–3.) In a sense this is the new defense budget, the one that addresses the most serious threats to our security.[65]

Unfortunately, the United States continues to focus on building an ever-stronger military, largely ignoring the threats posed by continuing environmental deterioration, poverty, and population growth. Its 2008 military expenditures totaled $607 bil-

Table 10–2. *Plan B Budget: Additional Annual Expenditures Needed to Meet Social Goals and to Restore the Earth*

Goal	Funding
	(billion dollars)
Basic Social Goals	
Universal primary education	10
Eradication of adult illiteracy	4
School lunch programs for 44 poorest countries	6
Assistance to preschool children and	
pregnant women in 44 poorest countries	4
Reproductive health and family planning	17
Universal basic health care	33
Closing the condom gap	3
Total	77
Earth Restoration Goals	
Planting trees to reduce flooding	
and conserve soil	6
Planting trees to sequester carbon	17
Protecting topsoil on cropland	24
Restoring rangelands	9
Restoring fisheries	13
Protecting biological diversity	31
Stabilizing water tables	10
Total	110
Grand Total	187

Source: See endnotes 63 and 64.

Table 10–3. *Military Budgets by Country and for the World*
in 2008 and Plan B Budget

Country	Budget
	(billion dollars)
United States	607
China	85
France	66
United Kingdom	65
Russia	59
Germany	47
Japan	46
Italy	41
Saudi Arabia	38
India	30
All other	380
World Military Expenditure	1,464
Plan B Budget	187

Source: See endnote 65.

lion, 41 percent of the global total of $1,464 billion. Other lead-ing spenders included China ($85 billion), France ($66 billion), the United Kingdom ($65 billion), and Russia ($59 billion).[66]

As of mid-2009, direct U.S. appropriations for the Iraq war, which has lasted longer than World War II, total some $642 bil-lion. Economists Joseph Stiglitz and Linda Bilmes calculate that if all the costs are included, such as the lifetime of care required for returning troops who are brain-injured or psychologically shattered, the cost of war will in the end approach $3 trillion. Yet the Iraq war may prove to be one of history's most costly mistakes not so much because of fiscal outlay but because it has diverted the world's attention from climate change and the other threats to civilization itself.[67]

It is decision time. Like earlier civilizations that got into environmental trouble, we can decide to stay with business as usual and watch our modern economy decline and eventually collapse, or we can consciously move onto a new path, one that will sustain economic progress. In this situation, the failure to act is a de facto decision to stay on the decline-and-collapse path.

No one can argue today that we do not have the resources to do the job. We can stabilize world population. We can get rid of hunger, illiteracy, disease, and poverty, and we can restore the earth's soils, forests, and fisheries. Shifting 13 percent of the world military budget to the Plan B budget would be more than adequate to move the world onto a path that would sustain progress. We can build a global community where the basic needs of all people are satisfied—a world that will allow us to think of ourselves as civilized.

This economic restructuring depends on tax restructuring, on getting the market to be ecologically honest, as described earlier. The benchmark of political leadership will be whether leaders succeed in shifting taxes from work to environmentally destructive activities. It is tax shifting, not additional appropriations, that is the key to restructuring the energy economy in order to stabilize climate.

It is easy to spend hundreds of billions in response to terrorist threats, but the reality is that the resources needed to disrupt a modern economy are small, and a U.S. Department of Homeland Security, however heavily funded, provides only minimal protection from suicidal terrorists. The challenge is not to provide a high-tech military response to terrorism but to build a global society that is environmentally sustainable and equitable—one that restores hope for everyone. Such an effort would do more to combat terrorism than any increase in military expenditures or any new weapons systems, however advanced.

Just as the forces of decline can reinforce each other, so can the forces of progress. For example, efficiency gains that lower oil dependence also reduce carbon emissions and air pollution. Steps to eradicate poverty help stabilize population. Reforestation sequesters carbon, increases aquifer recharge, and reduces soil erosion. Once we get enough trends headed in the right direction, they will reinforce each other.

The world needs a major success story in reducing carbon emissions and dependence on oil in order to bolster hope in the future. If the United States, for instance, were to launch a crash program to shift to plug-in and all-electric hybrid cars while simultaneously investing in thousands of wind farms, Americans could do most of their driving with wind energy, dramatically reducing the need for oil.

With many U.S. automobile assembly lines currently idled, it would be a relatively simple matter to retool some of them to produce wind turbines, enabling the country to quickly harness its vast wind energy potential. This would be a rather modest initiative compared with the restructuring during World War II, but it would help the world to see that restructuring an economy is achievable and that it can be done quickly, profitably, and in a way that enhances national security both by reducing dependence on vulnerable oil supplies and by avoiding disruptive climate change.

What You and I Can Do

One of the questions I hear most frequently is, What can I do? People often expect me to talk about lifestyle changes, recycling newspapers, or changing light bulbs. These are essential, but they are not nearly enough. We now need to restructure the global economy, and quickly. It means becoming politically active, working for the needed changes. Saving civilization is not a spectator sport.

Inform yourself, read about the issues. If you want to know what happened to earlier civilizations that found themselves in environmental trouble, read *Collapse* by Jared Diamond or *A Short History of Progress* by Ronald Wright or *The Collapse of Complex Societies* by Joseph Tainter. If you found this book useful in helping you think about what to do, share it with others. It can be downloaded free of charge from the Institute's Web site, earthpolicy.org.[68]

Pick an issue that's meaningful to you, such as tax restructuring, banning inefficient light bulbs, phasing out coal-fired power plants, or working for streets in your community that are pedestrian- and bicycle-friendly, or join a group that is working to stabilize world population. What could be more exciting and rewarding than getting personally involved in trying to save civilization?

You may want to proceed on your own, but you might also

want to organize a group of like-minded individuals. You might begin by talking with others to help select an issue or issues to work on.

And communicate with your elected representatives on the city council or the national legislature. Aside from the particular issue that you choose to work on, there are two overriding policy challenges: restructuring taxes and reordering fiscal priorities. Write or e-mail your elected representative about the need to restructure taxes by reducing income taxes and raising environmental taxes. Remind him or her that leaving costs off the books may offer a Ponzi sense of prosperity in the short run but that it leads to collapse in the long run.

Let your political representatives know that a world spending more than $1 trillion a year for military purposes is simply out of sync with reality, not responding to the most serious threats to our future. Ask them if $187 billion a year, the Plan B budget, is an unreasonable expenditure to save civilization. Ask them if diverting one eighth of the global military budget to saving civilization is too costly. Remind them of how the United States mobilized during World War II.[69]

And above all, don't underestimate what you can do. Anthropologist Margaret Mead once said, "Never doubt that a small group of concerned citizens can change the world. Indeed, it is the only thing that ever has."[70]

In addition, it doesn't hurt to underpin your political efforts with lifestyle changes. But remember they supplement your political action; they are not a substitute for it. Urban planner Richard Register recounts meeting a bicycle activist friend wearing a t-shirt that said "I just lost 3,500 pounds. Ask me how." When queried he said he had sold his car. Replacing a 3,500-pound car with a 22-pound bicycle obviously reduces energy use dramatically, but it also reduces materials use by 99 percent, indirectly saving still more energy.[71]

Dietary changes can also make a difference. We learned that the climate footprint differences between a diet rich in red meat and a plant-based diet is roughly the same as the climate footprint difference between driving a large fuel-guzzling SUV and a highly efficient gas-electric hybrid. Those of us with diets heavy in fat-rich livestock products can do both ourselves and civilization a favor by moving down the food chain.[72]

Beyond these rather painless often healthily beneficial lifestyle changes, we can also think about sacrifice. During World War II the military draft asked millions of young men to risk the ultimate sacrifice. But we do not need to sacrifice lives as we battle to save civilization. We are called on only to be politically active and to make lifestyle changes. During the early part of World War II President Roosevelt frequently asked Americans to adjust their lifestyles. What contributions can we make today, in time, money, or reduced consumption, to help save civilization?

The choice is ours—yours and mine. We can stay with business as usual and preside over an economy that continues to destroy its natural support systems until it destroys itself, or we can adopt Plan B and be the generation that changes direction, moving the world onto a path of sustained progress. The choice will be made by our generation, but it will affect life on earth for all generations to come.

Notes

Chapter 1. Selling Our Future

1. Sandra Postel, *Pillar of Sand* (New York: W. W. Norton & Company, 1999), pp. 13–21.

2. Guy Gugliotta, "The Maya: Glory and Ruin," *National Geographic*, August 2007; Jared Diamond, *Collapse: How Societies Choose to Fail or Succeed* (New York: Penguin Group, 2005); Postel, op. cit. note 1, pp. 13–21; Joseph Tainter, *The Collapse of Complex Societies* (Cambridge, U.K.: Cambridge University Press, 1998).

3. U.N. Food and Agriculture Organization (FAO), "Soaring Food Prices: Facts, Perspectives, Impacts, and Actions Required," paper presented at the High-Level Conference on World Food Security: the Challenges of Climate Change and Bioenergy, Rome, 3–5 June 2008; historical wheat, corn, and soybean prices are Chicago Board of Trade futures data from TFC Commodity Charts, "Grain & Oilseed Commodities Futures," at futures.tradingcharts.com/grains_oilseeds.html, viewed 16 January 2009; current wheat, corn, and soybean prices are Chicago Board of Trade futures data from CME Group, "Commodity Products," various dates, at www.cmegroup.com; rice prices from Nathan Childs and Katherine Baldwin, *Rice Outlook* (Washington, DC: U.S. Department of Agriculture (USDA), Economic Research Service (ERS), 11 June 2009), p. 26.

4. U.N. General Assembly, "United Nations Millennium Declaration," resolution adopted by the General Assembly, 8 September 2000; FAO, "1.02 Billion People Hungry," press release (Rome: 19 June 2009).

5. U.N. Population Division, *World Population Prospects: The 2008 Revision Population Database*, at esa.un.org/unpp, updated 11 March 2009.

6. USDA, *Production, Supply and Distribution*, electronic database, at

www.fas.usda.gov/psdonline, updated 12 May 2009; U.N. Population Division, op. cit. note 5.

7. Ward's Automotive Group, *World Motor Vehicle Data 2008* (Southfield, MI: 2008), pp. 239–42; USDA, op. cit. note 6; F.O. Licht, "Too Much Too Soon? World Ethanol Production to Break Another Record in 2005," *World Ethanol and Biofuels Report*, vol. 3, no. 20 (21 June 2005), pp. 429–35; U.S. Department of Energy (DOE), Energy Information Administration (EIA), "World Crude Oil Prices," and "U.S. All Grades All Formulations Retail Gasoline Prices," at tonto.eia.doe.gov, viewed 31 July 2007.

8. Cropland losing topsoil is author's estimate; USDA, op. cit. note 6; FAO, *The State of Food and Agriculture 1995* (Rome: 1995), p. 175.

9. Lester R. Brown, *Outgrowing the Earth* (New York: W. W. Norton & Company, 2004), pp. 101–02; Peter H. Gleick et al., *The World's Water 2004–2005* (Washington, DC: Island Press, 2004), p. 88; U.N. Population Division, op. cit. note 5; Andrew England, "Saudis to Phase Out Wheat Production," *Financial Times*, 10 April 2008; John Briscoe, *India's Water Economy: Bracing for a Turbulent Future* (New Delhi: World Bank, 2005); World Bank, *China: Agenda for Water Sector Strategy for North China* (Washington, DC: April 2001), pp. vii, xi.

10. Shaobing Peng et al., "Rice Yields Decline with Higher Night Temperature from Global Warming," *Proceedings of the National Academy of Sciences*, 6 July 2004, pp. 9,971–75; J. Hansen, NASA's Goddard Institute for Space Studies, "Global Temperature Anomalies in 0.1 C," at data.giss.nasa.gov/gistemp/tabledata/GLB.Ts.txt, updated April 2009; "Summary for Policymakers," in Intergovernmental Panel on Climate Change, *Climate Change 2007: The Physical Science Basis. Contribution of Working Group I to the Fourth Assessment Report of the Intergovernmental Panel on Climate Change* (Cambridge, U.K.: Cambridge University Press, 2007), p. 13.

11. U.N. Environment Programme, *Global Outlook for Ice and Snow* (Nairobi: 2007); Lester R. Brown, "Melting Mountain Glaciers Will Shrink Grain Harvests in China and India," *Plan B Update* (Washington, DC: Earth Policy Institute, 20 March 2008); USDA, op. cit. note 6.

12. W. T. Pfeffer, J. T. Harper, and S. O'Neel, "Kinematic Constraints on Glacier Contributions to 21st-Century Sea-Level Rise," *Science*, vol. 321 (5 September 2008) pp. 1,340–43; James Hansen, "Scientific Reticence and Sea Level Rise," *Environmental Research Letters*, vol. 2 (24 May 2007); Environmental Change and Forced Scenarios Project, "Preliminary Finds from the EACH-FOR Project on Environmentally Induced Migration" (September 2008), p. 16; U.N. Development Programme, *Human Development Report 2007/2008* (New York: 2007), p. 100; World Bank, *World Development Report 1999/2000* (New York: Oxford University Press, September 1999); USDA, op. cit. note 6; U.N. Population Division, op. cit. note 5.

13. FAO, *FISHSTAT Plus*, electronic database, at www.fao.org, updated February 2009.

14. Wang Tao, Cold and Arid Regions Environmental and Engineering Research Institute (CAREERI), Chinese Academy of Sciences, e-mail to author, 4 April 2004; Wang Tao, "The Process and Its Control of Sandy

Desertification in Northern China," CAREERI, Chinese Academy of Sciences, seminar on desertification, held in Lanzhou, China, May 2002; "Scientists Meeting in Tunis Called for Priority Activities to Curb Desertification," *UN News Service*, 21 June 2006.

15. Noel Gollehon and William Quinby, "Irrigation in the American West: Area, Water and Economic Activity," *Water Resources Development*, vol. 16, no. 2 (2000), pp. 187–95; Sandra Postel, *Last Oasis* (New York: W. W. Norton & Company, 1997), p. 137; R. Srinivasan, "The Politics of Water," *Info Change Agenda*, issue 3 (October 2005); *Water Strategist*, various issues, at www.waterstrategist.com; "China Politics: Growing Tensions Over Scarce Water," *The Economist*, 21 June 2004.

16. USDA, op. cit. note 6; pre-1960 data from USDA, in Worldwatch Institute, *Signposts 2001*, CD-ROM (Washington, DC: 2001).

17. USDA, op. cit. note 6; pre-1960 data from USDA, op. cit. note 16.

18. USDA, op. cit. note 6; Kenneth G. Cassman et al., "Meeting Cereal Demand While Protecting Natural Resources and Improving Environmental Quality," *Annual Review of Environment and Resources*, November 2003, pp. 322, 350; Thomas R. Sinclair, "Limits to Crop Yield?" in American Society of Agronomy, Crop Science Society of America, and Soil Science Society of America, *Physiology and Determination of Crop Yield* (Madison, WI: 1994), pp. 509–32.

19. Peter M. Vitousek et al., "Human Appropriation of the Products of Photosynthesis," *BioScience*, vol. 36, no. 6 (June 1986), pp. 368–73.

20. USDA, op. cit. note 6; U.N. Population Division, op. cit. note 5.

21. *Financial Times*, "In Depth: The Global Food Crisis," at www.ft.com/foodprices, updated 6 May 2008; USDA, op. cit. note 6.

22. Office of the President, Republic of the Philippines, "RP Assured of 1.5 Million Metric Tons of Rice Supply from Vietnam Annually," press release (Manila: 26 March 2008); "Yemen to Seek Australian Food Cooperation," *WorldGrain.com*, 19 May 2008; "Indonesia Set to Become Major Rice Exporter Next Year," *WorldGrain.com*, 1 July 2008; "Bahrain to Own Rice Farms in Thailand," *TradeArabia*, online business newswire, 30 May 2008; Javier Blas, "Nations Make Secret Deals Over Grain," *Financial Times*, 10 April 2008; Maria Kolesnikova and Alaa Shahine, "Russia, Egypt Agree on Wheat Deals to Boost Shipments," *Bloomberg*, 23 June 2009.

23. GRAIN, *Seized! The 2008 Land Grab for Food and Financial Security* (Barcelona: October 2008); USDA, op. cit. note 6; "Libya Agrees Deal to Grow Wheat in Ukraine," *Reuters*, 27 May 2009.

24. Joachim von Braun and Ruth Meinzen-Dick, *"Land Grabbing" by Foreign Investors in Developing Countries*, Policy Brief No. 13 (Washington, DC: International Food Policy Research Institute, April 2009).

25. GRAIN, op. cit. note 23; von Braun and Meinzen-Dick, op. cit. note 24; "Buying Farmland Abroad: Outsourcing's Third Wave," *The Economist*, 21 May 2009.

26. GRAIN, op. cit. note 23; "Land Deals in Africa and Asia: Cornering Foreign Fields," *The Economist*, 21 May 2009; Javier Blas, "Saudis Get First Taste of Foreign Harvest," *Financial Times*, 4 March 2009; "Saudi's Hadco Eyes Sudan, Turkey in Food Security Push," *Reuters*, 17 February 2009; U.N. World Food Programme, "Countries," at www.wfp.org/

countries, viewed 4 June 2009.

27. "Saudis Invest $1.3 Billion in Indonesian Agriculture," *Reuters*, 24 March 2009; von Braun and Meinzen-Dick, op. cit. note 24.

28. Von Braun and Meinzen-Dick, op. cit. note 24; USDA, op. cit. note 6; U.N. Population Division, op. cit. note 5; "China 'May Lease Foreign Fields'," *BBC News*, 29 April 2008; Gurbir Singh, "China is Buying Farm Lands Abroad to Ensure Food Supplies at Home," *Business World* (New Delhi), 16 May 2008; "China Eyes Russian Farmlands in Food Push," *Russia Today* (Moscow), 11 May 2008; GRAIN, op. cit. note 23, p. 3; "Govt to Lease Land for FDI in Agriculture," *Myanmar Times*, 11–17 September 2006; U.N. World Food Programme, op. cit. note 26.

29. USDA, op. cit. note 6; GRAIN, op. cit. note 23, pp. 4, 5; "Buying Farmland Abroad," op. cit. note 25; Javier Blas, "Hyundai Plants Seoul's Flag on 50,000ha of Russia," *Financial Times*, 15 April 2009.

30. Erik Ansink and Arjan Ruijs, "Climate Change and the Stability of Water Allocation Agreements," *Fondazione Ene Enrico Mattei*, Working Paper No. 16.2007 (February 2007), pp. 21–23.

31. "Memorandum of Understanding on Construction of Agriculture Technology Transfer Center and Grain Production and Processing Base in the Philippines," available at www.newsbreak.com.ph/dmdocuments/special%20coverages/China%20Agri/Fuhua%20MOU.pdf, signed 15 January 2007; "China: 'Going Outward' for Food Security," *Stratfor*, 30 April 2008; Luzi Ann Javier, "China's Appetite for Filipino Paddies Breeds Farmer Opposition," *Bloomberg*, 21 February 2008; Tom Burgis and Javier Blas, "Madagascar Scraps Daewoo Farm Deal," *Financial Times*, 18 March 2009; "Zambia's Opposition Condemns Reported Chinese Biofuels Project," *Earth Times*, 2 April 2009.

32. GRAIN, op. cit. note 23, p. 10; "Buying Farmland Abroad," op. cit. note 25.

33. Amena Bakr, "Pakistan Offers Farmland to Foreign Investors," *Reuters*, 20 April 2009.

34. Michiyo Nakamoto and Javier Blas, "G8 Move to Halt 'Farmland Grabbing'," *Financial Times*, 26 May 2009; von Braun and Meinzen-Dick, op. cit. note 24.

35. USDA, op. cit. note 6; U.N. Population Division, op. cit. note 5.

36. "Cereal Offenders," *The Economist*, 27 May 2008; "Commodities Boom Recalls 70s Surge; Prices Not There Yet," *Dow Jones Newswires*, 27 June 2008; Fred H. Sanderson, "The Great Food Fumble," *Science*, vol. 188 (9 May 1975), pp. 503–09; U.S. Department of the Treasury, "Report on Foreign Holdings of U.S. Securities at End-June 2008," press release (Washington, DC: 30 April 2009); U.S. Department of the Treasury, "Major Foreign Holders of Treasury Securities," current and historical data tables, at www.treasury.gov/tic, updated 16 January 2009.

37. James Bandler and Nicholas Varchaver, "How Bernie Did It," *Fortune*, vol. 159, no. 10 (11 May 2009); "The Madoff Affair: Going Down Quietly," *The Economist*, 12 May 2009.

38. Angus Maddison, "Statistics on World Population, GDP and Per Capita GDP, 1–2006 AD," at www.ggdc.net/maddison, updated March 2009; Mathis Wackernagel et al., "Tracking the Ecological Overshoot of the Human Economy," *Proceedings of the National Academy of Sciences*,

vol. 99, no. 14 (9 July 2002), pp. 9,266–71; Global Footprint Network, WWF, and Zoological Society of London, *Living Planet Report 2008* (Gland, Switzerland: WWF, October 2008), p. 2.

39. Author's estimate based on previously cited figures for China and India, as well as other countries such as Saudi Arabia and Pakistan where water tables are falling due to overpumping.

40. FAO, *The State of World Fisheries and Aquaculture 2008* (Rome: 2009), p. 7; Ransom A. Myers and Boris Worm, "Rapid Worldwide Depletion of Predatory Fish Communities," *Nature*, vol. 432 (15 May 2003), pp. 280–83.

41. Paul Hawken, "Commencement Address to the Class of 2009," speech at University of Portland, Portland, OR, 3 May 2009.

42. Eric Pfanner, "Failure Brings Call for Tougher Standards: Accounting for Enron: Global Ripple Effects," *International Herald Tribune*, 17 January 2002.

43. Nicholas Stern, *The Stern Review on the Economics of Climate Change* (London: HM Treasury, 2006).

44. DOE, EIA, "Weekly Retail Gasoline and Diesel Prices," at tonto.eia. doe.gov/dnav/pet/pet_pri_gnd_dcus_nus_w.htm, viewed 5 June 2009.

45. International Center for Technology Assessment (ICTA), *The Real Cost of Gasoline: An Analysis of the Hidden External Costs Consumers Pay to Fuel Their Automobiles* (Washington, DC: 1998); ICTA, *Gasoline Cost Externalities Associated with Global Climate Change* (Washington, DC: September 2004); ICTA, *Gasoline Cost Externalities: Security and Protection Services* (Washington, DC: January 2005); Terry Tamminen, *Lives Per Gallon: The True Cost of Our Oil Addiction* (Washington, DC: Island Press, 2006), p. 60, adjusted to 2007 prices with Bureau of Economic Analysis, "Table 3—Price Indices for Gross Domestic Product and Gross Domestic Purchases," *GDP and Other Major Series, 1929–2007* (Washington, DC: August 2007); DOE, op. cit. note 44.

46. Munich Re, *Topics Annual Review: Natural Catastrophes 2001* (Munich, Germany: 2002), pp. 16–17; value of China's wheat and rice harvests from USDA, op. cit. note 6, updated 12 July 2007, using prices from International Monetary Fund, *International Financial Statistics*, electronic database, at ifs.apdi.net/imf.

47. "Forestry Cuts Down on Logging," *China Daily*, 26 May 1998; Erik Eckholm, "China Admits Ecological Sins Played Role in Flood Disaster," *New York Times*, 26 August 1998.

48. Fund for Peace and *Foreign Policy*, "The Failed States Index," *Foreign Policy*, July/August 2005, pp. 56–65.

49. Ibid.

50. Lydia Polgreen, "In Congo, Hunger and Disease Erode Democracy," *New York Times*, 23 June 2006; International Rescue Committee, *Mortality in the Democratic Republic of Congo: An Ongoing Crisis* (New York: January 2008), p. ii; Lydia Polgreen, "Hundreds Killed Near Chad's Border With Sudan," *New York Times*, 14 November 2006; "A Failing State: The Himalayan Kingdom Is a Gathering Menace," *The Economist*, 4 December 2004.

51. "The Indian Ocean: The Most Dangerous Seas in the World," *The Economist*, 17 July 2008; U.N. Office on Drugs and Crime, *World Drug Report*

2009 (Vienna: June 2009), p. 34; Ania Lichtarowica, "Conquering Polio's Last Frontier," *BBC News*, 2 August 2007.

52. Neil MacFarquhar, "Haiti's Woes Are Top Test for Aid Effort," *New York Times*, 31 March 2009; U.S. Central Intelligence Agency, *The World Fact-book*, at www.cia.gov/library/publications/the-world-factbook, updated 26 June 2009; Madeleine K. Albright and Robin Cook, "The World Needs to Step It Up in Afghanistan," *International Herald Tribune*, 5 October 2004; Desmond Butler, "5-Year Hunt Fails to Net Qaeda Suspect in Africa," *New York Times*, 14 June 2003; Emilio San Pedro, "U.S. Ready to Aid Mexico Drug Fight," *BBC News*, 2 March 2009.

53. Fund for Peace and *Foreign Policy*, "The Failed States Index," *Foreign Policy*, July/August issues, 2005–09.

54. Fund for Peace and *Foreign Policy*, "The Failed States Index," *Foreign Policy*, July/August 2007, pp. 54–63; Table 1–1 from Fund for Peace and *Foreign Policy*, "The Failed States Index," *Foreign Policy*, July/August 2009, pp. 80–93.

55. Fund for Peace and *Foreign Policy*, op. cit. note 53.

56. U.N. Population Division, op. cit. note 5; Fund for Peace and *Foreign Policy*, July/August 2009, op. cit. note 54; Richard Cincotta and Elizabeth Leahy, "Population Age Structure and Its Relation to Civil Conflict: A Graphic Metric," *Woodrow Wilson International Center for Scholars Environmental Change and Security Program Report*, vol. 12 (2006–07), pp. 55–58.

57. Fund for Peace and *Foreign Policy*, July/August 2009, op. cit. note 54.

58. Ibid.; U.N. Population Division op. cit. note 5.

59. Fund for Peace and *Foreign Policy*, July/August 2009, op. cit. note 54; U.N. Population Division, op. cit. note 5.

60. Fund for Peace and *Foreign Policy*, July/August 2009, op. cit. note 54; U.N. World Food Programme, op. cit. note 26.

61. *Financial Times*, op. cit. note 21; Carolyn Said, "Nothing Flat about Tortilla Prices: Some in Mexico Cost 60 Percent More, Leading to a Serious Struggle for Low-Income People," *San Francisco Chronicle*, 13 January 2007; Adam Morrow and Khaled Moussa al-Omrani, "Egypt: Rising Food Costs Provoke Fights Over Subsidised Bread," *Inter Press Service*, 26 March 2008; Raphael Minder, John Aglionby, and Jung-a Song, "Soaring Soybean Price Stirs Anger Among Poor," *Financial Times*, 18 January 2008; Joseph Delva and Jim Loney, "Haiti's Government Falls after Food Riots," *Reuters*, 12 April 2008.

62. Keith Bradsher, "High Rice Cost Creating Fears of Asian Unrest," *New York Times*, 29 March 2008; Kamran Haider, "Pakistani Troops Escort Wheat Trucks to Stop Theft," *Reuters*, 13 January 2008; Nadeem Sarwar, "Pakistan's Poor, Musharraf Reeling Under Wheat Crisis," *Deutsche Presse-Agentur*, 14 January 2008; Carlotta Gall, "Hunger and Food Prices Push Afghanistan to Brink," *New York Times*, 16 May 2008; U.N. World Food Programme, "Almost 6 Million Sudanese Await WFP Support in 2009," at www.wfp.org, 5 March 2009.

63. United Nations, "United Nations Peacekeeping Operations," background note, at www.un.org/Depts/dpko/dpko/bnote.htm, viewed 8 June 2009; North Atlantic Treaty Organization, "NATO in Afghanistan," at www.nato.int/issues/Afghanistan/index.html, updated 27 March 2009.

64. U.N. World Food Programme, op. cit. note 26.
65. Stephanie McCrummen, "In an Eastern Congo Oasis, Blood amid the Greenery," *Washington Post*, 22 July 2007.
66. U.N. Population Division, op. cit. note 5.
67. Harold G. Vatter, *The US Economy in World War II* (New York: Columbia University Press, 1985), p. 13; Alan L. Gropman, *Mobilizing U.S. Industry in World War II* (Washington, DC: National Defense University Press, August 1996); Doris Kearns Goodwin, *No Ordinary Time— Franklin and Eleanor Roosevelt: The Home Front in World War II* (New York: Simon & Schuster, 1994), p. 316.
68. U.N. Population Division, *World Population Prospects: The 2008 Revision, Extended Dataset,* CD-ROM (New York: 9 April 2009).
69. CalCars, "All About Plug-In Hybrids," at www.calcars.org, viewed 9 June 2009; General Motors, "Imagine: A Daily Commute Without Using a Drop of Gas," at www.chevrolet.com/electriccar, viewed 8 August 2008.
70. Larry Kinney, *Lighting Systems in Southwestern Homes: Problems and Opportunities*, prepared for DOE, Building America Program through the Midwest Research Institute, National Renewable Energy Laboratory Division (Boulder, CO: Southwest Energy Efficiency Project, June 2005), pp. 4–5; CREE LED Lighting, "Ultra-Efficient Lighting," at www.cree lighting.com/efficiency.htm, viewed 17 April 2009.
71. Denmark from Global Wind Energy Council (GWEC), "Interactive World Map," at www.gwec.net/index.php?id=126, viewed 29 May 2009, and from Flemming Hansen, "Denmark to Increase Wind Power to 50% by 2025, Mostly Offshore," *Renewable Energy Access*, 5 December 2006; GWEC, *Global Wind 2008 Report* (Brussels: 2009), p. 13, with European per person consumption from European Wind Energy Association, "Wind Power on Course to Become Major European Energy Source by the End of the Decade," press release (Brussels: 22 November 2004); China's solar water heaters from Werner Weiss, Irene Bergmann, and Roman Stelzer, *Solar Heat Worldwide: Markets and Contribution to the Energy Supply 2007* (Gleisdorf, Austria: International Energy Agency, Solar Heating & Cooling Programme, May 2009), p. 20; Iceland National Energy Authority and Ministries of Industry and Commerce, *Geothermal Development and Research in Iceland* (Reykjavik: April 2006), p. 16; share of electricity calculated by Earth Policy Institute using installed capacity from Ruggero Bertani, "World Geothermal Generation in 2007," *GHC Bulletin*, September 2007, p. 9; capacity factor from Ingvar B. Fridleifsson et al., "The Possible Role and Contribution of Geothermal Energy to the Mitigation of Climate Change," in O. Hohmeyer and T. Trittin, eds., *IPCC Scoping Meeting on Renewable Energy Sources, Proceedings* (Luebeck, Germany: 20–25 January 2008), p. 5; total electricity generation from "World Total Net Electricity Generation, 1980–2005," in DOE, EIA, *International Energy Annual 2005* (Washington, DC: 13 September 2007).
72. Se-Kyung Chong, "Anmyeon-do Recreation Forest: A Millennium of Management," in Patrick B. Durst et al., *In Search of Excellence: Exemplary Forest Management in Asia and the Pacific*, Asia-Pacific Forestry Commission (Bangkok: FAO Regional Office for Asia and the Pacific, 2005), pp. 251–59; Daniel Hellerstein, "USDA Land Retirement Programs," in USDA, *Agricultural Resources and Environmental Indicators*

2006 (Washington, DC: July 2006); USDA, ERS, *Agri-Environmental Policy at the Crossroads: Guideposts on a Changing Landscape,* Agricultural Economic Report No. 794 (Washington, DC: January 2001); USDA, op. cit. note 6.

73. Molly O'Meara, *Reinventing Cities for People and the Planet,* Worldwatch Paper 147 (Washington, DC: Worldwatch Institute, June 1999), p. 47; City of Amsterdam, "Bike Capital of Europe," at www.toamsterdam.nl, viewed 2 July 2009; Serge Schmemann, "I Love Paris on a Bus, a Bike, a Train and in Anything but a Car," *New York Times,* 26 July 2007; Transport for London, *Central London Congestion Charging: Impacts Monitoring* (London: various years).

Chapter 2. Population Pressure: Land and Water

1. Lester R. Brown, *The Twenty-Ninth Day* (New York: W. W. Norton & Company, 1978).

2. Grain area from U.S. Department of Agriculture (USDA), *Production, Supply and Distribution,* electronic database, at www.fas.usda.gov/psdonline, updated 9 April 2009; cropland losing topsoil is author's estimate based on Mohan K. Wali et al., "Assessing Terrestrial Ecosystem Sustainability," *Nature & Resources,* October–December 1999, pp. 21–33, and on World Resources Institute (WRI), *World Resources 2000–01* (Washington, DC: 2000).

3. U.N. Food and Agriculture Organization (FAO), *ResourceSTAT,* electronic database, at faostat.fao.org, updated April 2009; Lester R. Brown, "Melting Mountain Glaciers Will Shrink Grain Harvests in China and India," *Plan B Update* (Washington, DC: Earth Policy Institute, 20 March 2008).

4. Jacob W. Kijne, *Unlocking the Water Potential of Agriculture* (Rome: FAO, 2003), p. 26.

5. Lester R. Brown, *Outgrowing the Earth* (New York: W. W. Norton & Company, 2004), pp. 101–02.

6. Walter C. Lowdermilk, *Conquest of the Land Through 7,000 Years,* USDA Bulletin No. 99 (Washington, DC: USDA, Natural Resources Conservation Service, 1939).

7. Ibid., p. 10.

8. FAO, "FAO/WFP Crop and Food Assessment Mission to Lesotho Special Report," at www.fao.org, viewed 29 May 2002; U.N. Population Division, *World Population Prospects: The 2008 Revision Population Database,* at esa.un.org/unpp, updated 11 March 2009; Michael Grunwald, "Bizarre Weather Ravages Africans' Crops," *Washington Post,* 7 January 2003.

9. USDA, op. cit. note 2; U.N. World Food Programme (WFP), "Lesotho," at www.wfp.org/countries/lesotho, viewed 5 May 2009.

10. USDA, op. cit. note 2; FAO, *Global Forest Resources Assessment 2005* (Rome: 2006), p. 193; WFP, "Haiti," at www.wfp.org/countries/haiti, viewed 5 May 2009.

11. U.N. Environment Programme (UNEP), *Mongolia: State of the Environment 2002* (Pathumthani, Thailand: Regional Resource Centre for Asia and the Pacific, 2001), pp. 3–7; U.N. Population Division, op. cit. note 8; USDA, op. cit. note 2.

12. FAO, "More People Than Ever are Victims of Hunger," background note

(Rome: June 2009).

13. National Aeronautics and Space Administration Earth Observatory, "Dust Storm off Western Sahara Coast," at earthobservatory. nasa.gov, viewed 9 January 2005.

14. Paul Brown, "4x4s Replace the Desert Camel and Whip Up a Worldwide Dust Storm," *Guardian* (London), 20 August 2004.

15. Ibid.

16. Ann Schrader, "Latest Import from China: Haze," *Denver Post*, 18 April 2001; Brown, op. cit. note 14.

17. Howard W. French, "China's Growing Deserts Are Suffocating Korea," *New York Times*, 14 April 2002.

18. For number of dust storms in China, see Table 1–1 in Lester R. Brown, Janet Larsen, and Bernie Fischlowitz Roberts, *The Earth Policy Reader* (New York: W. W. Norton & Company, 2002), p. 13.

19. U.S. Embassy, "Desert Mergers and Acquisitions," *Beijing Environment, Science, and Technology Update* (Beijing: 19 July 2002), p. 2.

20. Asif Farrukh, *Pakistan Grain and Feed Annual Report 2002* (Islamabad, Pakistan: USDA Foreign Agricultural Service, 2003).

21. UNEP, *Africa Environment Outlook: Past, Present, and Future Perspectives* (Nairobi: 2002).

22. Land area estimate from Stanley Wood, Kate Sebastian, and Sara J. Scherr, *Pilot Analysis of Global Ecosystems: Agroecosystems* (Washington, DC: International Food Policy Research Institute and WRI, 2000), p. 3; FAO, *ProdSTAT*, electronic database, at faostat.fao.org, updated June 2009.

23. Number of pastoralists from FAO, *The State of Food Insecurity in the World 2003* (Rome: 2003), p. 15; Robin P. White, Siobhan Murray, and Mark Rohweder, *Pilot Analysis of Global Ecosystems: Grassland Ecosystems* (Washington, DC: WRI, 2000); U.N. Population Division, op. cit. note 8; FAO, op. cit. note 22; Southern African Development Coordination Conference, *SADCC Agriculture: Toward 2000* (Rome: FAO, 1984).

24. Government of Nigeria, *Combating Desertification and Mitigating the Effects of Drought in Nigeria*, Revised National Report on the Implementation of the United Nations Convention to Combat Desertification (Nigeria: April 2002); U.N. Population Division, op. cit. note 8; FAO, op. cit. note 22.

25. U.N. Population Division, op. cit. note 8; FAO, op. cit. note 22; Iranian News Agency, "Official Warns of Impending Desertification Catastrophe in Southeast Iran," *BBC International Reports*, 29 September 2002.

26. UNEP, *Afghanistan: Post-Conflict Environmental Assessment* (Geneva: 2003), p. 52.

27. FAO, op. cit. note 22.

28. Wang Tao et al., "A Study on Spatial-temporal Changes of Sandy Desertified Land During Last 5 Decades in North China," *Acta Geographica Sinica*, vol. 59 (2004), pp. 203–12.

29. Wang Tao, Cold and Arid Regions Environmental and Engineering Research Institute (CAREERI), Chinese Academy of Sciences, e-mail to author, 4 April 2004; Wang Tao, "The Process and Its Control of Sandy Desertification in Northern China," CAREERI, Chinese Academy of Sciences, seminar on desertification, Lanzhou, China, May 2002.

30. FAO, *The State of Food and Agriculture 1995* (Rome: 1995), p. 175; Rosamond Naylor et al., "Losing the Links between Livestock and Land," *Science*, vol. 310 (9 December 2005), pp. 1,621–22.

31. "The Great North American Dust Bowl: A Cautionary Tale," in Secretariat of the U.N. Convention to Combat Desertification, *Global Alarm: Dust and Sandstorms from the World's Drylands* (Bangkok: 2002), pp. 77–121; John Steinbeck, *The Grapes of Wrath* (New York: Viking Penguin, Inc., 1939).

32. FAO, op. cit. note 30, p. 175; David Christian, *Imperial and Soviet Russia: Power, Privilege, and the Challenge of Modernity* (New York: Palgrave Macmillan, 1997) p. 366; USDA, op. cit. note 2; France from USDA, Foreign Agricultural Service, *World Agricultural Production* (Washington, DC: April 2009), p. 7.

33. David Kaimowitz et al., *Hamburger Connection Fuels Amazon Destruction* (Jakarta, Indonesia: Center for International Forestry Research, 2004); Carlos R. Spehar, "Production Systems in the Savannahs of Brazil: Key Factors to Sustainability," in Rattan Lal, ed., *Soil Quality and Agricultural Sustainability* (Chelsea, MI: Ann Arbor Press, 1998), pp. 301–18; Daniel Nepstad, "Climate Change and the Forest," *Tomorrow's Amazonia: Using and Abusing the World's Last Great Forests* (Washington, DC: The American Prospect, September 2007); Geoffrey Lean, "A Disaster to Take Everyone's Breath Away," *Independent* (London), 24 July 2006.

34. Craig S. Smith, "Saudis Worry as They Waste Their Scarce Water," *New York Times*, 26 January 2003.

35. Andrew England, "Saudis to Phase Out Wheat Production," *Financial Times*, 10 April 2008; USDA, op. cit. note 2; U.N. Population Division, op. cit. note 8.

36. Michael Ma, "Northern Cities Sinking as Water Table Falls," *South China Morning Post*, 11 August 2001; Smith, op. cit. note 34; John Opie, *Ogallala: Water for a Dry Land*, 2nd ed. (Lincoln, NB: University of Nebraska Press, 2000), p. 3.

37. U.N. Population Division, op. cit. note 8; USDA, op. cit. note 2; Christopher Ward, "Yemen's Water Crisis," based on a lecture to the British Yemeni Society in September 2000, July 2001; Fund for Peace and *Foreign Policy*, "The Failed States Index," *Foreign Policy*, July/August 2009, pp. 80–93.

38. Ma, op. cit. note 36; share of China's grain harvest from the North China Plain based on Hong Yang and Alexander Zehnder, "China's Regional Water Scarcity and Implications for Grain Supply and Trade," *Environment and Planning A*, vol. 33 (2001), and on National Bureau of Statistics of China, *China Statistical Yearbook 2008*, electronic database, at www.stats.gov.cn/tjsj/ndsj/2008/indexeh.htm, viewed 9 June 2009.

39. Ma, op. cit. note 36.

40. World Bank, *China: Agenda for Water Sector Strategy for North China* (Washington, DC: April 2001), pp. vii, xi; U.N. Population Division, op. cit. note 8; USDA, op. cit. note 2.

41. Number of farmers and well investment from Peter H. Gleick et al., *The World's Water 2006–2007* (Washington, DC: Island Press, 2006), p. 148; number of wells and rate of aquifer depletion from Fred Pearce, "Asian Farmers Sucking the Continent Dry," *New Scientist*, 28 August 2004.

42. Pearce, op. cit. note 41.
43. USDA, op. cit. note 2; John Briscoe, *India's Water Economy: Bracing for a Turbulent Future* (New Delhi: World Bank, 2005); U.N. Population Division, op. cit. note 8.
44. USDA, *Agricultural Resources and Environmental Indicators 2000* (Washington, DC: February 2000), Chapter 2.1, p. 6; irrigated share calculated from FAO, op. cit. note 3; harvest from USDA, op. cit. note 2; Sandra Postel, *Pillar of Sand* (New York: W. W. Norton & Company, 1999), p. 77.
45. U.N. Population Division, op. cit. note 8; fall in water table from "Pakistan: Focus on Water Crisis," *U.N. Integrated Regional Information Networks News*, 17 May 2002.
46. "Pakistan: Focus on Water Crisis," op. cit. note 45; Sardar Riaz A. Khan, "Declining Land Resource Base," *Dawn* (Pakistan), 27 September 2004.
47. Chenaran Agricultural Center, Ministry of Agriculture, according to Hamid Taravati, publisher, Iran, e-mail to author, 25 June 2002; USDA, op. cit. note 2.
48. Deborah Camiel, "Israel, Palestinian Water Resources Down the Drain," *Reuters*, 12 July 2000; USDA, op. cit. note 2; "Palestinian Water Crisis Deepens," *BBC News*, 20 April 2009.
49. U.N. Population Division, op. cit. note 8; Tushaar Shah et al., *The Global Groundwater Situation: Overview of Opportunities and Challenges* (Colombo, Sri Lanka: International Water Management Institute, 2000); Karin Kemper, "Groundwater Management in Mexico: Legal and Institutional Issues," in Salman M. A. Salman, ed., *Groundwater: Legal and Policy Perspectives*, Proceedings of a World Bank Seminar (Washington, DC: World Bank, 1999), p. 117; U.N. Development Programme, *Human Development Report 2006* (Gordonsville, VA: Palgrave Macmillan, 2006), p. 146.
50. Water to make steel from Sandra Postel, *Last Oasis* (New York: W. W. Norton & Company, 1997), pp. 38–39; 1,000 tons of water for 1 of grain from FAO, *Yield Response to Water* (Rome: 1979).
51. Noel Gollehon and William Quinby, "Irrigation in the American West: Area, Water and Economic Activity," *Water Resources Development*, vol. 16, no. 2 (2000), pp. 187–95; Postel, op. cit. note 50, p. 137; Pramit Mitra, "Running on Empty: India's Water Crisis Could Threaten Prosperity," *South Asia Monitor*, no. 103 (Washington, DC: Center for Strategic and International Studies, 8 February 2007); R. Srinivasan, "The Politics of Water," *Info Change Agenda*, issue 3 (October 2005); U.N. Population Division, *World Urbanization Prospects: The 2007 Revision Population Database*, at esa.un.org/unup, updated 2008.
52. Srinivasan, op. cit. note 51; Pearce, op. cit. note 41.
53. "China Politics: Growing Tensions Over Scarce Water," *The Economist*, 21 June 2004.
54. Gollehon and Quinby, op. cit. note 51; *Water Strategist*, various issues, at www.waterstrategist.com.
55. Joey Bunch, "Water Projects Forecast to Fall Short of Needs: Study Predicts 10% Deficit in State," *Denver Post*, 22 July 2004.
56. Dean Murphy, "Pact in West Will Send Farms' Water to Cities," *New York Times*, 17 October 2003; Tim Molloy, "California Water District Approves Plan to Pay Farmers for Irrigation Water," *Associated Press*, 13

May 2004; USDA, National Agricultural Statistics Service (NASS), "Table 10. Irrigation 2002 and 1997," *2002 Census of Agriculture*, vol. 1 (Washington, DC: June 2004), pp. 318–26; USDA, NASS, "Table 10. Irrigation: 2007 and 2002," *2007 Census of Agriculture*, vol. 1 (Washington, DC: February 2009), pp. 372–80.

57. FAO, op. cit. note 50.
58. Grain from USDA, Foreign Agricultural Service, *Grain: World Markets and Trade* (Washington, DC: various years); USDA, op. cit. note 2.
59. Nile River flow from Postel, op. cit. note 44, p. 71; grain imports from USDA, op. cit. note 2; calculation based on 1,000 tons of water for 1 ton of grain from FAO, op. cit. note 50.
60. U.N. Population Division, op. cit. note 8; USDA, op. cit. note 2.
61. USDA, *Production, Supply and Distribution Country Reports* (Washington, DC: October 1990); USDA, op. cit. note 2; U.N. Population Division, op. cit. note 8.
62. "Time for Action on Sudan" (editorial), *New York Times*, 18 June 2004; "A First Step to Save Darfur" (editorial), *New York Times*, 3 August 2007; "Hearings to Identify Causes of Conflict Kick Off in Darfur, Reports UN-AU Mission," *UN News Service*, 22 June 2009.
63. U.N. Population Division, op. cit. note 8; FAO, op. cit. note 22.
64. U.N. Population Division, op. cit. note 8; Government of Nigeria, *Combating Desertification and Mitigating the Effects of Drought in Nigeria*, National Report on the Implementation of the United Nations Convention to Combat Desertification (Nigeria: November 1999); Somini Sengupta, "Where the Land is a Tinderbox, the Killing Is a Frenzy," *New York Times*, 16 June 2004.
65. Sengupta, op. cit. note 64.
66. Ibid.
67. James Gasana, "Remember Rwanda?" *World Watch*, September/ October 2002, pp. 24–32.
68. Ibid.
69. U.S. Census Bureau, Population Division, International Programs Center, *International Database*, at www.census.gov/ipc/www/idb, updated 15 December 2008; Gasana, op. cit. note 67.
70. Gasana, op. cit. note 67; Emily Wax, "At the Heart of Rwanda's Horror: General's History Offers Clues to the Roots of Genocide," *Washington Post*, 21 September 2002.
71. U.N. Population Division, op. cit. note 8; Gasana, op. cit. note 67.
72. U.N. Population Division, op. cit. note 8; Postel, op. cit. note 44, pp. 141–49.
73. U.N. Population Division, op. cit. note 8; Postel, op. cit. note 44, pp. 141–49.
74. U.N. Population Division, op. cit. note 8; Postel, op. cit. note 44, pp. 141–49; Southeastern Anatolia Project Regional Development Administration, *Latest Situation on Southeastern Anatolia Project* (Ankara: Republic of Turkey, Prime Ministry, June 2006), pp. 3–5.
75. O'Hara quoted in Michael Wines, "Grand Soviet Scheme for Sharing Water in Central Asia is Foundering," *New York Times*, 9 December 2002; Ivan Stanchin and Zvi Lerman, *Water in Turkmenistan* (Rehovot, Israel: Hebrew University of Jerusalem, 2007), p. 1.

76. F.O. Licht, "Too Much Too Soon? World Ethanol Production to Break Another Record in 2005," *World Ethanol and Biofuels Report*, vol. 3, no. 20 (21 June 2005), pp. 429–35; U.S. Department of Energy (DOE), "World Crude Oil Prices," and "U.S. All Grades All Formulations Retail Gasoline Prices," at tonto.eia.doe.gov, viewed 31 July 2007; USDA, *Production, Supply and Distribution*, electronic database, at www.fas.usda.gov/psdonline, updated 12 May 2009; USDA, *Feedgrains Database*, electronic database at www.ers.usda.gov/Data/feedgrains, updated 19 May 2009.

77. F.O. Licht, "World Fuel Ethanol Production," *World Ethanol and Biofuels Report*, vol. 7, no. 18 (26 May 2009), p. 365; "Biodiesel: World Production, by Country," table in F.O. Licht, *World Ethanol and Biofuels Report*, vol. 7, no. 14 (26 March 2009), p. 288; "EU Ministers Agree Biofuel Target," *BBC News*, 15 February 2007.

78. USDA, *Production, Supply and Distribution,* op. cit. note 76; corn for ethanol from USDA, *Feedgrains Database*, op. cit. note 76; historical wheat, corn, and soybean prices are Chicago Board of Trade futures data from TFC Commodity Charts, "Grain & Oilseed Commodities Futures," at futures.tradingcharts.com/grains_oilseeds.html, viewed 16 January 2009; current wheat, corn, and soybean prices are Chicago Board of Trade futures data from CME Group, "Commodity Products," various dates, at www.cmegroup.com; rice prices from Nathan Childs and Katherine Baldwin, *Rice Outlook* (Washington, DC: USDA, Economic Research Service, 11 June 2009), p. 26; Donald Mitchell, *A Note on Rising Food Prices*, Policy Research Working Paper 4682 (Washington, DC: World Bank Development Prospects Group, July 2008), pp. 16–17.

79. Lester R. Brown, "Distillery Demand for Grain to Fuel Cars Vastly Understated: World May be Facing Highest Grain Prices in History," *Eco-Economy Update* (Washington, DC: Earth Policy Institute, 4 January 2007); corn ethanol conversion is author's estimate, based on Keith Collins, chief economist, USDA, statement before the U.S. Senate Committee on Environment and Public Works, 6 September 2006, p. 8; energy content of ethanol relative to gasoline from Oak Ridge National Laboratory (ORNL), "Bioenergy Conversion Factors," at bioenergy.ornl.gov/papers/misc/energy_conv.html, viewed 3 August 2007; U.S. gasoline consumption from "Table 10. Energy Consumption by Sector and Source: Total United States," in DOE, Energy Information Administration, "Supplemental Tables to the Annual Energy Outlook 2009," at www.eia.doe.gov/oiaf/aeo/supplement/supref.html, updated March 2009; USDA, op. cit. note 2.

80. C. Ford Runge and Benjamin Senauer, "How Biofuels Could Starve the Poor," *Foreign Affairs*, May/June 2007.

81. Celia W. Dugger, "As Prices Soar, U.S. Food Aid Buys Less," *New York Times*, 29 September 2007; WFP, "Our Work: Operations List," at www.wfp.org/operations, viewed 9 June 2009; Edith M. Lederer, "U.N.: Hunger Kills 18,000 Kids Each Day," *Associated Press*, 17 February 2007.

82. Ward's Automotive Group, *World Motor Vehicle Data 2008* (Southfield, MI: 2008), pp. 239–42; income calculations from "Gross National Income Per Capita 2007, Atlas Method and PPP," table in World Bank, "Data— Quick Reference Tables," at siteresources.worldbank.org, updated 24

April 2009, and from U.N. Population Division, op. cit. note 8.

83. Patrick Barta, "Jatropha Plant Gains Steam in Global Race for Biofuels," *Wall Street Journal*, 24 August 2007; "Shell Boosts Stake in Iogen Cellulosic Ethanol," *Reuters*, 15 July 2008; FAO, *State of Food and Agriculture 2008* (Rome: 2008), p. 47.

84. The White House, "Remarks by the President on National Fuel Efficiency Standards," transcript (Washington, DC: Office of the Press Secretary, 19 May 2009); John M. Broder, "Obama to Toughen Rules on Emissions and Mileage," *New York Times*, 19 May 2009; corn ethanol conversion is author's estimate, based on Collins, op. cit. note 79, p. 8; energy content of ethanol relative to gasoline from ORNL, op. cit. note 79; U.S. gasoline consumption from "Table 10. Energy Consumption by Sector and Source: Total United States," op. cit. note 79; USDA, op. cit. note 2; CalCars, "All About Plug-In Hybrids," at www.calcars.org, viewed 9 June 2009.

85. USDA, op. cit. note 2; F.O. Licht, "World Fuel Ethanol Production," op. cit. note 77, p. 365.

86. "Scientists Meeting in Tunis Called for Priority Activities to Curb Desertification," *UN News Service*, 21 June 2006.

87. Alan Cowell, "Migrants Found off Italy Boat Piled with Dead," *International Herald Tribune*, 21 October 2003.

88. Ibid.

89. Roberta Russo, "UNHCR Steps up Efforts to Stem Gulf of Aden Crossings As Numbers Mount," *News Stories* (Geneva: U.N. High Commissioner for Refugees (UNHCR), 22 May 2009); Hélène Caux and William Spindler, "Dozens Dead or Missing in Gulf of Aden; Boat People Figures Rise," *News Stories* (Geneva: UNHCR, 4 November 2008).

90. Miranda Leitsinger, "African Migrants Die an Ocean Away," *Washington Post*, 2 June 2006; Mar Roman, "A New Record for Africans Risking Boat Route to Europe," *Washington Post*, 4 September 2006.

91. Ginger Thompson, "Mexico Worries About Its Own Southern Border," *New York Times*, 18 June 2006; Instituto Nacional de Migración, *Estadísticas Migratorias*, electronic database, at www.inami.gob.mx, updated 30 April 2009.

92. "Mexico's Immigration Problem: The Kamikazes of Poverty," *The Economist*, 31 January 2004.

93. Frank Bruni, "Off Sicily, Tide of Bodies Roils Immigrant Debate," *New York Times*, 23 September 2002; Flora Botsford, "Spain Recovers Drowned Migrants," *BBC News*, 25 April 2002; "Boat Sinks Off Coast of Turkey: One Survivor and 7 Bodies Found," *Agence France-Presse*, 22 December 2003; Mary Jordan and Kevin Sullivan, "Trade Brings Riches, But Not to Mexico's Poor," *Washington Post*, 22 March 2003; Robert McLeman and Barry Smit, "Climate Change, Migration and Security," Commentary No. 86 (Ottawa: Canadian Security Intelligence Service, 2 March 2004); number leaving rural areas from FAO, *PopSTAT*, electronic database, at faostat.fao.org/site/550/default.aspx, updated February 2009; Coalición de Derechos Humanos, "Arizona Recovered Bodies," at www.derechoshumanosaz.net, updated 15 June 2009.

94. Abandoned villages in India from Shah et al., op. cit. note 49; U.N. Population Division, op. cit. note 8.

95. Wang, e-mail to author, op. cit. note 29; Wang, "The Process and Its Con-

trol of Sandy Desertification in Northern China," op. cit. note 29.

96. Souhail Karam, "Drought-Hit North Africa Seen Hunting for Grains," *Reuters*, 15 July 2005; African Development Bank and Organisation for Economic Co-operation and Development, *African Economic Outlook 2007* (Tunis and Paris: 2007), p. 386.

97. Iranian News Agency, op. cit. note 25; Government of Nigeria, op. cit. note 64.

98. Brazil and Mexico from Heitor Matallo, "General Approach to the Costs of Desertification," presentation at International Workshop on the Cost of Inaction and Opportunities for Investment in Arid, Semi-Arid and Dry Sub-Humid Areas," Rome, 4–5 December 2006; see also Table 5–2 in Brown, op. cit. note 5, pp. 86–87.

99. Gordon McGranahan, Deborah Balk, and Bridget Anderson, "The Rising Tide: Assessing the Risks of Climate Change and Human Settlements in Low Elevation Coastal Zones," *Environment and Urbanization*, vol. 18, no. 1 (April 2007), pp. 17–37; International Institute for Environment and Development (IIED), "Climate Change: Study Maps Those at Greatest Risk from Cyclones and Rising Seas," press release (London: 28 March 2007).

Chapter 3. Climate Change and the Energy Transition

1. J. Hansen, NASA's Goddard Institute for Space Studies, "Global Temperature Anomalies in 0.1 C," at data.giss.nasa.gov/gistemp/tabledata/ GLB.Ts.txt, updated June 2009; Intergovernmental Panel on Climate Change (IPCC), *Climate Change 2007: The Physical Science Basis. Contribution of Working Group I to the Fourth Assessment Report of the Intergovernmental Panel on Climate Change* (Cambridge, U.K.: Cambridge University Press, 2007), pp. 13, 15.

2. IPCC, op. cit. note 1, pp. 5–7; U.N. Environment Programme (UNEP), *Global Outlook for Ice and Snow* (Nairobi: 2007), p. 103; W. T. Pfeffer, J. T. Harper, and S. O'Neel, "Kinematic Constraints on Glacier Contributions to 21st-Century Sea-Level Rise," *Science*, vol. 321 (5 September 2008), pp. 1340–43; "Sea Levels Will Rise 1.5 Metres by 2100," *NewScientist.com*, 16 April 2008; Stefan Rahmstorf, "A Semi-Empirical Approach to Projecting Future Sea-level Rise," *Science*, vol. 315 (19 January 2007), pp. 368–70.

3. IPCC, *Climate Change 2007: Impact, Adaptation and Vulnerability. Contribution of Working Group II to the Fourth Assessment Report of the Intergovernmental Panel on Climate Change* (Cambridge, U.K.: Cambridge University Press, 2007), pp. 241–45.

4. International Energy Agency (IEA), *Oil Market Report* (Paris: August 2001), includes oil, natural gas liquids, and processing gains; historical data from U.S. Department of Defense, *Twentieth Century Petroleum Statistics* (Washington, DC: 1945), cited in Christopher Flavin and Seth Dunn, "Reinventing the Energy System," in Lester R. Brown, Christopher Flavin, and Hilary French, *State of the World 1999* (New York: W. W. Norton & Company, 1999), p. 25; coal from Seth Dunn, "Coal Use Continues Rebound," in Lester R. Brown et al., *Vital Signs 1998* (New York: W. W. Norton & Company, 1998), pp. 52–53.

5. IEA, *Oil Market Report* (Paris: June 2009); Colin J. Campbell, e-mail to

Jignasha Rana, Earth Policy Institute, 18 June 2009.

6. IEA, *World Energy Outlook 2008* (Paris: 2008), p. 507.

7. Hansen, op. cit. note 1.

8. IPCC, op. cit. note 1, pp. 27, 135, 141, 542.

9. Concentration in 2008 from Pieter Tans, "Trends in Atmospheric Carbon Dioxide—Mauna Loa," NOAA/ESRL, at www.esrl.noaa.gov/gmd/ccgg/trends, viewed 7 April 2009; R. A. Houghton, "Carbon Flux to the Atmosphere from Land-Use Changes: 1850–2005," in Carbon Dioxide Information Analysis Center, *TRENDS: A Compendium of Data on Global Change* (Oak Ridge, TN: Oak Ridge National Laboratory, 2008); Josep G. Canadell et al., "Contributions to Accelerating Atmospheric CO_2 Growth from Economic Activity, Carbon Intensity, and Efficiency of Natural Sinks," *Proceedings of the National Academy of Sciences*, vol. 104, no. 47 (20 November 2007), pp. 18,866–70.

10. Sarah Simpson, "The Arctic Thaw Could Make Global Warming Worse," *Scientific American: Earth 3.0*, June 2009; Global Carbon Project, "Super-size Deposits of Frozen Carbon Threat to Climate Change," press release (Canberra, Australia: 1 July 2009).

11. Veerabhadran Ramanathan et al., *Atmospheric Brown Clouds: Regional Assessment Report with Focus on Asia* (Nairobi: UNEP, 2008), pp. 2, 10.

12. Ibid., pp. 393–96; Yun Qian et al., "Effects of Soot-Induced Snow Albedo Change on Snowpack and Hydrological Cycle in Western United States Based on Weather Research and Forecasting Chemistry and Regional Climate Simulations," *Journal of Geophysical Research*, vol. 114, issue D3 (14 February 2009); Jane Qiu, "The Third Pole," *Nature*, vol. 454 (24 July 2008, pp. 393–96); Frances C. Moore, "Climate Change and Air Pollution: Exploring the Synergies and Potential for Mitigation in Industrializing Countries," *Sustainability*, vol. 1, no. 1 (24 March 2009), pp. 43–54.

13. Elisabeth Rosenthal, "Third-World Soot Stove is Target in Climate Fight," *New York Times*, 16 April 2009.

14. IPCC, op. cit. note 1, pp. 13, 15; Thomas R. Karl, Jerry M. Melillo, and Thomas C. Peterson, eds., *Global Climate Change Impacts in the United States* (New York: Cambridge University Press, 2009), pp. 22–23.

15. A. P. Sokolov et al., "Probabilistic Forecast for 21st Century Climate Based on Uncertainties in Emissions (Without Policy) and Climate Parameters," *Journal of Climate*, in press.

16. International Alliance of Research Universities, *Climate Change: Global Risks, Challenges & Decisions*, Synthesis Report from International Scientific Congress (Copenhagen: University of Copenhagen, 2009), pp. 18–19.

17. "Awful Weather We're Having," *The Economist*, 2 October 2004; Richard Milne, "Hurricanes Cost Munich Re Reinsurance," *Financial Times*, 6 November 2004.

18. U.S. Department of Agriculture (USDA), *Production, Supply and Distribution*, electronic database, at www.fas.usda.gov/psdonline, updated 11 June 2007; Janet Larsen, "Record Heat Wave in Europe Takes 35,000 Lives," *Eco-Economy Update* (Washington, DC: Earth Policy Institute, 9 October 2003); USDA, National Agricultural Statistics Service, "Crop Production," news release (Washington, DC: 12 August 2005).

19. Janet Larsen, "Setting the Record Straight: More than 52,000 Europeans

Died from Heat in Summer 2003," *Eco-Economy Update* (Washington, DC: Earth Policy Institute, 26 July 2006); National Commission on Terrorist Attacks Upon the United States, *The 9/11 Commission Report* (Washington, DC: U.S. Government Printing Office, 2004).

20. National Center for Atmospheric Research and UCAR Office of Programs, "Drought's Growing Reach: NCAR Study Points to Global Warming as Key Factor," press release (Boulder, CO: 10 January 2005); Aiguo Dai, Kevin E. Trenberth, and Taotao Qian, "A Global Dataset of Palmer Drought Severity Index for 1870–2002: Relationship with Soil Moisture and Effects of Surface Warming," *Journal of Hydrometeorology*, vol. 5 (December 2004), pp. 1,117–30.

21. Susan Solomon et al., "Irreversible Climate Change Due to Carbon Dioxide Emissions," *Proceedings of the National Academy of Sciences*, vol. 106, no. 6 (10 February 2009), pp. 1,704–09.

22. Donald McKenzie et al., "Climatic Change, Wildfire, and Conservation," *Conservation Biology*, vol. 18, no. 4 (August 2004), pp. 890–902.

23. Camille Parmesan and Hector Galbraith, *Observed Impacts of Global Climate Change in the U.S.* (Arlington, VA: Pew Center on Global Climate Change, 2004); DeNeen L. Brown, "Signs of Thaw in a Desert of Snow," *Washington Post*, 28 May 2002.

24. Patty Glick, *Fish Out of Water: A Guide to Global Warming and Pacific Northwest Rivers* (Seattle, WA: National Wildlife Federation, March 2005); Elizabeth Gillespie, "Global Warming May Be Making Rivers Too Hot: Cold-Water Fish Will Struggle, Report Says," *Seattle Post-Intelligencer*, 24 March 2005.

25. Douglas B. Inkley et al., *Global Climate Change and Wildlife in North America* (Bethesda, MD: The Wildlife Society, December 2004); J. R. Pegg, "Global Warming Disrupting North American Wildlife," *Environment News Service*, 16 December 2004.

26. UNEP, op. cit. note 2; Gordon McGranahan et al., "The Rising Tide: Assessing the Risks of Climate Change and Human Settlements in Low Elevation Coastal Zones," *Environment and Urbanization*, vol. 18, no. 1 (April 2007), pp. 17–37.

27. Arctic Climate Impact Assessment (ACIA), *Impacts of a Warming Arctic* (Cambridge, U.K.: Cambridge University Press, 2004); "Rapid Arctic Warming Brings Sea Level Rise, Extinctions," *Environment News Service*, 8 November 2004.

28. J. R. Pegg, "The Earth is Melting, Arctic Native Leader Warns," *Environment News Service*, 16 September 2004; ACIA, op. cit. note 27, p. 8.

29. ACIA, op. cit. note 27; Steven C. Amstrup, Bruce G. Marcot, and David C. Douglas, *Forecasting the Range-wide Status of Polar Bears at Selected Times in the 21st Century* (Reston, VA: U.S. Geological Survey (USGS), 2007), p. 2.

30. Julienne Stroeve et al., "Arctic Sea Ice Decline: Faster than Forecast," *Geophysical Research Letters*, vol. 34 (May 2007); National Snow and Ice Data Center (NSIDC), "Arctic Sea Ice Shatters All Previous Record Lows," press release (Boulder, CO: 1 October 2007); R. Kwok et al., "Thinning and Volume Loss of the Arctic Ocean Sea Ice Cover: 2003–2008," *Journal of Geophysical Research*, vol. 114 (7 July 2009).

31. David Adam, "Meltdown Fear as Arctic Ice Cover Falls to Record Winter

Low," *Guardian* (London), 15 May 2006; Kevin Rollason, "Arctic to See First Ice-Free Summer in 2015," *Canwest News Service* (Canada), 6 December 2008; Vincent cited in David Ljunggren, "Arctic Summer Ice Could Vanish by 2013: Expert," *Reuters*, 5 March 2009; Stroeve quoted in "Arctic Ice Retreating 30 Years Ahead of Projections," *Environment News Service*, 30 April 2007.

32. NSIDC, "Processes: Thermodynamics: Albedo," at nsidc.org/seaice/processes/albedo.html, viewed 26 July 2007.

33. UNEP, op. cit. note 2.

34. J. L. Chen, C. R. Wilson, and B. D. Tapley, "Satellite Gravity Measurements Confirm Accelerated Melting of Greenland Ice Sheet," *Science*, vol. 313 (29 September 2006), pp. 1,958–60; Isabella Velicogna and John Wahr, "Acceleration of Greenland Ice Mass Loss in Spring 2004," *Nature*, vol. 443 (21 September 2006), pp. 329–31; S. B. Luthke et al., "Recent Greenland Ice Mass Loss from Drainage System from Satellite Gravity Observations," *Science*, vol. 314 (24 November 2006), pp. 1,286–89; "Gravity Measurements Confirm Greenland's Glaciers Precipitous Meltdown," *Scientific American*, 19 October 2006.

35. Paul Brown, "Melting Ice Cap Triggering Earthquakes," *Guardian* (London), 8 September 2007; Robert W. Corell, discussion with Jignasha Rana, Earth Policy Institute, 15 July 2009.

36. Ohio State University, "Greenland's Glaciers Losing Ice Faster This Year than Last Year, Which Was Record-Setting Itself," news release (Columbus, OH: 13 December 2008).

37. H. Jay Zwally et al., "Surface Melt-Induced Acceleration of Greenland Ice-Sheet Flow," *Science*, vol. 297 (12 July 2002), pp. 218–22.

38. U.S. Department of Energy (DOE), Energy Information Administration (EIA), "Antarctica: Fact Sheet," at www.eia.doe.gov, September 2000.

39. "Giant Antarctic Ice Shelves Shatter and Break Away," *Environment News Service*, 19 March 2002; Vaughan quoted in Andrew Revkin, "Large Ice Shelf in Antarctica Disintegrates at Great Speed," *New York Times*, 20 March 2002.

40. "Breakaway Bergs Disrupt Antarctic Ecosystem," *Environment News Service*, 9 May 2002; "Giant Antarctic Ice Shelves Shatter and Break Away," op. cit. note 39.

41. NSIDC, "Larsen B Ice Shelf Collapses in Antarctica," at nsidc.org/news/press/larsen_B/2002.html, 21 March 2002; "Breakaway Bergs Disrupt Antarctic Ecosystem," op. cit. note 40; "Giant Antarctic Ice Shelves Shatter and Break Away," op. cit. note 39.

42. University of Colorado at Boulder, "NASA, CU-Boulder Study Shows Vast Regions of West Antarctica Melted in Recent Past," press release (Boulder: 15 May 2007).

43. Peter Brown, "NASA Satellites Watch Polar Ice Shelf Break into Crushed Ice," *Scientific American*, July 2008.

44. NASA Earth Observatory, "Wilkins Ice Bridge Collapse," at earthobservatory.nasa.gov/IOTD/view.php?id=37806, posted 8 April 2009.

45. Michael Byrnes, "New Antarctic Iceberg Split No Threat," *Reuters*, 20 May 2002.

46. Robin McKie, "Scientists to Issue Stark Warning Over Dramatic New Sea Level Figures," *Guardian* (London), 8 March 2009; IPCC, op. cit. note 1,

p. 13; Pfeffer, Harper, and O'Neel, op. cit. note 2; USGS, *Synthesis and Assessment Product 3.4: Abrupt Climate Change* (Washington, DC: 2009), p. 9.

47. McGranahan et al., op. cit. note 26.
48. Ibid.
49. World Glacier Monitoring Service, University of Zurich, "Glacier Mass Balance Data 2006 and 2007," at www.geo.uzh.ch/wgms/mbb/mbb10/sum07.html, updated 30 January 2009.
50. Lester R. Brown, "Melting Mountain Glaciers Will Shrink Grain Harvests in China and India," *Plan B Update* (Washington, DC: Earth Policy Institute, 20 March 2008).
51. USDA, *Production, Supply and Distribution*, electronic database, at www.fas.usda.gov/psdonline, updated 12 May 2009.
52. IPCC, op. cit. note 3, pp. 493–94; Emily Wax, "A Sacred River Endangered by Global Warming," *Washington Post*, 17 June 2007.
53. Clifford Coonan, "China's Water Supply Could be Cut Off as Tibet's Glaciers Melt," *The Independent* (London), 31 May 2007; UNEP, op. cit. note 2, p. 131; rice irrigation from "Yangtze River–Agriculture," *Encyclopedia Britannica,* online encyclopedia, viewed 25 July 2007.
54. Qiu, op. cit. note 12.
55. UNEP, op. cit. note 2, p. 131; Mehrdad Khalili, "The Climate of Iran: North, South, Kavir (Desert), Mountains," *San'ate Hamlo Naql*, March 1997, pp. 48–53.
56. Lonnie Thompson, "Disappearing Glaciers Evidence of a Rapidly Changing Earth," American Association for the Advancement of Science Annual Meeting, San Francisco, February 2001; Lonnie Thompson, "Receding Glaciers Erase Records of Climate History," *Science News*, 14 February 2009; "The Peak of Mt Kilimanjaro As It Has Not Been Seen for 11,000 Years," *Guardian* (London), 14 March 2005; Bancy Wangui, "Crisis Looms as Rivers Around Mt. Kenya Dry Up," *East Africa Standard*, 1 July 2007.
57. Eric Hansen, "Hot Peaks," *OnEarth*, fall 2002, p. 8.
58. Leslie Josephus, "Global Warming Threatens Double-Trouble for Peru: Shrinking Glaciers and a Water Shortage," *Associated Press*, 12 February 2007; *Citation World Atlas* (Union, NJ: Hammond World Atlas Corporation, 2004); Thompson, "Receding Glaciers," op. cit. note 56.
59. Josephus, op. cit. note 58; U.N. Population Division, *World Population Prospects: The 2008 Revision Population Database*, at esa.un.org/unpp, updated 11 March 2009.
60. U.N. Population Division, *Urban Agglomerations 2007 Wall Chart*, at www.un.org/esa/population, updated June 2008; James Painter, "Peru's Alarming Water Truth," *BBC News*, 12 March 2007.
61. Giles Tremlett, "Climate Change Lays Waste to Spain's Glaciers," *Guardian* (London), 23 February 2009.
62. Anne Minard, "No More Glaciers in Glacier National Park by 2020?" *National Geographic News*, 2 March 2009.
63. Michael Kiparsky and Peter Gleick, *Climate Change and California Water Resources: A Survey and Summary of the Literature* (Oakland, CA: Pacific Institute, 2003); Timothy Cavagnaro et al., *Climate Change: Challenges and Solutions for California Agricultural Landscapes* (Sacramento,

CA: California Climate Change Center, 2006).

64. Michael J. Scott et al., "Climate Change and Adaptation in Irrigated Agriculture—A Case Study of the Yakima River," in UCOWR/NIWR Conference, *Water Allocation: Economics and the Environment* (Carbondale, IL: Universities Council on Water Resources, 2004); Pacific Northwest National Laboratory, "Global Warming to Squeeze Western Mountains Dry by 2050," press release (Richland, WA: 16 February 2004).

65. John E. Sheehy, International Rice Research Institute, e-mail to Janet Larsen, Earth Policy Institute, 1 October 2002; Pedro Sanchez, "The Climate Change–Soil Fertility–Food Security Nexus," speech, Sustainable Food Security for All by 2020, Bonn, Germany, 4–6 September 2002.

66. K. S. Kavi Kumar and Jyoti Parikh, "Socio-Economic Impacts of Climate Change on Indian Agriculture," *International Review for Environmental Strategies*, vol. 2, no. 2 (2001), pp. 277–93; U.N. Population Division, op. cit. note 59.

67. Mohan K. Wali et al., "Assessing Terrestrial Ecosystem Sustainability," *Nature & Resources*, October–December 1999, pp. 21–33.

68. Shaobing Peng et al., "Rice Yields Decline with Higher Night Temperature from Global Warming," *Proceedings of the National Academy of Sciences*, 6 July 2004, pp. 9,971–75; *Proceedings of the National Academy of Sciences*, "Warmer Evening Temperatures Lower Rice Yields," press release (Washington, DC: 29 June 2004).

69. Sheehy, op. cit. note 65; Sanchez, op. cit. note 65.

70. Tim P. Barnett et al., "Human-Induced Changes in the Hydrology of the Western United States," *Science*, vol. 319 (22 February 2008); T. M. Shanahan et al., "Atlantic Forcing of Persistent Drought in West Africa," *Science*, vol. 324 (17 April 2009); Marshall B. Burke, David B. Lobell, and Luigi Guarino, "Shifts in African Crop Climates by 2050, and the Implications for Crop Improvement and Genetic Resources Conservation," *Global Environmental Change*, in press.

71. U.N. Population Division, op. cit. note 59; Burke, Lobell, and Guarino, op. cit. note 70; Marlowe Hood, "Warming May Outstrip Africa's Ability to Feed Itself: Study," *Agence France-Presse*, 17 June 2009.

72. IEA, op. cit. note 6, pp. 221, 225; DOE, EIA, "How Dependent Are We on Foreign Oil?" at tonto.eia.doe.gov/energy_in_brief/foreign_oil_dependence.cfm, updated 23 April 2009; U.S. Bureau of the Census, "Most of Us Still Drive to Work Alone—Public Transportation Commuters Concentrated in a Handful of Large Cities," press release (Washington, DC: 13 June 2007); Peter Whoriskey, "GM to Build Small Car in U.S.," *Washington Post*, 29 May 2009.

73. Ayesha Rascoe, "U.S. Oil Demand in 2008 Hit a 10-year Low: Government," *Reuters*, 27 February 2009; DOE, EIA, *Short-Term Energy Outlook* (Washington, DC: 7 July 2009), p. 22; Ayesha Rascoe, "U.S. Public Transit 2008 Ridership Highest in 52 years," *Reuters*, 9 March 2009.

74. Campbell, op. cit. note 5; Michael T. Klare, "Entering the Tough Oil Era," *TomDispatch.com*, 16 August 2007.

75. Michael T. Klare, "The Energy Crunch to Come," *TomDispatch.com*, 22 March 2005; Jad Mouawad, "Big Oil's Burden of Too Much Cash," *New York Times*, 12 February 2005; Mark Williams, "The End of Oil?" *Technology Review*, February 2005; John Vidal, "The End of Oil Is Closer

Than You Think," *Guardian* (London), 21 April 2005.

76. James Picerno, "If We Really Have the Oil," *Bloomberg Wealth Manager*, September 2002, p. 45; Klare, op. cit. note 75; Richard C. Duncan and Walter Youngquist, "Encircling the Peak of World Oil Production," *Natural Resource Research*, vol. 12, no. 4 (December 2003), p. 222; Walter Youngquist, *GeoDestinies: The Inevitable Control of Earth Resources over Nations and Individuals* (Portland: National Book Company, 1997); A. M. Samsam Bakhtiari, "World Oil Production Capacity Model Suggests Output Peak by 2006–07," *Oil and Gas Journal*, 26 April 2004, pp. 18–20.

77. Fredrik Robelius, *Giant Oil Fields—The Highway to Oil* (Uppsala, Sweden: Uppsala University Press, 9 March 2007), pp. 81–84; Petrobras Brazil, "Production Goes on Stream in Tupi: Year I of a New Era," at www2.petrobras.com.br/Petrobras/ingles/area_tupi.asp, viewed 17 June 2009.

78. Guy Chazan and Neil King Jr., "Russian Oil Slump Stirs Supply Jitters," *Wall Street Journal*, 15 April 2008; data on declining Russian oil production in IEA, *Oil Market Report* (Paris: May 2009).

79. Vidal, op. cit. note 75.

80. Gargi Chakrabarty, "Shale's New Hope," *Rocky Mountain News*, 18 October 2004; Walter Youngquist, "Alternative Energy Sources," in Lee C. Gerhard, Patrick Leahy, and Victor Yannacone, eds., *Sustainability of Energy and Water through the 21st Century*, Proceedings of the Arbor Day Farm Conference, 8–11 October 2000 (Lawrence, KS: Kansas Geological Survey, 2002), p. 65.

81. Robert Collier, "Canadian Oil Sands: Vast Reserves Second to Saudi Arabia Will Keep America Moving, But at a Steep Environmental Cost," *San Francisco Chronicle*, 22 May 2005; Alberta Department of Energy, *Alberta's Oil Sands, 2008* (Edmonton, Alberta: June 2009); BP, *BP Statistical Review of World Energy 2009* (London: June 2009), p. 11; Robin Pagnamenta, "Canadian Oil-Sand Mines Stuck as Crude Price Plummets," *The Times* (London), 5 January 2009; Jad Mouawad, "Big Oil Projects Put in Jeopardy by Fall in Prices," *New York Times*, 16 December 2008.

82. Sheila McNulty, "Tar Sands Refinery Projects Face a Sticky Future," *Financial Times*, 5 January 2009; Collier, op. cit. note 81; Alfred J. Cavallo, "Oil: Caveat Empty," *Bulletin of the Atomic Scientists*, vol. 61, no. 3 (May/June 2005), pp. 16–18; Richard Heinberg, "The End of the Oil Age," *Earth Island Journal*, vol. 18, no. 3 (fall 2003).

83. IEA, op. cit. note 6, p. 507.

84. World Health Organization, "Air Pollution," *Fact Sheet 187* (Geneva: revised September 2000); Janet Larsen, "Coal Takes Heavy Human Toll: Some 25,100 U.S. Deaths from Coal Use Largely Preventable," *Eco-Economy Update* (Washington DC: Earth Policy Institute, 24 August 2004).

85. U.S. Environmental Protection Agency, Office of Science and Technology, "National Listing of Fish Advisories: 2005–06 National Listing," fact sheet (Washington, DC: July 2007).

86. Jonathan Watts, "Beijing Blames Pollutants for Rise in Killer Cancers," *Guardian* (London), 22 May 2007.

87. Barbara Demick, "China Blames Pollution for Surge in Birth Defects," *Los Angeles Times*, 2 February 2009; Steven Mufson, "Asian Nations

Could Outpace U.S. in Developing Clean Energy," *Washington Post*, 16 July 2009.

88. Keith Bradsher, "Green Power Takes Root in the Chinese Desert," *New York Times*, 2 July 2009.

89. IEA, op. cit. note 6, p. 507.

90. Paul Hawken, Commencement Address to the Class of 2009, University of Portland, Portland, OR, 3 May 2009.

Chapter 4. Stabilizing Climate: An Energy Efficiency Revolution

1. Global Wind Energy Council, *Global Wind 2008 Report* (Brussels: 2009), pp. 3, 56; Erik Shuster, *Tracking New Coal-Fired Power Plants* (Pittsburgh, PA: U.S. Department of Energy (DOE), National Energy Technology Laboratory, January 2009); "Nuclear Dips in 2008," *World Nuclear News*, 29 May 2009; 1 megawatt of installed wind capacity produces enough electricity to supply 300 homes from American Wind Energy Association, "U.S. Wind Energy Installations Reach New Milestone," press release (Washington, DC: 14 August 2006); number of homes calculated using average U.S. household size from U.S. Census Bureau, "2005–2007 American Community Survey 3-Year Estimates—Data Profile Highlights," at factfinder.census.gov/servlet/ACSSAFFFacts, viewed 9 April 2009, and population from U.S. Census Bureau, *State & Country QuickFacts*, electronic database, at quickfacts.census.gov, updated 20 February 2009.

2. Carbon dioxide pathway modeled using fossil fuel emissions from Tom Boden and Gregg Marland, "Global CO_2 Emissions from Fossil-Fuel Burning, Cement Manufacture, and Gas Flaring: 1751–2006" and "Preliminary 2006-07 Global & National Estimates by Extrapolation," both in Carbon Dioxide Information and Analysis Center (CDIAC), *Fossil Fuel CO_2 Emissions* (Oak Ridge, TN: Oak Ridge National Laboratory (ORNL), 2009), and from land use change emissions from R. A. Houghton, "Carbon Flux to the Atmosphere from Land-Use Changes," in CDIAC, *Trends: A Compendium of Data on Global Change* (Oak Ridge, TN: ORNL, 2008), with decay curve cited in J. Hansen et al., "Dangerous Human-Made Interference with Climate: A GISS ModelE Study," *Atmospheric Chemistry and Physics*, vol. 7 (2007), pp. 2,287–312; current concentration from Pieter Tans, "Trends in Atmospheric Carbon Dioxide–Mauna Loa," National Oceanic and Atmospheric Administration, Earth System Research Laboratory, at www.esrl.noaa.gov/gmd/ccgg/trends, viewed 7 April 2009.

3. James Hansen et al., "Target Atmospheric CO_2: Where Should Humanity Aim?" *Open Atmospheric Science Journal*, vol. 2 (15 October 2008), pp. 217–31.

4. Lester R. Brown, "Creating New Jobs, Cutting Carbon Emissions, and Reducing Oil Imports by Investing in Renewable Energy and Energy Efficiency," *Plan B Update* (Washington, DC: Earth Policy Institute, 11 December 2008).

5. S. Pacala and R. Socolow, "Stabilization Wedges: Solving the Climate Problem for the Next 50 Years with Current Technologies," *Science*, vol. 305 (13 August 2004), pp. 968–72.

6. Ibid.

7. International Alliance of Research Universities, *Climate Change: Global Risks, Challenges & Decisions*, Synthesis Report from International Scientific Congress (Copenhagen: University of Copenhagen, 2009).

8. U.S. Environmental Protection Agency (EPA) and DOE, "Energy Star Change a Light, Change the World," fact sheet (Washington, DC: 23 April 2007); Larry Kinney, *Lighting Systems in Southwestern Homes: Problems and Opportunities,* prepared for DOE, Building America Program through the Midwest Research Institute, National Renewable Energy Laboratory (NREL) (Boulder, CO: Southwest Energy Efficiency Project, June 2005), pp. 4–5.

9. Alice McKeown, "Strong Growth in Compact Fluorescent Bulbs Reduces Electricity Demand," *Vital Signs Online* (Washington, DC: Worldwatch Institute, 27 October 2008); "Alliance Calls for Only Energy-Efficient Lighting in U.S. Market by 2016, Joins Coalition Dedicated to Achieving Goal," press release (Washington, DC: Alliance to Save Energy, 14 March 2007); DOE, *Big Results, Bigger Potential: CFL Market Profile* (Washington, DC: Energy Star, March 2009).

10. Ministry for the Environment and Natural Resources, "World First! Australia Slashes Greenhouse Gases from Inefficient Lighting," press release (Canberra, Australia: 20 February 2007); Rob Gillies, "Canada Announces Greenhouse Gas Targets," *Associated Press*, 25 April 2007; European Parliament, "Incandescent Light Bulbs: Environment Committee Backs Phase-Out Plan," press release (Brussels: 17 February 2009).

11. International Energy Agency (IEA), *Light's Labour's Lost: Policies for Energy-efficient Lighting* (Paris: 2006), p. 375; Deborah Zabarenko, "China to Switch to Energy-Efficient Lightbulbs," *Reuters*, 3 October 2007; Greenpeace India, "India's Light Bulb Phase Out: Setting a Smart Example," press release (New Delhi: 25 February 2009).

12. Retailer rankings from Deloitte, *Feeling the Squeeze, Global Powers of Retailing 2009* (London: 2009); Walmart Stores Inc., "Greenhouse Gas Emissions Fact Sheet" (Bentonville, AR: 2009); Hillary Osborne, "Currys to Stop Selling Incandescent Bulbs," *Guardian* (London), 13 March 2007.

13. CREE LED Lighting, "Ultra-Efficient Lighting," at www.creelighting .com/efficiency.htm, viewed 17 April 2009; Navigant Consulting Inc., *Energy Savings Estimates of Light Emitting Diodes in Niche Lighting Applications* (Washington, DC: DOE, rev. October 2008); Anthony DePalma, "It Never Sleeps, But It's Learned to Douse the Lights," *New York Times*, 11 December 2005; "Mayor Villaraigosa, President Clinton Light the Way to a Greener LA," press release (Los Angeles, CA: Office of the Mayor, 16 February 2009).

14. "Smart LED Lighting Makes Parking Garages Greener, Safer," *Environment News Service*, 13 January 2009.

15. LED life calculated from EPA and DOE, op. cit. note 8, and from "Company Profile: Expanding LED Possibilities at Samsung Electromechanics," *LEDs Magazine*, April 2007.

16. IEA, op. cit. note 11, pp. 25, 29, 38; CREE LED Lighting, op. cit. note 13.

17. Energy savings from lighting efficiency calculated using IEA, op. cit. note 11, pp. 25, 29, and IEA, *World Energy Outlook 2008* (Paris: 2008), p. 507; coal-fired power plant equivalents calculated by assuming that an average plant has a 500-megawatt capacity and operates 72 percent of the time,

generating 3.15 billion kilowatt-hours of electricity per year.

18. Steven Nadel, *The Federal Energy Policy Act of 2005 and Its Implications for Energy Efficiency Program Efforts* (Washington, DC: American Council for an Energy-Efficient Economy, 2005).

19. John M. Broder, "Obama Orders New Rules to Raise Energy Efficiency," *New York Times*, 6 February 2009.

20. National Bureau of Statistics of China (NBS), *China Statistical Yearbook* (Beijing: various years), in e-mail to Jessie Robbins, Earth Policy Institute, from David Fridley, Lawrence Berkeley National Laboratory (LBNL), DOE, 4 June 2009.

21. "Final Energy Consumption," in LBNL, *China Energy Databook*, v. 7.0 (Berkeley, CA: October 2008); NBS, "Electricity Balance Sheet," in *China Statistical Yearbook 2008*, at www.stats.gov.cn/english, viewed 21 July 2009.

22. U.N. Population Division, *World Population Prospects: The 2008 Revision Population Database*, at esa.un.org/unpp, updated 11 March 2009; Greenpeace, "Your Energy Savings," at www.greenpeace.org/international/campaigns/climate-change/take_action/your-energy, viewed 28 May 2009.

23. Marianne Haug et al., *Cool Appliances: Policy Strategies for Energy Efficient Homes* (Paris: IEA, 2003); Ministry of Economy, Trade and Industry, *Top Runner Program: Developing the World's Best Energy-Efficient Appliances* (Tokyo: 2008).

24. Haug et al., op. cit. note 23; Alan K. Meier, *A Worldwide Review of Standby Power Use in Homes* (Berkeley, CA: LBNL, 2002).

25. Lloyd Harrington et al., *Standby Energy: Building a Coherent International Policy Framework—Moving to the Next Level* (Stockholm: European Council for an Energy Efficient Economy, 2007).

26. Meier, op. cit. note 24.

27. Geoffrey Lean and Jonathan Owen, "Giant Plasma TVs Face Ban in Battle to Green Britain," *The Independent* (London), 11 January 2009; California Energy Commission, "Frequently Asked Questions—FAQs Energy Efficiency Standards for Televisions," at www.energy.ca.gov/appliances/tv_faqs.html, viewed 29 April 2009.

28. IEA, op. cit. note 17, p. 507.

29. U.S. Green Building Council (USGBC), "Green Building Facts" (Washington, DC: April 2009).

30. Edward Mazria, "It's the Architecture, Stupid! Who Really Holds the Key to the Global Thermostat? The Answer Might Surprise You," *World and I*, May/June 2003; Clinton Foundation, "Energy Efficiency Building Retrofit Program," fact sheet (New York: May 2007).

31. Davis Langdon, *The Cost & Benefit of Achieving Green Buildings* (Sydney: 2007).

32. German Federal Ministry for the Environment, Nature Conservation and Nuclear Safety (BMU), *Heat from Renewable Energies: What Will the New Heat Act Achieve?* (Berlin: July 2008); BMU, *Consolidated Version of the Reasoning Behind the Act on the Promotion of Renewable Energies in the Heat Sector* (Berlin: August 2008).

33. DOE, "Transforming the Way Americans Use Energy" at energy.gov/recovery/energy_efficiency.htm, viewed 9 April 2009; DOE, "Secretaries Donovan and Chu Announce Partnership to Help Working

Families Weatherize Their Homes," press release (Washington, DC: 27 February 2009).

34. USGBC, "About LEED," fact sheet (Washington, DC: 2007).

35. USGBC, op. cit. note 29; USGBC, "LEED for New Construction" (Washington, DC: 2007).

36. USGBC, *LEED 2009 for New Construction and Major Renovations*, Version 3.0 (Washington, DC: April 2009).

37. Ibid.

38. USGBC, op. cit. note 29.

39. NREL, *The Philip Merrill Environmental Center, Chesapeake Bay Foundation: Highlighting High Performance* (Golden, CO: April 2002).

40. "Toyota Seeks Gold for New Green Buildings," *GreenBiz.com*, 23 April 2003; "The Green Stamp of Approval," *Business Week*, 11 September 2006.

41. Nick Carey and Ilaina Jonas, "Green Buildings Need More Incentives in US," *Reuters*, 15 February 2007; Alexander Durst, The Durst Organization, discussion with Jignasha Rana, Earth Policy Institute, 2 July 2009.

42. Carey and Jonas, op. cit. note 41.

43. Barnaby J. Feder, "Environmentally Conscious Development," *New York Times*, 25 August 2004.

44. World Green Business Council, "Established Green Building Councils" and "Emerging Green Business Councils," at www.worldgbc.org/greenbuilding-councils, viewed 10 April 2009; LEED-certified floor space from Marie Coleman, USGBC, e-mail to Jignasha Rana, Earth Policy Institute, 1 June 2009.

45. USGBC, op. cit. note 34; "Clinton Unveils $5 Billion Green Makeover for Cities," *Environment News Service*, 16 May 2007.

46. USGBC, op. cit. note 34; "Clinton Unveils $5 Billion Green Makeover for Cities," op. cit. note 45; USGBC, "The Clinton Climate Initiative and the U.S. Green Building Council Expand Global Partnership," press release (Washington, DC: 10 February 2009).

47. Clinton Foundation, "CCI Helps Retrofit Empire State Building," press release (New York: 6 April 2009); Molly Miller, "Leading Example for Energy Efficiency," press release (Boulder, CO: Rocky Mountain Institute, April 2009).

48. Brad Heavner, Environment Maryland, Testimony before the Subcommittee on Energy and Air Quality, Energy and Commerce Committee, U.S. House of Representatives, Washington, DC, 17 July 2008.

49. Mazria, op. cit. note 30; information on the 2030 Challenge at www.architecture2030.org.

50. Mazria, op. cit. note 30.

51. Ibid.

52. Yuri Kageyama, "Toyota US Hybrid Sales Surpass Million Units," *Associated Press*, 12 March 2009; National Highway Traffic Safety Administration, *Summary of Fuel Economy Performance* (Washington, DC: U.S. Department of Transportation, 30 March 2009).

53. Cost of electricity equivalent to a gallon of gas from Roger Duncan, "Plug-In Hybrids: Pollution-Free Transport on the Horizon," *Solar Today*, May/June 2007, p. 46.

54. Chris Gaylord, "Electric Cars Around the Corner," *Christian Science*

Monitor, 16 March 2009; Micheline Maynard, "Toyota Plans to Leapfrog G.M. with a Plug-In," *New York Times*, 12 January 2009; Norihiko Shirouzu, "Technology Levels Playing Field in Race to Market Electric Car," *Wall Street Journal*, 12 January 2009.

55. Maynard, op. cit. note 54; General Motors, "Imagine: A Daily Commute Without Using a Drop of Gas," at www.chevrolet.com/electriccar, viewed 8 August 2008.

56. Matthew Dolan and Joan Murphy, "Nissan, Ford Plan Electric Push Aided by U.S.; Demand is Uncertain," *Wall Street Journal*, 24 June 2009; Think, "Think Announces U.S. Factory Plans," press release (Snarøya, Norway: 12 March 2009); CalCars, "How Carmakers are Responding to the Plug-In Hybrid Opportunity," at www.calcars.org/carmakers.html, viewed 3 June 2009.

57. Michael Kintner-Meyer et al., *Impacts Assessment of Plug-in Hybrid Vehicles on Electric Utilities and Regional U.S. Power Grids—Part 1: Technical Analysis* (Richland, WA: DOE, Pacific Northwest National Laboratory, 2006).

58. Steve Hamm, "The Electric Car Acid Test," *Business Week*, 4 February 2008, pp. 42–46; Better Place, "Global Progress," at www.betterplace.com/global-progress, viewed 14 April 2009.

59. Hiroki Matsumoto, "The Shinkansen: Japan's High Speed Railway," testimony before the Subcommittee on Railroads, Pipelines and Materials (Washington, DC: Committee on Transportation and Infrastructure, 19 April 2007); Central Japan Railway Company, *Annual Report 2008*, at english.jr-central.co.jp/company/ir/annualreport/index.html, viewed 29 May 2009.

60. Matsumoto, op. cit. note 59.

61. Ibid.

62. Inaki Barron, "High Speed Rail: The Big Picture," testimony before the Subcommittee on Railroads, Pipelines and Materials (Washington, DC: Committee on Transportation and Infrastructure, 19 April 2007); Railteam, "European High Speed Rail Operators Launch Railteam," press release (Brussels: 2 July 2007); Bruce Crumley, "European Train Travel: Working on the Railroad," *Time*, 28 May 2009.

63. "Ave Madrid," *The Economist*, 5 February 2009.

64. "A High-Speed Revolution," *The Economist*, 5 July 2007.

65. Barron, op. cit. note 62.

66. Jack Kinstlinger, *Magnetic Levitation High Speed Rail Service Along the Eastern Seaboard* (Hunt Valley, MD: KCI Technologies, Inc., 2007).

67. Huang Xin, "China Starts Work on Beijing-Shanghai Express Railway," *Xinhua*, 18 April 2008.

68. John L. Mica, "Opening Statement: Rep. Shuster from Today's Hearing on High Speed Rail," press release (Washington, DC: Committee on Transportation and Infrastructure, 19 April 2007); *American Recovery and Reinvestment Act of 2009*, Public Law 111–5, 111th Congress, 1st session (6 January 2009).

69. *National Interstate and Defense Highways Act (1956)*, Public Law 627, Chapter 462, 84th Congress, 2nd session (27 June 1956).

70. "Californians Approve High-Speed Rail, Nix Fake Clean Energy Props," *Environment News Service*, 5 November 2008.

71. Gerhard Metschies, "Pain at the Pump," *Foreign Policy*, July/August 2007; Ward's Automotive Group, *World Motor Vehicle Data 2008* (Southfield, MI: 2008).

72. Office of the Press Secretary, "President Obama Announces National Fuel Efficiency Policy," press release (Washington, DC: 19 May 2009); Keith Bradsher, "China Is Said to Plan Strict Gas Mileage Rules," *New York Times*, 27 May 2009; Andrew C. Revkin, "Fuel Efficiency Standards: Not So Efficient?" *New York Times*, 19 May 2009.

73. Ernst Ulrich von Weizsäcker, Amory B. Lovins, and L. Hunter Lovins, *Factor Four: Doubling Wealth, Halving Resource Use* (London: Earthscan, 1997); Friedrich Schmidt-Bleek et al., *Factor 10: Making Sustainability Accountable, Putting Resource Productivity into Praxis* (Carnoules, France: Factor 10 Club, 1998), p. 5.

74. William McDonough and Michael Braungart, *Cradle to Cradle: Remaking the Way We Make Things* (New York: North Point Press, 2002); Rebecca Smith, "Beyond Recycling: Manufacturers Embrace 'C2C' Design," *Wall Street Journal*, 3 March 2005.

75. Rona Fried, "Recycling Industry Offers Recession-Proof Investing," *Solar Today*, July/August 2008, pp. 22–23.

76. Claude Mandil et al., *Tracking Industrial Energy Efficiency and CO_2 Emissions* (Paris: IEA, 2007), pp. 39, 59–61.

77. World Steel Association, *World Steel in Figures 2009* (Brussels: 2009); Mandil et al., op. cit. note 76, pp. 39, 59–61.

78. "Iron and Steel Scrap," in U.S. Geological Survey (USGS), *Mineral Commodity Summaries* (Reston, VA: U.S. Department of the Interior, 2009), pp. 84–85; "Steel Recycling Rates at a Glance," fact sheet (Pittsburgh, PA: Steel Recycling Institute, 2007); Mississippi Department of Environmental Quality, "Recycling Trivia," at www.deq.state.ms.us, viewed 17 October 2007.

79. One fourth the energy from Mandil et al., op. cit. note 76, p. 106; cut in energy use calculated from International Iron and Steel Institute (IISI), "Crude Steel Production by Process," *World Steel in Figures 2007*, at www.worldsteel.org, viewed 16 October 2007; McKinsey Global Institute, *Curbing Global Energy Demand Growth: The Energy Productivity Opportunity* (Washington, DC: May 2007).

80. "Cement," in USGS, op. cit. note 78, pp. 40–41; energy savings by adopting Japanese technologies from U.N. Environment Programme, *Buildings and Climate Change: Status, Challenges and Opportunities* (Paris: 2007), p. 19; energy saving from adopting dry-kiln process calculated from Mandil et al., op. cit. note 76.

81. Bus weight from John Shonsey et al., *RTD Bus Transit Facility Design Guidelines and Criteria* (Denver, CO: Regional Transportation District, February 2006); car weight from Stacy C. Davis and Susan W. Diegel, *Transportation Energy Data Book: Edition 26* (Oak Ridge, TN: ORNL, DOE, 2007), p. 415; car-to-bus ratio from American Public Transportation Association, *The Benefits of Public Transportation—An Overview* (Washington, DC: September 2002).

82. Mandil et al., op. cit. note 76, pp. 265–68.

83. Ljupka Arsova et al., "The State of Garbage in America," *BioCycle*, vol. 49, no. 12 (December 2008); Malia Wollan, "San Francisco to Toughen a

Strict Recycling Law," *New York Times*, 11 June 2009; Felicity Barringer, "A City Committed to Recycling is Ready for More," *New York Times*, 7 May 2008.

84. "New Hampshire Town Boosts Recycling with Pay-As-You-Throw," *Environment News Service*, 21 March 2007; population data from Town of Lyme Web site, at www.lymenh.gov, viewed 3 June 2009.

85. "New Hampshire Town Boosts Recycling," op. cit. note 84.

86. Finland in Brenda Platt and Neil Seldman, *Wasting and Recycling in the United States 2000* (Athens, GA: GrassRoots Recycling Network, 2000); Prince Edward Island Government, "PEI Bans the Can," at www.gov.pe.ca, viewed 15 August 2005; Brenda Platt and Doug Rowe, *Reduce, Reuse, Refill!* (Washington, DC: Institute for Local Self-Reliance, 2002); David Saphire, *Case Reopened: Reassessing Refillable Bottles* (New York: INFORM, Inc., 1994).

87. Sue McAllister, "Commercial Recycling Centers: Turning Debris into Treasure," *San Jose Mercury News*, 10 April 2007.

88. Brian Hindo, "Everything Old is New Again," *BusinessWeek Online*, 25 September 2006.

89. Junko Edahiro, Japan for Sustainability, e-mail to Janet Larsen, Earth Policy Institute, 16 October 2007; Tim Burt, "VW is Set for $500m Recycling Provision," *Financial Times*, 12 February 2001; Mark Magnier, "Disassembly Lines Hum in Japan's New Industry," *Los Angeles Times*, 13 May 2001.

90. "FT Report—Waste and the Environment: EU Tackles Gadget Mountain," *Financial Times*, 18 April 2007; Jeremy Faludi, "Pop Goes the Cell Phone," *Worldchanging*, 4 April 2006.

91. Rick Ridgeway, Environmental Initiatives and Special Media Projects, Patagonia, Inc., discussion with author, 22 August 2006; Patagonia, "Patagonia Announces Major Expansion of Garment Recycling Program," press release (Ventura, CA: 28 January 2008); Jen Rapp, Patagonia, e-mail to Jignasha Rana, Earth Policy Institute, 28 April 2009.

92. Hindo, op. cit. note 88.

93. Daniel Michaels, "Boeing and Airbus Compete to Destroy What They Built," *Wall Street Journal*, 1 June 2007.

94. Ibid.

95. "Gold Statistics," in T.D. Kelly and G.R. Matos, comps., *Historical Statistics for Mineral and Material Commodities in the United States: U.S. Geological Survey Data Series 140* (Reston, VA: USGS, U.S. Department of the Interior, 2008); World Steel Association, op. cit. note 77; gold ore calculated from New Jersey Mining Company Reserves & Resources, "Estimated Ore Reserves," at www.newjerseymining.com, updated 31 December 2006; steel ore from Mandil et al., op. cit. note 76, p. 115; carbon dioxide emissions calculated using Gavin M. Mudd, "Resource Consumption Intensity and the Sustainability of Gold Mining," 2nd International Conference on Sustainability Engineering and Science, Auckland, New Zealand, 20–23 February 2007; EPA, *Emission Facts: Average Annual Emissions and Fuel Consumption for Passenger Cars and Light Trucks* (Washington, DC: April 2000).

96. Catherine Ferrier, *Bottled Water: Understanding a Social Phenomenon* (Surrey, U.K.: WWF, 2001).

97. Oil consumption calculated using number of plastic water bottles from Jennifer Gitlitz et al., *Water, Water Everywhere: The Growth of Non-carbonated Beverages in the United States* (Washington, DC: Container Recycling Institute, February 2007); I. Boustead, *Eco-profiles of the European Plastics Industry: PET Bottles* (Brussels: PlasticsEurope, Association of Plastics Manufacturers, March 2005), pp. 4–9; DOE, Energy Information Administration, "Oil Market Basics: Demand," at www.eia.doe .gov/pub/oil_gas/petroleum/analysis_publications/oil_market_basics/de mand_text.htm, viewed 23 January 2006; Ward's Automotive Group, *Ward's World Motor Vehicle Data 2006* (Southfield, MI: 2006), p. 242; Pacific Institute, "Bottled Water and Energy," fact sheet (Oakland, CA: 2007).

98. "S.F. Mayor Bans Bottled Water at City Offices," *Associated Press*, 25 June 2007; Ross C. Anderson, Salt Lake City Mayor, national press telephone conference, Think Outside the Bottle Campaign, 9 October 2007.

99. Janet Larsen, "Bottled Water Boycotts: Back-to-the-Tap Movement Gains Momentum," *Plan B Update* (Washington, DC: Earth Policy Institute, 7 December 2007); John G. Rodwan, Jr., *Confronting Challenges: U.S. and International Bottled Water Developments and Statistics for 2008* (New York: Beverage Marketing Corporation, April/May 2009).

100. John Roach, "Plastic-Bag Bans Gaining Momentum around the World," *National Geographic News*, 4 April 2008.

101. Michael Goggin, "Curtailment, Negative Prices Symptomatic of Inadequate Transmission," *Wind Energy Weekly*, vol. 27, no. 1305 (5 September 2008).

102. Joint Coordinated System Plan, *Joint Coordinated System Plan '08 Report Volume 1: Economic Assessment*, at www.jcspstudy.org, 2008.

103. S. Massoud Amin and Clark W. Gellings, "The North American Power Delivery System: Balancing Market Restructuring and Environmental Economics with Infrastructure Security," *Energy*, vol. 31, issues 6–7 (May–June 2006), pp. 967–99; Bracken Hendricks, *Wired for Progress 2.0: Building a National Clean-Energy Smart Grid* (Washington, DC: Center for American Progress, April 2009), p. 31.

104. Helen Knight, "Renewable Energy: Will the Lights Stay On?" *New Scientist*, 11 October 2008, pp. 30–31; Repower America, "Unified National Smart Grid," at www.repoweramerica.org, viewed 30 June 2009.

105. Ashlea Ebeling, "What Would You Pay to Stay Cool?" *Forbes*, 15 August 2007.

106. Knight, op. cit. note 104.

107. Ibid.

108. Rebecca Smith, "Consumers: A Little Knowledge...," *Wall Street Journal*, 30 June 2008; U.S. Department of Labor, Bureau of Labor Statistics, Mid-Atlantic Information Office, *Average Energy Prices in the Washington-Baltimore Area: April 2009* (Philadelphia, PA: 1 June 2009); Ahmad Faruqui and Sanem Sergici, *BGE's Smart Energy Pricing Pilot Summer 2008 Impact Evaluation* (Cambridge, MA: The Brattle Group, 28 April 2009), pp. 1–2; Baltimore Gas and Electric Company, "Re: Supplement 437 to P.S.C. Md E-6 - Rider 26 - Peak Time Rebate," electronic filings to Public Service Commission of Maryland, 15 April and 22 June 2009.

109. The Edison Foundation, "Utility-Scale Smart Meter Deployments, Plans

& Proposals (IOUs)," issue brief (Washington, DC: May 2009).

110. Smart Meters, "Finland Leads Europe in Smart Grid Development," news release (Isle of Benbecula, Scotland: 16 January 2009).

111. Erik Olsen, "Smart Meters Open Market for Smart Apps," Green, Inc., at *Nytimes.com*, 7 October 2008.

112. IEA, op. cit. note 17, p. 506.

113. IEA, *World Energy Outlook 2006* (Paris: 2006), p. 492; IEA, op. cit. note 11, pp. 25, 29.

114. Natalie Mims, Mathias Bell, and Stephen Doig, *Assessing the Electric Productivity Gap and the U.S. Efficiency Opportunity* (Snowmass, CO: Rocky Mountain Institute, January 2009), pp. 6, 16–17.

115. Mandil et al., op. cit. note 76, pp. 39, 59–61, 95–96, 139–42.

Chapter 5. Stabilizing Climate: Shifting to Renewable Energy

1. U.S. Department of Energy (DOE), Energy Information Administration (EIA), *Crude Oil Production*, electronic database, at tonto.eia.doe.gov, updated 28 July 2008; American Wind Energy Association (AWEA), "Installed U.S. Wind Power Capacity Surged 45% in 2007: American Wind Energy Association Market Report," press release (Washington, DC: 17 January 2008); AWEA, *U.S. Wind Energy Projects*, electronic database, at www.awea.org/projects, updated 31 March 2009; future capacity calculated from Emerging Energy Research (EER), "US Wind Markets Surge to New Heights," press release (Cambridge, MA: 14 August 2008); coal-fired power plant equivalents calculated by assuming that an average plant has a 500-megawatt capacity and operates 72 percent of the time, generating 3.15 billion kilowatt-hours of electricity per year; residential consumption calculated using "Residential Sector Energy Consumption Estimates, 2005," in DOE, EIA, *Residential Energy Consumption Survey 2005 Status Report* (Washington, DC: 2007), with capacity factor from DOE, National Renewable Energy Laboratory (NREL), *Power Technologies Energy Data Book* (Golden, CO: August 2006); population from U.S. Census Bureau, *State & County QuickFacts*, electronic database, at quickfacts.census.gov, updated 20 February 2009.

2. "Clipper and BP to JV on 5,050-MW South Dakota Wind Project," *Wind Energy Weekly*, vol. 27, no. 1300 (1 August 2008); 1 megawatt (MW) of installed wind capacity produces enough electricity to supply 300 homes from AWEA, "U.S. Wind Energy Installations Reach New Milestone," press release (Washington, DC: 14 August 2006); average U.S. household size from U.S. Census Bureau, "2005–2007 American Community Survey 3-Year Estimates—Data Profile Highlights," at factfinder.census.gov/servlet/ACSSAFFFacts, viewed 9 April 2009, with population from Census Bureau, op. cit. note 1; electricity export from EER, op. cit. note 1; ITC Holdings Corp., "ITC Holdings Corp. Unveils Green Power Express," press release (Novi, MI: 9 February 2009); TransCanada, "TransCanada's Zephyr and Chinook Power Transmission Line," project brochure (Calgary, Alberta: April 2009); Quanta Technology, LLC, *Final Report on the Southwest Power Pool (SPP) Updated EHV Overlay Study* (Raleigh, NC: 3 March 2008), pp. 11–17; "A Window of North Atlantic Opportunity," *Windpower Monthly*, October 2008, pp. 21–22.

3. Mark Leftly, "Middle East to Fund Scotland's £5bn Power Grid," *Inde-*

pendent (London), 10 August 2008; currency conversion from www.bloomberg.com/invest/calculators/currency.html, 9 April 2009; "World Electricity Installed Capacity by Type (Million Kilowatts), January 1, 2006," in DOE, EIA, "International Energy Annual 2006—World Electricity Data," at www.eia.doe.gov/iea/elec.html, updated 8 December 2008.

4. "Algeria Aims to Export Power—Solar Power," *Associated Press*, 11 August 2007; William Maclean, "Algeria Plans Solar Power Cable to Germany—Paper," *Reuters*, 15 November 2007.

5. "World Electricity Installed Capacity by Type (Million Kilowatts)," in DOE, op. cit. note 3; David O'Byrne, "Electricity Generation: Fair Winds Blow for a Clean Alternative," *Financial Times*, 10 June 2008; Jan Dodd, "Strong Winds and High Prices in Turkey," *Windpower Monthly*, September 2008; project selection and permitting from Dr. Hilmi Güler, Turkish Minister of Energy and Natural Resources, discussion with author, 20 June 2008.

6. Peter Janssen, "The Too Slow Flow: Why Indonesia Could Get All Its Power from Volcanoes—But Doesn't," *Newsweek*, 20 September 2004; "Geothermal Power Projects to Cost \$US19.8 Bln, Official Says," *ANTARA News* (Jakarta), 9 July 2008; Gita Wirjawan, "The Oil Cycle: The Wheels are Turning Again," *Jakarta Post*, 12 March 2009.

7. D. L. Elliott, L. L. Wendell, and G. L. Gower, *An Assessment of the Available Windy Land Area and Wind Energy Potential in the Contiguous United States* (Richland, WA: Pacific Northwest National Laboratory, 1991); Cristina L. Archer and Mark Z. Jacobson, "The Spatial and Temporal Distributions of U.S. Winds and Wind Power at 80 m Derived from Measurements," *Journal of Geophysical Research*, vol. 108 (13 May 2003); China from C. L. Archer and M. Z. Jacobson, "Evaluation of Global Windpower," *Journal of Geophysical Research*, vol. 110 (30 June 2005), and from Jean Hu et al., "Wind: The Future is Now," *Renewable Energy World*, July–August 2005, p. 212; Indonesia based on 27,000 MW potential from Alimin Ginting, Indonesia Geothermal Association, "Geothermal Energy: Global Status, Market and Challenge for Developing in Indonesia," presentation to the Thematic Panel Discussion of LEAD International Training Session on Leadership and Climate Change, 26 November–1 December 2007, Jakarta-Bandung, Indonesia, and on International Energy Agency (IEA), *IEA Statistics*, electronic database, at www.iea.org/Textbase/stats/ index.asp, viewed 1 May 2009.

8. Lester R. Brown, "The Flawed Economics of Nuclear Power," *Plan B Update* (Washington, DC: Earth Policy Institute, 28 October 2008).

9. International Telecommunication Union, "Key Global Telecom Indicators for the World Telecommunication Service Sector," at www.itu.int/ITU-D/ict/statistics/at_glance/KeyTelecom99.html, updated 10 March 2009; Molly O. Sheehan, "Mobile Phone Use Booms," in Worldwatch Institute, *Vital Signs 2002* (New York: W. W. Norton & Company, 2002), p. 85.

10. "Historical USA PC Sales" and "Historical Worldwide PC Sales," tables in Computer Industry Almanac Inc., *Worldwide PC Market* (Arlington Heights, IL: September 2008); European Photovoltaic Industry Association (EPIA), *Global Market Outlook for Photovoltaics Until 2013* (Brus-

sels: April 2009), pp. 3–4; Global Wind Energy Council (GWEC), *Global Wind 2008 Report* (Brussels: 2009), p. 10.

11. Archer and Jacobson, "Evaluation of Global Windpower," op. cit. note 7; Hu et al., op. cit. note 7.

12. Elliott, Wendell, and Gower, op. cit. note 7; Archer and Jacobson, "The Spatial and Temporal Distributions of U.S. Winds," op. cit. note 7; offshore potential from NREL data cited in U.S. Minerals Management Service, *Survey of Available Data on OCS Resources and Identification of Data Gaps*, Report to the Secretary, U.S. Department of the Interior (Washington, DC: April 2009), pp. I–11 to I–14.

13. European Wind Energy Association (EWEA), "Seas of Change: Offshore Wind Energy," fact sheet (Brussels: February 2009); Garrad Hassan and Partners, *Sea Wind Europe* (London: Greenpeace, March 2004).

14. GWEC, op. cit. note 10, pp. 3, 10, 24.

15. Denmark from GWEC, "Interactive World Map," at www.gwec.net/index.php?id=126, viewed 29 May 2009; Germany from GWEC, op. cit. note 10, pp. 34–35.

16. Flemming Hansen, "Denmark to Increase Wind Power to 50% by 2025, Mostly Offshore," *Renewable Energy Access*, 5 December 2006.

17. GWEC, op. cit. note 10, pp. 33, 48–49.

18. AWEA, "U.S. Wind Energy Industry Installs Over 2,800 MW in First Quarter," press release (28 April 2009); AWEA, *U.S. Wind Energy Projects*, op. cit. note 1; AWEA and Solar Energy Industries Association, *Green Power Superhighways: Building a Path to America's Clean Energy Future* (Washington, DC: February 2009).

19. Southern California Edison, *The Tehachapi Renewable Transmission Project: Greening the Grid* (Los Angeles: March 2008); Paul Klein, Media Relations Group, Southern California Edison, discussion with Jonathan G. Dorn, Earth Policy Institute, 22 October 2007; "Clipper and BP to JV," op. cit. note 2; Carl Levesque, "Super-Size It: Mega-Wind Farm Proposals Proliferate," *Wind Energy Weekly*, vol. 27, no. 1303 (22 August 2008).

20. "Maine Legislature Unanimously Approves Wind Recommendations," *Wind Energy Weekly*, vol. 27, no. 1286 (1 August 2008); population from Census Bureau, op. cit. note 1; installed capacities from AWEA, *U.S. Wind Energy Projects*, op. cit. note 1; New York from Matthew L. Wald, "Wind Energy Bumps Into Power Grid's Limits," *New York Times*, 27 August 2008; "Oregon Siting Council Green-Lights 909-MW Wind Farm," *Wind Energy Weekly*, vol. 27, no. 1300 (1 August 2008).

21. Cape Wind, "Project at a Glance," at www.capewind.org/article24.htm, viewed 14 April 2009; Rhode Island from "Deepwater to Start Building R.I. Wind Farm in 2010," *Reuters*, 8 January 2009; "LIPA & Con Edison Eye Offshore Wind Power," *Renewable Energy World*, 25 March 2009; "Garden State Offshore Energy Wins Bid for Offshore Wind Farm," *Renewable Energy World*, 6 October 2008; "Bluewater Wind Signs Contract for Sale of Offshore Wind Power," *Renewable Energy World*, 24 June 2008; 1 MW of installed wind capacity produces enough electricity to supply 300 homes from sources cited in note 2.

22. Willett Kempton et al., "Large CO_2 Reductions Via Offshore Wind Power Matched to Inherent Storage in Energy End-Uses," *Geophysical Research Letters*, vol. 34 (24 January 2007); Steve Gelsi, "Green-Collar Pioneers Eye

Offshore Wind Riches," *MarketWatch*, 8 October 2008; Walt Musial, "Deepwater Offshore Wind Technology Research Requirements," poster prepared for AWEA WindPower 2005 Conference, Denver, CO, 12–18 May 2005.

23. U.N. Population Division, *World Population Prospects: The 2008 Revision Population Database*, at esa.un.org/unpp, updated 11 March 2009; Archer and Jacobson, "Evaluation of Global Windpower," op. cit. note 7; GWEC, op. cit. note 10, p. 22; "A Window of North Atlantic Opportunity," op. cit. note 2.

24. GWEC, op. cit. note 10, pp. 3, 24–27; Liming Qiao, Policy Director, GWEC, e-mail to J. Matthew Roney, Earth Policy Institute, 29 April 2009.

25. A 2-megawatt wind turbine operating 36 percent of the time generates 6.3 million kilowatt-hours of electricity per year; capacity factor from DOE, NREL, op. cit. note 1; wholesale electricity price from DOE, *Wholesale Market Data*, electronic database at www.eia.doe.gov/cneaf/electricity, updated 22 April 2009; Renewable Fuels Association, *Homegrown for the Homeland: Ethanol Industry Outlook 2005* (Washington, DC: 2005); corn per acre and ethanol per bushel approximated from Allen Baker et al., "Ethanol Reshapes the Corn Market," *Amber Waves*, vol. 4, no. 2 (April 2006), pp. 32, 34; conservative ethanol price of $2 per gallon based on F.O. Licht, "Biofuels," *World Ethanol and Biofuels Report*, vol. 7, no. 15 (14 April 2009), p. 318.

26. Wind royalties are author's estimates based on Union of Concerned Scientists (UCS), "Farming the Wind: Wind Power and Agriculture," fact sheet (Cambridge, MA: 2003).

27. Laurie Jodziewicz, AWEA, e-mail to author, 16 October 2007; GWEC and Greenpeace, *Global Wind Energy Outlook 2006* (Brussels: 2006).

28. GWEC, op. cit. note 10, pp. 9–10.

29. Ward's Automotive Group, *World Motor Vehicle Data 2008* (Southfield, MI: 2008), pp. 239–42; "Trillions in Spending Needed to Meet Global Oil and Gas Demand, Analysis Shows," *International Herald Tribune*, 15 October 2007.

30. David L. Lewis, "They May Save Our Honor, Our Hopes—and Our Necks," *Michigan History*, September/October 1993; Harry Braun, *The Phoenix Project: Shifting from Oil to Hydrogen with Wartime Speed*, prepared for the Renewable Hydrogen Roundtable, World Resources Institute, Washington, DC, 10–11 April 2003, pp. 3–4; Kathy Barks Hoffman, "GM Plant Shutdowns Further Hurt Michigan Budget," *Associated Press*, 23 April 2009.

31. EWEA, "Wind Now Leads EU Power Sector," press release (Brussels: 2 February 2009); Erik Shuster, *Tracking New Coal-Fired Power Plants* (Pittsburgh, PA: DOE, National Energy Technology Laboratory, January 2009); "Nuclear Dips in 2008," *World Nuclear News*, 29 May 2009; GWEC, op. cit. note 10, pp. 10, 56–57.

32. EPIA, op. cit. note 10, pp. 3–4.

33. Prometheus Institute and Greentech Media, "25th Annual Data Collection Results: PV Production Explodes in 2008," *PVNews*, vol. 28, no. 4 (April 2009), pp. 15–18.

34. IEA, *World Energy Outlook 2006* (Paris: 2006); "Power to the Poor," *The Economist*, 10 February 2001, pp. 21–23.

35. Sybille de La Hamaide, "Bangladesh Seeks World Bank Loan for Solar Power," *Reuters*, 26 April 2007.
36. "Solar Loans Light Up Rural India," *BBC News*, 29 April 2007.
37. Emissions include kerosene and other fuel lamps, from IEA, *Light's Labour's Lost: Policies for Energy-Efficient Lighting* (Paris: 2006), pp. 201–02; DOE, EIA, *International Petroleum Monthly*, at www.eia .doe.gov/ipm/supply.html, updated 13 April 2009.
38. "PV Costs Set to Plunge for 2009/10," *Renewable Energy World*, 23 December 2008; "PV Costs Down Significantly from 1998–2007," *Renewable Energy World*, 23 February 2009; Christoph Podewils, "As Cheap as Brown Coal: By 2010, a kWh of PV Electricity in Spain Will Cost Around 9¢ to Produce," *PHOTON International*, April 2007.
39. Ines Rutschmann, "A Country of Megawatt Parks," *PHOTON International* (September 2008), pp. 32–39; Cleantech America, Inc., "KRCD Enters Long Term, Zero Emission Solar Power Plan," press release (San Francisco, CA: 6 July 2007); Ehud Zion Waldoks, "IEC Approves Arava Company's Proposal for World's Largest Photovoltaic Field," *The Jerusalem Post*, 15 February 2009.
40. Matthew L. Wald, "Two Large Solar Plants Planned in California," *New York Times*, 15 August 2008.
41. China Technology Development Group Corporation, "CTDC to Build 30MW On-Grid Solar Power Station in Qaidam Basin," press release (Hong Kong: 2 January 2009); EPIA, op. cit. note 10, p. 10.
42. Svetlana Kovalyova, "Italy's Solar Power Flourishes with State Help," *Reuters*, 12 March 2009; EPIA, op. cit. note 10, p. 8; "Chapter 8.8: California Solar Initiative," in California State Legislature, *Statutes 2006*, SB1, Chapter 132 (Sacramento, CA: 21 August 2006); California Public Utilities Commission, *California Solar Initiative Program Handbook* (San Francisco, CA: January 2009), p. 91; Sara Parker, "Maryland Expands RPS: 1,500 MW Solar by 2022," *Renewable Energy Access*, 12 April 2007; New Jersey's Clean Energy Program, "FAQ: NJ Solar Financing Program," fact sheet (Newark, NJ: New Jersey Board of Public Utilities, 12 September 2007).
43. Calculated from EPIA, op. cit. note 10, pp. 3–4; people who lack electricity from IEA, op. cit. note 34.
44. Rainer Aringhoff et al., *Concentrated Solar Thermal Power—Now!* (Brussels, Almeria, and Amsterdam: European Solar Thermal Industry Association (ESTIF), IEA SolarPACES, and Greenpeace International, September 2005), p. 4; NREL, *U.S. Parabolic Trough Power Plant Data*, electronic database, at www.nrel.gov/csp/troughnet/power_plant _data.html, updated 25 July 2008; "Largest Solar Thermal Plant in 16 Years Now Online," *EERE Network News*, 13 June 2007; Solar Energy Industries Association, *US Solar Industry Year in Review 2008* (Washington, DC: March 2009), pp. 1, 7.
45. Lockheed Martin Corporation, "Lockheed Martin to Support Utility-Scale Solar Power Plant in Arizona," press release (Moorestown, NJ: 22 May 2009); Arizona Public Service, "APS, Starwood Energy to Collaborate on Major Concentrating Solar Plant," press release (Phoenix: 22 May 2009).
46. "Algeria Aims to Export Power," op. cit. note 4; Maclean, op. cit. note 4.

47. "Algeria Aims to Export Power," op. cit. note 4; Maclean, op. cit. note 4; Oak Ridge National Laboratory, "New Energy Algeria (NEAL)," at www.ornl.gov/sci/eere/international/neal_index.htm, viewed 17 April 2009.

48. Douglas Fischer, "Solar Thermal Comes Out of the Shadows," *The Daily Climate*, 20 November 2008; Jonathan G. Dorn, "Solar Thermal Power Coming to a Boil," *Plan B Update* (Washington, DC: Earth Policy Institute, 22 July 2008); "NRG Energy to Develop 500 MW of Solar Thermal," *Renewable Energy World*, 25 February 2009; Vanessa Lindlaw, Bright-Source Energy, e-mail to J. Matthew Roney, Earth Policy Institute, 3 June 2009.

49. Alok Jha, "Power in the Desert: Solar Towers Will Harness Sunshine of Southern Spain," *Guardian* (London), 24 November 2008; proposed plants from Dorn, op. cit. note 48; EER, "Global Concentrated Solar Power Markets & Strategies, 2009–2020," study announcement (Cambridge, MA: April 2009).

50. Renewable Energy Policy Network for the 21st Century (REN21), *Renewables 2007 Global Status Report* (Paris and Washington, DC: REN21 Secretariat and Worldwatch Institute, 2008), p. 14; DOE, Office of Energy Efficiency and Renewable Energy (EERE), "Concentrating Solar Power Funding Opportunity Announcement," news release (Washington, DC: 25 May 2007).

51. Mark S. Mehos and David W. Kearney, "Potential Carbon Emissions Reductions from Concentrating Solar Power by 2030," in Charles F. Kutscher, ed., *Tackling Climate Change in the U.S.—Potential Carbon Emissions Reductions from Energy Efficiency and Renewable Energy by 2030* (Boulder, CO: American Solar Energy Society, 2007), pp. 79–90; U.S. electricity consumption from DOE, EIA, *Electric Power Annual 2007* (Washington, DC: January 2009), p. 1; U.S. Department of the Interior, Bureau of Land Management, Nevada State Office, "Energy," Arizona State Office, "Arizona, the New Frontier!" and California Desert District, "Solar Energy Projects," all at www.blm.gov, updated 19 March 2009.

52. Christoph Richter, Sven Teske, and Rebecca Short, *Concentrating Solar Power Global Outlook 2009* (Amsterdam, Tabernas, and Brussels: Greenpeace International, SolarPACES, and ESTIF, May 2009), pp. 53–59.

53. Werner Weiss, Irene Bergmann, and Roman Stelzer, *Solar Heat Worldwide: Markets and Contribution to the Energy Supply 2007* (Gleisdorf, Austria: IEA, Solar Heating & Cooling Programme, May 2009), p. 21; "Sunrise or Sunset?" *China Daily*, 25 August 2008; Ryan Hodum, "Kunming Heats Up as China's 'Solar City'," *China Watch* (Washington, DC: Worldwatch Institute and Global Environmental Institute, 5 June 2007); Emma Graham-Harrison, "China Solar Power Firm Sees 25 Percent Growth," *Reuters*, 4 October 2007.

54. Rooftop solar water heaters have a capacity of 0.7 kilowatts per square meter and a capacity factor similar to rooftop photovoltaics (22 percent); nominal capacity from Weiss, Bergmann, and Stelzer, op. cit. note 53, p. 4; capacity factor from DOE, NREL, op. cit. note 1.

55. Ole Pilgaard, *Solar Thermal Action Plan for Europe* (Brussels, Belgium: ESTIF, 2007); Weiss, Bergmann, and Stelzer, op. cit. note 53, p. 21; U.N. Population Division, op. cit. note 23; Janet L. Sawin, "Solar Industry Stays

Hot," in Worldwatch Institute, *Vital Signs 2006–2007* (New York: W. W. Norton & Company, 2006).

56. Pilgaard, op. cit. note 55; Weiss, Bergmann, and Stelzer, op. cit. note 53, p. 21; U.N. Population Division, op. cit. note 23.

57. Uwe Brechlin, "Study on Italian Solar Thermal Reveals a Surprisingly High Contribution to EU Market: 130 MWth in 2006," press release (Brussels: ESTIF, 24 April 2007); Sawin, op. cit. note 55, p. 38; Les Nelson, "Solar-Water Heating Resurgence Ahead?" *Solar Today*, May/June 2007, p. 28; Pilgaard, op. cit. note 55; Ambiente Italia, *STO Database*, ProSTO Project Web site, at www.solarordinances.eu, viewed 3 June 2009.

58. Nelson, op. cit. note 57, p. 27; Larry Sherwood, *U.S. Solar Trends 2007* (Latham, NY: Interstate Renewable Energy Council, August 2008), p. 9; Jackie Jones, "Such an Obvious Solution," *Renewable Energy World*, 2 September 2008.

59. Weiss, Bergmann, and Stelzer, op. cit. note 53, p. 21; incentives from Jones, op. cit. note 58.

60. If in 2020 the 5 billion people in developing countries outside of China match China's 0.08 square meters of rooftop water and space heating capacity per person, this would add 400 million square meters to the world total. Assumptions based on Weiss, Bergmann, and Stelzer, op. cit. note 53, p. 21, and on U.N. Population Division, op. cit. note 23.

61. Nelson, op. cit. note 57, p. 26.

62. Ibid., p. 28; Ambiente Italia, op. cit. note 57.

63. EPIA, op. cit. note 10, p. 6; Richter, Teske, and Short, op. cit. note 52, p. 83; Shuster, op. cit. note 31.

64. Karl Gawell et al., *International Geothermal Development Directory and Resource Guide* (Washington, DC: Geothermal Energy Association (GEA), 2003); EER, *Global Geothermal Markets and Strategies 2009–2020* (Cambridge, MA: May 2009).

65. Geothermal growth rate calculated using Ruggero Bertani, "World Geothermal Generation in 2007," *GHC Bulletin*, September 2007, pp. 8–9, and EER, op. cit. note 64.

66. Bertani, op. cit. note 65, pp. 8–9; Kara Slack, *U.S. Geothermal Power Production and Development Update* (Washington, DC: GEA, March 2009); EER, op. cit. note 64; number of countries with geothermal power from Karl Gawell et al., *2007 Interim Report: Update on World Geothermal Development* (Washington, DC: GEA, 1 May 2007), p. 1; share of electricity calculated using installed capacity from Bertani, op. cit. note 65, p. 9; capacity factor from Ingvar B. Fridleifsson et al., "The Possible Role and Contribution of Geothermal Energy to the Mitigation of Climate Change," in O. Hohmeyer and T. Trittin, eds., *IPCC Scoping Meeting on Renewable Energy Sources, Proceedings* (Luebeck, Germany: 20–25 January 2008), p. 5, and from "World Total Net Electricity Generation, 1980–2005," in DOE, EIA, "International Energy Annual 2005—World Electricity Data," at www.eia.doe.gov/iea/elec.html, updated 13 September 2007.

67. World Bank, "Geothermal Energy," prepared under the PB Power and World Bank partnership program, www.worldbank.org, viewed 23 January 2003.

68. Jefferson Tester et al., *The Future of Geothermal Energy: Impact of Enhanced Geothermal Systems (EGS) on the United States in the 21st*

Century (Cambridge, MA: Massachusetts Institute of Technology, 2006); John W. Lund and Derek H. Freeston, "World-Wide Direct Uses of Geothermal Energy 2000," *Geothermics*, vol. 30 (2001), pp. 34, 46, 51, 53.

69. Tester et al., op. cit. note 68, pp. 1–4; Julian Smith, "Renewable Energy: Power Beneath Our Feet," *New Scientist*, 8 October 2008.

70. Rachel Nowak, "Who Needs Coal When You Can Mine Earth's Deep Heat?" *New Scientist*, 19 July 2008; Tester et al., op. cit. note 68.

71. UCS, "How Geothermal Energy Works," at www.ucsusa.org/clean_energy/renewable_energy_basics/offmen-how-geothermal-energy-works.html, viewed 22 April 2009; Slack, op. cit. note 66.

72. "Geothermal Power Projects to Cost $US19.8 Bln, Official Says," op. cit. note 6; Ed Davies and Karen Lema, "Geothermal-Rich SE Asia Struggles to Tap Earth's Power," *Reuters*, 30 June 2008; Bertani, op. cit. note 65, pp. 8–9; "Energy Dev Corp.: Bid to Become Top Geothermal Producer," *Agence France-Presse*, 14 January 2009; Geysir Green Energy, "Philippines," at www.geysirgreen energy.com/Operations-and-Development/asia/philippines, viewed 22 April 2009.

73. German Federal Institute for Geosciences and Natural Resources (BGR), "African Rift Geothermal Facility (ARGeo)," at www.bgr.de/geotherm/projects/argeo.html, viewed 22 April 2009; U.N. Environment Programme (UNEP), "Hot Prospect—Geothermal Electricity Set for Rift Valley Lift-Off in 2009," press release (Nairobi: 9 December 2008); Bertani, op. cit. note 65, pp. 8–9; DOE, op. cit. note 3.

74. Yoko Nishikawa, "Japan Geothermal Projects Pick Up After 20 Years: Report," *Reuters*, 4 January 2009; Bertani, op. cit. note 65, pp. 8–9; Lund and Freeston, op. cit. note 68, p. 46.

75. Werner Bussmann, "Germany: The Geothermal Market is Expanding," presentation to the Renewable Energy Exhibition, Lyon, Paris, 25–28 February 2009; Jane Burgermeister, "Geothermal Electricity Booming in Germany," *Renewable Energy World*, 2 June 2008; UNEP, op. cit. note 73.

76. DOE, EERE, "Energy Savers: Geothermal Heat Pumps," updated 24 February 2009, and "Energy Savers: Benefits of Geothermal Heat Pump Systems," updated 30 December 2008, both at www.energysavers.gov; Burgermeister, op. cit. note 75.

77. Iceland National Energy Authority and Ministries of Industry and Commerce, *Geothermal Development and Research in Iceland* (Reykjavik, Iceland: April 2006), p. 16; World Bank, op. cit. note 67.

78. Lund and Freeston, op. cit. note 68, pp. 34, 51, 53.

79. World Bank, op. cit. note 67.

80. Ibid.

81. Lund and Freeston, op. cit. note 68, pp. 46, 53.

82. United States from Tester et al., op. cit. note 68; Japan based on assumption that Enhanced Geothermal Systems could double 72,000 MW potential, from Hirofumi Muraoka et al., "Assessment of Hydrothermal Resource Potentials in Japan 2008," *Abstract of Annual Meeting of Geothermal Research Society of Japan* (Kanazawa, Japan: 2008); Hirofumi Muraoka, National Institute of Advanced Industrial Science and Technology, e-mail to J. Matthew Roney, Earth Policy Institute, 13 July 2009.

83. Stephen R. Gliessman, *Agroecology: The Ecology of Sustainable Food Systems*, 2nd ed. (Boca Raton, FL: CRC Press, 2006), p. 256; Pew Center

on Global Climate Change, "Climate TechBook: Solar Power," fact sheet (Arlington, VA: May 2009); Richter, Teske, and Short, op. cit. note 52, pp. 18–19.

84. Ralph P. Overend and Anelia Milbrandt, "Potential Carbon Emissions Reductions from Biomass by 2030," in Kutscher, op. cit. note 51, pp. 112–30; DOE, op. cit. note 51, p. 24.

85. Swedish Energy Agency, *Energy in Sweden 2008* (Eskilstuna, Sweden: December 2008), pp. 96, 111.

86. Population data from Census Bureau, op. cit. note 1; Anders Rydaker, "Biomass for Electricity & Heat Production," presentation at Bioenergy North America 2007, Chicago, IL, 16 April 2007.

87. Oglethorpe Power Corporation, "Oglethorpe Power Announces Plans to Build Biomass Electric Generating Facilities," press release (Tucker, GA: 18 September 2008).

88. World Alliance for Decentralized Energy, *Bagasse Cogeneration—Global Review and Potential* (Washington, DC: June 2004), p. 32; sugar production from U.S. Department of Agriculture (USDA), *Production, Supply and Distribution*, electronic database, at www.fas.usda.gov/psdonline, updated 9 April 2009.

89. Waste to Energy Conference, "Power and Heat for Millions of Europeans," press release (Bremen, Germany: 20 April 2007); Confederation of European Waste-to-Energy Plants, "2008 Country Reports on Waste Management," at www.cewep.eu, viewed 23 July 2009; Jeffrey Morris, "Comparative LCAs for Curbside Recycling Versus Either Landfilling or Incineration with Energy Recovery," *International Journal of Life Cycle Assessment*, vol. 10, no. 4 (July 2005), pp. 273–84.

90. Puget Sound Energy, "King County, PSE, and Bio Energy-Washington Teaming Up to Generate Green Energy from Landfill Gas," press release (Seattle, WA: 6 April 2009).

91. Ray C. Anderson, presentation at Chicago Climate Exchange, Chicago, IL, 14 June 2006.

92. F.O. Licht, "World Fuel Ethanol Production," *World Ethanol and Biofuels Report*, vol. 7, no. 18 (26 May 2009), p. 365; F.O. Licht, "Biodiesel: World Production, by Country," *World Ethanol and Biofuels Report*, vol. 7, no. 14 (26 March 2009), p. 288.

93. F.O. Licht, "World Fuel Ethanol Production," op. cit. note 92, p. 365; Bill Guerin, "European Blowback for Asian Biofuels," *Asia Times*, 8 February 2007.

94. Timothy Searchinger et al., "Use of U.S. Croplands for Biofuels Increases Greenhouse Gases through Emissions from Land-Use Change," *Science*, vol. 319 (29 February 2008), pp. 1,238–40.

95. Joseph Fargione et al., "Land Clearing and the Biofuel Carbon Debt," *Science*, vol. 319 (29 February 2008), pp. 1,235–38.

96. "Biofools," *The Economist*, 11 April 2009; P. J. Crutzen et al., "N2O Release from Agro-biofuel Production Negates Global Warming Reduction by Replacing Fossil Fuels," *Atmospheric Chemistry and Physics*, vol. 8 (29 January 2008), pp. 389–95; industry reaction from Lauren Etter, "Ethanol Craze Cools As Doubts Multiply," *Wall Street Journal*, 28 November 2007; R. W. Howarth and Stefan Bringezu, eds., *Biofuels: Environmental Consequences and Interactions with Changing Land Use*, Pro-

ceedings of the Scientific Committee on Problems of the Environment (SCOPE) International Biofuels Project Rapid Assessment, 22–25 September 2008 (Ithaca, NY: Cornell University, 2009), pp. 1–13.

97. DOE, EERE, "Starch- and Sugar-Based Ethanol Feedstocks," at www.afdc.energy.gov/afdc/ethanol/feedstocks_starch_sugar.html, updated 4 February 2009; DOE and USDA, *Biomass as Feedstock for a Bioenergy and Bioproducts Industry: The Technical Feasibility of a Billion-Ton Annual Supply* (Washington, DC: April 2005); Jason Hill et al., "Environmental, Economic, and Energetic Costs and Benefits of Biodiesel and Ethanol Biofuels," *Proceedings of the National Academy of Sciences*, vol. 103, no. 30 (25 July 2006), pp. 11,206–10; M. R. Schmer et al., "Net Energy of Cellulosic Ethanol from Switchgrass," *Proceedings of the National Academy of Sciences*, vol. 105, no. 2 (15 January 2008), pp. 464–69; Purdue University, Department of Agricultural Communication, "Fast-Growing Trees Could Take Root as Future Energy Source," press release (West Lafayette, IN: 23 August 2006).

98. J. E. Campbell, D. B. Lobell, and C. B. Field, "Greater Transportation Energy and GHG Offsets from Bioelectricity than Ethanol," *Science,* vol. 324 (22 May 2009), pp. 1,055–57; DOE and USDA, op. cit. note 97, pp. i–ii.

99. Nic Lane, *Issues Affecting Tidal, Wave, and In-Stream Generation Projects* (Washington, DC: Congressional Research Service, 26 November 2008).

100. IEA, *World Energy Outlook 2008* (Paris: 2008), p. 165; IEA, *Member Countries and Countries Beyond the OECD*, electronic database, at www.iea.org/Textbase/country/index.asp, viewed 23 April 2009; International Rivers Network, "Frequently Asked Questions about Dams," fact sheet (Berkeley, CA: 2004).

101. "Rural Areas Get Increased Hydro Power Capacity," *Xinhua*, 7 May 2007.

102. Jason Palmer, "Renewable Energy: The Tide is Turning," *New Scientist*, 11 October 2008; European Commission, "Tidal Energy—Promising Sites Worldwide," ATLAS project Web site, at ec.europa.eu/energy/atlas/html/tidalsites.html, viewed 24 June 2009; ABS Energy Research, *The Ocean Energy Report* (London: 2009), pp. 13–23.

103. Choe Sang-Hun, "South Korea Seeks Cleaner Energy Sources," *International Herald Tribune*, 9 May 2007; Choe Sang-Hun, "As Tides Ebb and Rise, South Korea Prepares to Snare Them," *International Herald Tribune*, 31 May 2007; ABS Energy Research, op. cit. note 102, pp. 13–23; Lunar Energy, "British Firm Announces World's Largest Tidal Power Development," press release (East Yorkshire, U.K.: 11 March 2008); IEA, Implementing Agreement on Ocean Energy Systems (IEA-OES), *2008 Annual Report* (Lisbon, Portugal: February 2009), p. 83.

104. Palmer, op. cit. note 102; Choe, "As Tides Ebb and Rise," op. cit. note 103; ABS Energy Research, op. cit. note 102, pp. 13–23; "World Electricity Installed Capacity by Type (Million Kilowatts), January 1, 2006," in DOE, op. cit. note 3.

105. "Issued Hydrokinetic Projects Preliminary Permits," table in Federal Energy Regulatory Commission, "Hydropower-Industry Activities," at www.ferc.gov/industries/hydropower/indus-act/hydrokinetics.asp, updated 2 July 2009; Mike Hoover, Oceana Energy Company, e-mail to J.

Matthew Roney, 30 June 2009.

106. Robert Silgardo et al., *Finavera Renewables Inc.: Where There is Wind There is a Wave* (Toronto, ON: Dundee Securities Corporation, 18 June 2007); "Issued Hydrokinetic Projects Preliminary Permits," op. cit. note 105; San Francisco from Tom Zeller, Jr., "Wave Power for San Francisco?" Green Inc., at *Nytimes.com*, 27 February 2009.

107. Pelamis Wave Power, "Aguçadoura," at www.pelamiswave.com, viewed 23 April 2009; Mario de Queiroz, "Portugal: Waves of Energy Come Ashore," *Inter Press Service*, 24 September 2008; "Wave Hub Names Fourth Developer for Wave Energy Farm," *Renewable Energy Access*, 15 May 2007; European Commission, *Report on the Workshop on Hydropower and Ocean Energy—Part I: Ocean Energy* (Brussels: 13 June 2007), pp. 1, 3; IEA, op. cit. note 7; "Aquamarine to Develop 1 GW of Ocean Energy," *Renewable Energy World*, 24 February 2009; wave potential from World Energy Council, *2007 Survey of Energy Resources* (London: 2007), p. 544; "World Electricity Installed Capacity by Type (Million Kilowatts), January 1, 2006," in DOE, op. cit. note 3.

108. REN21, *Renewables Global Status Report: 2009 Update* (Paris and Washington, DC: REN21 Secretariat and Worldwatch Institute, 2009), p. 23; Lila Buckley, "Hydropower in China: Participation and Energy Diversity Are Key," *China Watch* (Washington, DC: Worldwatch Institute and Global Environmental Institute, 24 April 2007); "Rural Areas Get Increased Hydro Power Capacity," op. cit. note 101; Pallavi Aiyar, "China: Another Dammed Gorge," *Asia Times*, 3 June 2006; Gary Duffy, "Brazil Gives Amazon Dams Go-Ahead," *BBC News*, 10 July 2007; Patrick McCully, *Before the Deluge: Coping with Floods in a Changing Climate* (Berkeley, CA: International Rivers Network, 2007), pp. 22–23.

109. DOE, EIA, *Annual Energy Outlook 2009* (Washington, DC: March 2009), p. 74; National Hydropower Association, "NHA Applauds President Obama and Congress for Turning to Hydro in the Stimulus," press release (Washington, DC: 19 February 2009).

110. Table 5–1 by Earth Policy Institute, with 2020 goals cited throughout chapter and with 2008 figures calculated using the following sources: wind from GWEC, op. cit. note 10, p. 10; rooftop solar electric systems and solar electric power plants from EPIA, op. cit. note 10, p. 3, and from Rutschmann, op. cit. note 39; geothermal electricity from EER, op. cit. note 64; biomass electricity and heat and hydropower, including tidal and wave power, from REN21, op. cit. note 108, p. 23; rooftop solar water and space heaters from Weiss, Bergmann, and Stelzer, op. cit. note 53, p. 21; geothermal heat from Tester et al., op. cit. note 68, p. 9.

111. "'Wind Can Power Up Entire Nation'," *China Daily*, 18 June 2009; Rujun Shen and Tom Miles, "China's Wind-power Boom to Outpace Nuclear by 2020," *China Daily*, 20 April 2009.

112. Table 5–2 by Earth Policy Institute with existing fossil fuel and nuclear capacity from "Existing Capacity by Energy Source, 2007," and "Planned Nameplate Capacity Additions from New Generators, by Energy Source, 2008 through 2012," in DOE, op. cit. note 51, p. 25, and from Shuster, op. cit. note 31; renewables based on data and growth rates from AWEA, EPIA, GEA, DOE, Navigant Consulting, NREL, USDA, and Electric Power Research Institute.

113. "Texas to Spend Billions on Wind Power Transmission Lines," *Environment News Service*, 18 July 2008; Eileen O' Grady, "Texas Finalizes Plan to Expand Wind Lines," *Reuters*, 29 January 2009; residential supply calculated as described in note 2.

114. TransCanada, op. cit. note 2.

115. Scott DiSavino, "ITC Proposes Project to Move Wind Power to Chicago," *Reuters*, 9 February 2009; ITC Holdings Corp., op. cit. note 2; DOE, "Locke, Chu Announce Significant Steps in Smart Grid Development," press release (Washington, DC: 18 May 2009).

116. Cristina L. Archer and Mark Z. Jacobson, "Supplying Baseload Power and Reducing Transmission Requirements by Interconnecting Wind Farms," *Journal of Applied Meteorology and Climatology*, vol. 46 (November 2007), pp. 1,701–17.

117. Janice Massy, "Grand Vision on Paper: Blueprint for a European Supergrid," *Windpower Monthly*, December 2008, p. 37; Alok Jha, "Solar Power from Saharan Sun Could Provide Europe's Electricity, Says EU," *Guardian* (London), 23 July 2008; David Strahan, "From AC to DC: Going Green with Supergrids," *New Scientist*, 14–20 March 2009; Paul Rodgers, "Wind-fuelled 'Supergrid' Offers Clean Power to Europe," *Independent* (London), 25 November 2007.

118. Strahan, op. cit. note 117; Emmet Curley, Mainstream Renewable Power, discussion with J. Matthew Roney, Earth Policy Institute, 2 July 2009; The ABB Group, "The NorNed HVDC Link," at www.abb.com, updated 28 May 2009.

119. DESERTEC Foundation, "12 Companies Plan Establishment of a Desertec Industrial Initiative," press release (Munich: 13 July 2009); potential generating capacity estimated by author, based on Initiative's stated goal of meeting a substantial portion of the producer countries' electricity needs and 15 percent of Europe's electricity needs by 2050, using IEA, op. cit. note 100, pp. 506-07, with capacity factor from DOE, NREL, op. cit. note 1.

120. Edwin Clark, former senior economist, White House Council on Environmental Quality, letter to author, 25 July 2001; Joseph E. Aldy and Robert N. Stavins, Harvard Project on International Climate Agreements, "Economic Incentives in a New Climate Agreement," prepared for The Climate Dialogue, Copenhagen, Denmark, 7–8 May 2008.

121. Kate Galbraith, "Europe's Way of Encouraging Solar Power Arrives in the U.S.," *New York Times*, 12 March 2009; Karlynn Cory, Toby Couture, and Claire Kreycik, *Feed-in Tariff Policy: Design, Implementation, and RPS Policy Interactions* (Golden, CO: NREL, March 2009), p. 1; REN21, op. cit. note 50, p. 23; Database of State Incentives for Renewables & Efficiency, "Rules, Regulations, & Policies for Renewable Energy," updated April 2009, and "Federal Incentives for Renewables and Efficiency," updated 19 February 2009, electronic databases, both at www.dsireusa.org.

Chapter 6. Designing Cities for People

1. U.N. Population Division, *World Urbanization Prospects: The 2007 Revision Population Database*, electronic database, at esa.un.org/unup, updated 2008.

2. Urban population in 1900 from Mario Poläse, "Urbanization and Development," *Development Express*, no. 4, 1997; U.N. Population Division, *World Urbanization Prospects: The 2007 Revision* (New York: February 2008).

3. Molly O'Meara, *Reinventing Cities for People and the Planet*, Worldwatch Paper 147 (Washington, DC: Worldwatch Institute, June 1999), pp. 14–15; U.N. Population Division, op. cit. note 2, pp. 8–10; U.N. Population Division, *World Population Prospects: The 2008 Revision Population Database*, electronic database, at esa.un.org/unpp, updated 11 March 2009.

4. Christopher Flavin, "Hearing on Asia's Environmental Challenges: Testimony of Christopher Flavin," Committee on International Relations, U.S. House of Representatives, Washington, DC, 22 September 2004; Subir Bhaumik, "Air Pollution Suffocates Calcutta," *BBC News*, 3 May 2007; David Schrank and Tim Lomax, *2007 Urban Mobility Report* (College Station, TX: Texas Transportation Institute, September 2007), p. 1.

5. Francesca Lyman, "Twelve Gates to the City: A Dozen Ways to Build Strong, Livable, and Sustainable Cities," *Words and Pictures Magazine*, Issue 5, 2007; Lisa Jones, "A Tale of Two Mayors: The Improbable Story of How Bogota, Colombia, Became Somewhere You Might Actually Want To Live," *Grist Magazine*, 4 April 2002.

6. Claudia Nanninga, "Energy Efficient Transport—A Solution for China," *Voices of Grassroots*, November 2004; Enrique Peñalosa, "Parks for Livable Cities: Lessons from a Radical Mayor," keynote address at the Urban Parks Institute's Great Parks/Great Cities Conference, Chicago, 30 July 2001; Susan Ives, "The Politics of Happiness," *Trust for Public Land*, 9 August 2002; Jones, op. cit. note 5.

7. Peñalosa, op. cit. note 6.

8. Lara de Lacerda Santos Rodrigues, Curitiba City Government, e-mail to J. Matthew Roney, Earth Policy Institute, 24 July 2009.

9. O'Meara, op. cit. note 3.

10. Los Angeles from Sandra Postel, *Last Oasis*, rev. ed. (New York: W. W. Norton & Company, 1997), p. 20; Joel Simon, *Endangered Mexico* (San Francisco: Sierra Club Books, 1997); Chinese Ministry of Water Resources, *Country Report of the People's Republic of China* (Marseilles, France: World Water Council, 2003), pp. 60–61.

11. U.S. Department of Agriculture, Foreign Agricultural Service, *Grain: World Markets and Trade* and *Oilseeds: World Markets and Trade* (Washington, DC: various issues).

12. Richard Register, "Losing the World, One Environmental Victory at a Time—And a Way to Solve That Problem," essay (Oakland, CA: Ecocity Builders, Inc., 31 August 2005); Richard Register, *Ecocities: Rebuilding Cities in Balance with Nature: Revised Edition* (Gabriola Island, BC: New Society Publishers, 2006).

13. Register, "Losing the World, One Environmental Victory at a Time," op. cit. note 12; population estimate from U.S. Census Bureau, *State & County Quickfacts*, electronic database, at quickfacts.census.gov, updated 5 May 2009.

14. Register, "Losing the World, One Environmental Victory at a Time," op. cit. note 12.

15. Berliner Verkehrsbetriebe (BVG), "Means of Transport & Routes," at

www.bvg.de, viewed 11 May 2009.

16. Jay Walljasper, "Unjamming the Future," *Ode*, October 2005, pp. 36–41; Breakthrough Technologies Institute, *Transport Innovator* newsletter (various issues); Victoria Transport Policy Institute, "Bus Rapid Transit," *Online TDM Encyclopedia*, updated 22 July 2008; Institute for Transportation & Development Policy (ITDP), "China Bus Rapid Transit," at www.chinaBRT.org, updated 1 May 2009.

17. Bernardo Baranda, "Insurgentes Sur BRT Line Opens in Mexico City," ITDP, at www.itdp.org, 24 June 2008; Bernardo Baranda, "Mexico City Opens Second BRT Corridor," ITDP, at www.itdp.org, 21 December 2008; Karl Fjellstrom, "Guangzhou BRT Construction Begins," ITDP, at www.itdp.org, 17 December 2008; Karl Fjellstrom, ITDP, e-mail to J. Matthew Roney, Earth Policy Institute, 25 May 2009.

18. Tehran Public & International Relations Department, "Tehran Mayor Inaugurates 1st BRT Line," at www.tehran.ir, viewed 17 May 2009; Victoria Transport Policy Institute, op. cit. note 16; Breakthrough Technologies Institute, op. cit. note 16.

19. Molly O'Meara Sheehan, "Making Better Transportation Choices," in Lester R. Brown et al., *State of the World 2001* (New York: W. W. Norton & Company, 2001), p. 116.

20. William D. Eggers, Peter Samuel, and Rune Munk, *Combating Gridlock: How Pricing Road Use Can Ease Congestion* (New York: Deloitte, November 2003); Tom Miles, "London Drivers to Pay UK's First Congestion Tax," *Reuters*, 28 February 2002; Randy Kennedy, "The Day the Traffic Disappeared," *New York Times Magazine*, 20 April 2003, pp. 42–45; James Savage, "Congestion Charge Returns to Stockholm," *The Local*, 1 August 2007; currency conversion from www.oanda.com/convert/classic.

21. Transport for London, *Central London Congestion Charging: Impacts Monitoring* (London: various years).

22. "Milan to Impose 'Pollution Charge' on Cars," *Reuters*, 23 July 2007; "Milan Introduces Traffic Charge," *BBC News*, 2 January 2008; Malia Wollan, "San Francisco Studies Fees to Ease Traffic," *New York Times*, 3 January 2009; "Thousands Demonstrate Against Kyiv Mayor's Policies," *Radio Free Europe/Radio Liberty*, 12 February 2009; Paul Melia, "Drivers Facing Congestion Charge within Three Years," *Independent* (Dublin), 27 January 2009; Mathew Dearnaley, "Road Tolls a Hot Potato Since the Harbour Bridge," *New Zealand Herald*, 26 August 2008.

23. Serge Schmemann, "I Love Paris on a Bus, a Bike, a Train and in Anything but a Car," *New York Times*, 26 July 2007; Katrin Bennhold, "A New French Revolution's Creed: Let Them Ride Bikes," *New York Times*, 16 July 2007.

24. Steven Erlanger, "A New Fashion Catches on in Paris: Cheap Bicycle Rentals," *New York Times*, 13 July 2008; City of Paris, "Vélib: Subscriptions and Prices," at www.en.velib.paris.fr, viewed 12 May 2009; Alexandra Topping, "Free Wheeling: Paris's New Bike System," *Washington Post*, 23 September 2007; number of trips as of May 2009 from JCDecaux press officer, discussion with J. Matthew Roney, 14 May 2009.

25. Schmemann, op. cit. note 23; La Fédération de Paris du Parti Socialiste, ed., *Ce Que Nous Avons Fait Ensemble* (Paris: Office of Mayor Bertrand Delanoë, 2007), pp. 20–25; program expansion from JCDecaux press offi-

cer, op. cit. note 24; Alok Jha, "Boris Johnson Unveils Blueprint for London's 'Cycling Revolution'," *Guardian* (London), 27 April 2009.

26. John Ritter, "Narrowed Roads Gain Acceptance in Colo., Elsewhere," *USA Today*, 29 July 2007; John Ritter, "'Complete Streets' Program Gives More Room for Pedestrians, Cyclists," *USA Today*, 29 July 2007.

27. National Complete Streets Coalition, "Complete the Streets: Who We Are," at www.completestreets.org/whoweare.html, viewed 16 August 2007; AARP, "About AARP," at www.aarp.org/aarp/About_AARP, viewed 12 May 2009; Ritter, "Narrowed Roads," op. cit. note 26.

28. National Complete Streets Coalition, "Illinois Passes Complete Streets Law," press release (Washington, DC: 16 October 2007); Stefanie Seskin, National Complete Streets Coalition, e-mail to J. Matthew Roney, Earth Policy Institute, 28 May 2009; Office of Congresswoman Doris Matsui, "Congresswoman Matsui and Senator Harkin Introduce Bill to Make Streets Safer and Encourage Healthier America," press release (Washington, DC: 12 March 2009).

29. U.S. Department of Transportation, Federal Highway Administration, *Nationwide Personal Transportation Study: Transportation Characteristics of School Children* (Washington, DC: July 1972), p. 3; American Academy of Pediatrics, Committee on Injury, Violence, and Poison Prevention and Council on School Health, "Policy Statement: School Transportation Safety," *Pediatrics*, vol. 120, no. 1 (July 2007), pp. 213–20; International Walk to School, "About the Walk," at www.iwalkto school.org/about.htm, viewed 12 May 2009.

30. Car trip reduction is author's estimate.

31. O'Meara, op. cit. note 3, p. 45.

32. J. Matthew Roney, "Bicycles Pedaling into the Spotlight," *Eco-Economy Indicator* (Washington, DC: Earth Policy Institute, 12 May 2008); Ward's Automotive Group, *World Motor Vehicle Data 2008* (Southfield, MI: 2008), pp. 239–42; German Eslava, "1st in EU: Italian Government Spurs Bike Sales with Incentives," *Bike Europe*, at www.bike-eu.com, 28 April 2009; Jack Oortwijn and Jan-Willem van Schaik, "European Bike Season Kicks Off with Record Highs," *Bike Europe*, at www.bike-eu.com, 12 May 2009; Jan-Willem van Schaik, "Giant Targets 10% Growth in 2009," *Bike Europe*, at www.bike-eu.com, 21 April 2009.

33. Calculated by Earth Policy Institute from U.N. Population Division, op. cit. note 3, from 3.44 persons per Chinese household in Bingham Kennedy, Jr., *Dissecting China's 2000 Census* (Washington, DC: Population Reference Bureau, June 2001), and from National Bureau of Statistics of China data cited in Jme McLean, "Backpedal to the Future: China's Strength is in Its Bicycles," *E Magazine*, at www.emagazine.com/view/?3729, viewed 15 January 2008; ownership from Netherlands Ministry of Transport, Public Works and Water Management and Fietsberaad, *Cycling in the Netherlands* (The Hague and Utrecht: 2009), p. 14.

34. Chinese bicycle production compiled from United Nations, *Yearbook of Industrial Statistics* (New York: various years) and from *Industrial Commodity Statistics Yearbook* (New York: various years); "World Players in the Bicycle Market 2000–2007," in John Crenshaw, *Bicycle Retailer and Industry News*, e-mail to J. Matthew Roney, Earth Policy Institute, 9 May 2008; cars in China from Ward's Automotive Group, op. cit. note 32.

35. Percent of police forces calculated from Matthew Hickman and Brian A. Reaves, *Local Police Departments, 2003* (Washington, DC: U.S. Department of Justice, Bureau of Justice Statistics, May 2006), pp. 3, 13; arrest rate from a member of the Washington, DC, police force, discussion with author.

36. Katie Zezima, "With Free Bikes, Challenging Car Culture on Campus," *New York Times*, 20 October 2008.

37. Ibid.

38. Glenn Collins, "Old Form of Delivery Thrives in New World of E-Commerce," *New York Times*, 24 December 1999.

39. O'Meara, op. cit. note 3, pp. 47–48; John Pucher and Ralph Buehler, "Making Cycling Irresistible: Lessons from the Netherlands, Denmark, and Germany," *Transport Reviews*, vol. 28, issue 4 (July 2008), pp. 495–528.

40. Pucher and Buehler, op. cit. note 39.

41. Cornelia Dean, "Bicycle Evangelist with the Wind Now at His Back," *New York Times*, 13 January 2009.

42. O'Meara, op. cit. note 3, pp. 47–48; Fietsberaad, "Amsterdam: for the First Time More Transfers by Bike than by Car," at www.fietsberaad.nl, 22 January 2009.

43. Walljasper, op. cit. note 16; Interface for Cycling Expertise (I-ce), "Bicycle Partnership Program," at www.bikepartners.nl, viewed 12 May 2009.

44. O'Meara, op. cit. note 3, pp. 47–48; Japan from author's personal observation.

45. Jonathan Weinert, Chaktan Ma, and Chris Cherry, "Transition to Electric Bikes in China: History and Key Reasons for Rapid Growth," *Transportation*, vol. 34, no. 3 (May 2007), pp. 301–18; Austin Ramzy, "On the Streets of China, Electric Bikes Are Swarming," *Time*, 14 June 2009; "India 2007: LEVs to Grow to 70,000 Units," *Bike Europe*, at www.bike-eu.com, 15 May 2008; Vietnam News Agency, "Helmet Aversion, Petrol Boost Bicycle Sales," *Viet Nam News*, 8 October 2007; Elliot Gluskin, Gluskin Townley Group, discussion with J. Matthew Roney, Earth Policy Institute, 16 June 2009; Jack Oortwijn, "E-Bikes Beat the Crisis," *Bike Europe*, 8 April 2009.

46. Sunita Narain, "The Flush Toilet is Ecologically Mindless," *Down to Earth*, 28 February 2002, pp. 28–32; dead zones from Robert J. Diaz and Rutger Rosenberg, "Spreading Dead Zones and Consequences for Marine Ecosystems," *Science*, vol. 321 (15 August 2008), pp. 926–29; World Health Organization (WHO), *World Health Report 2007* (Geneva: 2007), p. 4; U.N. Food and Agriculture Organization (FAO), *The State of Food Insecurity in the World 2005* (Rome: 2005).

47. Narain, op. cit. note 46.

48. Ibid.

49. U.S. Environmental Protection Agency (EPA), "Water Efficiency Technology Factsheet—Composting Toilets" (Washington, DC: September 1999); Jack Kieffer, Appalachia—Science in the Public Interest, *Humanure: Preparation of Compost from the Toilet for Use in the Garden* (Mount Vernon, KY: ASPI Publications, 1998).

50. EPA, op. cit. note 49; EPA, "Wastewater Virtual Tradeshow Technologies," at www.epa.gov/region1/assistance/ceitts/wastewater/techs.html,

updated 14 April 2009; people lacking sanitation from WHO and UNICEF Joint Monitoring Programme for Water Supply and Sanitation, *Progress on Drinking Water and Sanitation: Special Focus on Sanitation* (Geneva and New York: 2008), p. 2.

51. Rose George, "Yellow is the New Green," (editorial), *New York Times*, 27 February 2009.

52. Tony Sitathan, "Bridge Over Troubled Waters," *Asia Times*, 23 August 2002; "Singapore Opens Fourth Recycling Plant to Turn Sewage into Water," *Associated Press*, 12 July 2005; Randal C. Archibold, "From Sewage, Added Water for Drinking," *New York Times*, 27 November 2007; Randal C. Archibold, "Los Angeles Eyes Sewage as a Source of Water," *New York Times*, 16 May 2008.

53. Peter H. Gleick, *The World's Water 2004–2005: The Biennial Report on Freshwater Resources* (Washington, DC: Island Press, 2004), p. 149.

54. Ibid.

55. "Farming in Urban Areas Can Boost Food Security," *FAO Newsroom*, 3 June 2005.

56. Ibid.

57. Jac Smit, "Urban Agriculture's Contribution to Sustainable Urbanisation," *Urban Agriculture*, August 2002, p. 13; Hubert de Bon, "Dry and Aquatic Peri-urban and Urban Horticulture in Hanoi, Vietnam," in René van Veenhuizen, ed., *Cities Farming for the Future—Urban Agriculture for Green and Productive Cities* (Philippines: ETC-Urban Agriculture, 2006), pp. 338–39.

58. Smit, op. cit. note 57, p. 13; pond coverage from Nitai Kundu et al., "Planning for Aquatic Production in East Kolkata Wetlands," in van Veenhuizen, op. cit. note 57, pp. 408–09; fish production from Stuart Bunting et al., "Urban Aquatic Production," in van Veenhuizen, op. cit. note 57, p. 386.

59. Smit, op. cit. note 57, p. 12.

60. "Gardening for the Poor," *FAO Newsroom*, 2004; P. Bradley and C. Marulanda, "A Study on Microgardens That Help Reduce Global Poverty and Hunger," *Acta Horticulturae* (ISHS), vol. 742 (2007), pp. 115–23.

61. Katherine H. Brown and Anne Carter, *Urban Agriculture and Community Food Security in the United States: Farming from the City Center to the Urban Fringe* (Venice, CA: Community Food Security Coalition, October 2003), p. 10.

62. Ibid., p. 7.

63. Ibid.

64. U.N. Population Division, op. cit. note 3; U.N. Population Division, op. cit. note 2, p. 1.

65. Hari Srinivas, "Defining Squatter Settlements," Global Development Research Center Web site, at www.gdrc.org/uem/define-squatter.html, viewed 9 August 2005.

66. Ibid.

67. O'Meara, op. cit. note 3, p. 39.

68. Rasna Warah, *The Challenge of Slums: Global Report on Human Settlements 2003* (New York: U.N. Human Settlements Programme, 2003).

69. Srinivas, op. cit. note 65.

70. E. O. Wilson, *Biophilia* (Cambridge, MA: Harvard University Press,

1984); S. R. Kellert and E. O. Wilson, eds., *The Biophilia Hypothesis* (Washington, DC: Island Press, 1993).

71. Theodore Roszak, Mary Gomes, and Allen Kanner, eds., *Restoring the Earth, Healing the Mind* (San Francisco: Sierra Club Books, 1995).

72. American Public Transportation Association (APTA), "Unlinked Passenger Trips by Mode (Millions)," in *2009 Public Transportation Fact Book, Part 2: Historical Tables* (Washington, DC: April 2009), pp. 1–2; APTA, *Public Transportation Ridership Report: Fourth Quarter 2008* (Washington, DC: 5 March 2009).

73. Ding Guangwei and Li Shishun, "Analysis of Impetuses to Change of Agricultural Land Resources in China," *Bulletin of the Chinese Academy of Sciences*, vol. 13, no. 1 (1999).

74. Ayres, McHenry & Associates, "Survey of Metro Atlanta Registered Voters Regarding Transportation Issues," conducted on behalf of Transit Planning Board (Alexandria, VA: March 2008); Molly O'Meara Sheehan, *City Limits: Putting the Breaks on Sprawl*, Worldwatch Paper 156 (Washington, DC: Worldwatch Institute, June 2001), p. 11; David Schrank and Tim Lomax, *2005 Urban Mobility Study* (College Station, TX: Texas Transportation Institute, May 2005); Luc Nadal, "Bike Sharing Sweeps Paris Off Its Feet," *Sustainable Transport*, fall 2007, pp. 8–13.

75. Jim Motavalli, "The High Cost of Free Parking," *E: The Environmental Magazine*, March–April 2005; Donald Shoup, *The High Cost of Free Parking* (Chicago: American Planning Association Planners Press, 2005), p. 591; Daniel B. Klein, "Free Parking Versus Free Markets," *The Independent Review*, vol. XI, no. 2 (fall 2006), pp. 289–97.

76. O'Meara, op. cit. note 3, p. 49; Donald C. Shoup, "Congress Okays Cash Out," *Access*, fall 1998, pp. 2–8.

77. Libby Nelson, "Broadway's Car-free Zones: This Space for Rent," *New York Times*, 9 July 2009; "Paris to Cut City Centre Traffic," *BBC News*, 15 March 2005; J. H. Crawford, "Carfree Places," at www.carfree.com, viewed 17 August 2007; see also J. H. Crawford, *Carfree Cities* (Utrecht, Netherlands: International Books, July 2000).

78. Yuri Kageyama, "Cars No Longer Coveted by Young," *Japan Times*, 4 January 2009; Japan Automobile Manufacturers Association, Inc., *Motor Vehicle Statistics of Japan 2008* (Tokyo: 2008), p. 8; Japan Automobile Manufacturers Association, Inc., "Forecast for Vehicle Demand 2009," at www.jama-english.jp/statistics/forecast/2009/081218.html, 18 December 2008; European Automobile Manufacturers' Association, "Passenger Cars: European Market at –4.9% in May," press release (Brussels: 16 June 2009); Bill Heenan, Steel Recycling Institute, discussion with J. Matthew Roney, Earth Policy Institute, 20 July 2009.

79. Kageyama, op. cit. note 78.

80. City of New York, *PlaNYC Progress Report 2009* (New York: Mayor's Office of Long-Term Planning & Sustainability, 2009), pp. 3–4, 30, 35, 38; City of New York, Mayor's Office of Operations, "PlaNYC/Sustainability Reports," at www.nyc.gov/html/ops/planyc/html/home/home.shtml, viewed 16 June 2009.

81. Kitson & Partners, "Babcock Ranch Florida—Embracing Nature," at www.babcockranchflorida.com/nature.asp, viewed 16 June 2009; Michael Grunwald, "A Solar-Powered Solution to Florida Sprawl," *Time*, 9 April

2009; Sydney Kitson, discussion with author, 14 May 2009.

82. Glover Park Group, "First Solar-Powered City to Fuel Clean Industry, Economic Recovery," press release (Washington, DC: 9 April 2009); Kitson & Partners, op. cit. note 81.

83. Kevin Bullis, "A Zero-Emissions City in the Desert," *Technology Review* (March/April 2009), pp. 56–63.

84. Ibid.

85. Adam Federman, "Roadkill: How NYC's Congestion Pricing Plan Crashed," *Earth Island Journal*, summer 2008, pp. 25–30; Robin Pogrebin, "Visions of Manhattan: For the City, 100-Year Makeovers," *New York Times*, 4 November 2006.

86. Federman, op. cit. note 85; Partnership for New York City, *Growth or Gridlock? The Economic Case for Traffic Relief and Transit Improvement for a Greater New York* (New York: December 2006), pp. 2–4.

Chapter 7. Eradicating Poverty and Stabilizing Population

1. U.N. General Assembly, "United Nations Millennium Declaration," resolution adopted by the General Assembly, 8 September 2000; World Bank, *Global Monitoring Report 2007: Millennium Development Goals* (Washington, DC: 2007), p. 39; World Bank, *Global Monitoring Report 2009: A Development Emergency* (Washington, DC: 2009), p. 17.

2. World Bank, "Millennium Development Goals—Country Tables," at www.developmentgoals.org, updated April 2009; U.N. Population Division, *World Population Prospects: The 2008 Revision Population Database*, at esa.un.org/unpp, updated 11 March 2009.

3. World Bank, op. cit. note 2; U.N. Population Division, op. cit. note 2; Jeffrey D. Sachs, "India Takes the Lead," *Korea Herald*, 4 August 2004; International Monetary Fund (IMF), *World Economic Outlook*, electronic database, www.imf.org, updated April 2009.

4. UNESCO, *Overcoming Inequality: Why Governance Matters, Education for All Global Monitoring Report 2009* (Paris: 2008), p. 195; Sara Miller Llana, "Brazil Becomes Antipoverty Showcase," *Christian Science Monitor*, 13 November 2008; World Bank, op. cit. note 2; U.N. Population Division, op. cit. note 2.

5. U.N. Statistics Division, *Millennium Development Goals Indicators*, electronic database, at mdgs.un.org/unsd/mdg/Data.aspx, updated 14 July 2009; World Bank, *Global Monitoring Report 2008: MDGs and the Environment* (Washington, DC: 2008), p. 2.

6. World Bank, *Global Economic Prospects: Commodities at a Crossroads 2009* (Washington, DC: 2009), pp. 11–12; World Bank, *Poverty Data: A Supplement to World Development Indicators 2008* (Washington, DC: 2008), p. 1.

7. U.N. Population Division, op. cit. note 2; G-8 leaders, "Gleneagles Communiqué on Africa, Climate Change, Energy and Sustainable Development," document from G-8 Summit, Gleneagles, Scotland, July 2005; fragile states from World Bank, *Global Monitoring Report 2007*, op. cit. note 1, p. 4.

8. U.N. General Assembly, op. cit. note 1.

9. World Bank, *Global Monitoring Report 2009*, op. cit. note 1, p. 14; U.N. Food and Agriculture Organization, "1.02 Billion People Hungry," press

release (Rome: 19 June 2009); U.S. Department of Agriculture (USDA), *Production, Supply and Distribution*, electronic database, at www.fas .usda.gov/psdonline, updated 12 May 2009; USDA, *Feedgrains Database*, electronic database at www.ers.usda.gov/Data/feedgrains, updated 19 May 2009; U.N. Population Division, op. cit. note 2.

10. UNESCO, op. cit. note 4, p. 65.

11. Martha Campbell et al., "Return of the Population Growth Factor," *Science*, vol. 315 (16 March 2007), pp. 1501–02; Martha Campbell, discussion with Janet Larsen, Earth Policy Institute, 8 October 2007; All Party Parliamentary Group on Population Development and Reproductive Health, *Return of the Population Growth Factor: Its Impact on the Millennium Development Goals* (London: Her Majesty's Stationery Office, January 2007), pp. 1–9.

12. World Bank, *Global Monitoring Report 2009*, op. cit. note 1, p. 19; Hilaire A. Mputu, *Literacy and Non-Formal Education in the E-9 Countries* (Paris: UNESCO, 2001), p. 5; Polly Curtis, "Lack of Education 'a Greater Threat than Terrorism': Sen," *Guardian* (London), 28 October 2003.

13. Paul Blustein, "Global Education Plan Gains Backing," *Washington Post*, 22 April 2002; World Bank, "World Bank Announces First Group of Countries for 'Education For All' Fast Track," press release (Washington, DC: 12 June 2002); Gene Sperling, "The G-8—Send 104 Million Friends to School," *Bloomberg News*, 20 June 2005.

14. United Nations, *Millennium Development Goals Report 2008* (New York: 2008), p. 14; World Bank, *Global Monitoring Report 2009*, op. cit. note 1, Annex.

15. Gene Sperling, "Toward Universal Education," *Foreign Affairs*, September/October 2001, pp. 7–13.

16. Gene Sperling, "Educate Them All," *Washington Post*, 20 April 2002.

17. U.K. Treasury, *From Commitment to Action: Education* (London: Department for International Development, September 2005).

18. UNESCO, *EFA Global Monitoring Report 2007: Strong Foundations* (Paris: 2006), p. 2; U.N. Commission on Population and Development, Thirty-sixth Session, Population, Education, and Development, press releases, 31 March–4 April 2003; UNESCO, "Winners of UNESCO Literacy Prizes 2003," press release, 27 May 2003.

19. George McGovern, *The Third Freedom: Ending Hunger in Our Time* (New York: Simon & Schuster: 2001), chapter 1.

20. Jeffrey Sachs, "A New Map of the World," *The Economist*, 22 June 2000; George McGovern, "Yes We CAN Feed the World's Hungry," *Parade*, 16 December 2001.

21. McGovern, op. cit. note 20.

22. Ibid.

23. Ibid.

24. World Bank, *Global Monitoring Report 2009*, op. cit. note 1, Annex; UNICEF, "Under-five Mortality Rate," at www.childinfo.org/mortalityunderfive.php, updated January 2009.

25. World Bank, *Global Monitoring Report 2009*, op. cit. note 1, p. 72.

26. Mustaque Chowdhury, *Health Workforce for TB Control by DOTS: The BRAC Case, Joint Learning Initiative Working Paper 5-2* (Global Health Trust, 2004).

27. Jeffrey D. Sachs and the Commission on Macroeconomics and Health, *Macroeconomics and Health: Investing in Health for Economic Development* (Geneva: World Health Organization (WHO), 2001); "UNICEF Lists Top Causes of Child Deaths," *Reuters*, 13 September 2007; Ruth Levine and the What Works Working Group, *Millions Saved: Proven Successes in Global Health* (Washington, DC: Center for Global Development, 2004).

28. Bill and Melinda Gates Foundation, "Global Health Program Fact Sheet" (Seattle, WA: 2009).

29. John Donnelly, "U.S. Seeks Cuts in Health Programs Abroad," *Boston Globe*, 5 February 2003.

30. Joint United Nations Programme on HIV/AIDS (UNAIDS), *Report on the Global AIDS Epidemic 2008* (Geneva: August 2008), pp. 15–16, 30.

31. Nita Bhalla, "Teaching Truck Drivers About AIDS," *BBC*, 25 June 2001; C. B. S. Venkataramana and P. V. Sarada, "Extent and Speed of Spread of HIV Infection in India Through the Commercial Sex Networks: A Perspective," *Tropical Medicine and International Health*, vol. 6, no. 12 (December 2001), pp. 1,040–61, cited in "HIV Spread Via Female Sex Workers in India Set to Increase Significantly by 2005," *Reuters Health*, 26 December 2001.

32. Mark Covey, "Target Soldiers in Fight Against AIDS Says New Report," press release (London: Panos Institute, 8 July 2002); "Free Condoms for Soldiers," *South Africa Press Association*, 5 August 2001; HIV prevalence rate from UNAIDS, op. cit. note 30, p. 215.

33. Condoms needed from Population Action International, "Why Condoms Count in the Era of HIV/AIDS," fact sheet (Washington, DC: 2008); cost per condom and condom distribution from United Nations Population Fund (UNFPA), *Donor Support for Contraceptives and Condoms for STI/HIV Prevention 2007* (New York: 2008).

34. Nada Chaya and Kai-Ahset Amen, with Michael Fox, *Condoms Count: Meeting the Need in the Era of HIV/AIDS* (Washington, DC: Population Action International, 2002); cost per condom from UNFPA, op. cit. note 33.

35. UNAIDS, "Global Facts and Figures," fact sheet (Geneva: August 2008); UNAIDS, op. cit. note 30, p. 135.

36. "AIDS Summit: The Economics of Letting People Die," *Star Tribune*, 16 July 2003.

37. Sachs and Commission on Macroeconomics and Health, op. cit. note 27; WHO, "Smallpox," fact sheet at www.who.int, viewed 10 October 2005.

38. WHO, "Polio Eradication: Now More Than Ever, Stop Polio Forever," at www.who.int/features/2004/polio/en, viewed 11 June 2009; Petina Dixon, Rotary International, discussion with Jignasha Rana, Earth Policy Institute, 6 July 2009; Bill and Melinda Gates Foundation, "Financial Innovation Will Buy Vaccine to Help Eradicate Polio Worldwide," press release (Seattle, WA: 29 April 2003).

39. "Wild Poliovirus 2000–2009," in WHO Global Polio Eradication Initiative, "Wild Poliovirus Weekly Update," at www.polioeradication.org, updated 3 June 2009; Donald G. McNeil, Jr., "Mecca Pilgrims May Be Spreading Polio, Experts Say," *New York Times*, 11 February 2005; Nigeria from WHO, *Global Polio Eradication Initiative: Annual Report 2006* (Geneva: 2007), p. 6.

40. "Wild Poliovirus 2000–2009," op. cit. note 39; "Pakistan Polio Drive is Suspended," *BBC News*, 8 August 2007; Isambard Wilkinson, "Taliban Blocks UN Polio Treatment in Pakistan," *Telegraph* (London), 27 March 2009.

41. Declan Butler, "$630-Million for Push to Eradicate Polio," *Nature News*, 21 January 2009; Barack H. Obama, "Remarks by the President on a New Beginning," speech at Cairo University, Cairo, Egypt, 4 June 2009.

42. Michele Barry, "The Tail of Guinea Worm—Global Eradication Without a Drug or Vaccine," *New England Journal of Medicine*, vol. 356, no. 25 (21 June 2007), pp. 2,561–64.

43. "Grants Push Guinea Worm to All-Time Low," news release (Atlanta, GA: The Carter Center, 20 January 2009); The Carter Center, "Distribution by Country of 4,647 Cases of Indigenous Cases of Dracunculiasis Reported During 2008," at www.cartercenter.org/health/guinea_worm/index.html, viewed 13 May 2009.

44. Tobacco deaths from WHO, "Chronic Obstructive Pulmonary Disease (COPD)," fact sheet (Geneva: November 2006); "The Tobacco Epidemic: A Crisis of Startling Dimensions," in *Message from the Director-General of the World Health Organization for World No-Tobacco Day 1998*, at www.who.int; air pollution from WHO, "Air Pollution," fact sheet 187 (Geneva: rev. September 2000).

45. Alison Langley, "Anti-Smoking Treaty Is Adopted by 192 Nations," *New York Times*, 22 May 2003; information on WHO Tobacco Free Initiative at www.who.int/tobacco/index.cfm; treaty goals and Bloomberg from Alexi A. Wright and Ingrid T. Katz, "Tobacco Tightrope—Balancing Disease Prevention and Economic Development in China," *New England Journal of Medicine*, vol. 356, no. 15 (12 April 2007), pp. 1,493–96.

46. Cigarette consumption from USDA, *Production, Supply and Distribution*, op. cit. note 9, and from Tom Capehart, *Tobacco Outlook* (Washington, DC: USDA, Economic Research Service (ERS), 24 April 2007); per capita estimates made with population from U.N. Population Division, op. cit. note 2; Daniel Yee, "Smoking Declines in U.S.—Barely," *CBS News*, 10 November 2004.

47. Betsy McKay, "Cigarette Tax Clouds Boosts Among States," *Wall Street Journal*, 8 February 2009.

48. Cigarette consumption from USDA, *Production, Supply and Distribution*, op. cit. note 9, and from Capehart, op. cit. note 46; per capita estimates made using population from U.N. Population Division, op. cit. note 2.

49. "Smoking Bans Around the World," *Reuters*, 10 January 2005; "New Zealand Stubs Out Smoking in Bars, Restaurants," *Reuters*, 13 December 2004.

50. "Bangladesh Bans Smoking in Many Public Places," *Reuters*, 15 March 2005; Italy from "Europeans Back Public Smoking Ban," *BBC News*, 31 May 2006; "England Smoking Ban Takes Effect," *BBC News*, 1 July 2007; France from Howard K. Koh et al., "Making Smoking History Worldwide," *New England Journal of Medicine*, vol. 356, no. 15 (12 April 2007), pp. 1,496–98; "French Cafes Set to Ban Smoking," *BBC News*, 28 December 2007; "Bulgaria Votes for Smoking Ban in Public Places," *Reuters*, 15 May 2009; Ivana Sekularac, "Smoking Ban Angers Cafes, Smokers in Croatia," *Reuters*, 6 May 2009.

51. "Connections between Diabetes and Alzheimer's Disease Explored," *Science Daily*, 11 May 2009.
52. "Cancer Most Lethal Illness in China Last Year," *China Daily*, 8 May 2007; Barbara Demick, "China Blames Pollution for Surge in Birth Defects," *Los Angeles Times*, 2 February 2009.
53. Sachs and Commission on Macroeconomics and Health, op. cit. note 27.
54. Countries with more than 1 million people and natural rate of increase of 0.4 percent or less retrieved from U.N. Population Division, *World Population Prospects: The 2008 Revision, Extended Dataset*, CD-ROM (New York: 9 April 2009).
55. Lesotho and Swaziland population data from Population Reference Bureau (PRB), *Datafinder*, electronic database, at www.prb.org.
56. U.N. Population Division, op. cit. note 54.
57. Ibid.
58. Ibid.
59. Program for Appropriate Technology in Health (PATH) and UNFPA, *Meeting the Need: Strengthening Family Planning Programs* (Seattle, WA: 2006), pp. 5–11; quote from All Party Parliamentary Group, op. cit. note 11, p. 22.
60. Janet Larsen, "Iran's Birth Rate Plummeting at Record Pace," in Lester R. Brown, Janet Larsen, and Bernie Fischlowitz-Roberts, *The Earth Policy Reader* (New York: W. W. Norton & Company, 2002), pp. 190–94.
61. Ibid.; see also Homa Hoodfar and Samad Assadpour, "The Politics of Population Policy in the Islamic Republic of Iran," *Studies in Family Planning*, March 2000, pp. 19–34, and Farzaneh Roudi, "Iran's Family Planning Program: Responding to a Nation's Needs," *MENA Policy Brief*, June 2002; Iran population growth rate from United Nations, *World Population Prospects: The 2004 Revision* (New York: 2005).
62. Larsen, op. cit. note 60.
63. Ibid.
64. Ibid.; population growth rates from PRB, *2005 World Population Data Sheet*, wall chart (Washington, DC: August 2005); U.N. Population Division, op. cit. note 2.
65. Pamela Polston, "Lowering the Boom: Population Activist Bill Ryerson is Saving the World—One 'Soap' at a Time," *Seven Days*, 21 August 2005.
66. Ibid.
67. Ibid.
68. Ibid.
69. Additional spending from J. Joseph Speidel et al., *Family Planning and Reproductive Health: The Link to Environmental Preservation* (San Francisco: Bixby Center for Reproductive Health and Research Policy, University of California, 2007), p. 10, and from J. Joseph Speidel, discussion with J. Matthew Roney, Earth Policy Institute, 16 October 2007.
70. PATH and UNFPA, op. cit. note 59, p. 18.
71. "Bangladesh: National Family Planning Program," *Family Planning Programs: Diverse Solutions for a Global Challenge* (Washington, DC: PRB, 1994); Speidel et al., op. cit. note 69, p. 10.
72. UNFPA, *The State of World Population 2004* (New York: 2004), pp. 14–15.
73. United Nations, op. cit. note 61; UNFPA, op. cit. note 72, p. 39.

74. Fund for Peace and *Foreign Policy*, "The Failed States Index," *Foreign Policy*, July/August issues, 2005–09; U.S. Department of State, "Background Note: Liberia," at www.state.gov/r/pa/ei/bgn/6618.htm, updated June 2009; María Cristina Caballero, "'Ma Ellen,' African Symbol of Hope, Returns to Harvard," *Harvard University Gazette*, 16 September 2006; "UN's Ban to Visit Liberia as Blue Helmets Prepare Pullout," *Agence France-Presse*, 20 April 2008.

75. Fund for Peace and *Foreign Policy*, op. cit. note 74; Fund for Peace, "Country Profile: Colombia," at www.fundforpeace.org, viewed 8 July 2009.

76. Commission on Weak States and U.S. National Security, *On the Brink: Weak States and U.S. National Security* (Washington, DC: Center for Global Development, 2004), p. 27.

77. The U.S. Commission on National Security in the 21st Century, *Road Map for National Security: Imperative for Change* (Washington, DC: February 2001), p. 53.

78. Commission on Weak States and U.S. National Security, op. cit. note 76, pp. 30–32.

79. Organisation for Economic Co-operation and Development (OECD), *Agricultural Policies in OECD Countries 2008: At a Glance* (Paris: 2008), p. 9; OECD, "Development Aid at its Highest Level Ever in 2008," press release (Paris: 30 March 2009); "The Hypocrisy of Farm Subsidies," *New York Times*, 1 December 2002.

80. "The Hypocrisy of Farm Subsidies," op. cit. note 79.

81. OECD, "Development Aid," op. cit. note 79; OECD, *OECD Statistics*, electronic database, at stats.oecd.org/wbos, updated 2009; "South Africa: Weaning States Off Subsidies," *Africa News*, 19 August 2005.

82. Julian Alston et al., *Impacts of Reductions in US Cotton Subsidies on West African Cotton Producers* (Boston: Oxfam America, 2007); OECD, op. cit. note 81; Elizabeth Becker, "U.S. Will Cut Farm Subsidies in Trade Deal," *New York Times*, 31 July 2004; Randy Schnepf, *U.S. Agricultural Policy Response to WTO Cotton Decision* (Washington, DC: Congressional Research Service, updated 8 September 2006).

83. Schnepf, op. cit. note 82; Randy Schnepf, *Brazil's WTO Case Against the U.S. Cotton Program: A Brief Overview* (Washington, DC: Congressional Research Service, 17 March 2009).

84. World Bank, *Global Economic Prospects*, op. cit. note 6, pp. 11–12.

85. "Ending the Cycle of Debt," *New York Times*, 1 October 2004; debt servicing from World Bank, *Little Data Book on External Debt in Global Development Finance 2007* (Washington, DC: 2007), p. 8; health care spending calculated from IMF, *World Economic and Financial Surveys: Regional Economic Outlook—Sub-Saharan Africa* (Washington, DC: September 2006), pp. 36, 43, from David Goldsbrough, "IMF Programs and Health Spending," presented at Global Conference on Gearing Macroeconomic Policies to Reverse the HIV/AIDS Epidemic, Brasília, 20 November 2006, and from U.N. Population Division, *World Population Prospects: The 2006 Revision Population Database*, at esa.un.org/unpp, updated 2007.

86. "G8 Finance Ministers' Conclusions on Development," Pre Summit Statement by G-8 Finance Ministers, London, 10–11 June 2005; Oxfam Inter-

national, "Gleneagles: What Really Happened at the G8 Summit?" *Oxfam Briefing Note* (London: 29 July 2005).

87. Oxfam International, "The View from the Summit—Gleneagles G8 One Year On," briefing note (Oxford, U.K.: June 2006).

88. World Bank, *Global Monitoring Report 2009*, op. cit. note 1, p. 8; U.N. World Food Programme, "Financial Crisis and High Food Prices," fact sheet (Rome: updated 11 June 2009).

89. World Bank, "Financial Crisis Could Trap 53 Million More People in Poverty," news release (Washington, DC: 12 February 2009); World Bank, *Global Economic Prospects*, op. cit. note 6, pp. 11–12; Robert Zoellick, "Seizing Opportunity from Crisis: Making Multilateralism Work," speech delivered at the Thomas Reuters Building, Canary Wharf, London, 31 March 2009.

90. Costs of meeting social goals in Table 7–1 based on the following sources: universal primary education from U.K. Treasury, op. cit. note 17; adult literacy campaign is author's estimate; school lunch program from McGovern, op. cit. note 20; assistance to preschool children and pregnant women is author's estimate of extending the U.S.'s Women, Infants, and Children program, based on ibid.; reproductive health and family planning from Speidel et al., op. cit. note 69, and from Speidel, op. cit. note 69; universal basic health care from Sachs and Commission on Macroeconomics and Health, op. cit. note 27; closing the condom gap estimated from UNFPA, op. cit. note 33, and from Population Action International, op. cit. note 33.

91. Sachs and Commission on Macroeconomics and Health, op. cit. note 27.

92. Jeffrey D. Sachs, *The End of Poverty: Economic Possibilities for Our Time* (New York: Penguin Group, 2005).

Chapter 8. Restoring the Earth

1. Craig A. Cox, "Conservation Can Mean Life or Death," *Journal of Soil and Water Conservation*, November/December 2004.

2. Ibid.

3. U.N. Food and Agriculture Organization (FAO), *The State of the World's Forests 2009* (Rome: 2009), pp. 109–15.

4. FAO, *ForesSTAT*, electronic database, at faostat.fao.org, updated 12 January 2009, using five-year averages; U.S. Environmental Protection Agency (EPA), *Municipal Solid Waste in the United States: 2007 Facts and Figures* (Washington, DC: 2008), p. 102.

5. FAO, op. cit. note 3, p. 129; Daniel M. Kammen, "From Energy Efficiency to Social Utility: Lessons from Cookstove Design, Dissemination, and Use," in José Goldemberg and Thomas B. Johansson, *Energy as an Instrument for Socio-Economic Development* (New York: U.N. Development Programme, 1995).

6. Kevin Porter, "Final Kakuma Evaluation: Solar Cookers Filled a Critical Gap," in Solar Cookers International, *Solar Cooker Review*, vol. 10, no. 2 (November 2004); "Breakthrough in Kenyan Refugee Camps," at solarcooking.org/kakuma-m.htm, viewed 30 July 2007.

7. FAO, *Agriculture: Towards 2015/30, Technical Interim Report* (Geneva: Economic and Social Department, 2000), pp. 156–57.

8. Alliance for Forest Conservation and Sustainable Use, "WWF/World

Bank Forest Alliance Launches Ambitious Program to Reduce Deforestation and Curb Illegal Logging," press release (New York: World Bank/WWF, 25 May 2005); WWF/World Bank Global Forest Alliance, *Annual Report 2005* (Gland, Switzerland, and Washington, DC: December 2006), p. 31.

9. Forest Stewardship Council (FSC), *Forest Stewardship Council: News & Notes*, vol. 7, issue 6 (July 2009); FSC, "Global FSC Certificates: Type and Distribution (March 2009)," PowerPoint Presentation, at www.fsc.org, June 2009.

10. A. Del Lungo, J. Ball, and J. Carle, *Global Planted Forests Thematic Study: Results and Analysis* (Rome: FAO Forestry Department, December 2006), p. 13; U.S. Department of Agriculture (USDA), *Production, Supply and Distribution*, electronic database, at www.fas.usda.gov/psdonline, updated 9 April 2009.

11. R. James and A. Del Lungo, "Comparisons of Estimates of 'High Value' Wood With Estimates of Total Forest Plantation Production," in FAO, *The Potential for Fast-Growing Commercial Forest Plantations to Supply High Value Roundwood* (Rome: Forestry Department, February 2005), p. 24; plantation area in "Table 4. Total Planted Forest Area: Productive and Protective—61 Sampled Countries," in Del Lungo, Ball, and Carle, op. cit. note 10, pp. 66–70.

12. Ashley T. Mattoon, "Paper Forests," *World Watch*, March/April 1998, pp. 20–28; USDA, op. cit. note 10.

13. FAO, op. cit. note 7, p. 185; Chris Brown and D. J. Mead, eds., "Future Production from Forest Plantations," *Forest Plantation Thematic Paper* (Rome: FAO, 2001), p. 9.

14. M. Davis et al., "New England—Acadian Forests," in Taylor H. Ricketts et al., eds., *Terrestrial Ecoregions of North America: A Conservation Assessment* (Washington, DC: Island Press, 1999); David R. Foster, "Harvard Forest: Addressing Major Issues in Policy Debates and in the Understanding of Ecosystem Process and Pattern," *LTER Network News: The Newsletter of the Long Term Ecological Network*, spring/summer 1996; U.S. Forest Service, "2006 Forest Health Highlights," various state sheets, at fhm.fs.fed.us, viewed 2 August 2007.

15. C. Csaki, "Agricultural Reforms in Central and Eastern Europe and the Former Soviet Union: Status and Perspectives," *Agricultural Economics*, vol. 22 (2000), pp. 37–54; Igor Shvytov, *Agriculturally Induced Environmental Problems in Russia*, Discussion Paper No. 17 (Halle, Germany: Institute of Agricultural Development in Central and Eastern Europe, 1998), p. 13.

16. Se-Kyung Chong, "Anmyeon-do Recreation Forest: A Millennium of Management," in Patrick B. Durst et al., *In Search of Excellence: Exemplary Forest Management in Asia and the Pacific, Asia-Pacific Forestry Commission* (Bangkok: FAO Regional Office for Asia and the Pacific, 2005), pp. 251–59.

17. Ibid.

18. Turkish Foundation for Combating Soil Erosion, at english.tema.org.tr, viewed 31 July 2007.

19. Reed Funk, letter to author, 9 August 2005.

20. U.S. Embassy, Niamey, Niger, "Niger: Greener Now Than 30 Years Ago," reporting cable circulated following national FRAME workshop, October

2006; Chris Reij, "More Success Stories in Africa's Drylands Than Often Assumed," presentation at Network of Farmers' and Agricultural Producers' Organisations of West Africa Forum on Food Sovereignty, 7–10 November 2006.

21. U.S. Embassy, op. cit. note 20; Reij, op. cit. note 20.
22. Vattenfall, *Global Mapping of Greenhouse Gas Abatement Opportunities up to 2030: Forestry Sector Deep-Dive* (Stockholm: June 2007), p. 1.
23. "Forest Area and Area Change," in FAO, op. cit. note 3, pp. 109–15.
24. Johanna Son, "Philippines: Row Rages Over Lifting of Ban on Lumber Exports," *InterPress Service*, 17 April 1998; John Aglionby, "Philippines Bans Logging After Fatal Floods," *Guardian* (London), 6 December 2004; Republic of the Philippines, "President Okays Selective Lifting of Log Ban," press release (Manila: 7 March 2005).
25. "Forestry Cuts Down on Logging," *China Daily*, 26 May 1998; Erik Eckholm, "China Admits Ecological Sins Played Role in Flood Disaster," *New York Times*, 26 August 1998; Erik Eckholm, "Stunned by Floods, China Hastens Logging Curbs," *New York Times*, 27 September 1998; Chris Brown, Patrick B. Durst, and Thomas Enters, *Forests Out of Bounds: Impacts and Effectiveness of Logging Bans in Natural Forests in Asia-Pacific* (Bangkok, Thailand: FAO Regional Office for Asia Pacific, 2001); John Aglionby, "Philippines Bans Logging After Fatal Floods," *Guardian* (London), 6 December 2004.
26. Geoffrey Lean, "A Disaster to Take Everyone's Breath Away," *The Independent* (London), 24 July 2006; Daniel Nepstad, "Climate Change and the Forest," *Tomorrow's Amazonia: Using and Abusing the World's Last Great Forests* (Washington, DC: The American Prospect, September 2007); S. S. Saatchi et al., "Distribution of Aboveground Live Biomass in the Amazon Rainforest," *Global Change Biology*, vol. 13, no. 4 (April 2007), pp. 816–37.
27. Intergovernmental Panel on Climate Change (IPCC), *Climate Change 2007: Mitigation of Climate Change. Contribution of Working Group III to the Fourth Assessment Report of the Intergovernmental Panel on Climate Change* (Cambridge, U.K.: Cambridge University Press, 2007), pp. 541–84; Vattenfall, op. cit. note 22, p. 16; sequestration per tree calculated assuming 500 trees per hectare, from U.N. Environment Programme (UNEP), Billion Tree Campaign, "Fast Facts," at www.unep.org/billiontreecampaign, viewed 10 October 2007; growing period from Robert N. Stavins and Kenneth R. Richards, *The Cost of U.S. Forest Based Carbon Sequestration* (Arlington, VA: Pew Center on Global Climate Change, January 2005), p. 10.
28. Carbon sequestration potential based on IPCC, op. cit. note 27, pp. 543, 559.
29. Johan Eliasch, *Climate Change: Financing Global Forests* (London: The Stationary Office Limited for Her Majesty's Stationery Office, 2008), pp. xvi–xvii, 69–80; McKinsey & Company, *Pathways to a Low Carbon Economy: Version 2 of the Global Greenhouse Gas Abatement Cost Curve* (London: 2009).
30. UNEP, Billion Tree Campaign, at www.unep.org/billiontreecampaign, viewed 13 July 2009; carbon sequestration assuming that three fourths of trees will be in tropics and one fourth in temperate regions, using seques-

tration rates in Vattenfall, op. cit. note 22, p. 16; UNEP, "Tree Planting Campaign Hits Four Billion Mark," press release (Nairobi: 10 June 2009).

31. UNEP, "The State of Paraná in Brazil Undertakes a Major Reforestation Project," at www.unep.org/billiontreecampaign/CampaignNews, viewed 12 October 2007; UNEP, "31 July—The Greenest Day of the Calendar in India and a Tree Planting Record by 600,000 Volunteers," at www.unep.org/Documents.Multilingual, viewed 12 October 2007.

32. Chang-Ran Kim, "Tokyo Turns to Rooftop Gardens to Beat the Heat," *Reuters*, 7 August 2002; Washington, D.C., program from Casey Trees, at www.caseytrees.org, viewed 17 June 2009.

33. Kathy Wolf, "Urban Forest Values: Economic Benefits of Trees in Cities," fact sheet (Seattle, WA: Center for Urban Horticulture, November 1998); Greg McPherson et al., "Municipal Forest Benefits and Costs in Five US Cities," *Journal of Forestry*, December 2005, pp. 411–16.

34. "The Great North American Dust Bowl: A Cautionary Tale," in Secretariat of the U.N. Convention to Combat Desertification, *Global Alarm: Dust and Sandstorms from the World's Drylands* (Bangkok: 2002), pp. 77–121.

35. Jeffrey Zinn, *Conservation Reserve Program: Status and Current Issues* (Washington, DC: Congressional Research Service, 8 May 2001); USDA, Economic Research Service, *Agri-Environmental Policy at the Crossroads: Guideposts on a Changing Landscape* (Washington, DC: 2001).

36. USDA, Natural Resources Conservation Service, *CORE4 Conservation Practices Training Guide: The Common Sense Approach to Natural Resource Conservation* (Washington, DC: August 1999); Rolf Derpsch, "Frontiers in Conservation Tillage and Advances in Conservation Practice," in D. E. Stott, R. H. Mohtar, and G. C. Steinhardt, eds., *Sustaining the Global Farm*, selected papers from the 10th International Soil Conservation Organization Meeting, at Purdue University and USDA-ARS National Soil Erosion Research Laboratory, 24–29 May 1999 (Washington, DC: 2001), pp. 248–54.

37. Rolf Derpsch and Theodor Friedrich, "Development and Current Status of No-till Adoption in the World," presentation for International Soil Tillage Research Conference, Izmir, Turkey, 16 June 2009; Conservation Technology Information Center, Purdue University, "National Tillage Trends (1990–2004)," from the 2004 *National Crop Residue Management Survey Data*; FAO, *Intensifying Crop Production with Conservation Agriculture*, at www.fao.org/ag, viewed 20 May 2003.

38. FAO, op. cit. note 37.

39. Souhail Karam, "Drought-Hit North Africa Seen Hunting for Grains," *Reuters*, 15 July 2005.

40. Godwin Nnanna, "Africa's Message for China," *China Dialogue*, 18 April 2007; International Institute for Sustainable Development, "African Regional Coverage Project," *Eighth African Union Summit—Briefing Note*, vol. 7, issue 2 (7 February 2007), p. 8; Federal Republic of Nigeria, Ministry of Environment, "Green Wall Sahara Programme," at www.greenwallsahara.org, viewed 17 October 2007; Anne Woodfine and Sandrine Jauffret, *Scope and Pre-Feasibility Study on the Great Green Wall for the Sahara and Sahel Initiative* (Hemel Hempstead, U.K.: HTPSE Ltd., June 2009).

41. Evan Ratliff, "The Green Wall of China," *Wired*, April 2003; Wang Yan, "China's Forest Shelter Project Dubbed 'Green Great Wall'," *Xinhua News Agency*, 9 July 2006; Sun Xiufang and Ralph Bean, *China Solid Wood Products Annual Report 2002* (Beijing: USDA, 2002); Jonathan Watts, "China Suspends Reforestation Project over Food Shortage Fears," *Guardian* (London), 23 June 2009.

42. Author's discussion with officials of Helin County, Inner Mongolia (Nei Monggol), 17 May 2002.

43. Ibid.

44. U.S. Embassy, *Grapes of Wrath in Inner Mongolia* (Beijing: May 2001).

45. A. Banerjee, "Dairying Systems in India," *World Animal Review*, vol. 79/2 (Rome: FAO, 1994).

46. Rattan Lal, "Soil Carbon Sequestration Impacts on Global Climate Change and Food Security," *Science*, vol. 304 (11 June 2004), pp. 1,623–27.

47. Partnership for Interdisciplinary Studies of Coastal Oceans, *The Science of Marine Reserves*, 2nd ed., International Version (Oregon and California: 2007).

48. Ibid.

49. W. Renema et al., "Hopping Hotspots: Global Shifts in Marine Biodiversity," *Science*, vol. 321, no. 5889 (1 August 2008), pp. 654–57.

50. "About the Papahānaumokuākea Marine National Monument," at hawaii reef.noaa.gov/about/welcome.html, viewed 8 May 2009; John M. Broder, "Bush to Protect Vast New Pacific Tracts," *New York Times*, 6 January 2009; "Establishment of the Marianas Trench Marine National Monument," Proclamation 8335, "Establishment of the Pacific Remote Islands Marine National Monument," Proclamation 8336, and "Establishment of the Rose Atoll Marine National Monument," Proclamation 8337, *Federal Register*, Vol. 74, No. 7 (12 January 2009); U.S. Fish and Wildlife Service, "Establishment of the Northwestern Hawaiian Islands Marine National Monument," at www.fws.gov/midway/presidential%20 proclamation.pdf, viewed 11 May 2009.

51. Population Reference Bureau, *Datafinder*, electronic database, at www.prb.org/DataFinder.aspx, updated 2008; Emma Young, "Ocean Biodiversity: Depths of Ignorance," *New Scientist*, 12 April 2008.

52. Andrew Balmford et al., "The Worldwide Costs of Marine Protected Areas," *Proceedings of the National Academy of Sciences*, vol. 101, no. 26 (29 June 2004), pp. 9,694–97; Tim Radford, "Marine Parks Can Solve Global Fish Crisis, Experts Say," *Guardian* (London), 15 June 2004.

53. Balmford et al., op. cit. note 52; Radford, op. cit. note 52.

54. Radford, op. cit. note 52; Richard Black, "Protection Needed for 'Marine Serengetis'," *BBC News*, 4 August 2003; Balmford et al., op. cit. note 52.

55. American Association for the Advancement of Science (AAAS), "Leading Marine Scientists Release New Evidence that Marine Reserves Produce Enormous Benefits within Their Boundaries and Beyond," press release (Washington, DC: 12 March 2001); "Scientific Consensus Statement on Marine Reserves and Marine Protected Areas," presented at the AAAS annual meeting, 15–20 February 2001.

56. AAAS, op. cit. note 55; "Scientific Consensus Statement," op. cit. note 55, p. 2.

57. R. J. Diaz, J. Nestlerode, and M. L. Diaz, "A Global Perspective on the

Effects of Eutrophication and Hypoxia on Aquatic Biota," in G. L. Rupp and M. D. White, eds., *Proceedings of the 7th Annual Symposium on Fish Physiology, Toxicology and Water Quality, Estonia, 12–15 May 2003* (Athens, GA: EPA, Ecosystems Research Division, 2004); UNEP, *GEO Yearbook 2003* (Nairobi: 2004); R. J. Diaz and R. Rosenberg, "Spreading Dead Zones and Consequences for Marine Ecosystems," *Science*, vol. 321 (15 August 2008), pp. 926–29.

58. WWF, *Hard Facts, Hidden Problems: A Review of Current Data on Fishing Subsidies* (Washington, DC: 2001), pp. ii; Balmford et al., op. cit. note 52; Radford, op. cit. note 52; fishery subsidy value includes "bad" subsidies and fuel subsidies as estimated in Fisheries Center, University of British Columbia, *Catching More Bait: A Bottom-Up Re-Estimation of Global Fisheries Subsidies* (2nd Version) (Vancouver, BC: 2006), p. 21.

59. U.N. Population Division, *World Population Prospects: The 2008 Revision Population Database*, at esa.un.org/unpp, updated 11 March 2009.

60. World Wide Fund for Nature (WWF), "Problems: Inadequate Protection," at www.panda.org, viewed 8 May 2009.

61. Conservation International, "Biodiversity Hotspots," at www.biodiversityhotspots.org, viewed 8 May 2009.

62. U.S. Fish and Wildlife Service, "The Endangered Species Act of 1973," at www.fws.gov/endangered, viewed 31 July 2007.

63. Table 8–1 from the following: planting trees to reduce flooding and conserve soil and protecting topsoil on cropland from Lester R. Brown and Edward C. Wolf, "Reclaiming the Future," in Lester R. Brown et al., *State of the World 1988* (New York: W. W. Norton & Company, 1988), p. 174, using data from FAO, *Fuelwood Supplies in the Developing Countries*, Forestry Paper 42 (Rome: 1983); planting trees to sequester carbon based on IPCC, op. cit. note 27, pp. 543, 559; restoring rangelands from UNEP, *Status of Desertification and Implementation of the United Nations Plan of Action to Combat Desertification* (Nairobi: 1991), pp. 73–92; restoring fisheries from Balmford et al., op. cit. note 52; protecting biological diversity from World Parks Congress, *Recommendations of the Vth IUCN World Parks Congress* (Durban, South Africa: 2003), pp. 17–19, and from World Parks Congress, "The Durban Accord," at www.iucn.org/themes/wcpa, viewed 19 October 2007; stabilizing water tables is author's estimate.

64. Chong, op. cit. note 16.

65. Brown and Wolf, op. cit. note 63, p. 175.

66. Runsheng Yin et al., "China's Ecological Rehabilitation: The Unprecedented Efforts and Dramatic Impacts of Reforestation and Slope Protection in Western China," in Woodrow Wilson International Center for Scholars, *China Environment Forum*, China Environment Series, Issue 7 (Washington, DC: 2005), pp. 17–32.

67. Brown and Wolf, op. cit. note 63, p. 176.

68. IPCC, op. cit. note 27, pp. 543, 559.

69. Brown and Wolf, op. cit. note 63, p. 173–74.

70. Ibid., p. 174.

71. Ibid.

72. Ibid.

73. Restoring rangelands from UNEP, op. cit. note 63, pp. 73–92, with figures converted from 1990 to 2004 dollars using implicit price deflators from

U.S. Department of Commerce, Bureau of Economic Analysis, "Table C.1. GDP and Other Major NIPA Aggregates," in *Survey of Current Business*, September 2005, p. D–48.

74. H. E. Dregne and Nan-Ting Chou, "Global Desertification Dimensions and Costs," in H. E. Dregne, ed., *Degradation and Restoration of Arid Lands* (Lubbock, TX: Texas Tech. University, 1992); restoring rangelands from UNEP, op. cit. note 63, pp. 73–92.

75. Balmford et al., op. cit. note 52.

76. World Parks Congress, *Recommendations*, op. cit. note 63, pp. 17–19; World Parks Congress, "The Durban Accord," op. cit. note 63.

77. Irrigated cropland from FAO, *ResourceSTAT*, electronic database, at faostat.fao.org, updated April 2009.

78. Jordan from Tom Gardner-Outlaw and Robert Engelman, *Sustaining Water, Easing Scarcity: A Second Update* (Washington, DC: Population Action International, 1997); Mexico from Sandra Postel, *Last Oasis* (New York: W. W. Norton & Company, 1997), pp. 150–51.

79. Sandra Postel, *Pillar of Sand* (New York: W. W. Norton & Company, 1999), pp. 230–35; Mexico from Postel, op. cit. note 78, pp. 167–68.

Chapter 9. Feeding Eight Billion People Well

1. U.S. Department of Agriculture (USDA), *Production, Supply and Distribution (PS&D)*, electronic database, at www.fas.usda.gov/psdonline, updated 12 May 2009; USDA, *Feedgrains Database*, electronic database at www.ers.usda.gov/Data/feedgrains, updated 19 May 2009.

2. U.N. Food and Agriculture Organization (FAO), "FAO-OECD to Weigh Investments Against Hunger," press release (Rome: 4 May 2009); Shenggen Fan and Mark W. Rosegrant, *Investing in Agriculture to Overcome the World Food Crisis and Reduce Poverty and Hunger* (Washington, DC: International Food Policy Research Institute (IFPRI), June 2008).

3. USDA, *PS&D*, op. cit. note 1; U.N. Population Division, *World Population Prospects, The 2008 Revision Population Database*, electronic database, at esa.un.org/unpp, updated 11 March 2009.

4. USDA, *PS&D*, op. cit. note 1.

5. Historical data compiled by Worldwatch Institute from FAO, *Fertilizer Yearbook* (Rome: various years), and by Earth Policy Institute from International Fertilizer Industry Association (IFA), *IFADATA*, electronic database at www.fertilizer.org/ifa/ifadata/search, retrieved 3 February 2009; current data from Patrick Heffer, *Medium-Term Outlook for World Agriculture and Fertilizer Demand 2007/08 – 2012/13* (Paris: IFA, June 2008), p. 34, and from IFA, *Fertilizer Consumption 2007/08 – 2012/13 Country Reports* (Paris: June 2008), pp. 8, 19, 21.

6. Irrigation data for 1950–60 compiled from Lester R. Brown, "Eradicating Hunger: A Growing Challenge," in Lester R. Brown et al., *State of the World 2001* (New York: W. W. Norton & Company, 2001), pp. 52–53; data for 1961–2007 from FAO, *ResourceSTAT*, electronic database at faostat.fao.org, updated April 2009.

7. Lester R. Brown, *Increasing World Food Output: Problems and Prospects*, Foreign Agricultural Economic Report No. 25 (Washington, DC: USDA, Economic Research Service (ERS), 1965), pp. 13–14; L. T. Evans, *Crop*

Evolution, Adaptation and Yield (Cambridge, U.K.: Cambridge University Press, 1993), pp. 242–44.

8. USDA, *PS&D*, op. cit. note 1; Margriet F. Caswell et al., *Agricultural Biotechnology: An Economic Perspective* (Washington, DC: USDA, ERS, 1998), p. 19; Kenneth G. Cassman and Adam J. Liska, "Food and Fuel for All: Realistic or Foolish?" *Biofuels, Bioproducts and Biorefining*, vol. 1, no. 1 (2007), pp. 18–23.

9. World Food Prize Foundation, "A World-Brand Name: Yuan Longping, The Father of Hybrid Rice," at www.worldfoodprize.org/laureates/yuan-spotlight.htm, viewed 15 July 2009.

10. USDA, *PS&D*, op. cit. note 1; FAO, *FAOSTAT*, electronic database, at faostat.fao.org, updated June 2009.

11. USDA, *PS&D*, op. cit. note 1.

12. IFA, *IFADATA*, op. cit. note 5; IFA, *Country Reports*, op. cit. note 5, pp. 8, 19, 21; USDA, *PS&D*, op. cit. note 1; USDA, National Agricultural Statistics Service (NASS), *Crop Production 2008 Summary* (Washington, DC: January 2009), p. 5.

13. USDA, *PS&D*, op. cit. note 1.

14. Lester R. Brown, *Eco-Economy* (New York: W. W. Norton & Company, 2001), pp. 145–46; Thomas R. Sinclair, "Limits to Crop Yield?" in American Society of Agronomy, Crop Science Society of America, and Soil Science Society of America, *Physiology and Determination of Crop Yield* (Madison, WI: 1994), pp. 509–32; USDA, *PS&D*, op. cit. note 1.

15. U.N. Population Division, op. cit. note 3; World Bank, "Malawi, Fertilizer Subsidies and the World Bank," at web.worldbank.org, viewed 14 July 2008; Celia W. Dugger, "Ending Famine, Simply by Ignoring the Experts," *New York Times*, 2 December 2007; USDA, *PS&D*, op. cit. note 1.

16. Ben Block, "African Leaders Pursue 'Malawi Miracle'," *Eye on Earth*, at www.worldwatch.org, 26 May 2009.

17. USDA, op. cit. note 12, pp. 5, 13.

18. USDA, *PS&D*, op. cit. note 1; 1950 data from USDA, in Worldwatch Institute, *Signposts 2001*, CD-ROM (Washington, DC: 2001).

19. Jorge Sanchez and Jiang Junyang, *China Grain and Feed Annual 2009* (Beijing: USDA, March 2009); USDA, *PS&D*, op. cit. note 1.

20. A. Govindian, *India Grain and Feed Annual 2009* (New Delhi: USDA, February 2009); USDA, *PS&D*, op. cit. note 1; U.N. Population Division, op. cit. note 3.

21. Richard Magleby, "Soil Management and Conservation," in USDA, *Agricultural Resources and Environmental Indicators 2003* (Washington, DC: February 2003), Chapter 4.2, p. 14.

22. USDA, *PS&D*, op. cit. note 1; Randall D. Schnepf et al., *Agriculture in Brazil and Argentina* (Washington, DC: USDA ERS, 2001), pp. 8–10.

23. Pedro Sanchez, "The Climate Change–Soil Fertility–Food Security Nexus," summary note (Bonn: IFPRI, 4 September 2001).

24. Edward Cody, "Chinese Lawmakers Approve Measure to Protect Private Property Rights," *Washington Post*, 17 March 2007; Jim Yardley, "China Nears Passage of Landmark Property Law," *New York Times*, 9 March 2007; Zhu Keliang and Roy Prosterman, "From Land Rights to Economic Boom," *China Business Review*, July–August 2006.

25. Land productivity from USDA, *PS&D*, op. cit. note 1, with pre-1961 data

from USDA, in Worldwatch Institute, op. cit. note 18; water requirements for grain production from FAO, *Yield Response to Water* (Rome: 1979).

26. Water use from I. A. Shiklomanov, "Assessment of Water Resources and Water Availability in the World," *Report for the Comprehensive Assessment of the Freshwater Resources of the World* (St. Petersburg, Russia: State Hydrological Institute, 1998), cited in Peter H. Gleick, *The World's Water 2000–2001* (Washington, DC: Island Press, 2000), p. 53; Sandra Postel and Amy Vickers, "Boosting Water Productivity," in Worldwatch Institute, *State of the World 2004* (New York: W. W. Norton & Company, 2004), pp. 51–52.

27. Wang Shucheng, discussion with author, Beijing, May 2004.

28. FAO, *Crops and Drops* (Rome: 2002), p. 17; Alain Vidal, Aline Comeau, and Hervé Plusquellec, *Case Studies on Water Conservation in the Mediterranean Region* (Rome: FAO, 2001), p. vii.

29. Postel and Vickers, op. cit. note 26, p. 53.

30. Sandra Postel et al., "Drip Irrigation for Small Farmers: A New Initiative to Alleviate Hunger and Poverty," *Water International*, March 2001, pp. 3–13.

31. Ibid.

32. "Punjab's Depleting Groundwater Stagnates Agricultural Growth," *Down to Earth*, vol. 16, no. 5 (30 July 2007).

33. R. Maria Saleth and Arial Dinar, *Water Challenge and Institutional Response: A Cross-Country Perspective* (Washington, DC: World Bank, 1999), p. 6; Comisión Nacional del Agua (CONAGUA), *National Water Program 2007–2012* (Coyoacán, Mexico: February 2008), p. 71.

34. World Bank and Swiss Agency for Development and Cooperation, Summary Report, Middle East and North Africa Regional Water Initiative Workshop on Sustainable Groundwater Management, Sana'a, Yemen, 25–28 June 2000, p. 19; Mei Xie, senior water resources specialist, World Bank Institute, e-mail to J. Matthew Roney, Earth Policy Institute, 10 July 2009.

35. USDA, *PS&D*, op. cit. note 1; Cynthia Guven and Sherif Ibrahim, *Egypt Grain and Feed Annual 2009* (Cairo: USDA, March 2009); "Rice Cropped for Water," *China Daily*, 9 January 2002; National Bureau of Statistics of China, *Statistical Data*, electronic database, at www.stats.gov.cn/english/statisticaldata/yearlydata, viewed 9 June 2009.

36. U.N. Population Division, op. cit. note 3; USDA, *PS&D*, op. cit. note 1; water calculation based on 1,000 tons of water for 1 ton of grain from FAO, op. cit. note 25.

37. USDA, *PS&D*, op. cit. note 1.

38. FAO, *1948–1985 World Crop and Livestock Statistics* (Rome: 1987); FAO, op. cit. note 10; U.N. Population Division, op. cit. note 3.

39. Conversion ratio for feed-to-poultry derived from data in Robert V. Bishop et al., *The World Poultry Market—Government Intervention and Multilateral Policy Reform* (Washington, DC: USDA, 1990); beef based on Allen Baker, Feed Situation and Outlook staff, ERS, USDA, discussion with author, 27 April 1992; pork from Leland Southard, Livestock and Poultry Situation and Outlook staff, ERS, USDA, discussion with author, 27 April 1992; fish from Rosamond Naylor et al., "Effect of Aquaculture on World Fish Supplies," *Nature*, vol. 405 (29 June 2000), pp. 1,017–24.

40. FAO, op. cit. note 10.
41. FAO, *FISHSTAT Plus*, electronic database, at www.fao.org, updated February 2009; Naylor et al., op. cit. note 39.
42. FAO, op. cit. note 41; Taija-Riitta Tuominen and Maren Esmark, *Food for Thought: The Use of Marine Resources in Fish Feed* (Oslo: WWF-Norway, 2003); Rosamond Naylor and Marshall Burke, "Aquaculture and Ocean Resources: Raising Tigers of the Sea," *Annual Review of Environmental Resources*, vol. 30 (November 2005), pp. 185–218.
43. FAO, op. cit. note 41.
44. S. F. Li, "Aquaculture Research and Its Relation to Development in China," in World Fish Center, *Agricultural Development and the Opportunities for Aquatic Resources Research in China* (Penang, Malaysia: 2001), p. 26; FAO, op. cit. note 41.
45. FAO, op. cit. note 10; FAO, op. cit. note 41.
46. Naylor et al., op. cit. note 39; W. C. Nandeesha et al., "Breeding of Carp with Oviprim," in *Indian Branch, Asian Fisheries Society, India*, Special Publication No. 4 (Mangalore, India: 1990), p. 1.
47. "Mekong Delta to Become Biggest Aquatic Producer in Vietnam," *Vietnam News Agency*, 3 August 2004; "The Mekong Delta Goes Ahead with the WTO," *Vietnam Economic News* Online, 8 June 2007; FAO, op. cit. note 41.
48. Naylor et al., op. cit. note 39; FAO, op. cit. note 41; USDA, NASS, *Catfish Production* (Washington, DC: 30 January 2009), pp. 17–20; U.N. Population Division, op. cit. note 3.
49. USDA, Foreign Agricultural Service, *Oilseeds: World Markets and Trade* (Washington, DC: May 2009).
50. USDA, *PS&D*, op. cit. note 1.
51. Historical data from USDA, in Worldwatch Institute, op. cit. note 18; USDA, *PS&D*, op. cit. note 1.
52. FAO, op. cit. note 10.
53. S. C. Dhall and Meena Dhall, "Dairy Industry—India's Strength in Its Livestock," *Business Line*, Internet Edition of *Financial Daily*, Hindu group of publications, 7 November 1997; see also Surinder Sud, "India Is Now World's Largest Milk Producer," *India Perspectives*, May 1999, pp. 25–26; A. Banerjee, "Dairying Systems in India," *World Animal Review*, vol. 79, no. 2 (1994).
54. FAO, op. cit. note 10; U.N. Population Division, op. cit. note 3.
55. Dhall and Dhall, op. cit. note 53; Banerjee, op. cit. note 53; FAO, op. cit. note 10.
56. John Wade, Adam Branson, and Xiang Qing, *China Grain and Feed Annual Report 2002* (Beijing: USDA, 2002); Gao Tengyun, "Treatment and Utilization of Crop Straw and Stover in China," *Livestock Research for Rural Development*, February 2000.
57. USDA, ERS, "China's Beef Economy: Production, Marketing, Consumption, and Foreign Trade," *International Agriculture and Trade Reports: China* (Washington, DC: July 1998), p. 28.
58. FAO, op. cit. note 10; FAO, op. cit. note 41; U.N. Population Division, op. cit. note 3.
59. U.N. Population Division, op. cit. note 3; China's economic growth from International Monetary Fund (IMF), *World Economic Outlook Data-*

base, at www.imf.org/external/pubs/ft/weo, updated April 2009; FAO, *FAOSTAT*, electronic database at faostat.fao.org, updated 30 June 2007.

60. Lisa McLaughlin, "Inner-City Farms," *Time*, 4 August 2008; Caryn Rousseau, "More Schools Cultivate Learning in Student Gardens," *Associated Press*, 17 November 2008; USDA, Agricultural Marketing Service, "Farmers Market Growth: 1994–2008," at www.ams.usda.gov, updated 22 September 2008.

61. Historical trend from Carolyn Dimitri, Anne Effland, and Neilson Conklin, *The 20th Century Transformation of U.S. Agriculture and Farm Policy* (Washington, DC: USDA, ERS, June 2005), p. 5; USDA, NASS, *2007 Census of Agriculture* (Washington, DC: February 2009), pp. 7, 64, 110–11; Andrew Martin, "Farm Living (Subsidized by a Job Elsewhere)," *New York Times*, 8 February 2009.

62. Martin, op. cit. note 61; USDA, op. cit. note 61, pp. 52, 66–67.

63. Marian Burros, "Obamas to Plant Vegetable Garden at White House," *New York Times*, 20 March 2009; Michael Pollan, "Farmer in Chief," *New York Times Magazine*, 12 October 2008.

64. Cristina Milesi et al., "Mapping and Modeling the Biogeochemical Cycling of Turf Grasses in the United States," *Environmental Management*, vol. 36, no. 3 (19 July 2005), pp. 426–38.

65. McLaughlin, op. cit. note 60; "Digging Their Way Out of Recession," *The Economist*, 26 February 2009; Adrian Higgins, "Community Gardens Need Room to Grow," *Washington Post*, 14 February 2008.

66. USDA, op. cit. note 60; current total from Joan Shaffer, USDA, Agricultural Marketing Service, discussion with J. Matthew Roney, Earth Policy Institute, 13 May 2009; Valerie Bauman, "More Farmers Markets to Accept Food Stamps," *Associated Press*, 26 August 2008.

67. Rousseau, op. cit. note 60; Mary MacVean, "Maria Shriver Says Edible Garden Will Be Planted in Capitol Park Flower Bed," *Los Angeles Times*, 27 March 2009.

68. Marian Burros, "Supermarket Chains Narrow Their Sights," *New York Times*, 6 August 2008; "Digging Their Way Out of Recession," op. cit. note 65.

69. Rich Pirog and Andrew Benjamin, *Checking the Food Odometer: Comparing Food Miles for Local Versus Conventional Produce Sales to Iowa Institutions* (Ames, IA: Leopold Center for Sustainable Agriculture, Iowa State University, July 2003); Michael Pollan, *In Defense of Food* (New York: The Penguin Group, 2008), pp. 157–58; Marc Xuereb, *Food Miles: Environmental Implications of Food Imports to Waterloo Region* (Waterloo, ON: Region of Waterloo Public Health, November 2005); Erika Engelhaupt, "Do Food Miles Matter?" *Environmental Science and Technology Online*, at pubs.acs.org, 16 April 2008.

70. "The Environment: Not on the Label," *The Economist*, 19 May 2007; John Waples, "Tesco Turns Itself into a Green Giant," *Sunday Times* (London), 31 May 2009; Tesco PLC, "Tesco Wins Green 'Gold Standard' Award," press release (Hertfordshire, U.K.: 5 June 2009); Miles Costello, "Tesco Reports Record £3 Billion Profit," *The Times* (London), 21 April 2009.

71. Lauren Etter, "Lofty Prices for Fertilizer Put Farmers in a Squeeze," *Wall Street Journal*, 27 May 2008; David A. Vaccari, "Phosphorus: A Looming

Crisis," *Scientific American*, June 2009, pp. 54–59.

72. Program for Appropriate Technology in Health and U.N. Population Fund, *Meeting the Need: Strengthening Family Planning Programs* (Seattle, WA: 2006), pp. 5–11.

73. Author's calculations from USDA, *PS&D*, op. cit. note 1; U.N. Population Division, op. cit. note 3.

74. USDA, *PS&D*, op. cit. note 1; U.N. Population Division, op. cit. note 3; FAO, *FAOSTAT*, electronic database at faostat.fao.org, updated May 2008.

75. Organisation for Economic Co-operation and Development, "Total Health Expenditure per Capita, US$ PPP," in *OECD Health Data 2008 – Frequently Requested Data*, at www.oecd.org, December 2008; FAO, op. cit. note 59.

76. Gidon Eshel and Pamela A. Martin, "Diet, Energy, and Global Warming," *Earth Interactions*, vol. 10, no. 9 (April 2006), pp. 1–17.

77. Poultry from data in Bishop et al., op. cit. note 39; beef from Baker, op. cit. note 39; fish from Naylor et al., op. cit. note 39.

78. Land area estimate from Stanley Wood, Kate Sebastian, and Sara J. Scherr, *Pilot Analysis of Global Ecosystems: Agroecosystems* (Washington, DC: IFPRI and World Resources Institute, 2000), p. 3.

79. Yields from USDA, NASS, *Agricultural Statistics 2008* (Washington, DC: 2008), pp. I-21, III-16.

80. USDA, *PS&D*, op. cit. note 1; USDA, *Feedgrains Database*, op. cit. note 1; U.N. Population Division, op. cit. note 3.

81. Money going to land acquisitions from Joachim von Braun, IFPRI, cited in Joe DeCapua, "Food Crisis Triggers Land Grab in Developing Countries," *Voice of America News*, 29 April 2009.

Chapter 10. Can We Mobilize Fast Enough?

1. Peter Goldmark, Environmental Defense Fund, e-mail to author, 28 June 2009.

2. Lester R. Brown, "Could Food Shortages Bring Down Civilization?" *Scientific American*, May 2009, pp. 50–57.

3. Mohammad Yunus and Karl Weber, *Creating a World Without Poverty* (New York: PublicAffairs, 2008), p. 105.

4. Øystein Dahle, discussion with author, State of the World Conference, Aspen, CO, 22 July 2001.

5. Norway, Costa Rica, and the Maldives from U.N. Environment Programme (UNEP), Climate Neutral Network, "Countries," at www.unep.org/climateneutral, viewed 24 June 2009; Olivia Lang, "Maldives Vows to be First Carbon-neutral Nation," *Reuters*, 15 March 2009.

6. UNEP, "UNEP Unveils the Climate Neutral Network to Catalyze a Transition to a Low Carbon World" press release (Nairobi: Climate Neutral Network, 21 February 2008).

7. Redefining Progress, "The Economists' Statement on Climate Change," at www.rprogress.org/publications/1997/econstatement.htm, viewed 26 June 2008.

8. Centers for Disease Control and Prevention, *Sustaining State Programs for Tobacco Control: Data Highlights 2006* (Atlanta, GA: 2006).

9. Campaign for Tobacco-Free Kids, "State Cigarette Excise Tax Rank and

Ratings," fact sheet (Washington, DC: 28 May 2009); Campaign for Tobacco-Free Kids, "Raising Cigarette Taxes Reduces Smoking, Especially Among Kids (And the Cigarette Companies Know It)," fact sheet (Washington, DC: 9 January 2009); Campaign for Tobacco-Free Kids, "Cigarette Tax Increases by State per Year 2000–2009," fact sheet (Washington, DC: 28 May 2009).

10. Gasoline indirect cost calculated based on International Center for Technology Assessment (ICTA), *The Real Price of Gasoline*, Report No. 3 (Washington, DC: 1998), p. 34, updated using the following: ICTA, *Gasoline Cost Externalities Associated with Global Climate Change: An Update to CTA's Real Price of Gasoline Report* (Washington, DC: September 2004), ICTA, *Gasoline Cost Externalities: Security and Protection Services: An Update to CTA's Real Price of Gasoline Report* (Washington, DC: January 2005), Terry Tamminen, *Lives Per Gallon: The True Cost of Our Oil Addiction* (Washington, DC: Island Press, 2006), p. 60, and Bureau for Economic Analysis, "Table 3—Price Indices for Gross Domestic Product and Gross Domestic Purchases," *GDP and Other Major Series, 1929–2007* (Washington, DC: August 2007); U.S. Department of Energy (DOE), Energy Information Administration (EIA), *This Week in Petroleum* (Washington, DC: various issues); EIA, "US Weekly Retail," *Retail Gasoline Historical Prices* (Washington, DC: 15 June 2009).

11. American Petroleum Institute, *State Gasoline Tax Report* (Washington DC: 1 April 2009); DOE, EIA, "Weekly (Monday) Retail Premium Gasoline Prices, Selected Countries," at www.eia.doe.gov/emeu, updated 16 June 2009; gasoline consumption from International Energy Agency (IEA), in World Resources Institute, "Energy and Resources: Energy Consumption by Source: Oil and Petroleum Products (2005)," *EarthTrends* electronic database, at www.earthtrends.wri.org, updated 2007.

12. U.S. Department of Agriculture, Economic Research Service, "Cigarette Price Increase Follows Tobacco Pact," *Agricultural Outlook*, January–February 1999.

13. Markus Knigge and Benjamin Görlach, *Effects of Germany's Ecological Tax Reforms on the Environment, Employment and Technological Innovation: Summary of the Final Report of the Project* (Berlin: Ecologic Institute for International and European Environmental Policy, August 2005); Michael Renner, Sean Sweeney, and Jill Kubit, *Green Jobs: Towards Decent Work in a Sustainable, Low Carbon World* (Nairobi: UNEP, 2008), p. 97.

14. Estimate of Swedish tax shifting based on Paul Ekins and Stefan Speck, "Environmental Tax Reform in Europe: Energy Tax Rates and Competitiveness," in Nathalie J. Chalifour et al., *Critical Issues in Environmental Taxation* (Oxford: Oxford University Press, 2008), pp. 77–105; Ministry of Finance, Sweden, "Taxation and the Environment," press release (Stockholm: 25 May 2005); household size from Target Group Index, "Household Size," *Global TGI Barometer* (Miami: 2005) and from U.N. Population Division, *World Population Prospects: The 2008 Revision Population Database*, at esa.un.org/unpp, updated 11 March 2009; Andrew Hoerner and Benoît Bosquet, *Environmental Tax Reform: The European Experience* (Washington, DC: Center for a Sustainable Economy, 2001); European Environment Agency, *Environmental Taxes: Recent Develop-*

ments in Tools for Integration, Environmental Issues Series No. 18 (Copenhagen: 2000); polls from David Malin Roodman, *The Natural Wealth of Nations* (New York: W. W. Norton & Company, 1998), p. 243.

15. Redefining Progress, op. cit. note 7; N. Gregory Mankiw, "Gas Tax Now!" *Fortune*, 24 May 1999, pp. 60–64.

16. Confederation of European Waste-to-Energy Plants, *Landfill Taxes and Bans* (Brussels: April 2007); Tom Miles, "London Drivers to Pay UK's First Congestion Tax," *Reuters*, 28 February 2002; Energy Council, *Energy Efficiency Policies and Indicators* (London: 2001), Annex 1; "DONG Satisfied with Electric Car Tax Relief," *Copenhagen Post*, 22 May 2009; Nick Kurczewski, "Scariest Place in the World to Buy a Car," *New York Times Wheels Blog*, 7 May 2008; Office of the Mayor, "Car Plate Prices Climb" (Shanghai: 21 June 2009).

17. South Australian Fisheries Management Series, *Management Plan for the South Australian Southern Zone Rock Lobster Fishery* (Adelaide, South Australia: 2007); South Australian Research and Development Institute, *Southern Zone Rock Lobster* (Jasus edwardsii) *Fishery*, assessment report to PIRSA (Adelaide, South Australia: 2008).

18. Edwin Clark, letter to author, 25 July 2001.

19. André de Moor and Peter Calamai, *Subsidizing Unsustainable Development* (San José, Costa Rica: Earth Council, 1997).

20. World Bank, *World Development Report 2003* (New York: Oxford University Press, 2003), pp. 30, 142; IEA, *World Energy Outlook 2006* (Paris: 2006), p. 279.

21. Belgium, France, and Japan from Seth Dunn, "King Coal's Weakening Grip on Power," *World Watch*, September/October 1999, pp. 10–19; Germany from UNEP, *Reforming Energy Subsides: Opportunities to Contribute to the Climate Change Agenda* (Nairobi: 2008), and from DOE, EIA, *International Energy Annual 2006* (Washington, DC: October 2008), Table 1.4; China, Indonesia, and Nigeria subsidy cuts from GTZ Transport Policy Advisory Service, *International Fuel Prices 2007* (Eschborn, Germany: April 2007), p. 3.

22. John Whitelegg and Spencer Fitz-Gibbon, *Aviation's Economic Downside*, 3rd ed. (London: Green Party of England & Wales, 2003); dollar conversion based on August 2007 exchange rate in International Monetary Fund, "Representative Exchange Rates for Selected Currencies in August 2007," *Exchange Rate Archives by Month*, at www.imf.org/external, viewed 16 August 2007; U.N. Population Division, op. cit. note 14.

23. Doug Koplow, *Subsidies in the U.S. Energy Sector: Magnitude, Causes, and Options for Reform* (Cambridge, MA: Earth Track, November 2006); Doug Koplow, Earth Track, e-mail to Jessie Robbins, Earth Policy Institute, 2 July 2009.

24. Fishery subsidy value includes "bad" subsidies and fuel subsidies as estimated in Fisheries Center, *Catching More Bait: A Bottom-Up Re-Estimation of Global Fisheries Subsidies* (2nd Version) (Vancouver, BC: University of British Columbia, 2006), p. 21.

25. Coal Moratorium NOW!, "Progress Towards a Coal Moratorium: 59 Coal Plants Cancelled or Shelved in 2007," press release (San Francisco: 17 January 2008); Mark Clayton, "Rising Construction Costs and Potential Climate Legislation in Congress Halt at Least 18 Proposed Power

Plants in the Past Nine Months," *Christian Science Monitor*, 25 October 2007; Janet Larsen, "Coal Takes Heavy Human Toll," *Eco-Economy Update* (Washington, DC: Earth Policy Institute, 24 August 2004).

26. Sierra Club, "Stopping the Coal Rush," online database, accessed 23 July 2009, at www.sierraclub.org/environmentallaw/coal/plantlist.asp; Kathleen Krust, Sierra Club, discussion with Jessie Robbins, Earth Policy Institute, 23 July 2009.

27. Opinion Research Corporation, *A Post Fossil-Fuel America: Are Americans Ready to Make the Shift?* (Princeton, NJ: October 2007).

28. Andrew Ross Sorkin, "A Buyout Deal That Has Many Shades of Green," *New York Times*, 26 February 2007; "Texas Decision Could Double Wind Power Capacity in the U.S.," *Renewable Energy Access*, 4 October 2007.

29. Timothy Gardner, "Florida Gov. Might Allow New Coal Power Plants," *Reuters*, 4 October 2007; Buck Parker, Earthjustice, letter to author, October 2007; Coal Moratorium NOW! op. cit. note 25.

30. Jim Jelter, "Coal Stocks Tumble on Citigroup Downgrade," *MarketWatch*, 18 July 2007; Steve James, "Coal Shares Fall After Merrill Downgrade," *Reuters*, 3 January 2008; Citigroup, "Leading Wall Street Banks Establish the Carbon Principles," press release (New York: 4 February 2008); Jeffrey Ball, "Wall Street Shows Skepticism Over Coal," *Wall Street Journal*, 4 February 2008; Jeffrey Ball, "Bank of America Puts a Price on Carbon," *Wall Street Journal*, 13 February 2008.

31. Martin Griffith, "Reid Fights New Coal-Fired Plants," (Salt Lake City) *Deseret News*, 26 August 2007; Nicholas D. Kristof, "The Big Melt," *New York Times*, 16 August 2007; Governor Jennifer M. Granholm, "Priorities for Michigan's Economic Future: Jobs, Education and Protecting Families," State of the State Address, 3 February 2009; State of Washington 60th Legislature, Climate Change—Mitigating Impacts, Engrossed Substitute Senate Bill 6001, Chapter 307, Laws of 2007, 22 July 2007; Carla Vigue, "Governor Says No to Coal for State Heating Plants in Madison," press release (Madison, WI: Office of the Governor, 1 August 2008); Audrey Chang, "California Takes on Power Plant Emissions: SB 1368 Sets Groundbreaking Greenhouse Gas Performance Standard," fact sheet (New York: Natural Resources Defense Council, August 2007); Gardner, op. cit. note 29.

32. Granholm, op. cit. note 31.

33. Kristen Lombardi, *Coal Ash: The Hidden Story: How Industry and the EPA Failed to Stop a Growing Environmental Disaster* (Washington, DC: Center for Public Integrity, 19 February 2009).

34. Ibid.; "Enviros Demand Locations of 44 'High Hazard' Coal Ash Sites," *Environmental News Service*, 19 June 2009.

35. James Hansen, "Why We Can't Wait," *The Nation*, 7 May 2007; Noelle Straub and Peter Behr, "Energy Regulatory Chief Says New Coal, Nuclear Plants May Be Unnecessary," *Greenwire*, 22 April 2009.

36. Supreme Court of the United States, *Massachusetts et al. v. Environmental Protection Agency et al.*, No. 05–1120, 549 U.S. 497, decided 2 April 2007, Washington, DC; Environmental Appeals Board, U.S. Environmental Protection Agency, "In Re: Deseret Power Electric Cooperative, PSD Permit No. PSD-OU-0002-04.00" (Washington, DC: 13 November 2008); David Biello, "EPA Ruling Halts All New Coal-Fired Power Plants," *Sci-*

entific American, 14 November 2008; Deborah Zabarenko, "EPA Finds Greenhouse Gases Endanger Health," *Reuters*, 23 March 2009.

37. Sierra Club, "Beyond Coal," at www.sierraclub.org/coal, viewed 25 June 2009.

38. Mathias Bell, Rocky Mountain Institute, e-mail to Jessie Robbins, Earth Policy Institute, 30 June 2009; Natalie Mims, Mathias Bell, and Stephen Doig, *Assessing the Electric Productivity Gap and the U.S. Efficiency Opportunity* (Snowmass, CO: Rocky Mountain Institute, January 2009).

39. Erik Shuster, *Tracking New Coal-Fired Power Plants* (Pittsburgh, PA: DOE, National Energy Technology Laboratory, January 2009); Julie Clendenin and Shawna Seldon, "Wind Energy Grows by Record 8,300 MW in 2008," press release (Washington, DC: American Wind Energy Association (AWEA), 27 January 2009); AWEA, *U.S. Wind Energy Projects*, electronic database, at www.awea.org/projects, updated 31 December 2008.

40. Henry Manczyk and Michael D. Leach, "Combined Heat and Power Generation and District Heating in Denmark: History, Goals, and Technology," at www.energy.rochester.edu/dk/manczyk/denmark.pdf, viewed 13 February 2008; "New Zealand Issues Ten-Year Ban on New Thermal Power Plants," *Power Engineering*, 11 October 2007; Global Wind Energy Council, *Global Wind 2008 Report* (Brussels: 2009); Jad Mouawad, "Chinese Clean Coal Will Be Critical, a Report Says," Green Inc. at *Nytimes.com*, 20 April 2009.

41. Table 10–1 calculated with the following: fossil fuel and transport carbon reductions using IEA, *World Energy Outlook 2008* (Paris: 2008), p. 507, industry reductions using IEA, *Tracking Industrial Energy Efficiency and CO_2 Emissions* (Paris: 2007), avoided deforestation and planting trees from Intergovernmental Panel on Climate Change (IPCC), *Climate Change 2007: Mitigation of Climate Change. Contribution of Working Group III to the Fourth Assessment Report of the Intergovernmental Panel on Climate Change* (Cambridge, U.K.: Cambridge University Press, 2007), pp. 543, 559, and soil carbon sequestration based on conservative estimates in Rattan Lal, "Soil Carbon Sequestration Impacts on Global Climate Change and Food Security," *Science*, vol. 304 (11 June 2004), pp. 1,623–27.

42. IEA, *World Energy Outlook 2008*, op. cit. note 41, p. 507.

43. R. A. Houghton, "Carbon Flux to the Atmosphere from Land-Use Changes: 1850–2005," in Carbon Dioxide Information Analysis Center (CDIAC), *TRENDS: A Compendium of Data on Global Change* (Oak Ridge, TN: Oak Ridge National Laboratory (ORNL), 2008); carbon sequestration based on IPCC, op. cit. note 41.

44. Lal, op. cit. note 41.

45. Carbon dioxide pathway modeled using fossil fuel emissions from Tom Boden and Gregg Marland, "Global CO_2 Emissions from Fossil-Fuel Burning, Cement Manufacture, and Gas Flaring: 1751–2006" and "Preliminary 2006–07 Global & National Estimates by Extrapolation," both in CDIAC, *Fossil Fuel CO_2 Emissions* (Oak Ridge, TN: ORNL, 2009), and from land use change emissions from Houghton, op. cit. note 43, with decay curve cited in J. Hansen et al., "Dangerous Human-Made Interference with Climate: A GISS ModelE Study," *Atmospheric Chemistry and*

Physics, vol. 7 (2007), pp. 2,287–312.

46. Federal Ministry for the Environment, Nature Conservation and Nuclear Safety, *Renewable Energy-Employment Effects: Impact of the Expansion of Renewable Energy on the German Labor Market* (Berlin: June 2006); "German Plan to Close Coal Mines," *BBC News*, 29 January 2007; Michael Levitin, "Germany Says Auf Wiedersehen to Nuclear Power, Guten Tag to Renewables," *Grist*, 12 August 2005.

47. Tim Weiner, *Legacy of Ashes: The History of the CIA* (New York: Doubleday, 2009), p. 429.

48. Surgeon General's Advisory Committee on Smoking and Health, *Smoking and Health* (Washington, DC: Office of the Surgeon General, 1964).

49. Cigarette consumption from U.S. Department of Agriculture (USDA), *Production, Supply and Distribution*, electronic database, at www.fas.usda.gov/psdonline, updated 31 August 2006, and from Tom Capehart, *Tobacco Outlook* (Washington, DC: USDA, Economic Research Service (ERS), 24 April 2007); American Cancer Society, "Guide to Quitting Smoking: Tobacco and Cancer," at www.cancer.org, updated 21 May 2009.

50. Duff Wilson, "Congress Passes Measure on Tobacco Regulation," *New York Times*, 13 June 2009; USDA, ERS, "Cigarette Price Increase Follows Tobacco Pact," *Agricultural Outlook*, January–February 1999.

51. DOE, EIA, *Annual Energy Outlook 2009 with Projections for 2030* (Washington, DC: March 2009); BP, *BP Statistical Review of World Energy 2009* (London: British Petroleum, June 2009); Sharon Silke Carty, "This Year's Auto Sales Forecast Falls to 10 Million," *USA Today*, 22 May 2009; cars scrapped from R. L. Polk & Co., "U.S. Vehicle Median Age Increased in 2008, According to Polk," press release (Southfield, MI: 3 March 2009).

52. U.S. Department of Transportation, *Summary of Fuel Economy Performance* (Washington, DC: 30 March 2009).

53. DOE, EIA, *Annual Energy Outlook 2007 with Projections for 2030* (Washington, DC:, February 2006); DOE, op. cit. note 51.

54. For information on mobilization, see Francis Walton, *Miracle of World War II: How American Industry Made Victory Possible* (New York: Macmillan, 1956).

55. Franklin Roosevelt, "State of the Union Address," 6 January 1942, at www.ibiblio.org/pha/7-2-188/188-35.html.

56. Harold G. Vatter, *The US Economy in World War II* (New York: Columbia University Press, 1985), p. 13; Alan L. Gropman, *Mobilizing U.S. Industry in World War II* (Washington, DC: National Defense University Press, August 1996).

57. Doris Kearns Goodwin, *No Ordinary Time—Franklin and Eleanor Roosevelt: The Home Front in World War II* (New York: Simon & Schuster, 1994), p. 316; "Point Rationing Comes of Age," *Business Week*, 19 February 1944.

58. "War Production—The Job 'That Couldn't Be Done'," *Business Week*, 5 May 1945; Donald M. Nelsen, *Arsenal of Democracy: The Story of American War Production* (New York: Harcourt, Brace and Co., 1946), p. 243.

59. Goodwin, op. cit. note 57, p. 316.

60. Grey quoted in Walton, op. cit. note 54.

61. Jeffrey Sachs, "One Tenth of 1 Percent to Make the World Safer," *Washington Post*, 21 November 2001.

62. Universal primary education from U.K. Treasury, *From Commitment to Action: Education* (London: Department for International Development, September 2005); adult literacy campaign is author's estimate; universal basic health care from Jeffrey D. Sachs and the Commission on Macroeconomics and Health, *Macroeconomics and Health: Investing in Health for Economic Development* (Geneva: World Health Organization, 2001); reproductive health and family planning from J. Joseph Speidel et al., *Family Planning and Reproductive Health: The Link to Environmental Preservation* (San Francisco: Bixby Center for Reproductive Health and Research Policy, University of California, 2007), p. 10, and from J. Joseph Speidel, discussion with J. Matthew Roney, Earth Policy Institute, 16 October 2007.

63. In Table 10–2, closing the condom gap estimated from Population Action International, "Why Condoms Count in the Era of HIV/AIDS," fact sheet (Washington, DC: 2008); cost per condom and condom distribution from United Nations Population Fund (UNFPA), *Donor Support for Contraceptives and Condoms for STI/HIV Prevention 2007* (New York: 2008); school lunch program from George McGovern, "Yes We CAN Feed the World's Hungry," *Parade*, 16 December 2001; assistance to preschool children and pregnant women is author's estimate of extending the U.S.'s Women, Infants, and Children program, based on United Nations, *World Population Prospects: The 2004 Revision* (New York: 2005); UNFPA, The *State of World Population 2004* (New York: 2004), p. 39.

64. In Table 10–2, restoring the earth budget compiled from the following: planting trees to reduce flooding and conserve soil and protecting topsoil on cropland from Lester R. Brown and Edward C. Wolf, "Reclaiming the Future," in Lester R. Brown et al., *State of the World 1988* (New York: W. W. Norton & Company, 1988), p. 174, using data from U.N. Food and Agriculture Organization, *Fuelwood Supplies in the Developing Countries*, Forestry Paper 42 (Rome: 1983); planting trees to sequester carbon from IPCC, op. cit. note 41, pp. 543, 559; restoring rangelands from UNEP, *Status of Desertification and Implementation of the United Nations Plan of Action to Combat Desertification* (Nairobi: 1991), pp. 73–92; restoring fisheries from Andrew Balmford et al., "The Worldwide Costs of Marine Protected Areas," *Proceedings of the National Academy of Sciences*, vol. 101, no. 26 (29 June 2004), pp. 9,694–97; protecting biological diversity from World Parks Congress, *Recommendations of the Vth IUCN World Parks Congress* (Durban, South Africa: 2003), pp. 17–19, and from World Parks Congress, "The Durban Accord," at www.iucn.org/themes/wcpa, viewed 19 October 2007; stabilizing water tables is author's estimate.

65. Table 10–3 compiled from Stockholm International Peace Research Institute (SIPRI), *Military Expenditure Database*, electronic database at www.sipri.org, updated 2009.

66. SIPRI, op. cit. note 65.

67. Amy Belasco, *The Cost of Iraq, Afghanistan and Other Global War on Terror Operations Since 9/11* (Washington, DC: Congressional Research Service, 15 May 2009); Linda Bilmes and Joseph Stiglitz, *The Economic*

Costs of the Iraq War: An Appraisal Three Years After the Beginning of the Conflict (Cambridge, MA: National Bureau of Economic Research, February 2006); Linda Bilmes and Joseph Stiglitz, "The $10 Trillion Hangover," *Harper's,* January 2009.

68. Jared Diamond, *Collapse: How Societies Choose to Fail or Succeed* (New York: Penguin Group, 2005); Ronald Wright, *A Short History of Progress* (New York: Carroll and Graf Publishers, 2005); Joseph A. Tainter, *The Collapse of Complex Societies* (Cambridge, U.K.: Cambridge University Press, 1988).

69. SIPRI, op. cit. note 65.

70. The Institute for Intercultural Studies, at www.interculturalstudies.org, viewed 8 July 2009.

71. Richard Register, e-mail to author, 16 October 2007.

72. Gidon Eshel and Pamela A. Martin, "Diet, Energy, and Global Warming," *Earth Interactions,* vol. 10, no. 9 (2006).

Index

Acknowledgments

If it takes a village to raise a child, then it takes the entire world to do a broad-based book on global issues. It begins with the work of thousands of scientists and research teams in many fields whose analyses we draw on. The process ends with the teams who translate the book into other languages. We are indebted to the thousands of researchers, to the 20 or so translation teams, and to countless others.

The research team at the Earth Policy Institute (EPI) is led by Janet Larsen, our Director of Research. They went through literally thousands of research reports, articles, and books—gathering, organizing, and analyzing information. In research and writing, Janet is my alter ego, my best critic, and a sounding board for new ideas.

J. Matthew Roney and Jignasha Rana anchored a heroic research effort, uncovering new and valuable data that raised this edition to a new level. Before moving to North Carolina with his family, Jonathan G. Dorn provided invaluable assistance in fleshing out the energy plan in both the previous edition and this one. Interns Jessie Robbins and Jessica Clarke contributed handily with data gathering, fact checking, and review comments. The unflagging enthusiasm and dedication of the research team allowed us to complete this book on time. I am deeply grateful to each of them.

Some authors write, but this one dictates. My thanks go to Consuela (Sway) Headrick who transcribed the many drafts and who, in the midst of preparation for this book, brought forth her own creation—a beautiful daughter, Rinay Steward.

Reah Janise Kauffman, our Vice President, not only manages the Institute, thus enabling me to concentrate on research, she also directs EPI's outreach effort. This includes, among other things, coordinating our worldwide network of publishers, organizing book tours, and working with the media. Reah Janise's productivity and versatility are keys to the Institute's success. Her value to me is evidenced in our 23 years of working together as a team.

Millicent Johnson, our Manager of Publications Sales, handles our publications department and serves as our office quartermaster and librarian. Millicent, who cheerfully handles the thousands of book orders, takes pride in her one-day turnaround policy.

A number of reviewers helped shape the final product. My colleagues at EPI reviewed several drafts and provided insightful comments and suggestions. Peter Goldmark, for many years publisher of the *International Herald Tribune* and now head of the climate program at the Environmental Defense Fund, used his rich experience to help us identify the strengths and weaknesses of the manuscript. Peter is simultaneously one of the book's strongest supporters and one of its most able critics.

Edwin (Toby) Clark, an engineer and economist by training, brought his decades of environmental experience as an environmental analyst at the Council on Environmental Quality and as an administrator at the U.S. Environmental Protection Agency to bear on the manuscript, providing both broad structural suggestions and detailed page-by-page commentary.

William Mansfield, a member of the EPI board who has a wealth of environmental experience, including several years as Deputy Director of the United Nations Environment Programme, provided many useful suggestions.

Doug and Debra Baker contributed their wide-ranging scientific knowledge, from physics to meteorology, to chapter-by-chapter critiques that were both constructive and encouraging. Maureen Kuwano Hinkle drew on 26 years of experience working on agricultural issues with the Environmental Defense Fund and the Audubon Society to provide valuable comments and encouragement along the way. Frances Moore, a former EPI researcher now in graduate school, lent her expertise with salient comments in the final weeks of the book's completion.

Also helping to shape the book near the end were Bridget Collins of the Patuxent Wildlife Research Center and Amy Heinzerling, our new colleague.

My thanks also to individuals who were particularly helpful in providing specific information for this edition: Mathias Bell, Euan Blauvelt, Colin J. Campbell, Martha M. Campbell, Marie Coleman, Robert W. Corell, Ken Creighton, John Crenshaw, Emmet Curley, Sandra Curtin, Rolf Derpsch, Junko Edahiro, Mark Ellis, David Fridley, Reed Funk, Nathan Glasgow, Bill Heenan, Michael Hoover, Ryde James, Egil Juliussen, Doug Koplow, Felix Kramer, Kathleen Krust, Rattan Lal, Alberto Del Lungo, Eric Martinot, Heitor Matallo, Hirofumi Muraoka, Jack Oortwijn, Richard Register, Lara de Lacerda Santos Rodrigues, William Ryerson, Adam Schafer, Richard Schimpf, Stefanie Seskin, John E. Sheehy, Kara Slack, J. Joseph Speidel, Jeff Tester, Jasna Tomic, Martin Vorum, Brian P. Wallace, Wang Tao, Sarah Williams, Walter Youngquist, and Paul Zajac.

As always, we are in debt to our editor, Linda Starke, who brings over 30 years of international experience in editing environmental books and reports to the table. She has brought her sure hand to the editing of not only this book, but all my books during this period.

The book was produced in record time thanks to the conscientious efforts of Elizabeth Doherty, who prepared the page proofs under a very tight deadline. The index was ably prepared by Kate Mertes.

We are supported by a network of dedicated translators and publishers for *Plan B* in 22 languages in addition to English—Arabic, Bulgarian, Chinese, Farsi, French, German, Hindi, Hungarian, Italian, Japanese, Korean, Marathi, Norwegian, Polish, Portuguese, Romanian, Russian, Slovenian, Spanish, Swedish, Thai, and Turkish. There are three publishers in English (U.S.A./Canada, U.K./Commonwealth, and India/South Asia), two in Spanish (Spain and Latin America), and two in Chinese (mainland and Taiwan).

These translations are often the work of environmentally committed individuals. In Iran, the husband and wife team of Hamid Taravati and Farzaneh Bahar, both medical doctors, head an environmental nongovernmental organization (NGO) and translate EPI's publications into Farsi. Their translation of

Plan B earned them a national book award. The ministries of environment and agriculture regularly purchase copies in bulk for distribution to staff.

In China, Lin Zixin has arranged the publication of my books in Chinese for more than 20 years. Premier Wen Jiabao and Pan Yue, Deputy Minister of the State Environmental Protection Administration, have quoted *Plan B 2.0* in public addresses and articles. The Chinese edition of *Plan B* received a coveted national book award in 2005 from the National Library of China.

In Japan, Soki Oda, who started Worldwatch Japan some 20 years ago, leads our publication efforts and arranges book promotional tours. He is indefatigable in his efforts and is already planning outreach for the Japanese edition of *Plan B 4.0*.

Gianfranco Bologna, with whom I've worked for over 25 years, arranges for publication of our books in Italy. As head of WWF–Italy, he is uniquely positioned to assist in this effort. He is joined in the translation effort by a team headed by Dario Tamburrano of the Amici de Beppe Grillo di Roma.

In Romania, former President Ion Iliescu started publishing our books some 20 years ago when he headed the publishing house Editura Tehnica. He takes pride in publishing the Romanian edition simultaneously with the English one. This is all made possible by the management skills of Roman Chirila at Editura Tehnica.

In Turkey, TEMA, the leading environmental NGO, which works especially on reforesting the countryside, has for many years published my books. Inspired by Ted Turner, they distributed 4,250 copies of *Plan B 3.0* to officials, academics, and other decisionmakers.

In South Korea, Yul Choi, founder of the Korean Federation for Environmental Movement and now head of the Korea Green Foundation, has published my books and oversees their launching through Doyosae Books Co.

Most remarkable are the individuals who step forward out of seemingly nowhere to publish and promote *Plan B*. For instance, Lars and Doris Almström translated *Plan B 3.0* and found an excellent publisher in Sweden. Inspired by the book and wanting to get a Plan B economy moving in Sweden, they established a Web site to promote EPI's work and to post the Swedish edition for free downloading at www.planb3.se.

Olav Randen, our Norwegian publisher, contacted us two months before I was scheduled to launch the Swedish edition of *Plan B 3.0*. With a Herculean effort, he translated and published the book so that I could launch his edition the day after the Swedish edition came out.

Pierre-Yves Longaretti and Philippe Vieille in France literally accepted the call to action in *Plan B 2.0* and not only translated the book but engaged a world-class publisher, Calman-Lévy. They further established an NGO, Alternative Planetaire, and a Web site to promote Plan B for France (www.alternative planetaire.com).

Bernd Hamm, a professor at the University of Trier, personally arranged for a German publisher, Kai Homilius Verlag, to publish *Plan B 2.0* Kai Homilius has now published *Plan B 3.0* and is preparing *Plan B 4.0* for release.

The Spanish editions of *Plan B 2.0* and *Plan B 3.0* in Latin America were spearheaded by Gilberto Rincon of the Centre of Studies for Sustainable Development in Colombia.

The Hungarian edition of *Plan B 3.0*, available electronically on our own Web site, resulted from the tireless efforts of David Biro, a school teacher in Hungary. And we are pleased to say that as this book was going to bed, Kossuth Publishing—excited by Biro's translation—contracted to publish *Plan B 4.0*.

Samir Menon and his colleagues at Globally Managed Services (GMS) produced the Hindi and English editions for India and arranged the outreach. GMS advises companies in the ASEAN region on how to balance the bottom line while conserving natural resources.

Those who are working to promote Plan B (see "People in Action" on our Web site) are gaining in both numbers and momentum.

I would also like to thank personally the members of our Plan B teams—the several thousand individuals who have purchased five or more copies of *Plan B*, *Plan B 2.0*, and *Plan B 3.0* for distribution to friends, colleagues, and opinion leaders. When we published the original *Plan B* six years ago, we noticed that about 700 individuals ordered a copy and then came back to order 5, 10, or 50 copies for distribution. With each subsequent edition, new buyers of multiple copies have joined in.

Ted Turner, who distributes copies of each *Plan B* to heads of state and their key cabinet members, the Fortune 500 CEOs, and members of Congress, has become the team captain. Turner distributed 5,500 copies of *Plan B 3.0*. National Plan B teams have emerged in Japan, led by Toshishige and Masatsugu Kurosawa, and in Turkey, led by TEMA.

We are delighted to announce that a film version of *Plan B 4.0* is in progress. Hal and Marilyn Weiner of ScreenScope are producing a two-hour film that is expected to air in the spring of 2010.

We are also indebted to our funders. Without their support this book would not exist. Among these are the Foundation for the Carolinas; the Rockefeller Brothers and United Nations Population funds; and the Farview, McBride Family, Laney Thornton, Shenandoah, Summit, Turner, and Wallace Genetic foundations.

Earth Policy is also supported by individual donors. I would like in particular to thank Ray Anderson, Charles Babbs, Junko Edahiro, John Robbins, and Jeremy Waletzky for large personal gifts. Other personal donors include Doug and Debra Baker, Peter Carter, Judith Gradwohl, Maureen Hinkle, Elaine Marszalek, Peter Seidel, and many others.

Finally, my thanks to the team at W. W. Norton & Company: Amy Cherry, our book manager; Devon Zahn, who put the book on a fast-track production schedule; Ingsu Liu, Art Director for the book jacket; Bill Rusin, Marketing Director; and Drake McFeely, President, with special thanks for his support. It is a delight to work with such a talented team and to have been published by W. W. Norton for more than 30 years.

And thanks to you, our readers. In the end, the success of this book depends on you and your help in implementing Plan B.

Lester R. Brown

About the Author

Lester R. Brown is President of Earth Policy Institute, a non-profit, interdisciplinary research organization based in Washington, D.C., which he founded in May 2001. The purpose of the Earth Policy Institute is to provide a plan for saving civilization and a roadmap of how to get from here to there.

Brown has been described as "one of the world's most influential thinkers" by the *Washington Post*. The *Telegraph of Calcutta* called him "the guru of the environmental movement." In 1986, the Library of Congress requested his papers for its archives.

Some 30 years ago, Brown helped pioneer the concept of environmentally sustainable development, a concept he uses in his design of an eco-economy. He was the Founder and President of the Worldwatch Institute during its first 26 years. During a career that started with tomato farming, Brown has authored or coauthored many books and been awarded 24 honorary degrees. His books have appeared in more than 40 languages.

Brown is a MacArthur Fellow and the recipient of countless prizes and awards, including the 1987 United Nations Environment Prize, the 1989 World Wide Fund for Nature Gold Medal, and Japan's 1994 Blue Planet Prize for his "exceptional contributions to solving global environmental problems." In 1995, Marquis *Who's Who*, on the occasion of its fiftieth edition, selected Lester Brown as one of 50 Great Americans. Most recently he was awarded the Presidential Medal of Italy and the Borgström Prize by the Royal Swedish Academy of Agriculture and Forestry. He holds three honorary professorships in China, including one at the Chinese Academy of Sciences. He lives in Washington, D.C.

If you have found this book useful and would like to share it with others, consider joining our
Plan B Team.

To do so, order five or more copies at our bulk discount rate at www.earthpolicy.org

This book is not the final word. We will continue to unfold new issues and update the analysis in our
Plan B Updates.
Follow this progress by subscribing to our free, low-volume electronic listserv.
Please sign up at www.earthpolicy.org to get these four-page Updates by e-mail as they are released.

Past Plan B Updates and all of the Earth Policy Institute's research, including this book, are posted on our Web site www.earthpolicy.org for free downloading.

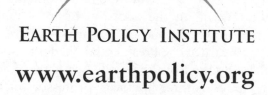

EARTH POLICY INSTITUTE
www.earthpolicy.org